SECOND THOUGHTS

4th edition

To our mothers . . .

Mary Ruane, a much treasured and loved source
of second thoughts and knowledge

Lina Cerulo, who convinced the men in the family
that girls deserved a college education too

SECOND THOUGHTS

Seeing Conventional Wisdom Through the Sociological Eye

4th edition

Janet M. Ruane
Montclair State University

Karen A. Cerulo
Rutgers University

PINE FORGE PRESS
An Imprint of Sage Publications, Inc.
Los Angeles • London • New Delhi • Singapore

For information:

Pine Forge Press
A SAGE Publications Company
2455 Teller Road
Thousand Oaks, California 91320
E-mail: order@sagepub.com

SAGE Publications India Pvt. Ltd.
B 1/I 1 Mohan Cooperative
Industrial Area
Mathura Road, New Delhi 110 044
India

SAGE Publications Ltd.
1 Oliver's Yard
55 City Road
London EC1Y 1SP
United Kingdom

SAGE Publications
Asia-Pacific Pte. Ltd.
33 Pekin Street #02-01
Far East Square
Singapore 048763

Printed in the United States of America.

Library of Congress Cataloging-in-Publication Data

Ruane, Janet M.,
Second thoughts : seeing conventional wisdom through the sociological eye/Janet M. Ruane, Karen A. Cerulo.—4th ed.
　　p. cm.
Includes bibliographical references and index.
ISBN-13: 978-1-4129-5653-6 (pbk.)
　　1. Sociology. 2. Sociology—Quotations, maxims, etc. 3. Maxims.
I. Cerulo, Karen A. II. Title.

HM585.R867 2008
301—dc22   2007052867

This book is printed on acid-free paper.

08　09　10　11　12　　10　9　8　7　6　5　4　3　2　1

Acquisitions Editor:	Benjamin Penner
Editorial Assistant:	Nancy Scrofano
Production Editor:	Karen Wiley
Copy Editor:	Gail Naron Chalew
Proofreader:	Andrea Martin
Typesetter:	C&M Digitals (P) Ltd.
Indexer:	Gloria Tierney
Cover Designer:	Edgar Abarca
Marketing Manager:	Jennifer Reed Banando

Contents

The Sociological Perspective

*In this introduction, we discuss the roots of conventional
wisdom. We also contrast such knowledge with that acquired
via the sociological perspective. In this way, we introduce
students to a sociological mode of thinking.*

Concepts Defined and Applied

Conventional wisdom; social patterns; social context; cultural
value; self-fulfilling prophecy; sociological imagination.

Methods

*Americans like to "run the numbers." No matter what the
realm— sports, business, politics, or entertainment—numbers
often provide the bottom line. Why is our faith in numbers so
strong? Conventional wisdom tells us that numbers don't lie. Is
such wisdom accurate? Can we be confident in the "realities"
claimed by national polls, social scientific surveys, and other
quantitative studies? In this essay, we note several important
elements to consider in establishing the "truth" of numbers.*

Concepts Defined and Applied

Population; sample; representative sample; survey research;
valid measure; reliable measure; operationalization; value-free
researcher; ethnocentrism.

Culture

Conventional wisdom suggests that competition and achievement go hand in hand. In this essay, however, we highlight the many studies that show the benefits of cooperation over competition. In so doing, we review American cultural values, strategies of action, and the connection of these elements to both positive and negative outcomes.

Concepts Defined and Applied

Cultural value; strategies of action; dialectic; prejudice; culture against people.

We frequently hear it said: Children are our future. They are our most valuable resource. Here, we present research suggesting otherwise. Children may be the most overlooked, the most neglected segment of the population despite current talk of family values and the future of American youth.

Concepts Defined and Applied

Infant mortality rates; social indicators; ideal culture; real culture; cultural inconsistency; conflict theorists; power; social policies; replacement level fertility.

Social Structure

In this essay, we explore various social statuses—age, education, gender, income, race, religion—noting the ways in which these factors can guide something as seemingly individualistic as Cupid's arrow.

Concepts Defined and Applied

Social status; norms of homogamy; endogamy; socioeconomic status; self-esteem.

cure to AIDS. This essay addresses the inconsistencies often found between what we pay for work and the value we place on it.

Concepts Defined and Applied

Income; Davis-Moore thesis; functional analysis; conflict theorists; wealth; power; occupational prestige; occupational prestige scale; stratification system.

This essay documents the impact of income on issues of mortality and life chances. Money, with all its alleged downfalls, can still mean the difference between life and death.

Concepts Defined and Applied

Mortality rates; socioeconomic status; infant mortality rates; life expectancy; negative life events; life chances; functional analysis.

In the past 40 years, women have made great strides toward equality with men. But have they journeyed far enough? Here, we focus on gender relations in the home, the schools, and the workplace, illustrating the gains and losses faced by women and men in the current era.

Concepts Defined and Applied

Gender socialization; gender typing; stereotypes; longitudinal data; sex segregation; pay gap; gender scripts.

Is the United States a level playing field for all Americans despite race? In this essay, we review the many arenas of continued segregation and racism in the United States. Furthermore, we explore the basis for determining one's race, noting that with all of the implications the classification holds, categorizing race is, at best, a tenuous process.

Concepts Defined and Applied

Social status; status set; race; racism; prejudice; discrimination; racial steering; linguistic profiling; concentrated-poverty neighborhoods; multiracial schools; paired testing; social construction of reality; reification; social context; achieved status; ascribed status; master status; identity; life chances; social minority.

Deviance, Crime, and Social Control

In recent decades, Americans have wrestled with a growing fear of violence. Is that fear justified? Here, we review the state of violence in America, and we explore those instances in which the public's fears of violence are justified and those in which they are exaggerated. As such, the essay explores the many problems surrounding the detection and perception of danger and crime.

Concepts Defined and Applied

Uniform Crime Reports Index for Serious Crime; victimization studies; social construction of reality; cultural value; fear of strangers.

There's no social ill that the law can't fix . . . or at least that is what many Americans believe. In this essay, we review various social functions of the law. We also consider whether or not we are overly dependent on this tool of formal social control.

Concepts Defined and Applied

Social control; norms; informal social control; formal social control; social engineering; moral entrepreneurs; civil lawsuits; class action suits; tolerance; social context.

. . . except, of course, when reporting your income, revealing your age, sparing the feelings of another—the list can go on and on. In this essay, we explore the conditions under which lying is viewed as normal. In so doing, we use lying as a case study that aptly demonstrates both the pervasiveness and the relative nature of deviance.

the least understood dimensions of welfare and explore exactly where welfare moneys are going.

Concepts Defined and Applied

Aid to Families with Dependent Children (AFDC); Temporary Assistance to Needy Families (TANF); poverty threshold; poverty; public assistance programs; social insurance programs; intergenerational upward mobility; out-group; in-group; social reproduction theory; structural functionalism; social functions.

"Why don't you go back where you came from?" This angry cry seems to be getting more and more familiar as the United States faces the highest levels of immigration in its history. Is immigration ruining this nation? This essay reviews the historical impact and future trends of immigration in the United States.

Concepts Defined and Applied

Prejudice; immigrant groups; illegal aliens; legal permanent residents (LPRs or "green card recipients"); aliens; legal immigrants; naturalized citizens; temporary legal migrants; refugees and asylees; unauthorized migrants; cultural value; in-group; out-group; assimilation; multiculturalism; cultural capital.

Social Institutions: Media and Technology

This essay examines new communication technologies and explores their role in contemporary social life. We begin by considering the ways in which technology has changed the development of community and intimacy. We explore as well the impact of new technologies on our definitions of social relations, social actors, and the public and private spheres.

Concepts Defined and Applied

New communication technologies; digital divide; e-philanthropy; direct communication; mediated communication; social relations.

Preface

It is not uncommon for those assigned to teach entry-level sociology courses to experience some trepidation, even dread, about the teaching task ahead. In many ways, intro to sociology is a "tough sell." Some students perceive the discipline as nothing more than a "rehash" of the obvious; it speaks to everyday life, something many students believe they already know and understand. Other students confuse sociology courses with disciplines such as psychology or social work; they take our courses hoping to "figure out the opposite sex," learn to better "work the system," or overcome their personal problems with regard to deviant behavior or family relations. To muddy the waters even more, many intro students are likely to be in our courses not because of some desire to learn sociology but because the courses satisfy a general education requirement. Taking all of these factors into account, sociology instructors can face substantial resistance. Getting students to "adjust" their visions of the world so as to incorporate the sociological eye is no small feat.

Despite these challenges, it remains essential to achieve success in entry-level sociology courses. From an instrumental point of view, the discipline recruits future sociologists from these courses, thus mandating a sound foundation. Furthermore, departments may gain significant institutional resources by keeping intro course enrollments up. Intellectual concerns also contribute to the importance of entry-level courses. Many sociology instructors believe that intro courses offer a guaranteed "dividend" for the student: The sociological vision represents an essential tool for understanding and surviving our increasingly complex social world. Thus, intro courses provide instructors with a valuable opportunity to plant and nurture the sociological imagination in each new cohort of college students. Thought of in this way, failing the intro student can carry long-term social costs.

Second Thoughts offers a "tried and true" approach to successfully nurturing sociological thinking in the newcomer. The book provides a vehicle with which to initiate dialogue; it allows instructors to meet their students on "common ground." Each chapter in this book begins with a shared idea—a conventional wisdom that both instructors and students have encountered by virtue of being consumers of popular culture. Once this common footing is established, *Second Thoughts* introduces relevant sociological concepts and theories that "mesh" with each conventional wisdom. Sociological ideas and perspective are used to explain, qualify, and sometimes debunk conventional wisdom.

At the conclusion of each chapter, we provide a vehicle by which students can apply their new sociological knowledge beyond the classroom. We have incorporated a set of exercises linked to the subject matter covered in the chapter. The exercises, too, are grounded in the familiar. We encourage students to turn to everyday, common resources for some firsthand learning experiences.

Our own classroom experiences prove that the "familiar" is a "user-friendly" place to jump-start discussion, thus laying the foundation for critical thinking and informed analysis. In the classroom, we also have found the "familiar" to be a useful tool with which to delineate the sociological vision. This book attempts to pass along some of the fruits of our own learning. In pushing beyond the familiar, *Second Thoughts* also exposes students to the sociological advantage. At minimum, readers will accrue the benefits that come from taking time to give conventional ideas some important "second thoughts."

Acknowledgments

There are, of course, a number of people who have contributed to this book. First and foremost, we would both like to acknowledge the students encountered in the many sociology courses taught at SUNY Stony Brook, Rutgers University, and Montclair State University. These students challenged us to make the sociological imagination a meaningful and desirable option on students' learning agendas. Thanks also go to our wonderful research assistant, Jennifer Hemler, an extremely talented graduate student at Rutgers. Her inquisitiveness, tenacity, and professionalism brought great improvements to this edition of *Second Thoughts*. Thanks also to our primo reference librarian, Maureen Gorman. In addition, we are grateful to the following reviewers for their careful readings and productive suggestions on various drafts of the manuscript:

Edward Brent
University of Missouri, Columbia

Katherine D. Walker
College of William and Mary

Adrian J. Tan
Southern Methodist University

Annette Schwabe
Florida State University

Martha Mazzarella
Bowling Green State University

Nick Kontogeorgopoulos
University of Puget Sound

David L. Brunsma
University of Missouri, Columbia

Margaret J. Weinberger
Bowling Green State University

Thanks also go to our wonderfully supportive editor, Ben Penner, and to the solid support staff at Pine Forge, including Nancy Scrofano, Karen Wiley, and Gail Naron Chalew. We would also like to thank several family members and friends (Mary Agnes, Anne, Mary Jane, Joan, and Sam) for consistently asking about "the book" and thus encouraging us to stick with the program and to stay on schedule.

Introduction:
The Sociological Perspective

In this introduction, we discuss the roots of conventional wisdom. We also contrast such knowledge with that acquired via the sociological perspective. In this way, we introduce students to a sociological mode of thinking.

Conventional wisdom is a part of our everyday lives. We are exposed to its lessons from early childhood, and we encounter its teachings until the day we die. Who among us was not taught, for example, to "be fearful of strangers" or that "beauty is only skin deep"? Similarly, we have all learned that "stress is bad for our well-being" and that "adult life is simply incomplete without children."

Conventional wisdom comes to us in many forms. We encounter it via folk adages, "old wives' tales," traditions, and political or religious rhetoric. We find it in advice columns, cultural truisms, and the tenets of "common sense." **Conventional wisdom** refers to that body of assertions and beliefs that is generally recognized as part of a culture's "common knowledge." These cultural lessons are many, and they cannot be taken lightly. They are central to American society, and they are frequently the source of our beliefs, attitudes, and behaviors.

To be sure, conventional wisdom often contains elements of truth. As such, it constitutes a starting point for knowledge (Mathisen 1989; Ruane 2005). Consider, for example, this well-known truism: "Actions speak louder than words." Many laboratory studies indeed have shown that those assessing an individual who says one thing but does another are influenced more strongly by the individual's actions (Amabile and Kabat 1982; Bryan and Walbek 1970; Ekman and Frank 1993; Ekman, O'Sullivan, Friesen, and

Scherer 1991; Van Overwalle 1997). Similarly, a long line of research supports the adage that warns, "Marry in haste, repent at leisure." When we define *haste* as "marrying too young or marrying too quickly," we find that those who "marry in haste" report less satisfaction over the course of the marriage and experience higher divorce rates than those who make a later or a slower decision (Furstenburg 1979; Glenn and Supancic 1984; Grover, Russell, and Schumm 1985; Kitson, Babri, and Roach 1985; Martin and Bumpass 1989; National Marriage Project 2006).

Placing complete faith in conventional wisdom, however, can be risky. Social patterns and behaviors frequently contradict the wisdoms we embrace. Many studies show, for instance, that adages encouraging the "fear of strangers" often are misguided; most crimes of personal violence are perpetrated by those we know (see Essay 15). Similarly, research documents that beauty may be merely "skin deep," but its importance cannot be underestimated. Physically attractive individuals fare better than those of more average appearance in almost all areas of social interaction (see Essay 10). Many studies suggest that stress is not always "bad for one's well-being"; it can sometimes be productive for human beings (see Essay 5). And despite all of the accolades to the presence of children in our lives, research shows that many adults report their highest levels of lifetime happiness take place *before* they have children or *after* their children leave home (see Essay 3).

Second Thoughts: Seeing Conventional Wisdom Through the Sociological Eye addresses the gaps that exist between conventional wisdom and social life. The book reviews several popular conventional wisdoms, noting the instances in which such adages cannot be taken at face value. Each of the following essays uses social research to expose the gray area that is too often ignored by the bottom-line nature of conventional wisdom. In so doing, *Second Thoughts* demonstrates that social reality is generally much more involved and complex than these cultural truisms imply. The book suggests that reviewing conventional wisdom with a sociological eye can lead to a more complete, detailed understanding of social life.

When Conventional Wisdom Isn't Enough

Although there may well be a kernel of truth to much of conventional wisdom, too often these adages present an incomplete picture. Why is this the case? The answer stems, in part, from the source of most conventional wisdom.

Much of the conventional wisdom we embrace originates from a particular individual's personal experiences, observations, or reflections. Often such adages emerge from a highly specific circumstance; they are designed to address a particular need or event as experienced by a certain social group at a specific place or historical moment. For example, consider this well-known adage: "There's a sucker born every minute!" P. T. Barnum coined this now-familiar phrase. But recall Barnum's personal circumstance—he was one of the most famous circus masters in history. When one considers Barnum's unique history, both the source and the limits of his wisdom become clear.

Now consider this maxim: "Don't switch horses in midstream." Abraham Lincoln originated this quote. (His actual words were, "It is not best to swap horses when crossing streams.") But note that Lincoln's frequently cited advice actually represents the political rhetoric of a historical moment. Lincoln coined the phrase as a kind of campaign slogan when seeking reelection to the U.S. presidency.

Finally, consider the famous quotation, "Good fences make good neighbors." Robert Frost forwarded this thought in his 1914 poem, "Mending Wall." Contrary to popular belief, however, Frost never intended to promote social separatism—quite the opposite. In "Mending Wall," Frost criticized the character who uttered the adage, writing, "He will not go behind his father's saying"—in other words, the character will not break with tradition. In so doing, Frost suggested that the wisdom linking good fences to good neighbors was that of *another* generation in a *former* time; it was not wisdom for all time.

Each of these examples shares a common thread. In each case, conventional wisdom was born of a particular experience or a specific social situation. The wisdom took root and grew as it resonated with other people who faced similar events and circumstances. Yet each of these examples also illustrates an inherent weakness of conventional wisdom. The "truth" revealed by such wisdom is tied to the particular circumstances of every maxim's origin. This characteristic can make conventional wisdom a precarious source of generalized knowledge. Because such wisdom is individualistic or situation-specific information, it may not carry the general applications that most people assume of it.

For the sociologist, reliable knowledge mandates that we move beyond individualistic or circumstantial information. Sociologists contend that there is more to the story than any one person's life or the lives of one's associates reveal.

Can one safely conclude that my experiences with an aging parent or my neighbors' experiences in raising their four-year-old will provide others with sufficient knowledge for handling the events of their lives? It is difficult to say. If these experiences are atypical, the wisdom they provide will offer little in the way of general conclusions regarding the treatment of elderly parents or four-year-olds. The wisdom will fail to transcend one individual's personal world. Similarly, wisdom born of experience may or may not transcend various social contexts. The maxim "Delay is the best remedy for anger" may prove fruitful in a variety of social sites: romance, work, friendship, and parenting. Yet the adage that instructs you to "keep your cards close to the vest" may lead to success on the job, but spell failure for a personal relationship.

Although your life may convince you that "birds of a feather flock together," my experience may reveal that "opposites attract." One situation may convince you that "haste makes waste," although another may convince you to "strike while the iron is hot." To be sure, experientially based or situation-specific information offers us knowledge, but that knowledge presents a fragmented, and thus incomplete, picture of the broader social world.

Relying on individualistic, circumstantial information can prove especially problematic when pursuing information regarding broad social patterns. Consider for a moment the ways in which one's geographic location might influence a person's estimate of general population patterns. The life experiences of Maine residents might lead them to conclude that 97% of the U.S. population is White. Such an estimate would greatly exaggerate the racial homogeneity of the nation. In contrast, the experiences of those living in our nation's capital (Washington, D.C.) might lead them to estimate that only 38% of the U.S. population is White, a vast underestimation of population homogeneity. (Across the United States, White Americans make up 80.2% of the population.) Based on their experience, Californians would have no trouble believing that Hispanics are now the largest minority in the United States (Hispanics constitute 35% of California's population). Yet the experiences of those in Mississippi, Alabama, or Louisiana would identify Blacks, not Hispanics, as the largest minority group. (Blacks constitute 37%, 26%, and 33% of Mississippi's, Alabama's, and Louisiana's population, while Hispanics constitute 1.7%, 2.3%, and 2.8% of Mississippi's, Alabama's and Louisiana's population, respectively.) On the basis of experience, residents of Alaska or Wyoming would never guess that the United States averages 80 inhabitants per square mile. Alaska averages one inhabitant per square mile, while Wyoming averages five. And experience might leave residents of Kentucky or Mississippi baffled by Californians' or New Yorkers' concerns over the number of foreign-born individuals entering the nation and settling in their states: 1.4% of Mississippi's population and 2% of Kentucky's population are foreign-born, whereas 26% of California's population and 20% of New York's population hail from other nations (U.S. Census Bureau 2007a).

The point we are trying to make here is really quite simple. Accurate knowledge about society requires us to move beyond the limitations of experientially based conventional wisdom. That leap represents one of the most compelling features of sociology. Sociologists are interested in social patterns. **Social patterns** are general trends that can be seen only when we force ourselves to stand back and look beyond any one, two, or three cases. In essence, sociologists search for the "big picture": the view that emerges when many individual stories are aggregated into a whole.

The sociologist's emphasis on patterns does not necessarily mean that she or he is never interested in personal stories and experiences. Rather, sociology's strength lies in its ability to place or situate individual stories in a social context. **Social context** refers to the broad social and historical circumstances surrounding an act or an event. Once the sociologist discovers the general trends within a particular group or society, she or he is in a better position to assess the relative meaning of any one individual's personal experiences. General patterns must be documented before we can assess one's personal experiences as typical or as exceptional.

Obstacles to the Sociological Vision

Approached in this way, the task of sociology sounds straightforward and even appealing. The discipline encourages us to move beyond the personal and adopt a broader social vision—a vision that promises to improve the accuracy of our knowledge. With such gains at stake, why do so many approach the sociological vision with skepticism or confusion?

Certain obstacles can make it difficult to adopt a sociological view of the world. For example, the sociological vision contrasts with Americans' longstanding cultural value of individualism. A **cultural value** is a general sentiment regarding what is good or bad, right or wrong, desirable or undesirable. In the United States, we like to think of ourselves as special and unique individuals. We view ourselves as "masters of our own fates." Thus, the notion that our behaviors follow patterns or are the product of social forces is at odds with an individualistic mentality. To illustrate this point, consider our typical reactions to a serious and growing problem in the United States today: obesity.

Our individualistic mentality encourages us to see obesity as a problem of the person, an issue involving one's self-control or self-restraint: Thus, individuals are overweight because of their personal eating habits, their lack of exercise, their laziness, or their emotional baggage. Contrast such thinking with the sociological perspective. A sociological view of obesity encourages us to push beyond the individual; it forces us to look at obesity in light of broader social patterns and contexts. In analyzing obesity, for example, a sociologist would consider the following facts: More than

66% of Americans are overweight; children are the age group most at risk; the poor and working poor are more likely to be overweight than other economic groups; and our obesity epidemic is a relatively recent phenomenon, largely a product of the last 40 years. The sociological perspective urges us to "connect the dots" between these facts. In doing so, we discover some important social patterns and social structural sources of the American obesity problem. For instance, when one adopts the sociological perspective, it becomes easier to see that changes in farm, trade, and economic policies during the past few decades have contributed to our national bulk problem. During the 1970s, Secretary of Agriculture Earl Butz pushed for significant changes in the production, pricing, importing, and exporting of grains and oils, which helped bring down the cost of food for consumers. In the same period, discoveries and innovations in food science and manufacturing led to major reductions in food production costs. But as we are now learning, these changes came on the back of high-fructose sweeteners with questionable health properties and unexpected metabolic costs. Adopting a sociological perspective also helps us discover that Americans' attitudes toward food have changed considerably. During the past three decades, our growing love affair with snack foods, fast foods, and super-sizes has put more and more "between meals" and "away from home" calories into consumers' stomachs. And school budget cuts, changes in physical education curricula, and increasing hours of television viewing all mean that more and more of the calories we consume stay with us (Critser 2003). With the sociological vision, we can appreciate that our obesity problem is not just one of individual control. Rather, obesity is the product of larger developments in politics, food production, marketing, and lifestyles.

Cultural values, such as those that champion individual control, are not the only obstacle to the sociological perspective. Adopting the sociological vision also can be hindered by our general preference for "certain" rather than "probable" answers. The study of large-scale patterns commits sociologists to predictions that are based on odds or probabilities. In other words, sociologists can identify outcomes that individuals from particular groups and places, or in particular circumstances, are *likely* to face. However, they cannot predict the definitive outcome for any one individual. In a culture that favors definitive answers for specific cases (usually, our own), this feature ensures a certain amount of resistance to the sociological approach. Indeed, sociology instructors often note a familiar complaint among newcomers to the field: If sociology can't predict what will happen to me, then what good is it?

Developing a sociological vision also can be undermined by the dynamic quality of social existence. Social reality is not static—it changes constantly. So just when we think we know the patterns, new ones may be emerging. In addition, the very act of examining social phenomena can inevitably influence the entity we are studying. (If you need a concrete example of this effect, think about how sensitive the stock market is to people's ideas about the economy.) Such dynamics mean that sociologists' work, in a sense, is never done. Furthermore, the conclusions they reach must often remain tentative and open to change. Unlike a physics formula or a mathematical proof, sociological knowledge is rarely final. That dynamic quality often leaves the onlooker questioning its legitimacy.

Another obstacle facing the sociological viewpoint is doubt about the value of *socially* informed knowledge. As conventional wisdom indicates, many people trust only their own personal experiences to teach them about the world, arguing that such knowledge works for them. And, in a certain sense, sociologists must concede the point. Often, it does *appear* as if personal experience is more relevant, or truer, than sociological knowledge. Consider the fact that, as thinking human beings, we have some capacity to create our own social reality. If we think people are not trustworthy, for example, we won't trust them, and we certainly won't give them the chance to prove us wrong. This course of action, no matter how ill conceived, serves to substantiate our own life experiences and to validate our own personally informed knowledge. In clinging to such a stance, we create a self-fulfilling prophecy. A **self-fulfilling prophecy** is a phenomenon whereby that which we believe to be true, in some sense, becomes true for us. In this way, self-fulfilling prophecies make personal experience seem like the clear victor over social knowledge.

Finally, the sociological viewpoint often is ignored by those who believe they already possess sociological expertise. One of the earliest figures in American sociology, William Graham Sumner (1963) noted the tendency of people to think they know sociology by virtue of living in societies. "Being there" affords the opportunity to make social observations, and arguably, social observations are the ingredients of which sociology is made. Thus, "being there" mistakenly is deemed by many as sufficient for generating social knowledge and sociological insights. As our previous discussion indicates, however, personal experience is not the same as the sociological perspective.

If you consider all of these obstacles, you will better understand why the sociological vision is not more readily pursued or adopted by all. It requires effort to move beyond our personal views or experiences and develop what C. Wright Mills called "the sociological imagination." **Sociological imagination** refers to the ability to see and evaluate the personal realm in light of the broader social/cultural and historical arenas.

Why Read This Book?

By introducing this broader picture of reality, *Second Thoughts* encourages readers to step back and sharpen their analytic focus on the familiar. The essays that follow highlight the complex reality of modern-day society—a complexity often missed when we restrict our knowledge to personal experience and the common knowledge or popular assumptions born of those experiences.

Second Thoughts also introduces readers to many concepts central to sociology. In this way, the book can serve as an initiation into the ways in which sociologists frame the world around them. For those who find their sociological eye activated, we provide some of the tools needed for additional research. Each essay concludes with several suggested readings that elaborate on key concepts and ideas introduced in the essay. Furthermore, each essay includes several reliable sources from which facts and figures were derived.

Readers may also find that some of the information presented here moves them beyond curiosity and toward action. To assist such individuals, we close many chapters with the names and URLs of organizations where individuals might further pursue their interests. These listings are not meant as publicity for any body or any cause. Rather, we offer them as preliminary leads, as starting blocks for those who feel directed toward change.

In moving through the text, it will become clear that we have organized *Second Thoughts* according to topics typically covered in introductory-level courses. Those who wish to consider broader applications of this material should consult the "concepts covered" sections in the table of contents. These lists suggest a variety of issues for which one might use a specific conventional wisdom to "jump-start" critical thinking and discussion.

In Closing

When we open our eyes and carefully examine the world around us, we must concede that the realities of social life often run contrary to our stock of common knowledge. In the pages that follow, we aim to highlight some of these contradictions and, in so doing, to demonstrate that reviewing conventional wisdom with a sociological eye can provide a valuable "correction" to our vision of the world around us.

Learning More About It

To learn more about developing a sociological vision, see Peter Berger's classic book *Invitation to Sociology* (New York: Anchor, 1963). C. Wright Mills also provides a brilliant theoretical treatise on this subject in *The Sociological Imagination* (London: Oxford, 1959). A more recent and very readable treatment of these issues is offered by Earl Babbie in *What Is Society? Reflections on Freedom, Order, and Change* (Thousand Oaks, CA: Pine Forge, 1994).

A compelling and humanistic introduction to sociology and its core concepts is offered in Lewis Coser's classic work, *Sociology Through Literature: An Introductory Reader* (Englewood Cliffs, NJ: Prentice Hall, 1963).

For a more thorough and very engaging discussion of America's obesity problem, read Greg Critser's *Fat Land: How Americans Became the Fattest People in the World* (Boston: Houghton Mifflin, 2003) or Eric Schlosser's *Fast Food Nation* (New York: Harper Perennial, 2005).

Public Agenda Online is a nonpartisan organization that offers users a chance to access public opinion studies on major social issues. The site also provides educational materials on various policy issues. You will find Public Agenda Online at http: //www.publicagenda.org

Exercises

1. Think about the social arrangements of your life—that is, your family relations, your neighborhood, your school, and work experiences. If your knowledge of the world were restricted to just these arenas, identify five important facts that you would fail to know.

2. The media give us one view of our social world. Select one week's worth of prime-time TV programs and use them to learn about U.S. society. Put together coding sheets that will allow you to collect basic data on all the program characters you encounter; that is, record each character's age, education, ethnicity, family status, family size, gender, occupational level, race, residence patterns, and so on. Tabulate summary statistics from your data. For example, determine the percentage of characters that are male and female, the average education level, and so on. Obtain a national or world almanac from your local or university library and compare the data you obtain via TV with comparable real-life demographics for the U.S. population. What can you conclude about the media's picture of American society? How did your particular selections of prime-time programming bias or influence your data?

3. Visit the Census Bureau's State and County Quick Facts page: http://quickfacts.census.gov/qfd/states/23000.html and compile a list of additional facts that clearly show how state (or county) context affects our "social vision."

Methods

Essay 1

Conventional Wisdom Tells Us . . . Numbers Don't Lie

Americans like to "run the numbers." No matter what the realm—sports, business, politics, or entertainment—numbers often provide the bottom line. Why is our faith in numbers so strong? Conventional wisdom tells us that numbers don't lie. Is such wisdom accurate? Can we be confident in the "realities" claimed by national polls, social scientific surveys, and other quantitative studies? In this essay, we note several important elements to consider in establishing the "truth" of numbers.

Numbers are everywhere. Indeed, in today's world it is virtually impossible to avoid statistical calculations, data sets, measurements, and projections. We judge the quality of our athletes by their "numbers"—their hits, their home runs, their stolen bases. We use numbers to gauge our financial futures. The Dow is up; the NASDAQ falls. Such numbers drive our investment decisions. The percentages gathered in public opinion polls guide both policymakers and citizen voters in making critical political decisions, and numbers form the cornerstone of research models in fields as diverse as education, medicine, the social sciences, and quantum physics.

Numbers, data, and statistics: Why is our commitment to these entities so strong? Many believe that numbers provide us with precision and objectivity. With numbers, we count rather than guesstimate; we measure rather than suppose; we capture reality rather than assume it. Armed with an empirical blueprint of the day's occurrences, many believe that we move one step closer to seeing the way things *really* are. In essence, many believe that numbers provide us with truth (Babbie 2006; Best 2001, 2004; Healey 2005).

Is this conventional wisdom about numbers accurate? Is it true that numbers don't lie? Can we be confident in the "realities" presented by national polls, social scientific surveys, and other quantitative studies?

To be sure, some of the numbers we see and read may indeed provide us with accurate pictures of the world. Yet the "truth" of numbers cannot be taken for granted. Before one can feel comfortable with the conclusions drawn from any body of data, one must consider several research-related factors. As we find ourselves increasingly bombarded with more and more numbers, we would do well to take a little extra time to review certain aspects of every study's design. By posing certain key questions in evaluating numerical findings, one can better gauge the veracity of any statistical claim.

In assessing the truth of numbers, one must first raise this question: *Exactly whom do the numbers in question represent?* This concern focuses our attention on issues of sampling.

Social researchers generally wish to draw conclusions about groups of people or things. For example, a researcher may wish to learn something about all women in the United States, or about first graders enrolled in New Jersey's public schools, or about Asian Americans living in Los Angeles. Similarly, a researcher may be interested in the content of *Time* magazine covers published from 1975 to 2005; he or she may wish to study the characters appearing in second-grade readers published in 1950 versus those published in 2000. Such groups of interest constitute what researchers call a **population**. A population is a collection of individuals, institutions, events, or objects about which one wishes to generalize or describe.

While social scientists are interested in populations, constraints such as time and money make it difficult, if not impossible, to study an entire population. Consequently, researchers often work with a **sample**; that is, a portion of the population. When selecting a sample, ideally researchers strive to select a **representative sample**. A representative sample refers to a group that mirrors the characteristics of the larger population of interest. With a representative sample, a researcher can make accurate inferences about a large population while working with a small, manageable group.

Representative samples are critical to the truthfulness of numbers. If researchers use nonrepresentative samples to make inferences or generalizations about a population, their conclusions may be misleading or erroneous. The following example helps illustrate the problem. Suppose that you wish to study dating habits among the students at your college. In particular, you are interested in the ways in which students meet potential partners. To research the issue, you choose a campus dorm and interview the first 20 people who leave the dorm one Thursday evening. Based on the answers offered by your 20 subjects, can you draw conclusions about the college population at large? Unfortunately, the answer is no. Because you took no steps to ensure that your sample was representative, your 20 subjects will provide only a limited picture of overall college dating practices. For example, if your subjects were members of a coed dorm, then their experiences could differ significantly from those of noncoed dorm residents. The fact that you are interviewing people *leaving* the dorm on a Thursday night may also prove significant. Those residents who choose to stay in for the night may exhibit very different dating patterns from those who leave the dorm. Similarly, the dating experiences of your 20 dorm residents may differ quite dramatically from the experiences of students commuting to your college from home or from an off-campus residence. By drawing a sample of college students based on convenience, you failed to represent the general character of the entire student body systematically. Therefore, the data you collect will tell us something about the 20 individuals who live in a particular dorm. However, the numbers generated from these 20 interviews cannot provide a useful picture of overall student dating practices.

Attention to sampling represents a first step in determining the "truthfulness" of numbers. However, if we wish to confirm the veracity of data, we must ask other questions as well. For example, *"How were a researcher's numbers collected?"* A researcher's data collection methods and measurement instruments will tell us much about the ultimate value of her or his research conclusions.

Consider, for example, the area of public opinion research. In today's world, there is scarcely a day when some dimension of public opinion is absent from the news. Public opinion reports typically result from a data collection method known as survey research. **Survey research** involves the administration of a carefully designed set of questions; the questions are posed during a face-to-face interview, during a telephone interview, or via a written or an online questionnaire.

If survey researchers construct their questions thoughtfully and subjects answer those questions honestly, then surveys should provide us with an accurate picture of the world, right? Maybe, but maybe not. Questionnaire design presents social scientists with one of the most difficult and challenging tasks of research. Because of this, even the most experienced researchers can fall prey to design problems that may inadvertently influence the accuracy of their numbers.

For example, recent research convincingly shows that the ordering of survey questions can dramatically affect respondents' answers to the questions they are asked. In other words, exposure to one question on an interview schedule can influence a respondent's interpretations and responses to subsequent survey questions. Keeping this phenomenon in mind, imagine a survey designed to solicit likeability ratings for various public figures. In such a survey, a subject's rating for one individual—say, Hillary Clinton—will vary significantly depending on where and when Mrs. Clinton is presented for evaluation. Hillary Clinton may prove quite likable if she is rated immediately following congressional colleagues such as Trent Lott or Tom DeLay. However, she may not fare as well if rated immediately following other first ladies such as Jacqueline Kennedy or Barbara Bush. In essence, the "numbers" on Hillary Clinton are strongly tied to the instrument by which her likeability is gauged. In survey research, the series of individuals considered by a respondent can make an impact on a respondent's perception of any one person (Cerulo 1998; Meyers and Crull 1994; Saris and Gallhofer 2007; Tanur 1992; Tourangeau, Couper, and Conrad 2004).

The ordering of survey questions can have other important effects as well. Methodology experts such as Earl Babbie note that the ordering of survey questions can sometimes alter a respondent's perception of current events. Such effects must be considered in evaluating the "truth" of numbers. Suppose, for example, that a survey researcher questions a respondent regarding the dangers of violent crime. After several questions on this topic, imagine that the researcher then asks the respondent a seemingly unrelated question: "What do you believe to be the single greatest threat to public stability?" Under these conditions, it is highly likely that the respondent will nominate violent crime more often than any other social problem. Why? The researcher's initial questions on violent crime can unintentionally focus the respondent on a specific set of concerns. By directing the respondent's attentions toward one particular subject, the researcher can inadvertently blind the respondent to other areas of consideration (Babbie 2006; Saris and Gallhofer 2007).

The ordering of questions represents one important element of data collection, but in judging the veracity of survey numbers, it is also critical to consider the specific questions that generated the numbers. All too often, critical information is lost in the reporting of survey results. For example, responses can be generalized in ways that misrepresent the questions posed in a survey. Similarly, answers to different questions may be reported and used to suggest changes in public attitudes. Thus, to correctly interpret the actual information that survey numbers provide, we must carefully trace survey data to its original source.

The following example helps illustrate the importance of tracing survey data to its source. In the early 1990s, the American Jewish Committee commissioned the Roper organization to survey Americans' attitudes on the Holocaust. One of the questions posed in the Roper survey read as follows: "Does it seem possible or does it seem impossible to you that the Nazi extermination of the Jews never happened?" Twenty-two percent of Roper's respondents answered that it was possible that the extermination never happened. (Roper was working with a representative sample of American adults.) Many Jewish leaders were stunned by the survey's results. The numbers suggested that approximately one in five Americans were terribly misinformed about the Holocaust. Researchers were surprised by these results as well. Hence, they decided to redo the survey. Again, researchers questioned a representative sample of American adults. This time, however, they posed the Holocaust question in a slightly different way. Respondents were asked, "Do you believe that the Holocaust: (a) definitely happened, (b) probably happened, (c) may have happened, (d) probably did not happen, (e) definitely did not happen." In the second survey, only 2.9% of those questioned said that the Holocaust "definitely" or "probably" did not happen (Kifner 1994:A12; Ruane 2004).

What happened here? Did Americans dramatically change their position on the Holocaust between the first and second surveys? On the surface, it may seem that way, but by tracing the data to its source, we can comfortably eliminate that possibility. The shift in Americans' attitudes toward the Holocaust is connected to the change in the researchers' survey questions. In the first survey, researchers posed a confusing question to respondents: "Does it seem possible or does it seem impossible to you that the Nazi extermination of the Jews never happened?" Consider the poor wording of this question. Choosing the seemingly positive response "possible" resulted in respondents expressing a negative view on the authenticity of the Holocaust. In essence, a poorly designed question resulted in a flawed measurement of attitudes. In the second survey, the Holocaust question was worded more clearly. Thus, the second survey produced very different results. Moreover, the clarity of the second survey question suggests that its results are a more accurate representation of American attitudes.

The Holocaust example highlights some other important benefits of tracing data to its source. In checking the source, we verify the quality of the data collection process. For example, examining a survey's original question allows us to assess the validity of a researcher's measurement tools. A **valid measure** is one that accurately captures or measures the concept or property of interest to the researcher. Examining a survey's original question also provides some sense of a measure's reliability. A **reliable measure** proves consistent and stable from one use to the next. The greater the validity and reliability of a researcher's measures, the greater the confidence we can have in the data generated.

Tracing data to its source represents an important step in determining the veracity of numbers. However, in reviewing numbers, it is equally important to consider the issues behind the questions as well. When we review a single study or when we compare the findings from two or more studies, it is important to ask, *What did the researcher hope to measure, and how did she or he operationalize that concept?* **Operationalization** refers to the way in which a researcher defines and measures the concept or variable of interest. Without a full understanding of a researcher's operationalizations, those reviewing a study's findings may misinterpret the researcher's intentions. Under such circumstances, a researcher's conclusions can be inadvertently applied to issues beyond the scope of the study. Similarly, when a researcher's operationalizations are misunderstood, projects addressing different concepts may be mistakenly compared, creating conflict and confusion.

For example, in Essay 15, you will read about two important studies of criminal activity: the *FBI Uniform Crime Reports* and the *National Crime Victimization Survey*. Both studies represent highly reputable data analysis projects. Both studies address the annual incidence of crime in the United States. Yet each study presents completely different estimates of crime. For example, while the *Uniform Crime Reports* estimate approximately 469.2 violent crimes per every 100,000 Americans (U.S. Department of Justice 2006d), the *National Crime Victimization Survey* estimates 2,006 violent crimes per every 100,000 Americans—over four times the number recorded by the FBI (U.S. Department of Justice 2006a, 2006b)!

Which report presents the "true" number of crimes? If we failed to note the ways in which each study operationalizes crime, we would probably conclude that one set of numbers is in error. But by examining each study's operationalizations, we learn that the numbers in both reports are credible. The *Uniform Crime Reports* are based on crimes reported to the police. Thus, to be counted in the FBI's statistics, a crime must be known to and officially recorded by some police agency. In contrast, estimates forwarded in the *National Crime Victimization Survey* are based on the self-reports of a nationally representative sample. Note that crimes self-reported by victims may be completely unknown to the police. Furthermore, a violent crime's classification in the *National Crime Victimization Survey* remains solely in the hands of the "victim." Thus, in some cases, a victim's report of a "crime" may not meet the normal standards of the law.

When we consider the very different ways in which these two studies measure violent crime, it becomes easy to understand the discrepancy between the two data sources. The FBI statistics capture "official crime" as reported by the police. In contrast, the *National Crime Victimization Survey* offers "unofficial crime" as reported by ordinary citizens. In essence, each study presents a different operationalization of crime. Each study provides us with different dimensions of violent crime in the United States.

Whom do research numbers represent? How did the researcher collect his or her numbers? How were concepts operationalized? All of these questions should be posed by those assessing the veracity of data. But a complete assessment of data requires one additional question as well: *Who is conducting the research?* Most researchers strive to remain value-free when conducting their work. A **value-free researcher** is one who keeps personal values and beliefs out of the collection and interpretation of data. In some cases, certain ideologies or self-interests can color the nature of a project. For example, should one believe numbers that document cigarettes' effects on health if one learns that the study generating such numbers is funded by a major tobacco company? Similarly, can one feel comfortable with data that suggest racial differences in IQ if one knows that the researcher presenting such conclusions is an avowed White Supremacist? The motives and interests of those executing or sponsoring a study must be carefully considered before one can determine the "truth" behind the numbers.

It is important to note that even the best of researchers—scholars trying to maintain a value-free stance—can unintentionally allow certain biases to color their interpretations of data. Researchers are, after all, social beings. They carry with them certain cultural assumptions and understandings. When executing research, these assumptions and understandings can unknowingly influence that which falls within a researcher's "viewfinder." Anthropologists have been especially effective at uncovering situations in which a researcher's vision is unintentionally distorted. How does such a thing happen?

Imagine a researcher who is interested in studying modes of interpersonal, nonverbal communication. She or he observes and records such exchanges among both American and non-American dyads (a dyad is a group of two). Now suppose that in observing interactions among non-American dyads, the researcher notes several instances in which one member of the dyad sticks out her or his tongue at the other member. Within American culture, such a gesture generally suggests teasing and mockery. Some researchers would allow this American standard to guide their interpretation of these observations of non-Americans. But were the researcher to impose the "American" meaning on interpretations of *all* tongue-sticking incidents, she or he would forward data that were biased by ethnocentrism. **Ethnocentrism** is a tendency to view one's own cultural experience as a universal standard. When ethnocentrism intrudes on research, one's data can present a completely false picture. Consider the fact that sticking out one's tongue in South China, for example, is a sign of deep embarrassment. Among inhabitants of the Caroline

Islands, the gesture is used to frighten demons away. In New Caledonia, sticking out one's tongue at another carries a wish for wisdom and vigor. And in India, the gesture is a sign of incredible rage.

As data consumers, we should make a reasonable effort to learn the cultural background of the researcher. We may also wish to explore the researchers' efforts to overcome their own biases, for if we remain unaware of their cultural "blinders," we can fall prey to the same misinterpretations made by the professional observer.

In this essay, we have provided much instruction; we have issued many warnings. In light of this stance, you may feel completely doubtful of the conventional wisdom on numbers. How can numbers ever be trusted? But keep in mind that as a research project unfolds, a careful researcher is asking the very same questions posed in this essay. A careful scholar is attending to the veracity of data even as they are produced. When one couples a careful researcher with an astute data consumer, the product can be a set of numbers that sheds much light on aspects of the social world.

Learning More About It

Janet Ruane offers an engaging and very readable discussion of good methodological technique in *Essentials of Research Methods* (Malden, MA: Blackwell, 2005).

Earl Babbie ponders the problems of doing research in *Observing Ourselves: Essays in Social Research* (Prospect Heights, IL: Waveland Press, 1998).

The Gallup organization offers some firsthand insight into selecting a representative sample, formulating questions, and so on. Visit its Web site at <http://www.gallup.com> and click on the link for the "Gallup Polls."

Nora Cate Schaeffer and Stanley Presser instruct us on good questionnaire design in "The Science of Asking Questions," *Annual Review of Sociology* 29:65–88, 2003.

Joel Best provides a fascinating guide to thinking critically about numbers and spotting "bad" statistics in *Damned Lies and Statistics: Untangling Numbers from the Media, Politicians, and Activists* (Berkeley: University of California Press, 2001) and *More Damned Lies and Statistics: How Numbers Confuse Public Issues* (Berkeley: University of California Press, 2004).

Jane Miller discusses the ins and outs of reporting statistics in *Writing About Numbers: Effective Presentation of Quantitative Information* (Chicago: University of Chicago Press, 2004).

Exercises

1. Earlier in this essay, we described a study exploring dating patterns of college students. The essay presented the "wrong way" to draw a sample for such a project. Briefly describe one possible method for drawing a better, more representative sample of a college student community.

2. Consult a sociology dictionary for a definition of alienation. Then, visit the Web site for the General Social Survey (GSS; <http://www.icpsr.umich.edu/ gss/home.htm>) and find the questions used on the GSS to measure alienation. (Once you've accessed the GSS home page, click on Site Map, then Subject Index, and then Alienation.) Assess the adequacy of the GSS questions relative to your working definition of alienation.

3. Visit the Web site PollingReport.com. Find several surveys that address the same "topic," but ask slightly different questions. Do the differences in polling numbers offer any insight into the meaning of statistical data's validity?

Culture

Essay 2

Conventional Wisdom Tells Us . . . Winning Is Everything

Conventional wisdom suggests that competition and achievement go hand in hand. In this essay, however, we highlight the many studies that show the benefits of cooperation over competition. In so doing, we review American cultural values, strategies of action, and the connection of these elements to both positive and negative outcomes.

Think back to the last Little League, soccer, or professional hockey game you attended. Or take note of the stores and businesses that celebrate the "salesperson of the week." Now consider the mega-dollar spending and the "hardball" tactics embraced by contenders for national political office. And who can forget the thrill of victory and the agony of defeat as read on the faces of the most recent World Series, Super Bowl, or Olympic contenders?

These snapshots of American life remind us that competition is central to our culture. As children, we are taught to play hard and fight to win. As adults, we learn to value winning. We equate winning with the most talented or the "best man," and we regularly remind ourselves that "nice guys finish last." In the United States (as well as in most capitalist societies), the emphasis is on beating one's opponent. (And as recent scandals in professional baseball and football reveal, some feel that steroids or other forms of cheating are legitimate strategies by which to accomplish that goal.) We want to be the one "on top," the "king of the hill," the one left standing after a "fair fight." Al Davis, managing partner of the Oakland Raiders NFL team captures the sentiment: "Just win, baby!" (as quoted in Wetzel 2007).

The conventional wisdom on competition represents a **cultural value**. A cultural value is a shared sentiment regarding what is good or bad, right or wrong, desirable or undesirable. In the United States, competition is a positive cultural value (Aronson 1980; Cavanagh 2005; Hunt 2000; Stinchcombe 1997:13–15; Williams 1970). Yet despite our commitment to healthy competition, research shows that the practice may not always be in our best interest. A growing literature suggests that in many areas of social life, cooperation leads to more profitable outcomes than does competition.

Social psychologists David and Roger Johnson reviewed nearly 200 studies on human performance. The results of their research indicate that cooperation promotes higher individual achievement, higher group productivity, better problem solving, and more effective learning than do competitive strategies of interaction. These same studies show that the more cooperative people are, the better their performance. Thus, when group members periodically take the time to review their efforts while executing a task or attempting to solve a problem—that is, when group members reflect on their actions, ensure the equal distribution of responsibility, and protect open communication channels—the benefits afforded by cooperative strategies often increase (Johnson and Johnson 1989, 2002; also see Alper, Tjosvold, and Law 2000; Bendor and Swistak 1997; De Dreu, Weingart, and Kwon 2000; Jensen, Johnson, and Johnson 2002; Johnson and Johnson 2005; Kohn 1986; Madrid, Canas, and Ortega-Medina 2007; Muthusamy, Wheeler, and Simmons 2005; Quiggin 2006; and Wilkinson and Young 2002).

The success of cooperation stems from the strategies of action that it stimulates. **Strategies of action** are the means and methods social actors use to achieve goals and fulfill needs. Research indicates that the cooperative stance allows individuals to engage in more sophisticated and advanced thinking and reasoning than that which typically occurs in competitive environments. Social psychologists refer to these sophisticated thinking strategies as higher-level reasoning and metacognitive strategies.

Why do cooperative environments enable sophisticated thinking? Research suggests that interaction within cooperative settings typically evolves according to a process that sociologists refer to as a dialectic. A **dialectic** is a process by which contradictions and their solutions lead participants to more advanced thought. The dialectic process consists of three steps. In Step 1, thesis, the group experiences conflict. Here, members propose different ideas, opinions, theories, and information regarding the task or problem at hand. This conflict or disequilibrium sparks Step 2, antithesis. In antithesis, members actively search for more information and additional views, thus maximizing their knowledge about the task or problem they face. When the search is complete, the group begins Step 3, synthesis. Synthesis is a period in which group members reorganize and reconceptualize their conclusions in a way that merges the best thinking of all members (Cerulo 2006: Chapter 7; De Dreu et al., 2000; Enns 2005; Glassman 2000; Johnson and Johnson 1989, 2002; Malley, Beck, and Adorno 2001; Wichman 1970).

In addition to bettering group and individual performance, cooperation—according to more than 180 studies—enhances the quality of interpersonal relationships. Friends, workers, and intimates who cooperate with one another rather than competing report feeling greater levels of acceptance from their colleagues and partners. As a result, cooperators become more caring and committed to their relationships. Furthermore, those involved in cooperative relationships report higher self-esteem and less psychological illness than those who compete with their friends, colleagues, and partners. Indeed, competitiveness has been repeatedly linked to psychological pathology (Combs 1992; Finlinson, Austin, and Pfister 2000; Johnson and Johnson 1989, 2002, 2005; Jurd 2005; Kohn 1986; Muthusamy et al. 2005; Wilson 2000).

Some studies also link cooperation to diminished feelings of prejudice. **Prejudice** refers to the prejudgment of individuals on the basis of their group memberships. For example, individuals who cooperate with those whom they previously had stigmatized or negatively stereotyped report an increased liking toward such individuals. In contrast, individuals placed in competitive situations with members of a previously stigmatized group report a greater dislike for their competitors. On the basis of such studies, many researchers suggest that interracial, interethnic, and intergender cooperative tasks should become a regular "orientation" strategy in workplaces, schools, civic groups, and neighborhood organizations. Many believe that such cooperation "exercises" could help reduce prejudice and bigotry in the sites of our daily interactions (Aronson and Cope 1968; Aronson and Thibodeau 1992; Holtz and Miller 2001; Jehn and Shah 1997; Johnson and Johnson 2000; McConahay 1981; Peterson 2007; Rabois and Haaga 2002; Slavin and Madden 1979; Stapel and Koomen 2005; Vanman, Paul, and Ito 1997). Indeed, several researchers have documented such outcomes as they pertain to periods of economic development, civil rights movements, and political revolutions (Deutscher and Messner 2005; Mihailescu 2005; Miller 2006; United Nations 2005).

If cooperation leads to so many benefits, why do social actors continue to choose the competitive stance? The persistence of competition is a good example of the power of cultural values and the ways in which cultural values can promote a phenomenon that sociologists refer to as **culture against people**. Culture works against people when the beliefs, values, or norms of a society lead to destructive or harmful patterns of behavior. When it comes to the value of competition, the culture-against-people phenomenon couldn't be any stronger. Indeed, research conducted over the past several decades suggests that, even when individuals are made fully aware that they have more to gain by cooperating with others than by competing with them, they often continue to adopt competitive strategies of action (Deutsch and Krauss 1960; Hargreaves-Heap and Varoufakis 2005: Chapter 5; Houston et al. 2000; Kelley and Stahelski 1970; Miceli 1992; Minas et al. 1960; Schopler et al. 1993; Schultz and Pruitt 1978; Van Avermaet et al. 1999).

In one experiment, for example, a college professor told his students that they were participating in an investment research project for the *Wall Street Journal*. The project consisted of several simple exercises. In each exercise, students in the class would be asked to write a number, either 1 or 0, on a slip of paper. Before casting their votes, students were informed that the number of "1" votes cast by class members would determine a financial "payoff" for each student. The professor explained that each exercise was designed such that a unanimous class vote of 1 would maximize every class member's payment as well as the total class "pot." The class was also instructed that a single 0 vote could increase one voter's payoff, but such split votes would always result in a smaller payment for the remaining class members, as well as a smaller payment for the class overall.

Here is a concrete example of the payoff schedule. If 30 people wrote the number 1, a total of $36.00 would be evenly divided by the class—$1.30 for each class member. But if 29 people chose 1 and one person chose 0, only $35.30 would be paid to the class. The one individual who voted 0 would be paid $1.66; the 29 students who voted 1 would each receive only $1.16. Now, consider a situation in which 10 students choose the number 0 and 20 choose the number 1. Here, the class would divide only $29.00. Students choosing 0 would each receive $1.30, but those choosing 1 would receive only $.80. (The professor provided students with a breakdown of all possible payoffs before the class voting began.)

The professor took several votes in his class, allowing class members to debate strategies before each vote. Yet even when the entire class recognized and agreed that a unanimous 1 vote would be the fairest and most lucrative strategy overall, several class members continued to vote 0 in an effort to maximize their own individual gain (Bishop 1986).

Similar results have emerged from experiments conducted in laboratory settings. The Prisoner's Dilemma, for example, is an experimental game designed to test an individual's preference for cooperative versus competitive strategies. The game is based on a hypothetical problem faced by two suspects and a district attorney, all gathered in a police station. The district attorney believes that both suspects have committed a crime but has no proof connecting the suspects to the crime. Thus, he separates the two, telling each prisoner that he has two alternatives: confess to committing the crime in question, or not confess. Prisoners are told that if neither confesses, both will be convicted of only a minor offense and receive only a minor punishment (1 year in prison). If both confess, each will be convicted of a major crime and face fairly severe penalties (10 years in prison). If only one of the prisoners confesses, the confessor will receive full immunity, while the nonconfessor will receive the maximum penalty allowed by law (15 years in prison).

The Prisoner's Dilemma is designed to encourage cooperation. Clearly, silence on the part of both prisoners maximizes the favorable chances of each one. Yet in experimental trials, prisoners repeatedly favor competition. When faced with both the cooperative and competitive options, players consciously choose confession—the strategy that offers them the potential to maximize their own gain. In other words, players choose to compete even when such a strategy proves riskier than cooperation (Hargreaves-Heap and Varoufakis 2005: Chapter 5; Houston et al. 2000; Kollock 1998; Rapoport 1960; Schopler et al. 1993; Van Avermaet et al. 1999).

The *Wall Street Journal* experiment (devised by three economists, Charles Plott, Mark Isaac, and James Walker), the Prisoner's Dilemma, and other similar games and experiments all illustrate the way in which our cultural value of competition can work against people. These examples suggest that, even when a goal can be realized best via a common effort, significant numbers of individuals will espouse cooperation but act in a competitive way. Significant numbers of individuals will act to maximize their own gain rather than acting in the best interest of the group as a whole—even if that maximization proves risky and the payoff uncertain.

Can we overcome the allure of competition? Are there any circumstances that motivate individuals to choose the cooperative path? For decades, experimental work has suggested that those faced with some type of external threat will abandon their competitive stance and ban together with others in cooperative strategies of defense or protection (Blake and Moulton 1979; Deutsch and Krauss 1960; Dion 1979; Lanzetta 1955; Sherif 1966; Sherif et al. 1961; Wilder and Shapiro 1984). Recently, these findings have been replicated in real-world settings, particularly in studies devoted to the aftermath of natural disasters or terrorist attacks (Cerulo 2006: Chapter 7; Halbert 2002; Heeren 1999; Press 2007; Turkel 2002). Equally exciting is a growing line of research that examines the role of cooperation in capitalism. For centuries, economists have argued that competition is essential to a sustainable, dynamic economy. However, a number of current studies suggest that locally, nationally, or globally, the healthiest economies are those that find a balance between competition and cooperation within institutional structures (Amodeo 2001; Brandenburger and Nalebuff 1996; Deutsch 2000; Deutscher and Messner 2005; Moore 1997; Royo 2006; Wisman 2000). Thus, in the final analysis, working together may be the most profitable strategy of all.

Learning More About It

Those interested in a thorough examination of the conditions that foster cooperation and in learning how to promote cooperation should consult Robert Axelrod's *The Evolution of Cooperation* (New York: Penguin, 2006).

The notion of "culture against people" stems from a line of work that includes Philip Slater's *The Pursuit of Loneliness: American Culture at the Breaking Point* (Boston: Beacon Press, 1970); Richard Sennett's *The Fall of Public Man* (New York: Knopf, 1977); and Robert Bellah and colleagues' *Habits of the Heart: Individualism and Commitment in American Life* (Berkeley: University of California Press, 1985).

Several interesting articles linking cooperation to successful economies can be found in *The Handbook of Conflict Resolution: Theory and Practice,* 2nd edition, edited by Morton Deutsch, Peter T. Coleman, and Eric C. Marcus (San Francisco: Jossey-Bass, 2006).

A good review of cooperation and competition as exercised by children can be found in Jacques F. Richard and colleagues' "Cooperation and Competition," in *Blackwell Handbook of Child Social Development,* edited by P. K. Smith and C. H. Hart, pp. 515–532 (Malden, MA: Blackwell Publishers, 2002).

The following organizations can help you learn more about cooperation:

Cooperative Learning Center
60 Peik Hall, University of Minnesota, Minneapolis, MN 55455,
http://www.co-operation.org

Future Problem Solving Program (Fosters creative thinking in
    problem-solving efforts)
http://www.fpsp.org

Grace Contrino Abrams Peace Education Foundation
http://www.peaceeducation.com

Institute on Global Conflict and Cooperation
http://igcc.ucsd.edu/contact.php

Up With People (Builds understanding and cooperation among those
of different cultures through a special educational program)
http://www.upwithpeople.org

Exercises

1. To determine the cultural importance of competition, try the following "experiment." Solicit several friends or relatives to join you in some traditionally competitive activity, such as basketball, bowling, cards, or tennis. Vary the conditions of play with each individual you choose. For example, use normal game rules with some of your "subjects"; tell others that you don't want to play for points or keep score. Note the different reactions, if any, to the different conditions of play. Does playing without keeping score affect the willingness of some to participate? Affect the quality of interaction? Do you note any effects of gender or age on the reactions you observe?

2. Explore the significance of competition for college grading. Prepare a serious proposal that testing be conducted under conditions of cooperation rather than competition. (Cooperative conditions might include group testing, open discussion during the exam, or an adjustment in grade calculation methods such that each student's grade is an average of her or his actual performance as well as the performance of the best and worst students in the class.) Conduct a limited survey of your colleagues. Do they support or reject such a proposal? What reasons do they offer for their position? Is their reasoning consistent with American values on competition? On cooperation?

3. Access the online site of the U.S. Senate, http://www.senate.gov/, and review the recent history of some political issue or debate. Based on your review, would you say that the workings of the Senate are more reflective of competition or cooperation? What is your evidence?

Essay 3

Conventional Wisdom Tells Us . . . Children Are Our Most Precious Commodity

We frequently hear it said: Children are our future. They are our most valuable resource. Here, we present research suggesting otherwise. Children may be the most overlooked, the most neglected segment of the population despite current talk of family values and the future of American youth.

Children—who doesn't love them? In the United States, we refer to children as "our nation's future." Our conventional wisdom celebrates them as society's most precious commodity. And national opinion polls repeatedly document that Americans consider children one of life's true rewards. Witness how our popular icons—Madonna or Angelina Jolie—can cause a media frenzy over their efforts to adopt and garner that reward. Indeed, couples who want children but cannot have them are ensured the sympathies and support of their fellow members of society. In contrast, couples who don't want children frequently find themselves objects of contempt or suspicion.

Much of today's political rhetoric is fueled by the cultural value America places on children. Citizens and elected officials are urged to "act now" in the long-term interest of the nation's youth. Politicians vow to cut today's

Photo 3.1   Copyright Anne
Glassman.
Reprinted by
permission of
Anne Glassman.

spending and spare our children and grandchildren a troubled and debt-laden tomorrow.
Many advocate curbing Social Security and
Medicare costs so as to protect benefits for
future generations. Global warming is frequently discussed with an eye to the environmental legacy we will leave our heirs.
Such prescriptions underscore the importance of children in our youth-oriented
society.

Threats to our children can mobilize
American sentiments in a way that few
other issues can. Consider some landmark
moments of the past few decades that
joined American citizens together in public
outrage: the bombing of a federal building in Oklahoma City; school shootings
at Columbine High School, "Virginia
Tech," or that one-room schoolhouse in
Pennsylvania's Amish country; the Amber
Hagerman kidnapping, which inspired the
creation of the Amber Alert system; the
murder and rape of Megan Kanka, which
resulted in Megan's Law; or the sensational
kidnapping of Madeleine McCann,
allegedly stolen from a hotel room while
her parents enjoyed dinner in the hotel
restaurant. In such instances, public out-
rage was fueled in large measure by the fact that these acts threatened
and/or took the lives of so many children.

Can we take the pro-child rhetoric of conventional wisdom at face value?
How do our pro-child sentiments compare with the realities of American
children's lives? A review of worldwide infant mortality rates offers one perspective on the matter. **Infant mortality rates** gauge the number of deaths per
1,000 live births for children under one year of age. Such statistics represent
a commonly consulted measure, or social indicator, of a society's behavior
toward its children. **Social indicators** are quantitative measures or indices of
social phenomena.

Despite the pro-child sentiments of American culture, the United States
trails many other nations in the fight against infant mortality. To be sure,
infant deaths typically are highest within less developed nations of the world

Photo 3.2   Copyright Karen A. Cerulo. Reprinted by permission of
Karen A. Cerulo.

community, such as Afghanistan, Liberia, Angola, or the Congo. Yet the
U.S. infant mortality rate—6 deaths for every 1,000 live births—is comparable to that found in Cuba, Croatia, and Poland—nations with far less wealth
or international power than the United States (see Figure 3.1). A variety of
other major (and minor) industrial nations, such as Finland, Japan, Slovenia,
France, Germany, Greece, Spain, and Austria, have been more effective than
the United States in fighting infant deaths. Indeed, the U.S. infant mortality
rate is higher than the summary rate (5) for all industrialized countries
(UNICEF 2007a).

Child inoculation rates are another informative measure of a society's
behavior toward its children. As we entered the new millennium, 20% of
two-year-olds failed to have the full series of childhood vaccinations. Nearly
a decade later, the United States has yet to reach its goal of a 90% immunization rate (Children's Defense Fund 2006). And while recent UNICEF data
indicate that 92% of one-year-olds in the United States are fully immunized
against polio, that figure lags behind rates found in far less developed nations,
such as Trinidad and Tobago (97%), Botswana (97%), Cyprus (98%), Cuba
(99%), Kazakhstan (99%), and Sri Lanka (99%; UNICEF 2006).

Figure 3.1   Infant Mortality Rate for the United States and Selected Countries
of the World

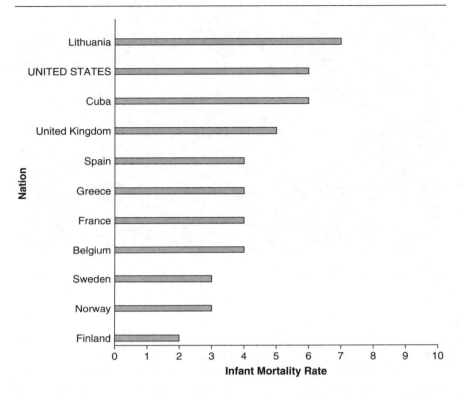

SOURCE: UNICEF Child Mortality Rates. http://www.childinfo.org/areas/childmortality/
infantdata.php

NOTE: Infant mortality rate refers to the number of deaths of children under one year of age per
1,000 live births.

The wealthiest nation in the world doesn't guarantee a healthy start to all of
its newborns. Eight percent of U.S. babies are born at a low birth weight, a
number that has been *increasing* in recent years (Martin et al. 2006). This 8%
rate is higher than that found in many other countries of the world: Republic of
Korea and Sweden (both 4%); Cuba, Denmark, and Norway (all 5%); Spain
and Switzerland (both 6%); and Germany, France, and Kuwait (all at 7%; see
the Federal Interagency Forum on Child and Family Statistics 2006; UNICEF
2007b). And every day in the United States, more than 1,800 newborns join the
ranks of the uninsured in America (Children's Defense Fund 2007).

Figure 3.2   "Select" Moments in the Lives of U.S. Children

- **Every 36 seconds** a baby is born into poverty.
- **Every 36 seconds** a child is confirmed as abused or neglected.
- **Every 47 seconds** a baby is born without health insurance.
- **Every minute** a baby is born to a teen mother.
- **Every 2 minutes** a baby is born at low birth weight.
- **Every 19 minutes** a baby dies before his first birthday.
- **Every 3 hours** a child or teen is killed by a firearm.
- **Every 4 hours** a child or teen commits suicide.
- **Every 6 hours** a child is killed by abuse or neglect.
- **Every 18 hours** a mother dies in childbirth.

SOURCE: Children's Defense Fund: *Moments in America for Children*, May 2007. http://www
.childrensdefense.org/site/PageServer?pagename=research_national_data_moments

To be sure, it is not easy nor is it safe to be young in America (see Figure 3.2). Consider, for example that *for each day of 2003,* fifteen 10- to 24-year-olds were murdered in the United States. (Most were killed by guns.) Indeed, in the United States, gunfire kills a child or teen every three hours (Children's Defense Fund 2007). Homicide is the leading cause of death for Blacks in this age group, and it is the second leading cause of death for 10- to 24-year-old Hispanics. Note too that in 2004, more than 750,000 of those aged 10–24 received emergency room treatment for injuries from violence. And America's love of automobiles can be lethal for children. Injuries from car accidents are the leading cause of death for U.S. children. And of those children under 14 who are killed in auto accidents, nearly half were unrestrained passengers (Centers for Disease Control and Prevention 2007a).

These facts and figures on the physical well-being of U.S. children unveil glaring discrepancies between what we say and what we do with regard to children. However, the discrepancies extend well beyond the realm of health and mortality. Although conventional wisdom celebrates the child, the reality is that millions of American children confront poverty and its many ills throughout their childhood. Currently, slightly more than 18% of those under 18 years old are living in poverty; for those 6 years of age or younger the rate climbs to 20%. (Contrast these figures with 13.3% of the overall population and 10% of the 65+ population living below the poverty level; see, e.g., Children's Defense Fund 2006, National Center for Children in Poverty 2007, U.S. Census Bureau 2005a). Between 2000 and 2005, the number of children living in poverty rose by 11% (Fass and Cauthen 2006). If we compare the United States to a select group of industrialized, market economy countries (what are known as "rich" OECD nations), our record on fighting childhood poverty is truly dismal. Among the OECD nations, the

United States ranks the highest in per capita income. Yet it has the highest childhood poverty rate (21.9%). Among the "rich" OECD nations, the United States also has the distinction of having the lowest social expenditures for fighting poverty (Economic Policy Institute 2005).

It should also be noted that for many poverty scholars, official poverty rates fail to capture economic hardship in the United States. This is because the poverty level is calculated using what many consider an outdated metric. (That metric is based on 1950s data and assumes that the average family spends one-third of its income on food.) Using the official equation, the poverty level for a family of four is approximately $20,700. But for many, this figure is unrealistically low. It fails to give sufficient weight to the growing and disproportional impact of non-food family expenses such as health care, child care, housing costs, transportation expenses, and so on. Critics argue that a family of four needs about twice the official poverty level to meet its basic needs (or approximately $40,000 a year). Families with this level of income, however, are classified by the U.S. Census Bureau as "low income" rather than as impoverished. If we were to revise our poverty statistics to utilize these new income cutoffs, we would find almost 40% of U.S. children living in "impoverished" conditions (Fass and Cauthen 2006).

To fully understand the plight of our nation's children, consider these images. In a "group portrait" of the U.S. poor, more than one-third of the faces would belong to children (U.S. Conference of Catholic Bishops 2006). More than 9 million children—almost one in eight—have no health insurance. One in six children are born to mothers who did not receive any prenatal care in the first trimester (Children's Defense Fund 2007).

Living conditions play a role in this group portrait of the poor. Financially speaking, two-parent families represent the most favorable condition for children. But the percentage of children under 18 living in such households has fallen from 77% in 1980 to 67% in 2005. Today 23% of children under the age of 18 live in mother-only families. Such arrangements can exact a heavy cost for children: 31% of the children in mother-only families live in poverty. Contrast this with the fact that only 6% of children in married couple families are poor (Federal Interagency Forum on Child and Family Statistics 2006; U.S. Census Bureau 2006a, POV10). The high poverty rate for children in single-mother families is in part due to "deadbeat dads." For families below the poverty level, child support constitutes 30% of the family income (Turetsky 2005). In divorced families, child support constitutes about one-quarter of total family income. It is responsible for lifting about half a million children out of poverty each year (Center for Law and Social Policy 2007). More than 17 million children are due more than $100 billion in child support. The Association for Children for the Enforcement of Support reports that only 53% of owed child support is collected (Association for Children for Enforcement of Support 2008).

Poverty undermines the education of our children as well. Before entering kindergarten, children in the highest socioeconomic groups have cognitive scores that are 60% above the average scores for children in the lowest socioeconomic group. As children move through the system, the effects of poverty persist. Low-income third graders with undereducated parents have vocabularies of about 4,000 words. In contrast, their peers from middle-income families with well-educated parents have vocabularies of 12,000 words (Klein and Knitzer 2007). Note too that poor children are more likely to be retained in a grade, and they have high school dropout rates that are six times higher than their wealthy peers. By age 24, almost half of young adults raised in affluent families have graduated from college, compared to only 7% of their low-income counterparts. The conditions of poverty attack the schools themselves. High-poverty schools are more likely to be over-crowded than schools attended by wealthier children. And classes in these high-poverty schools are 77% more likely to be assigned to teachers who did not major in the fields in which they are teaching (Children's Defense Fund 2005b; U.S. Department of Education 2006).

For many children, poverty goes hand in hand with homelessness; nationally, about 40% of the homeless population consists of children under 18 years of age. Further, families with children are among the fastest-growing segments of the homeless population (National Coalition for the Homeless 2006). These conditions have prompted at least one writer to observe that child poverty is one of our country's most stunning failures (Madrick 2002).

But even among children who have a roof over their heads, life is not always easy. National surveys suggest rates of physical and sexual child abuse that are completely inconsistent with America's pro-child rhetoric. The U.S. Department of Health and Human Services estimates that approximately 900,000 children (or a rate of 12.1 per 1,000) were victims of abuse and neglect in 2005. Sixty-three percent of these children experienced neglect, 7% were physically abused, and 9% were sexually abused. During 2005, approximately 1,500 children died from abuse and neglect (Administration for Children and Families 2005).

While it may be hard to fathom mistreating helpless babies and infants, note that it is the *youngest* children who are the most vulnerable to abuse and neglect. Almost 29% of victims of abuse and neglect are between 0 and 3 years of age, and more than half of all victims are under 7 years of age (Children's Defense Fund 2005a). The youngest children also experience the highest rates of fatalities. In 2005, more than three-quarters of those children killed were under 4 years of age (Administration for Children and Families 2005).

As children make their way into the school system, danger persists. Student days are certainly not carefree days for children. Thirty percent of sixth to tenth graders have reported being the targets or the perpetrators of bullying (Centers for Disease Control 2006a). At the high school level, nearly 8% were threatened or injured *on school property,* and nearly 14% were in a physical fight *on school property.* Almost 30% had their property stolen or deliberately damaged *while in school* (Centers for Disease Control 2006a). In the United States, school grounds simply don't offer students a sufficiently safe haven.

Alcohol and drugs play a role in the lives of our schoolchildren as well. Forty-three percent of students reported drinking alcohol on one or more days in the preceding month. Twenty-five percent have engaged in heavy drinking (five or more drinks in a row). Twenty-six percent had first consumed alcohol before the age of 13. With regard to drugs, 9% of eighth graders, 17% of tenth graders, and 23% of twelfth graders report using illicit drugs in the previous 30 days. Sex is a factor to be reckoned with as well. Nearly 47% of high school students have already had sexual intercourse, and 34% are currently sexually active (Centers for Disease Control 2006a; Federal Interagency Forum on Child and Family Statistics 2006).

Our schools also appear to fail our children with regard to academic achievement. Since the early days of the American space program, many have voiced concern regarding the performance levels of American schoolchildren. These concerns are well grounded. While U.S. fourth graders earn higher scores in reading literacy than students from 23 other countries, they earn lower math scores than students from 11 countries. U.S. high school students are consistently outperformed by students in Asian and European countries in math and science (U.S. Department of Education 2006, Special Analysis). Eleven percent of 16- to 18-year-olds are functioning at a *below* basic literacy rate (Kutner et al. 2007). The U.S. mean prose literacy score for those with a high school degree was near the bottom of a 19-country list (18th out of 19—see the National Institute for Literacy 2007a). Across the nation, the average high school graduation rate is 74% (U.S. Department of Education 2006, Indicator 28).

We may idealize childhood (especially in our memories). But these everyday patterns suggest that the reality for today's U.S. children is often anything but ideal. Indeed, despite our pro-child stance, many children find childhood too difficult to endure. The suicide rate among American youth increased by 240% from the early 1950s to the late 1970s. Among contemporary youth, 17% of today's high school students report that they have seriously considered suicide in the last year, and 13% report having made a suicide plan. It is no wonder then that suicide is the third leading cause of death for 15- to 24-year-olds (Centers for Disease Control and Prevention

2007b). On an average day in the United States, five children or teens will take their own lives (Children's Defense Fund 2007).

What meaning can we draw from the discrepancies between conventional wisdom's view of children and the way children actually are treated? Are we simply a nation of hypocrites? We gain some perspective on the issue when we consider a distinction sociologists draw between ideal culture and real culture. **Ideal culture** comprises the values, beliefs, and norms each society claims as central to its modus operandi. In other words, ideal culture has to do with aspirations, the ends or goals of our behaviors. In contrast, **real culture** refers to those values, beliefs, and norms we actually execute or practice. Thus, real culture has to do with behaviors or the means to a society's ends.

Your own life experiences have surely taught you that humans have a remarkable capacity to be inconsistent: We can say one thing and do another. In fact, Americans have a cultural prescription reflecting this capacity: "Do as I say, not as I do." When sociologists examine the fit between ideal and real culture, they are exploring the "Say one thing, do another" phenomenon as it occurs at the social level.

For a society to achieve perfect agreement between its ideal and real cultures, it must achieve both consensus on goals and agreement regarding the appropriate methods for achieving those goals. That is, ideal and real cultures are in balance only when a society is free of contradiction between what it says and what it does. If a society cannot synchronize its goals and behaviors, then it experiences a condition sociologists refer to as cultural inconsistency. **Cultural inconsistency** depicts a situation in which actual behaviors contradict cultural goals. Cultural inconsistency indicates an imbalance between ideal and real cultures.

Why do cultural inconsistencies emerge in a society? Conflict theorists offer one possible answer. **Conflict theorists** analyze social organization and social interactions by attending to the differential resources controlled by different sectors of a society. These theorists suggest that the inability to balance ideal and real cultures has much to do with the broader issues of power and social policy. **Power** is the ability of groups and/or individuals to get what they want even in the face of resistance. **Social policies** are officially adopted plans of action.

In American society, social policies often guide social behaviors, or what we are referring to as real culture. Yet social policies rarely emerge from a consensus of the general population; they are rarely directed toward ideal culture. Rather, such prescriptions inevitably are influenced by the actions and relative power of various sectors of the population: special interest groups, political action committees, lobbyists, and so on.

By definition, special interest groups promote or advance the cause of certain segments of the population, such as the New Christian Right, senior citizens, tobacco manufacturers, or trial lawyers. Thus, these groups are unduly responsive to the interests of the few—and necessarily ignore the broader interests of the larger population. Special interest groups vie to prescribe social policy. Ultimately, then, social policy generally reflects the particularized goals of groups sufficiently powerful to influence it.

Lacking control of economic resources or access to the political ballot denies children, as a collective, the typical tools of power. Furthermore, age works against the self-serving collective actions of children. Children are dependents; they must rely on adults to act as their advocates. As a result, the interests and rights of children always will be weighed against those of parents, families, and society at large. The child's voice always will be rendered via an intermediary's perspective.

The drawbacks of the child's indirect political presence are aptly illustrated when we review efforts to combat child abuse in the United States. History reveals a parade of policies consistent with child advocates' views and beliefs regarding the best interests of children. For example, child advocates of the early 1800s believed that abused and neglected children were at risk of delinquency; such advocates saw abused children as threats to society. As a result, social and reform policies of the period demanded the institutionalization of abused children. Protecting society was deemed "action in the best interest of the child." In the early 1900s, the newly emerging professions of social work and clinical psychology argued that promoting and protecting intact families would best serve the interests of children. Such policy recommendations remanded abused children to the very sites of their mistreatment (Pfohl 1977).

In the current era, many child advocates continue to cling to the family protection theme. The Family Research Council, for example, is an advisory group that has worked for the past 25 years to promote traditional family values. This group rejects any efforts to view children and their rights as an issue separate from the context of the family; they are dedicated to the primacy of paternal authority (Gusdek 1998). The Family Research Council's position, as well as those of other groups before them, makes the political plight of children clear. Without the ability to organize and lobby solely on their own behalf, children will always be one critical step removed from the social policy process—and the gap between the ideal and real cultures that frame childhood in America will continue to exist.

Given the cultural inconsistency that exists in American society's stance toward children, isn't it hypocritical to continue to espouse the ideals we hold? Should an honorable society promote ends it cannot meet?

Sociologically speaking, there are several important reasons to maintain the concept of an ideal culture even when society fails to practice what it preaches. First, a gap between goals and behaviors—that is, a gap between ideal and real cultures—does not diminish the value of a society's ideals. We can honestly place a high value on children even though our behaviors may fall short of the ideal. Ideals, goals, and values are aspirations, and as such, they are frequently not achieved.

Second, changing ideal culture to fit a society's actual practices might indeed bring an end to cultural inconsistency. However, such a change would not alter an important fact: Children literally are the future of any group or society. For a society to survive, individuals must be persuaded to reproduce themselves. In preindustrial days, economic necessity was an attractive incentive for reproduction. Children furnished valuable labor power to colonial families. Children were valuable sources of family income in the early days of industrialization as well. In the industrialization era, children regularly took their places alongside older workers in factories and sweatshops (LeVine and White 1992; Zelizer 1985).

Today, the economic incentives attached to childbearing have changed dramatically. Children are no longer regarded as valuable labor power or income sources for families. Furthermore, the cost of having and raising children in our society has risen dramatically over the years. In a middle-income two-parent, two-child household, it is estimated that 42%–50% of total household expenditures are attributable to the children. The U.S. Department of Agriculture estimates that the expense of raising one child born in 2006 is close to $190,000 for the lowest income families, just over $260,000 for middle-income families, and just over $381,000 for the highest income families! These lifetime expense estimates do not include the cost of a college education. Parents who agree to assist with college costs must be prepared to spend tens of thousands of dollars more to cover college tuition and room and board (Lino 2007).

Changes in lifestyles and priorities, education, and career commitments render the decision to have children more problematic today than at earlier points in America's history. Individuals no longer automatically equate children with personal fulfillment and happiness. Surveys reveal that many married adults report that their highest levels of marital satisfaction occurred before they had children or after their children left home. Indeed some researchers assert that for a growing number of adults, having children is no longer a defining life event (National Marriage Project 2006). The economic and personal costs of child rearing may account for the steady decrease in average family size during the past century. The latest census figures put the average family size at 3.2 for 2006 (U.S. Census Bureau 2006b). Furthermore, surveys indicate that Americans no longer fantasize about "having a house full of children." *USA Today* has reported that 52% of Americans say the ideal family size is two or fewer children (*USA Today* 2003). Trend analysis for the last several years reveals that more and more Americans are citing "two" as the ideal number of children (General Social Survey 2000).

Delayed childbearing also accounts for part of the decline in average family size. Women in the United States are waiting longer to marry (U.S. Census Bureau 2004a) and to have children, and such delays ultimately translate into fewer total births (Martin et al. 2006). In addition, increases in education levels, career aspirations, satisfaction with present life situations, and more reliable birth control all appear to be making it easier for some couples to remain childless (Bennett, Bloom, and Craig 1992; Dalphonse 1997; Wu and MacNeill 2002). The latest census data indicates that 44.6% of women of childbearing age are childless (Dye 2005). In 2004, among those women who were nearing the end of their childbearing years (ages 40–44), 20% remained childless, a twofold increase over the percent childless in 1976 (National Marriage Project 2006). A growing trend toward singlehood among the young and middle-aged further complicates overall U.S. fertility patterns. Since 1970, there has been a steady increase in the percentage of males and females who have never married: In 2005, 31% of males and 25.5% of females 15 years and older fell into the "never-married" category. When we consider all of these changes and trends, it isn't too surprising to see that at present, only 21.5% of U.S. households embody the traditional nuclear family, that is, married couples with children under age 18 (U.S. Census Bureau 2007b).

Any society interested in its own survival must keep a watchful eye on such developments. In 2002, the U.S. birth rate reached its lowest level since birth records were first kept in the early 1900s: 13.9 births per 1,000 persons, a decline of 17% since 1990 (Zitner 2003)! With this drop, the United States teetered on joining the growing ranks of countries with below replacement-level fertility: Austria, Ireland, Japan, Lithuania, Portugal, South Korea, and Taiwan. **Replacement-level fertility** is the level needed for a population to continually renew itself without increasing. Currently, replacement-level fertility is about 2.1 children per woman. In 2005, the U.S. total fertility rate was 2.0 (Haub 2007).

Many population experts regard lower birth rates as foreshadowing dangerous population decline. In general, low fertility produces shrinking labor forces. Declining birth rates also mean that the burden of supporting the social programs for a nation's aging and retiring population will fall on fewer and fewer shoulders. And the longer low fertility rates exist, the harder it becomes to reverse population declines (McDonald 2001; Zitner 2003). Some suspect that the sluggish U.S. economy will further reduce our birth rate and bring us closer to the "zero population growth" situation of other industrialized countries of the world; others see our fertility rates settling into a stabilizing trend (Haub 2003, 2007).

Somewhat ironically, then, nations with increasingly geriatric populations can ill afford record low birth rates—the older a population, the greater its stake in achieving higher birth rates. Viewed in this light, maintaining an ideal culture that values children makes good sense, even when we sometimes fail to practice what we preach. Placing a high premium on children is one important way to ensure that individuals continue to make a financial investment in children and it is a policy that is being adopted by many industrialized countries (Haub 2007). By doing so, these countries are promoting the critical raw material for societal survival. While once a rather academic subject matter, discussion of world fertility issues is now finding its way into the mainstream press. The *Population Reference Bureau* now has a Web site that allows users to monitor fertility conditions of low-fertility countries of the world. The U.S. fertility rate, while holding somewhat steady in the last few years, deserves our attention (Haub 2007).

American conventional wisdom on children seems at odds with our behaviors and actions. But this cultural inconsistency is not likely to disappear soon. Indeed, even if the costs of having and raising children continue to increase and the structures of our families continue to change, pro-child rhetoric may grow even stronger in the United States in the days ahead.

Learning More About It

For a very readable review of sociological perspectives on childhood, see William Cosaro's book *The Sociology of Childhood* (Thousand Oaks: Sage, 2005).

The Child Trends Data Bank offers a collection of pertinent indicators for monitoring trends in child and family welfare: http://www.childtrendsdatabank.org/about.cfm.

The Children's Welfare League of America offers online national and state fact sheets on the status of America's children at http://www.cwla.org/advocacy. Scroll down the page and follow the links for the "National" or the "State" sheets.

D. Russell Crane and Tim B. Heaton provide a collection of articles addressing family and poverty. See the *Handbook of Families and Poverty* (Thousand Oaks, CA: Sage, 2007).

The National Center for Children in Poverty offers a link to demographic profiles of children in each of the 50 states: http://www.nccp.org/profiles/.

For an interesting perspective on historical responses to child abuse in the United States, see Stephen J. Pfohl's "The Discovery of Child Abuse" (*Social Problems* 24:3:310–323, 1977). Murray Straus and Denise Donnelly offer a thorough review of corporal punishment and its effects on children in *Beating the Devil Out of Them: Corporal Punishment in American Families and Its Effects on*

Children (New Brunswick, NJ: Transaction Publishers, 2001). And Sylvia I. Mignon, Calvin J. Larson, and William M. Holmes provide a comprehensive review of family violence—one that offers an integrated theoretical explanation (sociology, psychology, and biology). See *Family Abuse: Consequences, Theories, and Responses* (Boston: Allyn & Bacon, 2002).

Viviana Zelizer offers a fascinating historical review on the social value of children in *Pricing the Priceless Child* (New York: Basic Books, 1985).

A review of the issue of low fertility and its global spread can be found in S. Philip Morgan and Miles Taylor's article, "Low Fertility at the Turn of the Twenty-First Century" (*Annual Review of Sociology*, 2006, 32:375–399).

To learn more about the promise of education, especially for girls, consult UNICEF's "The State of the World's Children: 2004": http://www.unicef.org/sowc04/.

For a discussion on the discrepancy between goals and the paths we choose to achieve them, see Robert Merton's classic 1938 work, "Social Structure and Anomie" (*American Sociological Review* 3:672–682).

The following organizations and sites can help you learn more about children in society:

The Administration for Children and Families
http://www.acf.dhhs.gov

Children's Defense Fund
http://www.childrensdefense.org

Exercises

1. Take a look at the age statistics in Figure 3.3. Pay particular attention to the relative size of the various age groups and the corresponding implications for population trends over the next 25 years. What does the graph suggest is a likely development with regard to our pro-child culture?

2. Select three family TV programs whose cast of characters includes children. Monitor the content of the programs for a two- to three-week period, noting program incidents and themes. On the basis of your observations, do the programs emphasize ideal or real culture in their portrayal of children in our society? What factors can you suggest that might account for your findings?

Figure 3.3   Age and Gender Distribution of the U.S. Population, 1997 and 2025

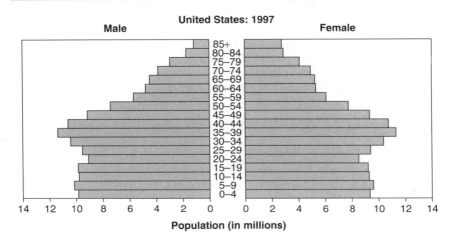

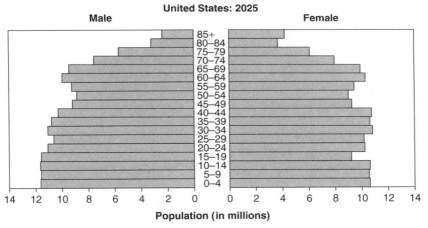

SOURCE: U.S. Bureau of the Census. 2007c. "International Data Base." http://www.census .gov/ipc/www/idb/.

3. Visit and view the state fact sheets about children posted on the Child Welfare League of America Web page http://www.cwla.org/advocacy/statefact sheets/statefactsheets06.htm:

   • What are the states (if any) where the poverty rate for children under 18 is lower than the overall poverty rate for the entire state? What were your most surprising findings? Least surprising? Which states appear to be making the most progress against childhood poverty? What's your evidence? Speculate about the factors that seem to account for progress.

4. Sample some TV commercials from early morning children's programming. Use the information to assemble a "social profile" of U.S. children. How does this profile (i.e., race, economic status, living arrangements, etc.) compare with the picture provided by the National Center for Children in Poverty (http://www.nccp.org/profiles/)?

Social Structure

Essay 4

Conventional Wisdom Tells Us ... Love Knows No Reason

In this essay, we explore various social statuses—age, education, gender, income, race, religion—noting the ways in which these factors can guide something as seemingly individualistic as Cupid's arrow.

L ove: that invigorating, addictive sensation, the emotional roller-coaster ride that signals the wonder of being human. Conventional wisdom locates love in the world of passion; adages describe it as an experience that can make us irrational, impetuous, and often oblivious to the real-life events that surround us. There is nothing logical about love. Love bows to emotion, not reason.

The conventional wisdom on love is not easily shaken. One might even say it stands shoulder to shoulder with the laws of the land! For example, in 1974, the National Science Foundation awarded an $84,000 grant for a social scientific investigation into the experience of love. But upon hearing of the grant, then Senator William Proxmire blasted the investment from the floor of the U.S. Senate, saying,

> I'm against this, not only because no one—not even the National Science Foundation—can argue that falling in love is a science; not only because I'm sure that even if they spend 84 million or 84 billion they wouldn't get an

answer that anyone would believe. *I'm also against it because I don't want the answer!* (quoted in Harris 1978, our emphasis)

Proxmire embraced the conventional wisdom on love—for him, love knows no reason. Is his assumption supported? Is the fall into love strictly an emotional journey? Does Cupid's arrow defy reason or direction and truly strike us senseless?

Despite romantic visions, research indicates that the experience of falling in love is much more logical than we might like to admit. Although Cupid's arrow may contain the magic that joins two hearts, Cupid's aim appears to be highly selective, and heavily influenced by the social status of his targets. **Social status** refers to the position or location of an individual with reference to characteristics such as age, education, gender, income, race, and religion. Consider the love-and-marriage game. Our choices for the "love of our lives" generally occur along highly predictable lines (Blackwell and Lichter 2004; Buss et al. 2001; Gardyn 2002; Kalmijn 1991, 1994, 1998; Kalmijn and Flap 2001; McPherson, Smith-Lovin, and Cook 2001; Ono 2006; Schwartz and Scott 2007: Chapter 5; U.S. Census Bureau 2004b). Indeed, these choices are guided by "rules" that sociologists refer to as norms of homogamy. **Norms of homogamy** encourage interaction between individuals occupying similar social statuses.

Research shows that the large majority of Americans fall in love and marry mates within four years of their own age (U.S. Census Bureau 2004b). Furthermore, the look of love seems routinely reserved for those of like races, religions, and classes. For example, fewer than 5% of all U.S. marriages are interracial, and only about a quarter of American marriages occur between people of different religions (Bisin, Topa, and Verdier 2002; Gardyn 2002; U.S. Census Bureau 2004b). Approximately 60% of all American marriages unite people of the same social class, and more than 80% of all U.S. marriages join people who are no more than one socioeconomic class apart (Gardyn 2002; Holman, Larson, and Olsen 2001; Hout 1982; U.S. Census Bureau 2004b).

Cupid's arrow also is typically reserved for those with similar educational backgrounds, similar intelligence levels, and similar physical appearances. And, apparently, Cupid's flights are amazingly short. Research documents a 50/50 chance that individuals will marry people who live within walking distance of their homes or their jobs (Gardyn 2002; Mulford et al. 1998; Sprecher and Regan 2002; U.S. Census Bureau 2004b).

When it comes to love and marriage, research suggests that "birds of a feather seem to flock together," while "opposites rarely attract." Star-crossed lovers may exist in principle, but in practice the stars of love are likely to be carefully charted by social forces—and thus glitter in the eyes of a social peer. Such patterns lead sociologists to characterize both romantic love and marriage as endogamous phenomena. **Endogamy** is a practice restricted by shared group membership; it is an "in-group" phenomenon. What explains the endogamous nature of love? Endogamy generally results from a societal wish to maintain group and class boundaries. In some cases, these boundaries are formally stated. Certain religious groups, for example, strongly urge their members toward intrafaith marriages. Similarly, traditional caste systems generally prohibit marriage between individuals of different castes. In other settings, however, boundary maintenance occurs via more informal channels, where certain key social players may quietly enforce endogamy in love and marriage.

In U.S. society, parents and peers often play the role of enforcer. It is not uncommon for family and friends to threaten, cajole, wheedle, and even bribe individuals in the direction of a "suitable" mate. Suitability generally translates into a partnership based on similar social profiles. Thus, the "American way" of marriage places the most personal decisions of one's life—falling in love and getting married—under "group control." This subtle control serves as a vehicle by which endogamy can be maintained.

Like romantic love, the development and expression of platonic love or friendship are also heavily influenced by the social location of its participants. Research shows that friendship formation is largely a product of one's daily interaction patterns rather than of chance or "good chemistry."

Friendships tend to develop with the people we see most often—those with whom we work, those enrolled in the same classes, or members of our churches, health clubs, and so on. Similarly, friendships tend to form among those who are in close geographic proximity to us, as opposed to those who are farther away—that is, the people in the same apartment complex or those who live in the same neighborhood as we do (Carley and Krackhardt 1996; Festinger, Schachter, and Back 1950; Giordano 2003; McPherson et al. 2001; Monge and Kirste 1980, Pahl and Pevalin 2005; Spencer and Pahl 2006).

Like romantic love, the platonic love of friendship grows best out of similarity. We tend to build the strongest friendships with those who hold attitudes similar to our own. We also tend to connect with those who share our physical and social characteristics—appearance, income, education level, race, and so on. In the case of friendship, familiarity breeds attraction rather than contempt (Adams and Allan 1998; Allan 1998a; Diamond and Dube 2002; Giordano 2003; McPherson et al. 2001; Pahl and Pevalin 2005; Spencer and Pahl 2006).

Interestingly, our feelings about friendship—the way we define and express it—differ in systematic ways on the basis of our socioeconomic status. **Socioeconomic status** refers to a particular social location—one defined with reference to education, occupation, and financial resources. Studies show, for example, that working-class Americans conceive of friendship as an exchange of goods and services. Gifts and favors come to indicate the strength of a friendship bond. In contrast, material exchange is absent from middle-class definitions of friendship. Middle-class individuals frequently view friendship as an emotional or intellectual exchange; they may also conceive of friendship simply as the sharing of leisure activities.

The "faces" of our friends also differ by social class. Thus, if you are a member of America's working class, your friends are highly likely to be relatives—siblings, cousins, parents, and so on. In contrast, middle-class individuals prefer nonblood relations for friends. Furthermore, among working-class people, friendships are overwhelmingly same sex, whereas middle-class people are more open to cross-gender friendships. Finally, if you are from America's working class, your friendships are likely to be local. Thus, working-class friends interact, on average, once a week or more. In contrast, middle-class individuals have as many long-distance friendships as they do local ones. Because middle-class life in America often involves high levels of geographic mobility, members of the middle class are more likely than their working-class counterparts to maintain friendships after individuals move out of the immediate geographic area. This distance factor carries a downside, however. Middle-class friends generally report less frequent contact than their working-class counterparts (Allan 1989, 1998b; Bleiszner and Adams 1992; Elles 1993; Fischer 1982; Giordano 2003; Gouldner and Strong 1987; Liebler and Sandefur 2002; Rawlins 1992; Spencer and Pahl 2006; Walker 1995).

The patterned nature of love also emerges in matters of self-love, or what social scientists refer to as self-esteem. **Self-esteem** refers to the personal judgments individuals make regarding their own self-worth. Like romantic and platonic love, love of self appears quite systematically tied to an individual's social situation.

On the level of experience, for example, many studies show that self-esteem is directly tied to the love expressed toward that individual by her or his significant others. Not surprisingly, when significant others give positive feedback, self-esteem increases. Conversely, consistently negative feedback from significant others lowers self-esteem (Amato and Fowler 2002; Dolgin and Minowa 1997; Jaret, Reitzes, and Shapkina 2005; Mruk 2006; Voss, Markiewicz, and Doyle 1999). Similarly, the character of one's social or work environment clearly influences self-esteem. Those who are situated among optimistic people in positive, upbeat environments have been shown repeatedly to enjoy better self-esteem than those who find themselves in negative environments with depressed or disgruntled colleagues (Cross and Vick

2001; Mruk 2006; Ross and Broh 2000). Finally, various social attributes can influence levels of self-love or self-esteem, with members of upper classes and racial majority groups routinely faring better than the poor or those in racial minorities (Coopersmith 1967; De Cremer 2001; Felson and Reed 1986, 1987; Gergen 1971; Keefe and Berndt 1996; McLeod and Owens 2004; Mruk 2006).

Romantic love, platonic love, self-love—when findings from these areas are considered together, we must concede that love, in its various forms, is a highly structured phenomenon. There is much rhyme and reason regarding how we find it, define it, experience it, and express it. And that logic is tied to aspects of our social backgrounds and our social locations. Knowing this, we might do better to trade our notions of the irrational heart for knowledge of the social organization of the heart. Indeed, the study of love reminds us that even the most personal of experiences can succumb to the systematic influence of the social.

Learning More About It

For informative and very readable studies on romantic coupling in America, see *The Mating Game: A Primer on Love, Sex, and Marriage* by Pamela C. Regan (Thousand Oaks: Sage Publications, 2002), *Seven Stories of Love* by Marcia Millman (New York: HarperCollins, 2002), or *Talk of Love: How Culture Matters* by Ann Swidler (Chicago: University of Chicago Press, 2001).

For recent reviews of literature on the social similarities of lovers and friends, see "Birds of a Feather," a 2001 article by Miller McPherson, Lynn Smith-Lovin, and James M. Cook (*Annual Review of Sociology* 27:415–444), Peggy Giordano's 2003 piece "Relationships in Adolescence" (*Annual Review of Sociology* 29: 257–281), or Nijole Benokraitis's *Marriages and Families: Changes, Choices, and Constraints* (Upper Saddle River, NJ: Prentice Hall, 2007).

For an interesting and still timely look at the social aspects of friendship, see Lillian Rubin's *Just Friends: The Role of Friendship in Our Lives* (New York: HarperCollins, 1993). A more recent treatment of the social patterns of friendship can be found in *Rethinking Friendship: Hidden Solidarities Today,* by Liz Spencer and Ray Pahl (Princeton, NJ: Princeton University Press, 2006).

Most sociological work on self-esteem is steeped in the writings of Charles Horton Cooley. His classic works include *Human Nature and Social Order* (New York: Scribner, 1902) and *Social Organization* (New York: Charles Scribner, 1909). A very readable review of recent research on self-esteem can be found in Christopher Mruk's book *Self-Esteem: Research, Theory, and Practice,* 3d edition (New York: Springer, 2006).

Exercises

1. Identify the top three traits you desire in a friend. Do these traits correspond to the friendship trends cited here for (a) your social class of origin or (b) the social class to which you aspire? Now, repeat the exercise, this time considering the top three traits that you desire in a spouse. Do your answers suggest the influence of homogamy?

2. Using yourself (if appropriate) and your married friends as case studies, discuss how the rules of homogamy either apply or do not apply in these individuals' selections of marriage partners. Collect similar information about your parents, aunts, and uncles, and compare it with what you found about yourself and your friends. Do you see any important generational changes in the rules for marital homogamy? Are there rule variations that can be linked to class or educational factors?

Essay 5

Conventional Wisdom Tells Us . . . Stress Is Bad for Your Well-Being

Or is it? This essay reviews the conditions under which stress can prove beneficial in one's everyday activities. In so doing, we highlight the importance of considering social context in assessing social behaviors.

Stress has become a regular feature of modern-day existence. Finding a parking space at the mall, hooking up a new home entertainment system, navigating the university's new automated registration system, correcting an error on your credit card bill—in today's fast-paced, high-tech environment, stress can weave its way into even the most routine tasks.

Modernization and technological advancement have stress-related costs. To be sure, these phenomena make possible amazing strides, including increased life-spans, greater geographic mobility, and heightened industrial and agricultural productivity. Yet these changes also actively alter a society's social structure. **Social structure** refers to the organization of a society—the ways in which social statuses, resources, power, and mechanisms of control combine to form a framework of operations.

Thus, for many, a society's "amazing strides" may translate into commuter marriages, single parenthood, long widowhoods, or "downsized" work environments—conditions often associated with increased stress. In addition, such advances may expand the ranks of the poor, trigger rapid population growth, and increase competition for resources. Such structural changes can increase the day-to-day stress experienced by those in certain social locations. **Social location** is an individual's total collection of social statuses; it pinpoints an individual's social position by simultaneously considering age, education, gender, income, race, and so on.

The pervasiveness of stress makes it important to weigh conventional wisdom's dire warnings on the subject. Will the benefits of modernization ultimately cost us our physical, mental, or emotional health? Just what toll does stress take on our overall well-being?

The links between stress and well-being are complex because the effects of stress vary by social context (Cockerham 2006: 63–83; Jacobson 1989; Lennon 1989; Pearlin 1989; Pearlin and Skaff 1996; Pearlin et al. 2005; Roxburgh 2005). **Social context** refers to the broad social and historical circumstances surrounding an act or an event. For example, consider the links between stress and health. Many studies link stress to serious physical problems: cancer, heart disease, mental illness, and emotional depression. Research also suggests that stress can trigger increases in smoking, drinking, drug use, and other hazardous behaviors (American Heart Association 2007a; House 2002; Lantz et al. 2005; Pearlin et al. 1981; Ross and Huber 1985; Stenson 2003; Wheaton 1983). However, these negative effects are largely confined to contexts in which stress is chronic. **Chronic stress** refers to the relatively enduring problems, conflicts, and threats that individuals face on a daily basis. Most researchers agree that chronic stress contexts, such as persistent financial woes, a bad marriage, and constant exposure to crime, violence, overcrowding, or even noise, are harmful to our well-being. In contrast, sporadic, short-term stress generally proves less detrimental to well-being (American Institute of Stress 2007; American Psychological Association 2004; Aneshensel 1992; House et al. 1986; Kristenson et al. 2004; Pearlin 1989).

Now consider the stress generated by certain life events—retirement, children leaving home, the death of a spouse, major changes in the workplace, and so on. Conventional wisdom suggests that such events can be the most stressful experiences of our lives. Again, however, research reveals that the stress associated with these life events varies with the social context in which the event occurs. For example, retirement actually has been shown to alleviate stress if one is leaving an unpleasant or difficult job. Similarly, when a child leaves home, stress actually decreases for those parents who perceived their family relationships to be troubled or strained. And major changes in the workplace can prove beneficial if those changes challenge and tap workers' knowledge and skills rather than threatening their security. To determine the level of stress associated with any life event, one must explore the circumstances and activities that precede and/or accompany the event; one must assess the life event within its proper social context (Aneshensel 1992; Burton 1998; Cockerham 2006: 63–83; Jacobson 1989; Lennon 1989; Martin and Svebak 2001; Mirowsky and Ross 1989; Pearlin 1989; Simon 1997; Simon and Marcussen 1999; Thoits 1983; Verhaeghe et al. 2006; Wheaton 1982).

In assessing the conventional wisdom on stress, it also is important to note that the negative effects of stress are not inevitable. Research documents several coping mechanisms that can temper or even cancel the negative impact of stress on one's well-being. For example, individuals who enjoy strong social support networks often are protected from the harmful consequences of stress. A **social support network** consists of family, friends, agencies, and resources—entities that actively assist individuals in coping with adverse or unexpected events. Studies document, for instance, that widows and widowers who have close friends or confidants report much less stress from the death of a spouse than individuals who lack such support. Similarly, the stress of divorce appears greatly diminished for those with close friends, confidants, or new romantic interests. And research on children shows that increased parental contact can mitigate the stress experienced by children when families are forced to geographically relocate (Boardman 2004; Cockerham 2006: 63–83; Cohen 2004; Hagan, MacMillan, and Wheaton 1996; House et al. 1986; Kessler, Price, and Wortman 1985; Lin, Ye, and Ensel 1999; Mui 2001; Roussi, Vagia, and Koutri 2007; Thoits 1995; Treharne, Lyons, and Tupling 2001; Wheaton 1982, 1990; Zimmer-Gembeck and Locke 2007).

Certain resources also can influence the experience of stress. Research indicates that relaxation techniques can buffer individuals from the negative impact of stress. Similarly, problem-solving strategies or strategies that can physically or mentally distance one from the site of stress can help mitigate its harmful effects. Research also indicates significant stress reduction among optimists or those who learn to deemphasize the negative aspects of a stress-producing role. And those who perceive some level of personal control over their environment experience less stress than those who feel little or no control (Affleck, Tennen, and Apter 2000; Caplan and Schooler 2007; Chan 2002; Danner, Snowden, and Friesen 2001; Frazier et al. 2000; Nes and Segerstrom 2006; Pham, Taylor, and Seeman 2001; Simon 1997; Thoits 1994, 1995, 2006; Von Ah, Kang, and Carpenter 2007).

Coping mechanisms can offer protection from stress. However, some contend that modern lifestyles may make it difficult for individuals to put these "safeguards" into effect. For example, the geographic mobility that characterizes modern society may place friends and family out of one's immediate reach. Similarly, increased access to information may create a mental overload that eats away at one's relaxation time, and technological advancements that allow one to merge work and home sites may make mental distancing strategies difficult to execute (Hochschild 1997/2001, 2003a; Nippert-Eng 1996; Pearson 1993; Philipson 2002; Robinson 2003).

The successful enactment of coping mechanisms may be largely related to the kinds of social relationships that characterize one's social environment. Ferdinand Tonnies (1855–1936) analyzed such relationships using two distinct categories: Gemeinschaft and Gesellschaft. **Gemeinschaft** refers to an environment in which social relationships are based on ties of friendship and kinship. **Gesellschaft** refers to an environment in which social relationships are formal, impersonal, and often initiated for specialized or instrumental purposes. Modern social environments, with their emphasis on privacy and individuality, reflect the Gesellschaft environment. As such, the social resources from which coping mechanisms develop may not be readily available to modern women and men.

Are there contexts in which stress positively influences our well-being? Social psychologists have demonstrated that task-oriented stress often can lead to visibly productive consequences. **Task-oriented stress** refers to short-term stress that accompanies particular assignments or settings. Individuals who report feeling completely comfortable or relaxed during the execution of certain mental tasks remember and absorb less information than those who experience moderate levels of task-oriented stress. Indeed, moderate levels of task-oriented stress have been linked to enhanced memory of facts and skills and increased learning ability—important attributes in our post-industrial, knowledge-based society. This suggests that the nervous tingles you experience in studying for the law boards, your driving test, or a public speaking engagement may serve you better than a lackadaisical stance (Driskell, Johnston, and Salas 2001; Ellis 1972; Mughal, Walsh, and Wilding 1996; Nelson and Simmons 2005; Nemours Foundation 2004; Quick et al. 2003; U.S. Department of the Army 2003). Social psychologists have also demonstrated that stress can promote self-improvement. This is because stressful events encourage (or force) individuals to acquire new skills, reevaluate their positions, and reconsider their priorities. In this way, stress may serve as a catalyst for personal growth (Calhoun and Tedeschi 2001; Quick et al. 2003; Tennen and Affleck 1999; Verhaeghe et al. 2006).

Studies also show that stress can work through other physiological or psychological states to produce quite unexpected, and quite positive, behavioral outcomes. For example, when stress leads to a state of emotional arousal such as anxiety or fear, stressed individuals are more likely to befriend or bond with others. (This may explain why your student colleagues always seem more approachable on the day of a big exam.) Furthermore, when stress leads to anxiety or fear, stressed individuals demonstrate a greater tendency to like and interact with people whom they usually dislike or around whom they typically feel uncomfortable. This "benefit" extends to people who differ from the stressed individual in terms of race, socioeconomic status, and personality. In light of these findings, some researchers contend that under the right circumstances, stress may aid the cause of achieving interracial, intergenerational, or interclass affiliations (Kulik and Mahler 1990; Kulik, Mahler, and Moore 1996; Latané and Glass 1968; Olbrich 1986; Rofé 2006; Schachter 1959).

The links between stress and affiliation hold true at the collective level as well. Where disasters strike communities at large—be they hurricanes, floods, or terrorist attacks—victims' most common response involves affiliation. While stereotypes of disaster suggest that victims succumb to mass panic and hysteria, studies repeatedly show that disaster victims are much more likely to bond together and work toward mutual survival and recovery (Mawson 2005; Quarantelli 2001; Tierney, Bevc, and Kuligowsky 2006; Tierney, Lindell, and Perry 2001).

It is interesting to note that stress that proves detrimental to the well-being of individuals sometimes may prove productive for societies at large. Consider one such example in the area of chronic stress. Chronic stress can emerge from a particular type of long-term situation, a condition sociologists refer to as role conflict. **Role conflict** occurs when social members occupy two or more social positions that carry opposing demands. Military chaplains, working parents, and student teachers all provide examples of potentially conflicting role combinations. Roles that carry opposing demands create a tug-of-war within individuals—a persistent strain characteristic of chronic stress.

Although role conflict can take its toll on an individual's well-being, it sometimes proves the source of positive social change. For example, when role conflict is routinized by changing cultural or economic demands, the resulting stress can actually trigger needed social restructuring. Routinized role conflict can lead societies to institute changes that positively alter the playing field of social interaction. For example, the conflict and stress that emerged from the working-parent role combination served to revolutionize America's work environment. Methods such as flex-time, in-house day care, and work-at-home options—originally antidotes to the stress of role conflict—are now a productive dimension of work in the United States.

We can take this analysis of the positive consequences of stress one step further. The phenomenon of stress need not be confined to individual-level inquiries; societies as a whole also can experience stress. Sociologists refer to this type of stress as social strain. **Social strain** develops when a social event or trend disrupts the equilibrium of a society's social structure. For example, an economic depression may generate social strain by forcing increases in unemployment and exacerbating poverty. In essence, the depression event disrupts expected patterns of resource distribution. Similarly, a large increase in a society's birth rate may place strain on various social institutions. Schools, hospitals, or prisons may suddenly be presented with more clients than they were designed to serve.

Sociologists such as Talcott Parsons (1951/1964) or Lewis Coser (1956), although coming from different perspectives, both suggested that social strain creates an opportunity for societal change and growth. (Note that Coser refers to the phenomenon of strain as "social conflict.") With their writings, both Parsons and Coser established a view of society that continues to guide contemporary social thinkers. Social strain is important because it disrupts the status quo. Thus, it can force societies to work at reestablishing smooth operations. For example, the strain placed on the U.S. stratification system by the civil rights movement of the 1950s and 1960s resulted in positive strides toward racial and ethnic equality in America. Similarly, consider the growing demands that U.S. entitlement programs currently place on the nation's economic system. Many credit such strain with prompting much-needed public discourse on major budget reforms.

Is stress harmful to our well-being? Taken as a whole, current research on stress paints a less dismal picture than that promoted by conventional wisdom. To be sure, stress is frequently harmful, and it is rarely a pleasant experience. Yet its consequences do not necessarily jeopardize personal health and happiness. In fact, when one views stress in context, or at the level of societies at large, it sometimes proves to be a useful social resource.

Learning More About It

For a good summary of current findings and controversies within the social science literature on stress, see Leonard Pearlin and colleagues' 2005 article "Stress, Health, and the Life Course: Some Conceptual Perspectives" (*Journal of Health and Social Behavior.* 46:2:205–219), or William C. Cockerham's chapter "Social Stress," in his book *Medical Sociology* (10th edition, Upper Saddle River, NJ: Prentice Hall, 2006).

Several interesting experiments document the positive consequences of stress for individuals. Schachter's *The Psychology of Affiliation* (Stanford, CA: Stanford University Press, 1959) represents a classic among such studies.

Stress and conflict within social systems are wonderfully addressed in Lewis Coser's classic, yet still relevant, theoretical treatise, *The Functions of Social Conflict* (Glencoe, IL: Free Press, 1956).

Want to learn something about the history of stress in the marketplace and its "commerce" value? Visit Stress.inc at http://findarticles.com/p/articles/mi_m0ISW/is_263/ai_n13790761 for information, quizzes, and amusing tidbits on the subject.

The following organizations can help you learn more about stress:

The American Institute of Stress
http://www.stress.org

National Mental Health Association
http://www.nmha.org

Exercises

1. Research suggests that stress can increase an individual's likelihood of affiliating with others. Can stress function in a similar way at the societal level? To test the hypothesis that social stress increases social solidarity, see if periods of economic recession or a nation's involvement in a major war is associated with any indicators of increased group cohesion. Using a source like the Information Please Almanac, track membership rates in five national organizations for years before and after the economic recession of the 1970s or World War II.

2. Compare two weeks' worth of "Letters to the Editor" prior to the September 11, 2001, terrorist attacks in America; the declaration of war on Iraq in 2003; Hurricane Katrina; or a well-publicized murder or accident in your hometown—with two weeks' worth of "Letters to the Editor" after such an event. Analyze the content of letter writers' remarks concerning their personal feelings and reactions to these events. What does your analysis show regarding the social consequences of stress?

Essay 6

Conventional Wisdom Tells Us ... The "Golden Years" Are Tarnished Years

---

Growing old—no one looks forward to it. Yet this essay illustrates that our worst fears about growing old may be largely unfounded, simply products of a "master status" for which we have been inadequately prepared.

A ging is a curious phenomenon. When we are young, we can't wait to be older—or at least old enough to drive, get a good job, and make our own decisions. When we finally reach adulthood, many of us continue to yearn for a later stage in life, a time when we can begin to capitalize on the lessons of youth, a time when we can enjoy the fruits of our labors. Retirement looks like a pretty good deal from the vantage point of youth. Indeed, one national study found that 88% of Americans 6 to 15 years away from retirement believe that retirement will be a very happy period in their life, and 76% believe it will be a time when they will achieve their dreams (Ameriprise Financial 2006). A recent American Association of Retired Persons (AARP) study found much the same thing; 75% of the 50+ population were confident in their retirement futures (American Association of Retired Person [AARP] 2007).

Eventually, however, there comes a time when the benefits of aging seem less clear cut. We begin to view age as a liability, perhaps even as a thing to be feared. For many, the dread comes with the appearance of their first gray hairs (Graham 2002), and suddenly, we become more attuned to the very negative conventional wisdom on aging. The young are warned never to "trust anyone over 30." Those in their forties and fifties frequently are characterized as "over the hill." Children and adolescents see their parents as "old fogies." And children aren't alone on this matter. In general, Americans tend to perceive men and women as "old" once they have reached the age of 63 (Abramson and Silverstein 2006). Advanced age is often viewed as a liability for many practices and occupations. After all, "you can't teach an old dog new tricks." And retiring is often equated with "being put out to pasture." Interestingly, these images are aided by the law. The Age Discrimination in Employment Act protects employees *aged 40 and over* from age discrimination! Organizations such as AARP also fuel the fires of conventional wisdom. Note that this organization opens its membership ranks to those *50 and older!*

Thus, despite early desires to "be older," many Americans ultimately develop a rather negative view of growing old. Many picture old age as a time of loneliness, vulnerability, sickness, and anger. Many overestimate senility and the number of accidents that befall the elderly (Abramson and Silverstein 2006). And there is a widespread perception that the aging of America, especially the aging of the Baby Boomers, poses a social and economic problem. Are such images accurate? Is conventional wisdom's negative stance on growing old justified? Research suggests that the "negative press" on aging is not fully supported by the facts. In reviewing several studies on the elderly, one finds many inconsistencies between the public perceptions and the social realities of old age in America.

Consider, for instance, the image of old age as a lonely, isolated existence. It is true that the elderly make up a relatively large portion of single-occupant households in the United States, but in 2005 only 30% of the elderly lived alone. (That's 7.7 million women and 2.9 million men.) Nearly 72% of older men and 42% of older women lived with their spouses in 2005; about 13% lived with other relatives; and many elderly were still caregivers. In 2005 about 445,000 grandparents aged 65 and over had primary responsibility for their grandchildren, with those grandchildren living under their roofs (Administration on Aging 2007; Centers for Disease Control 2007c).

For those elderly who do live alone, such living arrangements seem to reflect a personal preference rather than a forced choice. Of those 50 and older who live in homes that will meet their changing physical needs, 95% indicate a desire to remain in those homes. Indeed even when homes don't meet the physical needs of an aging population, most residents (62%) still express a desire to keep living in them (Kochera and Guterbock 2005). Elderly Americans report that they want to stay at home, and they wish to do so for as long as possible. In fact, 82% of those 65 and older think it is somewhat to very likely that they will be able to stay in their current homes for the rest of their lives (AARP 2003a). These figures suggest that the elderly value their independence. More than two-thirds of older parents who have children over the age of 34 report not wanting to live with their children—even if they were to need assistance and care (*Health and Medicine Work* 2002). And an AARP report finds that even older disabled people express a strong preference for living independently in their own homes (AARP 2003b).

In addition to living arrangements, several other behavioral patterns contradict the loneliness stereotype. Today's seniors are connected. In 2006, 52% of those aged 65–74 used the Internet; 24% of those over 75 did so. Only 8% of those aged 65–74 reported missing social engagements because of lack of transportation (AARP 2007). Seniors were committed volunteers: those 65 and older average 96 hours of volunteer work each year compared to 52 hours by the general population (National Governors Association 2006). Senior citizens also reported active companionship in a variety of settings, not the least of which is the family. In 2006, 77% of those aged 65–74 and 73% of those 75 and over reported being very satisfied with the amount of contact maintained with family, friends, and neighbors (AARP 2007). While the elderly are not a transient population, their desire to relocate closer to friends and family is an increasingly important reason for moving (Kochera and Guterbock 2005). Perhaps a more telling trend is the return of the "whole" family vacation—family traveling with and staying with family. In 2002, 35% of grandparents joined their grandchildren on a family trip (Mencimer 2002).

In general, research shows that parents and adult children do have a high sense of mutual normative obligation (Johnson 2000; Rossi and Rossi 1990; Umberson 1996). Caregiving for the elderly is clearly a family affair. In recent years, reliance on paid caregiving has decreased; the majority of care for the frail elderly is provided by family and friends. Forty-six percent of those aged 50–64 report providing unpaid help to friends or relatives 50 years of age and older (AARP 2007). And as previously mentioned, many elderly continue in the caregiver role for their children and grandchildren. The latest census data indicate that more than 6% of children under 18 are living in a grandparent-headed home (Goyer 2006).

Loneliness is only one of the many misconceptions we have about old age. Conventional wisdom also paints the elderly as frequent victims of violent crime. Yet violent crime against the elderly has declined drastically over the past 35 years. In fact, age and violent victimization are inversely related—as age goes up, victimization goes down. Those between the ages of 50 and 64, for example, are five times more likely to be victims of violent crime than those over the age of 65. Individuals between the ages of 25 and 34 are ten times more likely to be victimized. And note that when the elderly are victims of crime, they are likely to be victims of property crime rather than violent crime (U.S. Department of Justice 2006a). Yet, the "crime myth" that surrounds old age is not without its consequences; the myth generates a great deal of anxiety among the elderly (although less today than previously; see Abramson and Silverstein 2006). Of those 65 and older, 71% think that there is more crime today than a year ago, a percentage higher than that reported for any other age group (*Sourcebook of Criminal Justice Statistics* 2005). Survey data also indicate that an overwhelming majority of older voters think it important for the state to make communities safer by reducing crime, and seven out of ten would be likely to vote for candidates who support such initiatives (Dinger 2006).

Another fear of aging centers on increased poverty. At one point in U.S. history, there was a firm basis for this fear. Until the 1970s, the elderly were more likely than any other age group to live in poverty. While the poverty rate for the population at large was only 13%, a full 25% of those 65 and older were classified as poor. But changes in the Social Security system—in particular, changes linking benefits to cost-of-living increases—have helped reduce the percentage of elderly living in poverty. Today the poverty rate for those over 65 years of age hovers around 10%. Thus, current poverty rates for the elderly are below the national poverty rate of 12.6% (Administration on Aging 2007; U.S. Census Bureau 2006a).

Images of physical and mental deterioration also pervade public perceptions of old age. To be sure, aging does result in some changes on the physical front. Arthritis, hypertension, hearing impairment, and heart disease are frequently occurring chronic conditions of the elderly. Yet it is important to note that health, not disease, is the norm for older Americans (see Figure 6.1). Seventy-six percent of Whites, 60% of Blacks, and 62% of Hispanics aged 65 and over describe their health as good or excellent (Federal Interagency Forum on Aging-Related Statistics 2006; U.S. Department of Health and Human Services 2007a, Table 60). Only one-third of those 65 years of age and older report having *any* limitation in activity caused by chronic health conditions. About 6% of this age group (but only 2.9% for those 65–74) report needing help with personal care (what researchers call limitations in ADLs—activities of daily living); 11.5% of those 65 and older (and 5.5% of those 65–74) report needing help with routine activities (what researchers call limitations in IADLs—instrumental activities of daily living; IADLs include shopping, preparing meals, doing housework, and otherwise managing one's affairs independently). Less than 17% of those 65 and older have trouble seeing; only about 11% have trouble hearing (U.S. Department of Health and Human Services 2007a, Tables 58 & 59). And over the last decade, older Americans reported improvement in their ability to walk a quarter-mile, climb stairs, and reach up and over their heads (Federal Interagency Forum on Aging-Related Statistics 2006). In fact, more than a quarter (26.7%) of those aged 65–74 report engaging in three or more sessions of vigorous physical activity per week, a number very close to the overall 30% rate for the general public (U.S. Department of Health and Human Services 2007a, Table 72).

The elderly's desire for independence and their general good health help explain another important fact: Only 3.5% of the 65+ population live in nursing homes (Houser, Fox-George, and Gibson 2006). While the percentage of nursing home residents does increase with age, it is still the case that only 18.2% of those 85 and older are relegated to nursing home care (Administration on Aging 2007).

In terms of mental health, the elderly fare quite well. Most enjoy good mental health—the mental health problems that do arise are not part of the normal aging process per se. For many major mental disorders (schizophrenia; bipolar, obsessive-compulsive, panic, and borderline personality disorders), the average age of onset is in adolescence and early adulthood (Mental Health America 2007; National Institute of Mental Health 2006). Moderate

Figure 6.1   Percentage of Persons with ADL Limitations, by Age Groups: 2004

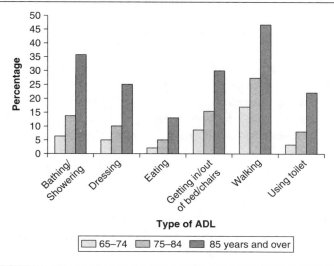

Type of ADL

65–74   75–84   85 years and over

SOURCE: Administration on Aging. (2007). *A Profile of Older Americans: 2006.* Available at http://www.aoa.gov/prof/Statistics/profile/2006/10.asp

to severe memory loss affects only 5% of those 65 to 69, 8% of those 70 to 74, and still only about a third of those aged 85 and over (Federal Interagency Forum on Aging-Related Statistics 2006). And although Alzheimer's disease is frequently associated with old age, it afflicts only 3% of those aged 65 to 74 (Mental Health America 2007). Overall, aging appears to bring an elusive mental benefit: The elderly, even with the changes associated with aging, are more likely to report being very satisfied with their lives than younger age groups. For the most part, anxieties about aging belong to the young, not the old. Those over 65 are less bothered by thoughts of death, less worried about their health, and less anxious about their future and about financial matters than are those aged 18–34 (Abramson and Silverstein 2006). A growing body of research is finding that **emotional regulation,** or the ability to maintain a positive affect, improves with age (American Psychological Association 2005). Surely some elderly must already know what research is confirming: A positive attitude toward aging is one of the things that keep us going (Kennedy, Mather, and Carstensen 2004; Levy et al. 2002).

The facts about old age in America seem to contradict "common knowledge." Why do such misconceptions exist? The concept of a master status may provide one flash of insight in the matter. A **master status** refers to a single social status that overpowers all other social positions occupied by an individual. A master status directs the way in which others see, define, and relate to an individual.

Master statuses are powerful identity tools because they carry with them a set of qualities or characteristics that they impose on those who occupy the status. For example, those who occupy the master status of doctor are assumed to be knowledgeable, wealthy, rational, and usually white and male. Similarly, those who occupy the master status of mother are presumed to be caring, nurturing, stable, and female.

In short, a master status and the traits and characteristics that accompany it have a tremendous capacity to influence what others "see" or assume to be true in their social interactions. Thus, although I can look at a doctor and see that she is not a male, the story doesn't end there. Expectations that stem from the master status "doctor" might nonetheless continue to influence my interaction with my doctor. I may question whether or not she possesses other key traits of the master status, such as knowledge or rationality. I may doubt her ability to diagnose.

During two periods in our lives, childhood and our senior years, age serves as a master status. In childhood, the master status of age is equated with such qualities as dependency, unbounded energy, innocence, inquisitiveness, irresponsibility, and the ability to be uninhibited. As senior citizens, the master status of age is associated with such characteristics as dependency, frailty, loneliness, stubbornness, and the lack of creativity.

In essence, age becomes a master status early and late in life due to a lack of competition. We begin to accumulate statuses more powerful than age only as we move out of childhood and through adolescence, young adulthood, and our middle-aged years. During life's middle stages, we embark on careers, take spouses, raise children, join clubs and associations, become homeowners, and pursue leisure-time or self-fulfilling interests. During life's middle stages, occupational and family statuses typically assume the master status position.

In our later years, we exit many of our occupational and family statuses. Children leave home, people retire, spouses die, and homes are sold. When such status losses occur, age and the characteristics associated with it once again return to the forefront of our identities.

Misconceptions about our golden years may also result from a lack of anticipatory socialization. **Anticipatory socialization** refers to socialization that prepares a person to assume a role in the future. Consider the fact that as children, we "play" at being mommies and daddies, teachers, and fire fighters. As we move through the early stages of our lives, anticipatory socialization provides a road map to the statuses of young adulthood and the middle years. High school and college put us through the paces via internships, apprenticeships, and occupational training. We receive on-the-job instruction when we are initiated into the workforce. Such preparation is simply not given to the tasks involved in senior citizenship. At no time in our lives are we schooled in the physiological changes and social realities that surround retirement, widowhood, or other events of old age.

This lack of anticipatory socialization should not surprise us. Preparing for old age would be inconsistent with typical American values and practices. We are an action- and production-oriented society. We generally don't prepare for doing less. As a society, we don't encourage role playing for any statuses that carry negative traits and characteristics, such as being old, criminal, terminally ill, widowed, and so on.

Switching our focus to a macro-level analysis provides additional insight regarding the misconceptions on aging. A **macro-level analysis** focuses on broad, large-scale social patterns as they exist across contexts or through time. Consider aging as a historical phenomenon. Old age in America is a relatively new event. In the first census, in 1790, less than 2% of the U.S. population was 65 or older; the median age was 16. (Historians suggest that these statistics probably characterized the population from the early 1600s to the early 1800s; see Fischer 1977.) Thus, old age was an uncommon event in preindustrial America. Those of the period could not reasonably expect to live into old age. Indeed, individuals who did reach old age were regarded as exceptional and often were afforded great respect. Life-earned experience and knowledge were valuable commodities in a preindustrial society (Fischer 1977).

The youthful age structure of early America meant the absence of retire-ment. Preindustrial societies consisted of home-based, labor-intensive enter-prises. Thus, the ability to produce, not age itself, was the relevant factor for working. Before the 20th century, most Americans worked until they died.

With the rise of modern society and industrialization, this pattern changed. The skills, experience, and knowledge of older workers did not res-onate with the demands and innovations of factory work. Younger and inex-perienced (that is, cheaper) workers were the better economic choice for employers. Such changes in the knowledge and economic base of American society had a profound impact on social and cultural views on aging (Watson and Maxwell 1977). With this shift, old age ceased to be exalted, and a youth-oriented society and culture began to develop.

The youth mentality of the industrial age is clearly articulated in one of the 20th century's most influential pieces of legislation: the Social Security Act of 1935. This act can be credited with setting the "old-age" cutoff at 65. (Note that older workers lobbied for a higher age cutoff and younger workers lobbied for a lower age cutoff at the time of the act's passage.) Furthermore, the act legally mandated that older workers must make way for younger ones. The directive has been successful. Only about 15% of older Americans are still in the workforce (Administration on Aging 2007).

The forced retirement instituted by the Social Security Act contributed to the negative image of old age. Retirement signifies both a social (occupational) and an economic "loss." Despite the reality of Social Security benefits, the elderly as a whole have a lower income than all other age groups except 15- to 24-year-olds (U.S. Census Bureau 2007d, Table 683). In 2005, the median income for the 65+ age group was $15,696 (Administration on Aging 2007). When one couples these losses with the natural physiological and social changes that accompany aging (increasing risk of chronic diseases, some vision and hearing impairment, relinquishment of parental and spousal roles, and so on), it becomes easier to understand the development of old age's negative image.

Before leaving this discussion, it is important to note that the analysis of old age in America must be qualified with reference to social context. **Social context** refers to the broad social and historical circumstances surrounding an act or an event. Those in certain social circumstances can find the aging experience to be a greater hardship than do others. Figure 6.2, for example, confirms that poverty among the elderly *as a whole* has diminished over the past 30 years. But some segments of that population still experience high poverty rates. Elderly women, elderly minority members, and, in particular, elderly Hispanic women living alone continue to suffer rates of poverty that exceed the national average (Administration on Aging 2007). Similarly, *overall,* the elderly experience high rates of emotional calm or peace of mind. However, such rates can vary widely among subgroups of the elderly population. For instance, while older Black females have suicide rates well below the national average, White men over 85 years of age have the highest suicide rate of any age group (National Institute of Mental Health 2006). These high rates have been attributed to the difficulty older males experience in coping with serious illness or the loss of a spouse (National Center for Injury Prevention and Control 2007).

Despite the multiple sources for our misconceptions on aging, all of our views on the matter may soon undergo significant revision. The changing age structure of the U.S. population helps explain why such a shift may occur. **Age structure** refers to the distribution that results from dividing a population according to socially defined, age-based categories: childhood, adolescence, young adulthood, middle age, and old age.

Since the early 1900s, the median age in America has risen steadily. So too has the proportion of our population that is 65 or older. Today, approximately 12% of the population is over 65. With the aging of Baby Boomers, these percentages will increase significantly. Figure 6.3 shows that by 2030, the elderly population should number 71.5 million—roughly twice the size

Figure 6.2   Poverty Among Various Segments of the U.S. Elderly, 2005

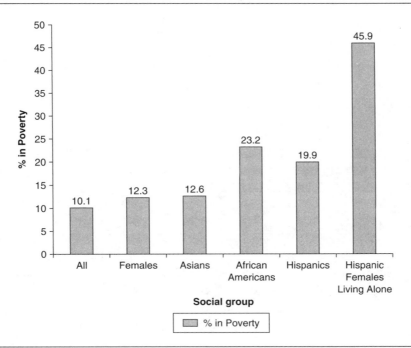

SOURCE: Administration on Aging. (2007). *A Profile of Older Americans: 2006.* Available at http://www.aoa.gov/prof/Statistics/profile/2006/2006profile.pdf

of the 2005 group. Those 65 and older will comprise about 20% of the population (Administration on Aging 2007). Now let's move the bar a little bit higher. Those 85 years or older are members of the fastest-growing cohort in both the United States and the world (Shalala 2003). In 2005, the 85+ age group numbered 5.1 million and was 42 times larger than it was in 1900 (Administration on Aging 2007)! Such fundamental changes to the age structure of our society will produce major consequences for both the image and the reality of old age.

The 65+ age group has the highest voter registration and turnout rates of any age group—71% of older Americans reported voting in 2004 (U.S. Census Bureau 2007d, Table 405). With such high civic-mindedness and with their increasing numbers, the elderly represent a powerful voting bloc. The elderly also benefit from the lobbying efforts of the largest interest group in politics today: the AARP (Cockerham 1997). Through its Web site, the AARP regularly offers its members a primer on Capitol Hill proceedings. The site also lists the daily and weekly schedules of both the U.S. Senate and the House of Representatives. Such organizational efforts are credited with increasing the political impact of elderly Americans (Button and Rosenbaum 1990).

The political clout of the elderly already has resulted in a significant reduction in the percentage of elderly living in poverty. Such clout also has

Figure 6.3   Older Population by Age: 1900–2050—Percent 65+ and 85+

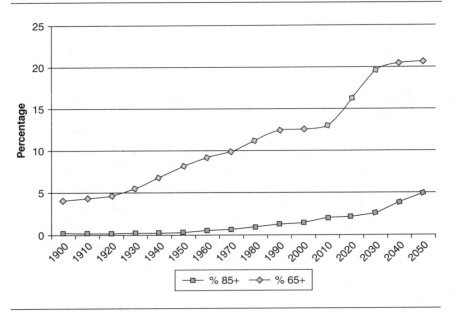

SOURCE: Table compiled by the U.S. Administration on Aging based on data from the U.S. Census Bureau. http://www.aoa.gov/prof/Statistics/online_stat_data/AgePop2050Chart-pct.asp

figured in positive changes with regard to medical care (via Medicare) and lifestyles of the elderly (tax breaks for people over 65). Indeed, the voting power of the old and "near-old" has helped make Social Security and some of its related assistance programs the "third rail" of American politics. To be sure, Social Security is the major source of income for the elderly. It is received by 89% of older persons and provides at least half of the total income for two-thirds of the elderly (Administration on Aging 2007; Congressional Budget Office 2003). Social Security benefits have been credited with saving about half of the elderly from the clutches of poverty in the past (Center on Budget and Policy Priorities 1998); the benefits are credited with saving about one-third of the elderly from poverty today (Leland and Wilgoren 2005). As the size and political power of the elderly continue to grow through the aging of the Baby Boomers, we should expect to see significant "corrections" in our social views of old age in America.

Indeed, we may be seeing signs of the change already. There is a new phenomenon being noted by students of pop culture: "eldercool." It seems that the twenty-something crowd are particularly apt to grant celebrity status to older individuals who are "cool" enough to speak their own minds and be their own authentic selves: Muhammad Ali, Clint Eastwood, Bob Barker (that's right, come on down), and Donald Rumsfield are but a few of the cool oldies (Dudley 2002). Elder cool may also be influencing the beauty industry. M.A.C. cosmetics, Christian Dior and Cover Girl, and Miu Miu have all turned to older women in their recent searches for beauty icons. Catherine Deneuve, age 62, was M.A.C.'s icon in 2006. Sharon Stone, age 48, became the new face of Christian Dior. And Christy Brinkley, age 50, is the latest "Cover Girl" (Tannen 2006). And let's not overlook how the "boys" of summer are aging. The 2007 season started with 21 "active roster" players who were over 40 years of age—Barry Bonds, Tom Glavine, Curt Schilling, Sammy Sosa, and Frank Thomas are but a few of them. (Roger Clemens isn't part of the count since he didn't sign with the Yankees until after the season began.) The 2007 season isn't a fluke, but reflects a trend in baseball for the last decade: More and more players are remaining in the game *and productive* into their 30s and 40s (Brown 2007).

Are the golden years tarnished? Research suggests not. We have used several sociological tools—master status, anticipatory socialization, macro historical analysis, and contextual analysis—to understand the discrepancy between the myths and realities of aging.

However, the story on aging in America is hardly complete. Perhaps more than any other social phenomenon, aging is an extremely dynamic process. Given recent and continuing population changes, it is more and more difficult to talk about a single elderly population. On any number of fronts (health, social, and financial), we need to differentiate the "young-old"

(65–75) from the "old" (75–85) and the "old-old" (85+). As previously mentioned, the last group is the one increasing at the fastest rate (President's Council on Bioethics 2005). The 85+ age group is expected to number 6.1 million in 2010 and 7.3 million in 2020 (Administration on Aging 2007). It is estimated today that roughly one-third of Americans will live to 85 and older (President's Council on Bioethics 2005). With these changes, many of us will be facing futures in which one-third of our lives will be spent in "old" and "old-old" age.

Think of the changes this will bring to family, economic, and social relations. As the elderly age into (and beyond) their 80s, their adult children (especially their daughters) will face greater demands for (and conflicts over) elder care (President's Council on Bioethics 2005). Today, the typical caregiver is a nonpaid 46-year-old daughter who works outside the home and still averages 20 hours of caregiving to her mother (Houser 2007). In the near future, a possible scenario will be a "young-old" daughter (who can't afford to retire) taking care of an "old-old" parent. Consider, too, the fact that Baby Boomers are fueling the projected increases in our elderly population, but this group may pose special problems with regard to caregiving. Currently spouses and children are the primary caregivers for the elderly. Baby Boomers might be "at risk" on these fronts with their high divorce rates and smaller families. Neither of these trends bode well for the caretaking possibilities of the next cohort of the elderly. Indeed it is estimated that by 2020 there will be 1.2 million people aged 65 and older who will have no living children, siblings, or spouses (Johnson, Toohey, and Wiener 2007; President's Council on Bioethics 2005).

What the future holds for a society experiencing increases in both average age and the absolute numbers of the elderly is unclear. Without breakthroughs in gerontology, living longer will most certainly mean living with chronic, disabling diseases currently associated with the "old-old." For instance, it is estimated that by 2050, the percentage of those 85+ suffering with Alzheimer's disease is expected to increase fourfold if no new cures or treatments are achieved (President's Council on Bioethics 2005). The likelihood of such breakthroughs, however, is undermined by current funding practices for aging-related medicine: In 2006 the National Institutes of Health allotted only 0.1% of its $28 billion budget to such studies (Matousek 2007). To be sure, medical advances are "keeping us young": Who hasn't heard that the 60s are the new 50s? But there is also a paradox of modern aging that deserves mentioning: We may indeed be younger longer, but we are also aged longer. Health care services and practices will surely need to be revamped and expanded to accommodate these changes. A recent Rand study estimates that 4 in 10 of us will die after an extended period of worsening debility. Future care of the elderly may entail giving many more than the eight years typically devoted to caregiving at present (President's Council on Bioethics 2005).

Finally, consider that when the Social Security Act was first passed, approximately 50 workers "supported" each Social Security recipient. Today, the burden of support falls on fewer than three workers for every retiree (see Figure 6.4). What will happen to this ratio in the not too distant future when the aging Baby Boomers hit retirement age and continue to live long, healthy lives? In 2004, nearly 42,000 centenarians were receiving Social Security benefits (Social Security Online 2006)! In the next 30 years, the number of retired workers is expected to double (U.S. Social Security Administration 2007). But with as dynamic a process as aging, any and all projections might very well be shaky. The most recent survey by the AARP, for instance, finds that our jittery economy is prompting big changes in Americans' retirement plans. Indeed, 79% of Baby Boomers plan to work in some capacity during retirement. More than one-fourth of current Baby Boomers expect to rely on Social Security for all of their retirement income (AARP 2004). A recent Putnam Investments study found that retirement can be a short-lived phenomenon: one-third of surveyed retirees returned to work after just 18 months of retirement. Indeed there may be a new group

Figure 6.4   Number of Workers Supporting Each Retiree: Ratio of Covered Workers to Social Security Beneficiaries

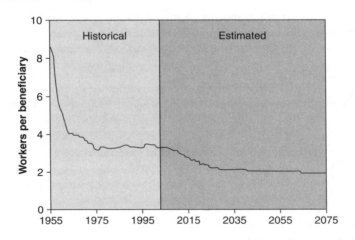

SOURCE: 2007 Annual Report of the Board of Trustees of the Federal Old-Age and Survivors Insurance and Disability Insurance Trust Funds, Table IV.B2. U.S. Social Security Administration, *Fast Facts & Figures About Social Security*, 2007. http://www.socialsecurity.gov/policy/docs/chartbooks/fast_facts/2007/fast_facts07.html#generalinfo emerging, "the working retired," who are estimated to comprise about one-third of retirees (Putnam Investments 2005).

To be sure, the "aging" story is one that will continue to evolve; it is a story that will continue to demand our attention. Thus, old age in America is an area to which all of us must apply careful "second thoughts."

Learning More About It

To learn more about the concept of master status, consult Everett C. Hughes's "Dilemmas and Contradictions of Status" (*American Journal of Sociology* 50(5):353–359, 1945); Howard Becker's *The Outsiders* (Glencoe, IL: Free Press, 1963); or J. L. Simmons's "Public Stereotypes of Deviants" (*Social Problems* 13:223–232, 1966).

To probe more deeply into the process of anticipatory socialization, check Robert K. Merton's *Social Theory and Social Structure* (Glencoe, IL: Free Press, 1957) or "Adult Socialization," by Jeylan T. Mortimer and Roberta G. Simmons (*Annual Review of Sociology* 4:421–454, 1978).

Todd Nelson's edited volume, *Ageism: Stereotyping and Prejudice Against Older Persons* (Cambridge, MA: MIT Press, 2002) examines the origins and consequences of negative stereotyping of the elderly.

For an informative and "in their own words" account of making one's home in assisted living facilities, see Jacquelyn Frank's *The Paradox of Aging in Place in Assisted Living* (Westport, CT: Bergin and Garvey, 2002).

Sociologist Robert Weiss presents "before and after" interviews with 89 retirees and gives us a chance to "hear" subjects' experiences of the retirement process in his book *The Experience of Retirement* (Ithaca, NY: Cornell University Press, 2005).

To see the latest research on emotions and the aging process, visit Laura Carstensen's "Life Span Development Lab" at Stanford University: http://psychology .stanford.edu/~lifespan/welcome.htm

The following organizations can help you to learn more about aging:

American Association of Retired Persons
http://www.aarp.org

National Aging Information Center, Administration on Aging
http://www.aoa.gov/naic/

Exercises

1. Try a little fact-finding yourself. Ask some friends and family members what they believe to be true about the financial and social situations of those 65 and older. For instance, what social characteristics do your "subjects" associate with the elderly? What percentage of the elderly do your subjects believe are still employed? Are the elderly financially secure? Are the elderly happy after retirement? After you've solicited several opinions, compare your results with your library's holdings on the latest census figures or with the results of a recent survey executed by the AARP. How do the social locations of your respondents influence their knowledge of the elderly?

2. It is not always possible to know in advance which status will emerge as one's master status. Consider the following individuals and try to identify the master status for each: Hillary Clinton, Rudy Guiliani, Barack Obama, Oprah Winfrey, Mother Theresa, Martha Stewart, Paris Hilton, and yourself. Be prepared to discuss your selections.

3. We've offered the concepts of master status and anticipatory socialization as useful devices for understanding conventional wisdoms regarding old age. Consider some of the other sociological ideas introduced in previous essays. Select and discuss two of them that you feel also offer insight into the misconceptions about old age. (Hint: Do the dynamics of a "self-fulfilling prophecy" feed a negative view of old age?)

4. Visit the AARP Web site (http://www.aarp.org/):
   - Click on the link for policy and research and then on the link for minorities. Scroll down through the list and access fact sheets regarding the financial security for aging Hispanics and Blacks. Which specific categories within each minority group are most vulnerable to any future insolvency of Social Security? Cite your evidence.

Culture Meets Social Structure

Essay 7

Conventional Wisdom Tells Us . . . Americans Are Becoming More and More Individualistic

This essay examines social relations in the United States, exploring in particular the characterization of contemporary Americans as increasingly isolated, disconnected, and dangerously individualistic. Here, we argue that social relations in the United States are more multifaceted than conventional wisdom suggests and are a result of the complex interplay of social structure and culture.

Community is dead! That is the cry of many a social commentator. Indeed, since the 1970s, a bevy of intellectuals have warned of a growing individualism in America. **Individualism** refers to the relational form that prioritizes the individual over any group, community, or institution.

Consider this timeline of claims. In 1976, author Tom Wolfe (1976:143) anointed the "Me Generation," a cohort of "zealous individualists" devoted only to the project of themselves. Three years later, Christopher Lasch (1979) proclaimed that a "culture of narcissism" had "carried the logic of individualism to the extreme of a war of all against all, the pursuit of happiness to the dead end of a narcissistic preoccupation with the self" (p. xv). Through the 1980s and 1990s, scholars wrote of rising selfishness, declining civility, suburban isolation, and the loss of community. By the millennium's end, many saw Americans as hopelessly disengaged—from everything but themselves. Indeed, political scientist Robert Putnam (1998, 2000; Putnam, Feldstein, and Cohen 2004) declared the "death of Civic America." Sociologist Amitai Etzioni (1996) described the United States as a nation "heavily burdened with the antisocial consequences of excessive individual liberty" (pp. xvii, xv). And sociologists Miller McPerson, Lynn Smith-Lovin, and Mathew Brashears (2006) warned that America was quickly becoming a nation of social isolates.

Are these analysts and intellectuals correct in their depictions of American society? In reviewing social life in the United States during the past four decades, do we indeed find that social relations have slowly moved from something approximating civic community to an anomic world of self-centered strangers? And if so, is such "me-centered" individualism a terminal condition or simply a social phase?

In exploring this issue, sociologist Karen A. Cerulo examined data on American attitudes and behaviors for the past four decades (1960–2000), including figures generated by the Gallup poll, the General Social Survey, and the U.S. Census. (For a full accounting of the study's data sources, see Cerulo 2002.) Cerulo contends that these data fail to confirm an unequivocal shift toward individualism. Rather, data on American attitudes and behaviors provide a very complex and multifaceted picture of U.S. social relations. **Social relations** refer to the types of connections and the patterns of interaction that structure the broader society. Thus, in response to those who depict social actors of the future as isolated, disconnected beings, Cerulo suggests a much more optimistic picture.

To be sure, there are several areas in which national-level data support increased individualism. For example, many point to the changing configuration of American families and households as an indicator of this phenomenon. And indeed during the past four decades, national data reveal an increase in the percentage of single people, divorced people, and one-person households in the U.S. population. Each of these trends suggests a greater propensity on the part of Americans to "go it alone." Several other indicators confirm the increased "me-centeredness" of this period. For example, when it comes to sociability, Americans generally have reduced the time they spent socializing with their immediate neighbors. In turn, Americans have increased the amount of time they devoted toward the very individualistic project of personal grooming. The data also show increases in certain attitudes that champion personal freedom. For example, public approval for suicide has increased during this period.

But while the indicators just reviewed suggest a definitive shift toward individualism, it is important to note that other national-level data question that trend. Many attitudes and behaviors of the period suggest only a "temporary flirtation" with individualism. Consider abortion, an act often cited as a hallmark of individual freedom. (Indeed, the individual's right to privacy was the basis for the Supreme Court ruling that legalized abortion at the federal level.) Both abortion rates and Americans' approval ratings for abortion increased from 1970 to 1980. But in 1981, abortion rates began to steadily decrease. After 1980, Americans' approval ratings for abortion proved rather erratic as well. Thus, the support for individual rights—at least in this area—was fleeting rather than permanent. Now consider violent crime rates. Murder rates in particular are often cited as a cue of excessive personal liberty, a hallmark of a dying community. However, the murder rates recorded for the period in question fail to display the linear increase that would confirm a growing individualism. While U.S. murder rates increased from 1965 to 1975, rates leveled off between 1976 and 1980. From 1981 to 2000, murder rates generally decreased. Finally, consider the popularity of various college majors during the period in question. Business, a field many feel is a trademark of the "me generation," increased in popularity from 1970 to 1985; however, the major saw a precipitous decrease in popularity after 1985. The number of majors in art, perhaps the extreme expression of individualism, actually declined during the 1970s and early 1980s, rebounding only slightly after 1985. Now consider majors in education and social science, which are prototypically nonindividualistic in thrust. While the number of such majors temporarily declined in the 1970s, that trend generally reversed after 1981. Taken together, these indicators suggest that the growth of individualistic attitudes and behaviors is not linear and absolute. Often, the growth of individualism is a short-lived, reversible phenomenon.

While some attitudes and behaviors suggest only a temporary shift toward individualism, note that others suggest no movement toward individualism at all. For example, in an increasingly individualistic society, we might expect community-oriented activities such as church membership and church attendance to decrease. Yet these behaviors have remained relatively stable over the past four decades. In a period of individualism, we also might expect more and more people to seek the independence of self-employment. Yet here, too, such rates have remained relatively stable. In an era of growing individualism, we might expect to find cues of decreased interaction with family and friends. (After all, we found that socializing with neighbors had declined.) Yet indicators of parent-child contact or social contacts between adults and their parents, siblings, and friends have displayed little change. In a period of individualism, we might expect to see increases in prototypically individualistic acts such as suicide. Yet suicide rates have remained stable as well. Note, too, that in an era of growing individualism, we might expect to see changes in Americans' reported levels of satisfaction with their communities. Similarly, we might expect people to lose faith in the communal spirit. Yet Americans' attitudes on these matters have remained relatively stable. In total, these data fail to support a growing individualism in America. Rather, the data suggest little change in many relevant attitudes and behaviors.

In reviewing American attitudes and behaviors during the past four decades, one final trend deserves noting. Several indicators clearly challenge any growth in individualism. Rather, much data suggest the sustenance or growth of communally oriented sentiments. For example, if individualism were truly surging, we might expect to see an increase in self-gratifying or what sociologist Robert Merton referred to as "retreatist" behaviors, such as smoking or alcohol and drug use. Yet such behaviors have generally decreased during the past four decades. During an era of individualism, we might expect to see individuals withdrawing their support from community-oriented causes, such as higher education, fraternal clubs, and organizations. Yet figures show that voluntary contributions to such causes have increased steadily during the period in question. In concert with voluntary spending, government expenditures on social welfare programs, Social Security, Medicare, and veterans benefits have consistently increased during this period as well. So, too, has public support for such spending (albeit in a jagged fashion). Taken together, these data indicate that many of Americans' attitudes and behaviors circa 1960 to 2000 were actually more "other-oriented" than they were "me-oriented."

To be sure, the indicators summarized here constitute only a portion of the many measures that tap social relations in America. We could, of course, increase the number of indicators we examine, but research suggests it would lead us to a similar end. For example, in a recent *New York Times* poll, researchers asked Americans how much importance they attached to 15 specific values. Some seemingly individualistic dimensions such as "being responsible for your own actions" and "being able to stand up for yourself" ranked among the most important values for those sampled. However, very close behind were more communally-oriented sentiments, such as "being able to communicate your feelings (to others)," "having faith in God," and "having children." In support of increased individualism, Americans ranked "having enough time for one's self" as more important than "being involved in the community." Yet in support of community, Americans ranked "being a good neighbor" as more important than "being financially secure" or "being physically attractive" (Cherlin 1999; also see Dubois and Beauvois 2005 and Spreafico 2005 for similar findings). Thus, it seems clear that Americans live a multifaceted existence. While Americans have indeed grown more individualistic in some regards, they have grown more community oriented in others, or simply exhibited no change in either direction. Indeed, a careful study of American attitudes and practices firmly suggests that American social relations are a highly complex phenomenon. (For additional support of this thesis, see Boase, Horrigan, Wellman, and Rainie 2006; Pahl and Spencer 2004; Radin 2006; Spencer and Pahl 2006; Wellman 2001; Wellman, Boase, and Chen 2002; Wuthnow 1998.)

Cerulo (2002, 2008) suggests that rather than labeling the United States as dangerously individualistic, we should think of American society as an entity that resides in a state of relational polyphony. **Relational polyphony** means that different relational forms—not just individualism—simultaneously constitute American society. Cerulo's work shows that one can enter American society at any point from 1850 to the present and find that four different relational forms coexist: individualism, pluralism, bilateralism, and communalism.

Recall that, earlier, we defined individualism as a relational form that prioritizes the individual over any group, community, or institution. Here, we define the remaining three relational forms. **Pluralism** emerges when social interactions are directed toward the peaceful coexistence of multiple groups. Various sectors of a society work to maintain mutual understanding; they work toward a system by which resources can be shared. Under pluralistic conditions, compromise and collaboration represent the dominant modes of social interaction. **Bilateral relations** suggest a condition in which a "them-versus-us" mentality guides social interaction. Dominance over or competition with the "other" represents social interaction's central goal. When bilateralism is in force, conflict and organized competition are the most frequent modes of interaction. Strong bonds are built with in-group members, while connections to out-group members are discouraged. In **communalism**, social actors become connected, albeit temporarily, via a specific task, event, or characteristic. During such periods, a sense of familiarity, "like-mindedness," or "we-ness" emerges. Similarities are stressed over differences; common knowledge is stressed over specialized knowledge. The good of the community takes precedence over the welfare of any subgroup or individual.

How can these relational forms coexist? We need only look at the present historical moment to understand the phenomenon. In today's society, for example, new communication technologies can greatly facilitate individualism. One can customize and insulate rather than commune, creating a "world of one." Via the portable Internet (as accessed via PDFs, cell phones, and iPods), one can downscale the scope of interaction, performing all one's routine tasks—banking, shopping, medical counseling, even romance—all without entering the physical community. In this way, contemporary

American society can be reduced to its most basic element, the individual, with each individual remaining only loosely or instrumentally connected—and, sometimes, disconnected.

At the same time, contemporary America is mapped according to pluralistic relations. Present-day society exists as a set of overlapping, interlocking "circles" (i.e., "Baby Boomers," "pro-lifers," gun-control supporters, Independents, etc.), and often social action is directed by the ways in which these circles configure and coalesce. Such pluralistic relations become quite visible—every four years—when the race for the White House heats up. Contemporary presidential candidates can no longer rely on person-to-person connections or blind party loyalty. Rather, successful candidates' constituencies must represent a coalition of compatible interest groups.

Of course, contemporary American society does periodically divide according to dualistic conflict. Certain events and issues pit White against Black, male against female, pro-life against pro-choice, big business against government, and so on. Such controversies force "either/or" choices and forge relations on the basis of social actors' bilateral affiliations. In the case of race, we saw this occur with the Rodney King trial, the O. J. Simpson case, the Duke lacrosse incident involving allegations of a racially charged rape, or the firing of shock jock Don Imus following racials slurs aimed at the Rutgers women's basketball team. Similarly, court cases such as the Microsoft antitrust trial or the Enron prosecution underscored the divide between government and big business. During such periods, social relations often develop in opposition rather than in conjunction with the "other."

And yet it is also true that, faced with certain social events, Americans will temporarily ignore social partitions and emphasize collective concerns. Actors band together (albeit for short, finite spans of time) in a single, targeted point of attention. Such like-mindedness enables actors to form communalistic relations, express shared perspectives, and support a common agenda. We witnessed such relations in widespread efforts aimed at solving national problems. Think back to recovery efforts following the September 11th terrorist attacks or those that followed Hurricane Katrina. Similarly, we witness communalistic relations in response to American human interest stories. Recall the intense collective focus that surrounded the deaths of Princess Diana or John F. Kennedy Jr., the Oklahoma City bombing or the executions of Timothy McVeigh and, later, Saddam Hussein. (Gallup polls showed that more than 80% of respondents reported paying very close attention to these stories; see Gallup 1976–2003; 2004–2007.)

And finally, we witness such relations in what sociologist Nina Eliasoph (1998) calls the "community of talk." **Communities of talk** revolve around topics about which the large majority of social members can fluently and affably converse: steroid scandals in the world of baseball, the latest winner of television's *American Idol,* or the most recent Britney Spears scandal. Far from the isolated existence attributed to contemporary Americans, communalistic relations infuse society with a sense of group-mindedness.

The aforementioned examples suggest that different relational forms—individualism, pluralism, bilateralism, and communalism—are all integral parts of American society. To be sure, the relative concentration of these forms shifts through time, just as the primary melody of a polyphonic composition shifts from voice to voice as the piece progresses. But it is the coexistence of these four relational forms—their harmony—that constitutes social relations in America.

If relational polyphony is the typical state of the American society, why have so many social commentators argued that one relational form, individualism, has come to dominate the United States? Three factors may help perpetuate claims of a growing individualism. First, some argue that researchers may be incorrectly measuring individualism's opposites—namely, community-oriented factors such as social connectedness and civic engagement. If, indeed, we are mis-measuring, and thus underestimating the communal side of social life, individualism will appear to be a more powerful phenomenon than it truly is in practice. In today's sophisticated academic world, the notion of measurement error may be difficult to fathom. Yet, mistakes in measuring social connectedness and civic engagement could be a byproduct of changing technological and economic environments. New environments carry with them new methods of joining together. But until researchers fully understand and acknowledge these new methods, they will fail to identify the scope and strength of contemporary social ties (Boase et al. 2006; Cerulo and Ruane 1998; Chayko 2002; Pahl 2005; Spencer and Pahl 2006; Wellman 2001; Wellman et al. 2002; Wuthnow 1998).

An overemphasis on individualism may also result from a predisposition in sociological analysis toward linear models of social relations. **Linear models** invoke a set of bipolar categories (such as communalism versus individualism) to capture changing social relations. Such models describe movement from one relational pole to the other as a unidirectional process, a transition typically triggered by the modernization of society. When we look at some of the linear models so central to sociological analysis (e.g., Tonnies's Gemeinschaft versus Gesellschaft, Durkheim's mechanical and organic solidarity, Simmel's small-town relations versus the metropolis, Habermas's or Gidden's distinctions between the public and private sphere), one argument forms a common thread: Modernization drives societies down a one-way path of development, triggering a steady progression from a "we-centered" to a "me-centered" experience. When so many central models promote a similar point of view, analysts can become blinded to empirical data that contradict that view.

We must also consider the role of culture in perpetuating claims of a growing individualism. **Culture** refers to the values, beliefs, symbols, objects, customs, and conventions that characterize a group or society's way of life. Cerulo (2002) shows that, in certain historical eras, one finds what we might call "cultural surges of individualism," eras in which individualistic images overpower the projection of other cultural themes. In the United States, one such surge occurred from 1970 to 1984. During this period, a wide variety of cultural sectors, such as music, best-sellers, film, theater, television, sports, education, law, and science, were saturated with images and messages of growing individualism. Yet it is important to note that the culture of the period did not reflect Americans' actual behaviors and attitudes. As we pointed out earlier in this essay, Americans of the era did not display a dramatic increase in individualistic practices. Rather, behavioral and attitudinal moves toward individualism were temporary or limited in scope. Thus, the sense of this period as an "era of individualism" must be viewed, in part, as a cultural construction. A **cultural construction** is an image of reality that may not necessarily reflect actual behaviors and attitudes.

Cultural constructions of individualism do not emerge without reason. Such surges appear to be a reaction to a social condition called diffuse instability. **Diffuse instability** refers to a widespread period of flux in which change and uncertainty are distributed across the social system. In reviewing decades of U.S. history and cultural production, one finds that cultural constructions of individualism are almost always associated with diffuse instability. In contrast, periods of stability rarely emphasize individualistic themes (Cerulo 2002). Why? It may be that during periods of social confusion and uncertainty, a culture of individualism provides a message of personal control—a message of survival. Cultural constructions of individualism suggest to social actors that in the face of adversity, the individual can fight back and prevail. When social life appears to be slowly eroding, individual initiative can turn the tide. As such, cultural constructions of individualism offer a coping mechanism of sorts, a prescription for personal action at a time when instability derails predictability and threatens established social patterns.

The research discussed in this chapter reminds us that the cultural and the social are not bound by a simple causal relationship. Culture does not simply reflect the social, or vice versa. Rather, each sphere develops in response to the progression of the other, suggesting the unique integrity of culture and society as well as the powerful symbiosis between the two. The study of individualism represents one avenue by which to study this symbiotic relationship. But only patient and extensive empirical inquiry will provide us with the full scope of this intricate interaction.

Learning More About It

For the definitive work on the decline of civic America, see Robert D. Putnam's *Bowling Alone: The Collapse and Revival of American Community* (New York: Simon and Schuster, 2000).

In concert with Putnam, a recent study suggests that Americans are losing their confidants and becoming increasingly isolated beings. For more information see Miller McPherson, Lynn Smith-Lovin, and Mathew E. Brashears' 2006 article, "Social Isolation in America: Changes in Core Discussion Networks over Two Decades" (*American Sociological Review* 71:3:353–375).

Karen A. Cerulo offers an opposing view in "Individualism . . . Pro Tem: Reconsidering U.S. Social Relations" in K. A. Cerulo (Ed.), *Culture in Mind: Toward a Sociology of Culture and Cognition* (pp. 135–171), New York: Routledge, 2002. She continues this line of thought in a 2008 follow-up piece entitled "Social Relations, Core Values and the Polyphony of the American Experience" (*Sociological Forum* 23:2:351–362).

For some interesting ideas on community building, see Amitai Etzioni's *Monochrome Society* (New York: New Forum Books, 2003) or Robert Putnam and colleagues' *Better Together: Restoring American Community* (New York: Simon and Schuster, 2004).

The U.S. Census Bureau offers a wide variety of indicators by which to "track" social relations in America. For trends in marriage, divorce, college majors, suicide, visiting neighbors, church attendance, violent crime, and many, many more, consult the *Statistical Abstracts of the United States* at http://www.census.gov/compendia/statab/

Exercises

1. In this essay, we mention a number of indicators used as cues of individualism. Check a recent volume of the *Statistical Abstracts of the United States.* Can you locate five additional indicators that could be added to the measures mentioned here? Defend your selection.

2. Relational polyphony can readily be seen in various TV programs. Select five different sitcoms and view two episodes of each show. Which form of social relations appears most often? Offer some interpretation of any patterns you observe.

3. Randomly select five "My Space" pages and analyze the postings that appear on them. Which of the four forms of social relations are represented in these online interactions? Support your answers.

Essay 8

Conventional Wisdom Tells Us . . . There's Nothing We Can Do About the Weather

"Mother Nature" may call lots of the shots when it comes to weather and climate. But "the elements" have a social and cultural side as well. In this essay, we focus the sociological eye on weather and climate, exploring the way in which factors such as modernization, profit motives, and our entrepreneurial values can both create climate problems . . . and solve them.

"Everybody talks about the weather," wrote Mark Twain, "but nobody does anything about it." It would be hard to quibble with Twain's observations on the social aspects of weather. The weather is a conversational constant—a "go to" topic when we are at a loss for words. On the job, on a date, in line at the division of motor vehicles, we can always resort to the weather when other topics of discourse elude us: Hot enough for you? Is it ever going to stop raining?

But Twain's quote also expresses the common belief that the weather is something beyond our control. Weather professionals can attest to the strength of this belief. Despite many accurate weather forecasts, meteorologists will tell you that the public tends to focus on and remember only their local weather person's big misses—the prediction of rain on a day that turns sunny or a warning of record snowfall when a mere dusting occurs. We don't think of our weather people as reliable. Yet we typically cut the weather people some slack because the weather—well, it just happens. We have to grin and bear it.

Despite the conventional wisdom on weather, we may be more involved in manufacturing it than we realize. And the manufacturing of weather is a very social phenomenon. For this reason, weather is a topic that deserves a second look—this time, a look guided by our sociological eye.

Let's begin by reviewing some terms. **Weather** refers to the atmospheric conditions of a given moment and place. In contrast, **climate** refers to the average weather conditions of a region over time. Weather can change quickly, from one hour to the next. (The earth's day to night cycle is a powerful driver of the weather.) Climate changes occur over longer periods of time—that is, years and decades.

Now let's consider some climate "facts." Statistics show that in 2005, we broke some records—those for warmest average global temperatures on the land and on ocean surfaces (National Climate Data Center 2007). The following year, 2006, proved the second warmest year on record for the United States and the fifth warmest year globally (National Oceanic and Atmospheric Administration 2007). At this writing, 2007 appears headed for record-breaking numbers as well. In the first six months of the year, the United States was dominated by above average warmth and dryness (National Climate Data Center 2007). These figures appear to be part of a larger trend. Eleven of the last 12 years number among the hottest years on record (Union of Concerned Scientists 2007a, 2007b). Since 1980, snow cover in the Northern Hemisphere has significantly declined. Sea ice areas in the Arctic have decreased, and ocean temperatures have increased. Our climate is changing and more and more scientists agree that human activity is responsible for that change (Baker 2006; Union of Concerned Scientists 2007a).

To understand our hand in changing the climate, we might first start with a review of a term that has been bandied about for the last decade or so: the "greenhouse effect." Despite some bad press, this phenomenon is, in itself, a good thing. The **greenhouse effect** refers to a natural phenomenon that makes life on earth possible. Our climate is basically driven by energy from the sun. In the normal flow of solar energy, the sun warms the earth's surface, and this energy is radiated back toward space as heat. As is the case with garden greenhouses that control heat loss, this radiated heat is "trapped" by an insulating blanket of gases. (We might think of "greenhouse" gases such as carbon dioxide, methane, and nitrous oxide as akin to the glass panes of greenhouses; see Figure 8.1.) The trapped heat keeps the earth's average surface temperature at approximately 60 degrees Fahrenheit. Without the greenhouse effect, the average temperature of the earth would be 0° F—far too low to sustain life. So far, this sounds quite positive. So why is the greenhouse effect a bad thing? The greenhouse effect begins to be a problem when too much heat is trapped by too many gases—a situation that scientists agree is now underway (Union of Concerned Scientists 2006a).

The climate changes we are witnessing are all indicative of a phenomenon known as **global warming**. Global warming refers to a rise in the earth's temperature due to the increase in greenhouse or heat-trapping gases in the atmosphere. To be sure, global warming is not a new phenomenon. The earth experienced a drastic rise in temperature after the last Ice Age. And over the course of the last century, the earth's temperature has increased by 1.4° F (Fitzpatrick 2006). During this same time period, the level of the sea has risen between 6 and 8 inches worldwide (Environmental Protection Agency 2004). By the end of the century, sea levels are expected to rise another 7–23 inches (Union of Concerned Scientists 2007a).

While these changes may sound modest, they are nonetheless significant. Consider that over the past 10,000 years, the earth's average temperature hasn't fluctuated by more than 1.8° F. The Ice Age saw average temperatures that were only 5–9 degrees cooler than today. If global warming continues on the order of 2- to 10-degree increases, we are likely to see increased coastal erosion, increased flooding and permanent inundation of some areas (think more Katrinas), disruption of agriculture in low-lying areas like the

Figure 8.1   The Greenhouse Effect

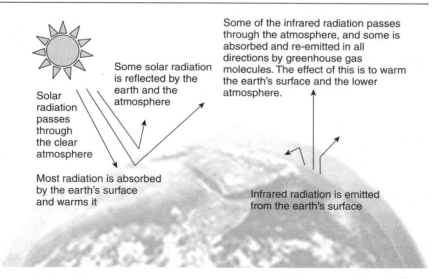

SOURCE: http://www.epa.gov/globalwarming/kids/greenhouse.html

Mississippi River delta, and increasing health threats from disease-carrying insects and rodents (Union of Concerned Scientists 2006a). Add to this list the fact that heat is the leading cause of weather-related deaths in the nation—excessive heat takes more lives each year than tornadoes, hurricanes, flooding, lightning, and cold weather combined (Allsopp 2006). To be sure rising temperatures demand our attention, and that attention should be focused on ourselves. The scientific community is increasingly in agreement that a primary source of global warming, especially over the last 50 years, is human activity (Union of Concerned Scientists 2007a).

The human impact on the environment is really not news. Indeed an entire field of study is devoted to this interaction—the field of **ecology**. Ecology entails the study of the interaction between organisms and the natural environment. Ecologists note that, in dealing with the environment, humans have a resource that greatly facilitates our influence—humans have **culture**. Culture refers to our design for living. It encompasses all the material and nonmaterial things and ideas we use to solve the problems of living. How does culture have an impact on the environment? Consider that humans' influence on the environment can range from low (i.e., in simple hunting and gathering societies) to high (i.e., in modern, industrialized nations). In large measure, it is the material aspect of culture, in particular the technological advances of modern societies, that produces the high-impact scenario.

Technology is often used as a way of taming or bending the natural environment to better suit our current needs. Necessity and material comfort are both mothers of invention and of cultural innovation. As populations and cities and suburbs grow, fields and forests give way to housing developments and malls and parking structures. Community schools, hospitals, factories, stores, roadways, bridges and tunnels, and theme parks are built. Growing populations present growing energy and utility demands that are met with ever expanding power grids and infrastructures. Waste management and pollution are inevitable byproducts of progress, and technology devises new ways to handle both. Our modern, technologically enhanced existence is second nature to most of us; many can't imagine life any other way. Currently, there are only a few individuals committing to "no impact" lifestyles: living their lives so as to have no net impact on the environment.[1] Not surprisingly then, the high environmental impact and environmental costs of modern society often go unrecognized.

Merton's work on manifest and latent functions and dysfunctions helps us understand our "blindness" to modernity's environmental costs. **Manifest functions** are obvious consequences or benefits of some social process. **Latent functions** are unrecognized positive outcomes. **Manifest dysfunctions** are obvious negative consequences of some social process. **Latent dysfunctions** are less than obvious negative outcomes. Any one event or social process might give rise to each of these categories of effects. For example, a manifest function of war is the defense of a nation. A latent function is the strengthening of in-group solidarity as the nation rallies round its war effort. A manifest dysfunction of war is the loss of lives and destruction of property that accompany war. A latent dysfunction of war might be the declining status of the warring nation.

Very often, the products and processes of modernity, while they yield immediate benefits, also present us with latent dysfunctions. So, for example, our interstate highway system obviously supports our mobility needs and helps us overcome the obstacle of distance. But our interstate highway system has also increased our dependence on the automobile and in turn our dependence on foreign oil. Similarly, chemicals and pesticides can make our lawn the envy of our neighbors, but they can also ruin local water tables, lakes, and streams. Unintended negative consequences are exactly what we seem to be facing with the global warming issue.

As Figure 8.2 reveals, two human activities—our increasing use of fossil fuels (coal, oil, and natural gas) and our land use practices (i.e., deforestation, landfills, agricultural activities, and development)—contribute significantly to the unexpected but nonetheless dangerous outcome: the buildup of heat-trapping gases. Our daily reliance on cars, our dependence on fossil-fuel-generated electricity, and our use of heating fuels for our homes collectively constitute the greatest source of human-caused greenhouse gas emissions. (If you average 20,000 miles a year on your car, you alone are responsible for contributing 20,000 pounds of carbon dioxide to the atmosphere—and more, of course, if you're driving an SUV and still more if you're driving a Hummer!)

Forests can help slow global warming by their sequestering function—their ability to remove carbon dioxide from the atmosphere. But when forests are cleared, carbon is released back into the atmosphere. Tropical deforestation is responsible for 20% of human-activity-based carbon dioxide emissions each year (Union of Concerned Scientists 2006b). Farms, landfills. and coal mines are the source of another greenhouse gas—methane. Methane accounts for about 10% of the U.S. greenhouse gas emissions. (And note that methane is 20 times more potent than carbon dioxide as a heat blanket; Solman 2006a.) If we continue with "business as usual" in our social and cultural practices, the forecast indicates significant climate change will result.

Global warming has caught the attention of much of the world. As of 2007, nearly 170 countries have ratified the Kyoto Protocol. This agreement sets binding targets for developed nations to reduce their greenhouse gas emissions by about 5% by 2012. On average, industrialized countries account for about one-half of global greenhouse gas emissions, so the Kyoto treaty is a step in the direction of stabilizing greenhouse gas (GHG)

Figure 8.2   Average Annual Carbon Dioxide Emissions by Various Sources

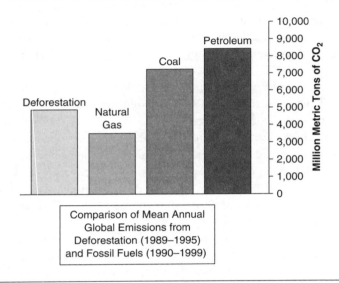

SOURCE: IPCC: U.S. Department of Energy http://www.ucsusa.org/global_warming/solutions/
recognizing-forests-role-in-climate-change.html

concentrations. The United Sates has both the distinction of being the single largest emitter of GHGs (see Figure 8.3) and the distinction of being one of the few major nations to refuse to ratify the Kyoto Protocol. President Bush opposed the protocol on two counts: the treaty's potential for harming the U.S. economy via revenue and job losses and its exemption of developing nations. Without U.S. participation, however, many fear that the power of the agreement to avert negative climate change will be seriously compromised.

The U.S. position on the Kyoto Protocol is consistent with the views of other global warming skeptics. The Global Climate Coalition (GCC) was founded in 1989 by 46 corporate and trade groups representing U.S. industry. The GCC launched an aggressive campaign against the Kyoto Protocol, claiming it was a flawed agreement that would hurt U.S. business interests. More recently, a novel by Michael Crichton casts doubt on the scientific claims about climate change. Crichton, however, is accused of hand selecting evidence that agrees with his position while ignoring the bulk of evidence that documents climate change. Skeptic groups must contend with the likes of the National Academy of Sciences, the American Geophysical Union, the American Meteorological Society, and the Intergovernmental Panel on Climate Change, all of which affirm that climate change is indeed occurring.

While the federal government has been slow to warm up to global warming, other sectors have been more responsive. Local and state governments

Figure 8.3   Fossil Fuel Usage per Capita (20 Largest Countries)

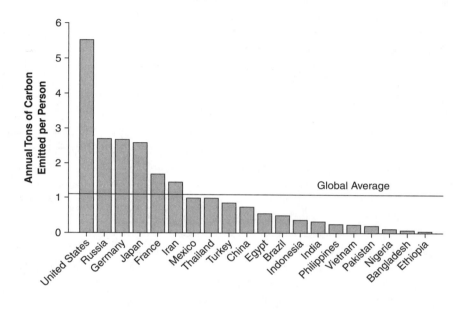

SOURCE: Global Warming Art. Figure prepared by Robert Rohde. http://www.globalwarmingart .com/wiki/Image:Global_Carbon_Emission_by_Type.png

and even big business have acted where the federal government has not. California has taken a series of steps to reduce greenhouse gas emissions: It has ordered automakers to reduce global warming emissions by 30%, it has instructed private utility companies to calculate GHG emissions, and it is requiring companies in its Public Employees Retirement System to join the Carbon Disclosure Project (and commit to public disclosure on carbon emissions). George Pataki, former governor of New York, leads a coalition of nine northeast states that is developing a mandatory cap system for regional power plants. Major corporations are also responding. In 2003, DuPont, Ford, IBM, and other major firms started the Chicago Climate Exchange. Members of the exchange have committed to reducing their greenhouse gas emissions by 4% and to trade credits with other exchange members that are not meeting these output goals (Collier 2005).

While culture has a hand in exacerbating the global warming problem, it may also play a role in slowing or even solving the crisis. The entrepreneurial spirit is one of the defining U.S. values. The ability to profit from global warming may be the very thing that reverses the warming pattern. The trading of greenhouse gas emissions is presenting entrepreneurs with new business opportunities. A **cap-and-trade system** uses the power of the market to create financial incentives for reducing emissions. (The system was used successfully in the 1990s to reduce sulfur dioxide emissions and combat the acid rain problem.) Dairy farmers, for instance, can earn credits for reducing their methane gas emissions below cap levels by converting cow manure into fertilizer. The credits they earn by reducing methane emissions can then be sold via the Chicago Climate Exchange. And who would want to buy these credits? Other exchange participants who have volunteered to reduce their emissions but have exceeded their caps. Buying credits from low emitters can set the balance right for high emitters and make for happy participants all around. One may ask: Why, absent the United States ratifying the Kyoto agreement, would *any* U.S. businesses volunteer to lower their greenhouse gas emissions? Again there appears to be an economic answer. Businesses are betting that consumers will agree that "green is better." As a result, they will pay more for greener industries and products (Solman 2006b).

The belief that greener is better is one force driving research on biofuels as an alternative to oil. Entrepreneurs are busy turning used cooking grease into biodiesel, and corn, soy, sugar cane, woodchips, and switchgrass into ethanol. Boosters see two major advantages to developing biofuels. Biofuels are cleaner fuel sources that will reduce greenhouse gas emissions. Biofuels are also *renewable* energy sources and might very well put us on a path to energy self-sufficiency (Solman 2006c). Furthermore, corporations are also discovering that the steps they take to reduce greenhouse gases can be cost saving. DuPont has reported saving $2 billion through its mitigation efforts; IBM has reported saving $791 million (Union of Concerned Scientists 2005). And for those gases that continue to escape into the air, some are hard at work on developing technologies that could neutralize harmful gases. A Columbia University scientist, Klaus Lachner, has been working on a device to trap and remove carbon dioxide from the air. He claims that 250,000 of these devices positioned around the world could seriously reduce the threat of global warming (Solman 2006d). Amidst this activity, one fact is becoming increasingly clear: The global warming trend may only cool down if business opportunities to combat it heat up.

If there is one additional harbinger of things to come on the global warming front, it may be gleaned from the insurance industry. Greener products or new gas-reducing technologies aren't the only source of big profits. The insurance industry also sees profits in global warming itself. Insurance companies regard global warming as a disaster waiting to happen and thereby as a way to sell more insurance. Smart consumers would do well to insure against global warming so that they can be in a position to recover from any economic losses (Solman 2006b). To be sure, the insurance we opt for might be in the form of a traditional policy (this would make the insurance industry happy). But the "insurance" we opt for might also be in the steps we take to reduce our carbon dioxide "footprint." (The term "footprint" is used by environmentalists to convey our personal contribution to carbon dioxide emissions.) Doing so allows us to finally take up Twain's challenge—namely, doing something about the weather or more precisely about the climate.

Learn More About It

For an in-depth discussion of the social side of environmental issues, see Michael Mayerfeld Bell's book *An Invitation to Environmental Sociology* (Thousand Oaks, CA: Sage, 2007).

The issue of global warming has finally made its way into the political arena thanks in part to Al Gore's documentary, "An Inconvenient Truth." More information about the film as well as educational curricula materials can be found at http://www.climatecrisis.net

You can calculate your own greenhouse gas emissions (or the size of your "footprint") by visiting the following EPA Web site: http://yosemite.epa.gov/oar/global warming.nsf/content/ResourceCenterToolsGHGCalculator.html

Those interested in learning more about "cap-and-trade" systems for combating pollution will find the following 2005 article by Mathers and Manion helpful: "How It Works: Cap-and-Trade Systems." *Catalyst* (Spring) 4:1. http://www.ucsusa.org/publications/catalyst/page.jsp?itemID=27226959

The following Web page offers a list of the top ten sources for environmental news: http://environment.about.com/od/activismvolunteering/tp/environews.htm

Exercises

1. Talk to 20 people—10 who drive SUVs and 10 who drive small economy cars. How many in each group recognize global warming as a serious problem? Do members of each group hold many social similarities—age, gender, socioeconomic status (SES), or political affiliation? Is there a predictable "social profile" linked to global warming believers and nonbelievers?

2. Visit some "going green" Web sites (e.g., "Living with Ed" at http://www.hgtv.com/hgtv/pac_ctnt_988/text/0,,HGTV_22056_56190,00.html) to get a good idea of green products and practices. Now try another brief survey. This time ask 20–30 people about their willingness to "go green." What's the social profile of those who are willing to "pay" for a green solution to global warming?

Note

1. Early in 2007, Americans were introduced to the "no impact man," a New Yorker vowing to live for one year in New York City without the taken-for-granted practices and products that have a negative impact on the environment. See http://noimpactman.com for more information.

Socialization and Identity

Essay 9

Conventional Wisdom Tells Us . . . What's in a Name? That Which We Call a Rose by Any Other Name Would Smell As Sweet

This essay explores the power of names, highlighting the central role of symbols and labels in the construction of identity.

Shakespeare's verse argues for substance over labels. It is a sentiment common to much of the conventional wisdom on names. You've heard the adages: "Sticks and stones may break my bones, but names will never hurt me" or "The names may change, but the story remains the same." And how about quips like "Call me anything, but don't call me late for dinner"? All these truisms consistently downplay the importance of names. Are the labels we give to people and things as inconsequential as conventional wisdom suggests? Do names really lack the power to influence or the force to injure? Would a rose really command such deep respect and awe if it were known as a petunia or a pansy?

A large body of social science literature suggests that conventional wisdom has vastly underestimated the significance of names. Indeed, names in our society function as powerful symbols. **Symbols** are arbitrary signs that come to be endowed with special meaning and, ultimately, gain the ability to influence behaviors, attitudes, and emotions.

The symbolic nature of names makes them much more than a string of alphabetics. Rather, names function as calling cards or personal logos. They signify important aspects of one's history and heritage; they pinpoint an individual's social location and group affiliations. Based on our names, others make important decisions regarding our nature and temperament. In this way, names serve as important markers of identity. **Identity** refers to those essential characteristics that both link us and distinguish us from other social players and thus establish who we are.

The link between names and identity helps explain why forgetting someone's name often is viewed as a social faux pas. Similarly, we view situations that preclude the linking of name to identity with great pathos. Consider the sadness that surrounds every tomb of an unknown or unnamed soldier. In settings where one's name remains unknown, it is not unusual for an individual to feel alienated or disconnected. Think of those large lecture courses in which neither the professor nor other students know your name.

Names contribute to the construction of identity in a variety of ways. A family surname, for example, provides instant knowledge of an individual's history. Surnames serve as road maps to the past; they guide us through an individual's lineage and archive one's traditional group affiliations and cultural ties. Thus, historically, children who were denied their father's surnames were denied legitimate social locations. Without this signifier to chronicle their paternal pasts, such children were considered faceless and anonymous, with no rightful place in their social environments (Brunet and Bideau 2000; Colantonio, Fuster, Ferreyras, and Lascano 2006; Isaacs 1975; Lloyd 2000; Nagata 1999; Sanabria 2001; Sapkidis 1998; Stevens 1999; Tait 2006). Surnames also tend to be indicators of one's ethnic background.

In the modern world, many states manipulate surnames in ways that forward their current national agendas. A governing body may, for example, create official policy that uses surnames to include or exclude particular communities in the national identity (Alcoff 2005; Scassa 1996; Stevens 1999; Tait 2006; Wang 2002). Consider the case of Japan. After annexing Korea in the 1900s, the Japanese government forced the first wave of Korean immigrants to adopt Japanese surnames. In this way, the government placed Koreans under both physical and symbolic control (Fukuoka 1998). In the White (British) controlled Jamaica of the 18th century, immigrants were an issue as well. But here, the immigrants were African slaves. Rather than assimilating the group, the government wished to mark that population's separation from Whites. Hence, upon their arrival in Jamaica, slaves were stripped of ancestral forenames and surnames. Furthermore, they were renamed using only common English forenames. These truncated labels marked slaves as a distinctive group. Their "missing" surnames also made it clear that slaves lacked the lineage of Whites (Burnard 2001; Prabhakaran 1999). In the contemporary era too, certain ethnic surnames place their "owners" in negative social space. In post-9/11 America, for example, research documents that those whose surnames suggested Arab lineage experienced a period of increased harassment, violence. and workplace discrimination. This milieu proved especially dangerous for pregnant Arab women. Indeed, the risk of a poor birth outcome (i.e., a stillbirth, a premature birth, a problematic delivery, etc.) proved significantly higher for Arab-named women than it did for non-Arab-named women (Lauderdale 2006).

A name's ability to pinpoint personal histories leads some individuals to abandon their family surnames and adopt new ones. A well-chosen replacement name can bring one closer to groups or social histories that seem more in vogue, more powerful, or more in tune with one's future aspirations and endeavors. The entertainment industry is rife with examples of the practice. Many performers readily acknowledge the necessity of name changes in building a successful career. Consequently, Marshall Bruce Mathers's fans now know him as rapper "Eminem." Brian Werner decided "Marilyn Manson" was better suited to a life of shock rock. And credit singer "Queen Latifah" for understanding that names such as Dana Owens are not the stuff of which pop idols are made. In particular, personalities with ethnic surnames often feel the need for more mainstream, English-sounding names. Thus, fans know Winona Horowitz as "Winona Ryder," Jennifer Anistopoulou as "Jennifer Aniston," and Carlos Irwin Estevez as "Charlie Sheen" (*World Almanac and Book of Facts*, 1998:352–353; www.famousnamechanges.net). When careers encounter "dry spots" or take a new direction, a name change can become the perfect "jump-start." Perhaps that explains why singer Prince evolved from "Prince" to "the artist formerly known as Prince" to ♀ and back to "Prince" or why Sean Combs moved from "Puff Daddy" to "Puffy" to "P Diddy" to "Diddy." Of course, name changing is not restricted to the famous. In many African nations, for example, one's name is *expected* to change with every significant life event—for example, puberty, marriage, or entering the life of a soldier (Brinkman 2004). Often, newly naturalized citizens choose to change their names, selecting something familiar within their adopted nation. Such name changing can be political in nature. For example, after the September 11, 2001, terrorist attacks on the United States, some Muslims began legally changing their names to avoid bias and discrimination (Donohue 2002; see Thompson 2006 for similar findings on Koreans).

In each of these cases, a name change became a tool for impression management. **Impression management** is a process by which individuals manipulate or maneuver their public images so as to elicit certain desired reactions. In the process of impression management, new surnames become the foundation upon which broadly targeted identities are constructed.

First or common names function as powerful symbols as well. No doubt, you have witnessed the care and consideration most parents-to-be take as they set about naming a newborn. Many parents start the process months before the child is born. Such care may represent a worthy investment, for research suggests that the selection of a personal name can have long-term consequences for a child. Several studies show that individuals assess others' potential for success, morality, good health, and warmth on the basis of names. Thus, when asked to rate other people on the basis of first names alone, subjects perceived "James" as highly moral, healthy, warm, and likely to succeed. In contrast, "Melvin" was viewed as a potential failure, lacking good character, good health, or human caring. Similarly, individuals with names that correspond to contemporary norms of popularity—currently these include Jacob, Michael, and Joshua for boys and Emily, Emma, and Madison for girls—are judged to be more intelligent and better liked than individuals with old-fashioned names such as Arnold, Earl, Fred, Betty, Judy, and Phyllis (Christopher 1998; Etaugh, Bridges, Cummings-Hill, and Cohen 1999; Feinson 2004; Gueguen, Dufourcq-Brana, and Pascual 2005; Joubert 1994; Karylowski et al. 2001; Liddell and Lycett 1998; Mehrabian 2001; Mirsky 2000; Rosenkrantz and Satran 2004; Twenge and Manis 1998; Wattenberg 2005).

Personal names can influence more than just the perception of performance and ability. Some studies show a significant association between uncommon, peculiar, undesirable, or unique names and actual outcomes such as low academic performance, low professional achievement, and psychological maladjustment (Banse 1999; Bruning, Polinko, Zerbst, and Buckingham 2000; De Schipper, Hirschberg, and Sinha 2002; Gueguen, Dufourcq-Brana, and Pascual 2005; Insaf 2002; Liddell and Lycett 1998; Marlar and Joubert 2002; Rosenkrantz and Satran 2004; Twenge and Manis 1998; Willis, Willis, and Grier 1982). Indeed, so strong is the influence of personal names that some nations actually regulate the process of naming. French law, for example, allows officials to reject any name deemed at odds with a child's well-being (Besnard and Desplanques 1993). The Canadian government has set similar standards, refusing to register unusual names for babies. So after trying to register the name "Ivory" for their daughter, two Quebec parents were told, "No! Ivory is only a brand of soap" (McLean 1998). Similar concerns emerged in Italy. In 2007, an Italian court ruled that a couple could not name their baby "Friday" and ordered that he be named "Gregory" – the patron saint for the day on which he was born (Pullella 2007). To be sure, naming concerns are a worldwide phenomenon. The New Zealand government rejected the request of Pat and Sheena Wheaton when they petitioned the government registry to name their son "4Real" (Reuters 2007a). In China, government officials discouraged one couple from naming their baby "@" (Reuters 2007b). And in the United States, the Marine Corps "pulled the plug" on Sgt. Cody C. Baker when they discovered that the soldier planned to change his name to one suggested by the highest bidder on his Web site, ChooseMyName.com. According to Marine officials, U.S. federal law prohibits military personnel from making such commercial endorsements (*New York Times* 2006).

Outside of the military, we don't fully regulate naming in the United States. However, there are limits, especially in the world of business. Nearly 100 years ago, the U.S. Supreme Court ruled that newcomers to the market could not use their personal names if those titles duplicated active names with high market recognition (Quigley 2003). So, if your name is Martha Stewart, Tommy Hilfiger, or Sarah Lee—sorry, you'll have to make a change before you enter the marketplace!

While laws on naming are somewhat rare, there are strong social norms that govern the practice of naming. **Norms** are social rules or guidelines that direct behavior; they are the "shoulds" and "should nots" of social action, feelings, and thought. In the United States, norms tell us that naming is a very personal affair. That may explain why Jason Black and Frances Schroeder drew the wrath of the public when they tried to "cash in" on the naming of their son. In 2001, the couple announced they were willing to sell a corporate buyer the right to name their child. People were aghast when they posted the "naming rights" on eBay and started the bidding at $500,000 (Goldiner 2001)! And it is worth noting that the couple got no takers. Not a single corporation wanted to get involved in the controversial scheme.

In charting the role of personal names, it is interesting to note that child name selection follows some predictable patterns. For example, naming patterns initiate and reinforce certain gender scripts. Parents quite frequently select trendy or decorative names for their daughters, for example, Chloe, Destiny, Lily, or Jade. In contrast, parents prefer traditional or biblical names for their sons—such as David, Ethan, Jacob, or Michael. (Think about it. How often have you met a man named after a flower, a season, or a concept?) Furthermore, although little boys frequently are given the names of their fathers or grandfathers, little girls rarely share a name with any family member (Lieberson 2000; Satran and Rosenkrantz 2003). Indeed, among some immigrant groups, straying from ethnic or family names for daughters (but not sons) is seen as a powerful means of achieving family assimilation within the host country (Sue and Telles 2007).

In addition to establishing identity, names often demarcate shifts in identity or changes in social status. In this way, names facilitate a process sociologists refer to as boundary construction. **Boundary construction** is the social partitioning of life experience or centers of interaction. When we cross the boundary from childhood to adulthood, for example, we often drop childlike nicknames—Mikey, Junior, or Princess—in favor of our full birth names. Similarly, when acquaintances become close friends, the shift is often signaled by a name change. Mr. or Ms. becomes "Bob" or "Susan"; William becomes "Bill," or Alison becomes "Ali" (Tait 2006).

A shift from singlehood to marriage, an occupation change, and a religious conversion are marked by name changes. Thus, in the occupational arena, "Ike," "the Gipper," and "W" all became "Mr. President" when they moved into their new status. In the religious realm, Siddhartha's conversion was signaled by his new name, "Buddha." With a similar experience, Saul became "Paul." In the modern day, a change in religion transformed Cassius Clay into "Muhammad Ali."

Name changes accompany the shifting identities of places as well. With the reemergence of Russia's nationhood, for example, the city of Leningrad reverted to "St. Petersburg." Similarly, with political reorganization, the plot of land once known as Czechoslovakia was renamed as the "Czech Republic" and "Slovenia." Political reorganization also resulted in renaming the place once known as Yugoslavia as "Bosnia," "Croatia," and "Serbia." Of course, the physical terrain of these areas remains the same. But new names serve to reconfigure each location's political identity. So important are names to place identities that naming struggles can be long lasting. For example, after more than 60 years of peaceful protest by its citizens, the Japanese government agreed to reinstate the prewar name for the island of Iwo Jima (now the famous site of one of World War II's bloodiest battles). The island's original inhabitants argued that Allied forces "hijacked" their identity when they renamed the land. With the island's name returned to Iwo Tu, the Japanese say that they have "reclaimed their identity" (Greimel 2007).

Changing place names often does more than mark an identity shift. Such changes can also function as tools of social control. Gonzalez Faraco and Murphy (1997) illustrate this condition as they trace the rise and fall of three socially transformative regimes in 20th-century Spain. The authors note that extensive changes to the street names of a town called "Almonte" served as a strategy by which each ruling body announced its relationship to the ruled. Indeed, the street names chosen by each regime proclaimed each government's intentions, methods, philosophy, and ethos. Thus, the Second Republic

(1931–1936) chose street names that promoted the regime's educational agenda. In contrast, Franco's oppressive dictatorship (1936–1975) employed intimidating street names. And the Socialist Democracy that followed the Franco regime adopted a clever set of symbolic compromises designed to heal the rifts between the nation's opposing "camps." Azaryahu and Kook (2002) tell a similar story in their study of street names in pre-1948 Haifa and post-1948 Umm el Fahm. The researchers show that the naming of streets in these locations represent variations on the theme of Arab-Palestinian identity. For example, street names in pre-1948 Haifa define Arab identity in the broadest meaning of the term, celebrating culture and politics, Catholics and Muslims, heroes and occasions that traverse locality and time. In contrast, street names in Umm el Fahm project a much narrower version of Arab-Palestinian identity. The overwhelming majority of these names highlight persons and events critical to early Islamic history. The differences one finds in Haifa and Umm el Fahm street names are important, for they reveal the interests and attitudes of local political elites. In studying them, one can concretize a political shift and track a period of changing ideologies. Finally, consider this example from the American South. In 1993, the New Orleans school board launched an effort to lead the population toward greater racial tolerance. The school board mandated that slave owners' names be removed from all city schools. Schools that bore the names of slave owners were renamed after racially tolerant individuals. The seriousness of the school board's intentions was dramatically illustrated in 1997 when President George Washington's (a slave owner) name was removed from one of New Orleans' schools. School board officials renamed the institution after Charles Drew, a pioneering black doctor. Spain, Palestine, the United States: These examples illustrate one common point. By reading the symbolic tapestry created by place names, we learn something about official identity formation in a region. We learn something as well about the ideological premises upon which such identities are built.

Beyond person and place, names can illustrate changing collective identities. In this regard, consider the experience of African Americans in the United States. Note that when the name "Negro" appeared in the United States, it was synonymous with the status of slave. To distance themselves from slavery, free African Americans of that period elected to call themselves "African" rather than "Negro." However, when a movement developed in the 1830s encouraging slaves and their descendants to return to Africa, free African Americans renamed themselves "Colored" or "People of Color." The color term was adopted to underscore disapproval of the "return to Africa" movement. Interestingly, "Black" was repeatedly rejected as a name for this collective and appeared on the scene only with the social and legal changes of the 1960s and 1970s (Isaacs 1975). Currently, the name "African

American" is favored, with many arguing that this change will emphasize African Americans' cultural heritage and help address problems such as racial disparity and poverty (Philogene 1999; Sangmpam 1999).

Postmodern theorists suggest that collective identities generated by shared group names can sometimes prove more harmful than helpful. **Postmodern theory** represents an approach that destabilizes or deconstructs fixed social assumptions and meanings. Collective names imply a unity of identity—a sameness—among all members of a group. In this way, collective names can mask the diversity that exists within groups. Collective names can lead us to conclude that all "Hispanics," "women," or "senior citizens" think or act in identical ways by virtue of their shared classifications. Postmodernists also warn that collective names can give a false sense of distinctiveness to groups. Labeling collectives suggests that "Whites" are profoundly different from "Blacks," "men" irreconcilably different from "women," and "nations" unique unto themselves (Collins 1990; Foucault 1971; Hacking 1995, 1999; Riley 1988; Smith 1991; Wong 2002).

Just as name changes symbolize shifts and movement, they can also function to immortalize certain identities. The name often becomes the tool of choice in poignant and permanent commemorations of extraordinary human efforts. Consider the American Immigrant Wall of Honor located at Ellis Island or the AIDS Memorial Quilt. Special individuals often are honored by attaching their names to buildings or streets. War memorials elicit heightened emotions by listing the names of those they honor. Witness the deeply moving response elicited by the Vietnam War Memorial in Washington, D.C., or the ceremonies for the September 11, 2001, terrorist attacks that have involved reading the victims' names.

Extraordinary athletes have their "numerical names," or numbers, retired, indicating that there will never be another Yankee "Number 7" (Mickey Mantle), another Jets "Number 12" (Joe Namath), or another Red Sox Number 22 (Roger Clemens). The retirement and return of the Chicago Bull's Michael Jordan provides an interesting example of this phenomenon. Recall that upon Jordan's 1993 exodus from basketball, "Number 23" was ceremoniously retired by his team. When he returned to the Bulls in 1994, his new beginning was signaled by the assignment of a new "name": "Number 45." These numerical names served to distinguish the old, proven Jordan from the new, mysterious Jordan. Indeed, the National Basketball Association viewed the boundary protected by these symbols to be so sacred that they fined Jordan heavily the first few times he tried to wear his old number during one of his "second-life" games.

Names can be used to indicate possession or ownership. It is not unusual for valuable belongings such as homesteads, boats, aircraft, cars, or pets to be named by their owners. In the same way, conquerors reserved the right to name the continents they discovered or acquired, as well as the indigenous people living there. Columbus, for example, named the indigenous people he met "Indians," a term that came to be used generically for all native peoples. Similarly, colonial populations were frequently renamed by those controlling them so as to reflect the cultural standards of the ruling power. In one case, a mid-19th-century Spanish governor replaced the Philippine surnames of his charges with Spanish surnames taken from a Madrid directory, as a method of simplifying the job of Spanish tax collectors (Isaacs 1975). Scientists, too, use names to mark their discoveries. Most of us are familiar with "Lucy," the name given to some of the oldest human remains known to contemporary scientists. Indeed, the naming of scientific discoveries is so important that scientists fight hard for the right to name. Witness the multiyear controversy that surrounded heavy elements 104 (discovered in the 1960s), 105 (discovered in the 1970s), and 107 through 109 (discovered in the early 1980s). These elements went nameless, in some cases for decades, because researchers in the field disagreed as to the parties responsible for their discovery. Similar controversies now surround the human genome project as companies and universities fight for the right to patent and trademark thousands of genes and gene fragments (Browne 1997; *Information Please Almanac* 1997:545; Pollack 2000).

Family names function as a sign of ownership as well. In bestowing their surnames on children, parents identify the children as "theirs." And historically, wives were expected to take the names of their husbands to indicate to whom the women "belonged" (Arichi 1999; Johnson and Scheuble 2002; Suarez 1997). These examples highlight a normative expectation: That which we name belongs to us. This expectation may help explain why adopted children are more likely to be named after a parent or relative than are biological children. In the absence of shared genes, names become a mode of establishing familial connection. And, indeed, research shows that namesaking generally strengthens the bond between father and child (Sue and Telles 2007). This link among males, surnames, and possession has been a difficult one to challenge. Interestingly, in places and times in which women have won . the right to keep their surnames upon marriage, the large majority choose to name their children in accord with the surnames of their husbands (Auerbach 2003; Furstenburg and Talvitie 1980; Johnson, McAndrew, and Harris 1991; Johnson and Scheuble 2002; Lloyd 2000; Stodder 1998).

Perhaps the importance of the power of naming is best revealed in research on labeling. **Labeling theory** is built around a basic premise known to sociologists as Thomas's theorem: If we define situations as real, they are real in their consequences. In other words, the names or labels we apply to people, places, or circumstances influence and direct our interactions and thus the emerging reality of the situation.

Thomas's theorem was well documented in a now-famous study of labeling practices in the classroom. After administering intelligence tests to students at the beginning of the academic year, researchers identified to teachers a group of academic "spurters"—that is, children who would show great progress over the course of the approaching school year. In fact, no such group really existed. Rather, researchers randomly assigned students to the spurter category. Yet curiously enough, when intelligence tests were readministered at the end of the academic year, the spurters showed increases in their IQ scores over and above the "nonspurters." Furthermore, the subjective assessments of the teachers indicated that the spurters surpassed nonspurters on a number of socioeducational fronts. The researchers credited these changes to the power of labels: When teachers came to define students as "spurters," they began to interact with them in ways that guaranteed their success (Rosenthal and Jacobson 1968; Schulman 2004).

A famous study in the area of mental health also demonstrates the enormous power of labels. David Rosenhan engaged colleagues to admit themselves to several psychiatric hospitals and to report symptoms of schizophrenia to the admitting psychologists. (Specifically, Rosenhan's colleagues were told to report "hearing voices.") Once admitted to the hospital, however, these pseudopatients displayed no signs of mental disorder. Rather, they engaged in completely normal behavioral routines. Despite the fact that the pseudopatients' psychosis was contrived, Rosenhan notes, the label "schizophrenia" proved more influential in the construction of reality than their actual behaviors. Hospital personnel "saw" symptomatic behaviors in their falsely labeled charges. The power of the label of schizophrenia caused some normal individuals to remain hospitalized for as long as 52 days (Rosenhan 1973; Schulman 2004).

The labeling phenomenon is not confined to what others "see" in us. Labels also hold the power to influence what we see in ourselves. Recent emphasis on politically correct (PC) speech is founded on this premise. The PC movement suggests that by selecting our labels wisely, we may lead people to more positive self-perceptions. There is, after all, a difference between calling someone "handicapped" and calling that person "physically challenged." The former term implies a fundamental flaw, whereas the latter suggests a surmountable condition. Many believe that applying such simple considerations to the use of positive versus negative labels can indeed make a critical difference in self-esteem levels. Others feel the shift to PC language is far more critical. Psychologists Brian Mullen and Joshua Smyth contend that negative ethnic labels are among several direct causes of increased suicide among the targets of such hate speech (Mullen and Smyth 2004).

Similar logic can be found within the literature on social deviants. Some contend that repeated application of a deviant label—class clown, druggie, slut, troublemaker, and so on—may lead to a self-transformation of the label's "target." Sociologists refer to this phenomenon as secondary deviance. **Secondary deviance** occurs when labeled individuals come to view themselves according to what they are called. In other words, the labeled individual incorporates the impressions of others into his or her self-identity. Thus, just as positive labels such as "spurter" can benefit an individual, negative or deviant labels can help ensure that an individual "lives down" to others' expectations (Lemert 1951; Schulman 2004).

The power of names and labels may be best demonstrated by considering the distrust and terror typically associated with "the unnamed." Namelessness is often synonymous with invisibility and exclusion. One can note several examples of this phenomenon. Historically, the Christian child was considered a nonperson until "it" received a name. Indeed, Christian children were not granted full rights to heaven until they were baptized and "marked" by a Christian name. The soul of a child who died before such membership cues could be bestowed was believed to be barred from heaven and condemned to perpetuity "in limbo." Indeed, the body of such a child could not be buried in sacred ground (Aries 1962).

Things that are unnamed can strike terror in social members because, in a very real sense, such things remain beyond our control. The most feared diseases, for example, are those that are so new and different they have not yet been named. The lack of a name implies unknown origins, and thus little hope for a cure. In contrast, the mere presence of a diagnosis, even one that connotes a serious condition, often is viewed as a blessing by patients. Think of the number of times you've heard a relieved patient or family member say, "At least now I know what the problem is."

Alzheimer's disease also illustrates the terror that accompanies namelessness. For many people, the most frightening aspect of Alzheimer's disease is its ability to steal from us the names of formerly familiar people and objects. Generally, our life experiences are rendered understandable via insightful naming and labeling.

In another realm, note that anonymous callers and figures can strike dread in their targets. The namelessness of these intruders renders them beyond our control. Wanted "John Does" are frequently perceived as greater threats than known criminals because of their no-name status. Recall the intensive search efforts for the suspect "John Doe II" following the Oklahoma City bombing. Similarly, note the frantic aura that surrounded the hunt for the unknown "Unabomber." And no time was wasted in putting names to faces after the

September 11, 2001, attacks. Fears of namelessness plague us in cyberspace as well. Anonymous communication forums or situations in which people use "fake" names and identities make Internet users uncomfortable and unsure of "who they're dealing with." In these settings, namelessness can threaten the development of trust (Marx 1999).

When we experience disruptive behaviors that appear new or unusual, our first step toward control involves naming. We coined the label "rumble," for example, to characterize the violent and frightening gang fights that began to erupt on urban streets in the 1950s. We applied the label "wilding" to the new and shocking acts of violence by packs of juveniles that emerged as a phenomenon of the 1980s. And we use the term "hacking" to describe those who harm Web sites and machinery by releasing unwanted computer viruses and worms. In essence, naming such phenomena provides us with a sense of control. In addition to control, naming people, places, objects, and events seems to make them more appealing. Thus, marketers work long and hard to get the right "brand name," one that will "hook" potential consumers. Nothing can hurt the image of a product more than locating it in the generic or no-name arena (Achenreiner and John 2003; Grassl 1999).

What's in a name? Obviously more than conventional wisdom implies. Names and labels can effectively reshape an individual's past, present circumstance, or future path. Indeed, research seems to leave little doubt: A rose by any other name . . . would somehow be different.

Learning More About It

For a fascinating examination of the social patterns of naming, see Stanley Lieberson's award winning book *A Matter of Taste* (New Haven, CT: Yale University Press, 2000). For a more lighthearted discussion, consult Linda Rosenkrantz and Pamela Redmond Satran's *Beyond Jennifer and Jason, Madison and Montana: What to Name Your Baby Now* (New York: St. Martin's Griffin, 2004).

Want to trace the popularity of a name or discover the most popular names of the day? Visit the Social Security Web site on names at http://www.ssa.gov/OACT/babynames/index.html

Harold Isaacs offers some interesting reflections on collective naming in his now classic treatise, *Idols of the Tribe* (Cambridge, MA: Harvard University Press, 1975). For an interesting discussion of postmodern perspectives on collective naming and identity, see James Wong's article, "What's in a Name: An Examination of Social Identities" (*Journal for the Theory of Social Behavior* 32(4):451–464, 2002).

For the classic work on impression management, see Erving Goffman's *The Presentation of Self in Everyday Life* (New York: Anchor, 1959). Howard Becker provides a highly readable discussion of labeling in *The Outsiders* (Glencoe, IL: Free Press, 1963). An informative discussion of labeling as it pertains to women comes from Edwin Schur in *Labeling Women Deviant* (Philadelphia: Temple University Press, 1984).

The following organizations and Web sites will help you learn more about names:

American Name Society (sponsors research on names)
http://www.wtsn.binghamton.edu/ANS

Ancestry.com (Web site facilitating genealogical research)
http://www.ancestry.com

Behind the Name (devoted to information on the history of names)
http://www.behindthename.com

Exercises

1. Choose one or two good friends and intentionally call them by the wrong name several times over the course of a day. Record your friends' reactions. What do these data tell you about the power of personal symbols?

2. Review some recent naming events—for example, the naming of new buildings on your campus, sport complexes, or airports. See if you detect any trends. Are the norms of naming time-bound? Class-bound? Gender-bound?

Essay 10

Conventional Wisdom Tells Us . . . Beauty Is Only Skin Deep

This essay documents the social advantages enjoyed by physically attractive individuals—tall, slim, and beautiful or handsome women and men. We also discuss the powerful role physical attractiveness can play in the construction of self-identity.

"Beauty is only skin deep," goes the old adage. It's a lesson we learn very early in our lives. From youth to old age, we are promised that, ultimately, we will be judged on the basis of our inner qualities and not simply by our appearance.

The conventional wisdom on beauty is echoed on many fronts. Religious doctrines teach us to avoid the vanity of physical beauty and search for the beauty within. Popular Broadway shows such as *Phantom of the Opera* or *Beauty and the Beast*, fairy tales like "The Ugly Duckling," or songs such as "I Love You Just the Way You Are" promote the notion that appearances are too superficial to seriously influence our fate. All in all, our culture warns us not to "judge a book by its cover," for "all that glitters is not gold."

The conventional wisdom on beauty is reassuring, but is it accurate? Do social actors really look beyond appearance when interacting with and evaluating one another?

One finds considerable **cultural inconsistency** surrounding the topic of beauty. Cultural inconsistency refers to a situation in which actual behaviors contradict cultural goals. Cultural inconsistency depicts an imbalance between ideal and real cultures. Although we say that appearances don't matter, our actions indicate something quite to the contrary. Indeed, a large body of research suggests that an individual's level of attractiveness dramatically influences others' assessments, evaluations, and reactions.

Several studies show that attractive individuals—tall, slim, and beautiful or handsome women and men—are better liked and more valued by others than individuals considered as unattractive (Buss et al. 2001; Langlois et al. 2000; Livingston 2001; Ludwig 2005; Olson and Marshuetz 2005; Patzer 2006; Zuckerman, Miyake, and Elkin 1995). Interestingly, these preferences begin shortly after birth and are amazingly widespread (Ramsey et al. 2004). In seeking friends, individuals prefer the companionship of attractive versus unattractive people (Marks, Miller, and Maruyama 1981; Patzer 2006; Reis, Nezlek, and Wheeler 1980; Sprecher and Regan 2002). In the workplace, attractive people are more likely to be hired and promoted than their unattractive competitors, even when an experienced personnel officer is responsible for the hiring (Cash and Janda 1984; Haas and Gregory 2005; Marlowe, Schneider, and Nelson 1996; Olson and Marshuetz 2005; Patzer 2006; Watkins and Johnston 2000). In courts of law, physically attractive defendants receive more lenient sentences than unattractive defendants (Abwender and Hough 2001; DeSantis and Kayson 1997; Erian et al. 1998; Vrij and Firmin 2002). Within the political arena, attractive candidates regularly garner more votes than unattractive candidates (Ottati and Deiger 2002; Sigelman, Sigelman, and Fowler 1987). And some studies suggest that students rate the performance of their physically attractive professors higher than that of their less attractive professors (Riniolo, Johnson, Sherman, and Misso 2006)!

Only in the search for a lifetime mate does the influence of physical attractiveness wane. Studies show that people tend to choose long-term partners whom they judge to be of comparable attractiveness (Kalick and Hamilton 1986; Kalmijn 1998; Keller and Young 1996; Murstein 1999; Wong, McCreary, Bowden, and Jenner 1991). However, "comparable" can be a pretty big category, and within it people shoot for the most attractive person they can get (Takeuchi 2006)!

The link between physical attractiveness and being liked and rewarded exists at all stages of the life cycle, including infancy and childhood. Studies show, for example, that attractive babies are held, cuddled, kissed, and talked to more frequently than unattractive babies. This pattern holds true even when one restricts the focus to mother-child interactions (Badr and

Abdallah 2001; Berscheid 1982; Leinbach and Fagot 1991; Weiss 1998). It is worth noting that babies apparently feel the same way about attractiveness. Studies show that newborns and young infants spend more time looking at pictures of attractive faces than they do pictures of unattractive faces (Ramsey et al. 2004; Rhodes et al. 2002; Riniolo et al. 2006; Rubenstein, Kalakanis, and Langlois 1999; Slater et al. 2000). When attractive children make their way to school, they tend to be more frequently praised and rewarded by teachers than their less attractive counterparts (Clifford and Walster 1973; Kenealy, Frude, and Shaw 1988; Olson and Marshuetz 2005; Pace et al. 1999; Patzer 2006; Wapnick, Mazza, and Darrow 2000). Furthermore, studies show that children themselves come to equate attractiveness with high moral character (K. K. Dion 1979; Dion and Berscheid 1974; Langlois and Stephan 1981; Ramsey and Langlois 2002). The typical children's fairy tale is one source of this lesson. Remember Cinderella and her evil stepsisters? Or Snow White and her wicked stepmother, who is disguised as an ugly witch? And how about Oz's beautiful, "good" witch of the North versus the ugly and "wicked" witch of the West? The stories of our youth regularly couple beauty with goodness, whereas ugliness is usually indicative of wickedness (Ramsey and Langlois 2002).

In addition to issues of liking, reward, and moral character, physically attractive individuals are perceived as having a host of other positive and highly desirable characteristics. Research shows that "beautiful people" are assumed to possess pleasing personalities, personal happiness, great intelligence, mental and physical competence, high status, trustworthiness, and high success in marriage. Furthermore, these perceptions persist even when the facts contradict our assumptions (Andreoletti, Zebrowitz, Leslie, and Lachman 2001; Chia and Alfred 1998; Dion 2001; Dion, Berscheid, and Walster 1972; Feeley 2002; Grant, Button, Hannah, and Ross 2002; Jackson, Hunter, and Hodge 1995; Jones, Hansson, and Phillips 1978; Ludwig 2005; Olson and Marshuetz 2005; Patzer 2006; Perlini, Marcello, Hansen, and Pudney 2001; Zaidel, Bava, and Reis 2003; Zebrowitz, Collins, and Dutta 1998).

Some researchers feel that our perceptions of attractive people and their lifestyles may create a **self-fulfilling prophecy** (Leonard 1996; Snyder 2001; Zebrowitz et al. 1998). A self-fulfilling prophecy is a phenomenon whereby that which we believe to be true, in some sense, becomes true for us. Thus, when we expect that handsome men or beautiful women are happy, intelligent, or well placed, we pave the way for expectation to become reality. This may explain why attractive individuals tend to have higher self-esteem and are less prone to psychological disturbances than are unattractive individuals (Jackson 1992; Patzer 2006; Rudd and Lennon 1999; Taleporos and McCabe 2002).

By contributing to a self-fulfilling prophecy, social reactions to physical appearance may endow handsome men and beautiful women with valuable cultural capital. **Cultural capital** refers to attributes, knowledge, or ways of thinking that can be converted or used for economic advantage. Cultural capital is a concept that was originally introduced by contemporary theorist Pierre Bourdieu. According to Bourdieu (1984), one accumulates cultural capital in conjunction with one's social status. **Social status** refers to the position or location of an individual with reference to characteristics such as age, education, gender, income, race, religion, and so on. The more privileged one's status, the better one's endowment of cultural capital.

Bourdieu argues that an individual's cultural capital works like a good investment. The capital itself—typically defined as family background, education, communication skills, and so on—has inherent value and gains for the individual's entry into "the market." "Working" one's cultural capital enables its "owner" to "buy" or accumulate additional social advantages.

The many studies reviewed in this essay suggest that physical attractiveness also forms another type of cultural capital that operates according to the same dynamic as the one described by Bourdieu. Physical attractiveness provides individuals with an extra resource in meeting life's demands. Beauty places individuals in a preferred, or more powerful, position (Boyatzis and Baloff 1998; Espino and Franz 2002; Greenhouse 2003; Haas and Gregory 2005; Hunter 2002; Koernig and Page 2001; Lynn and Simons 2000; Mehrabian 2000; Mulford et al. 1998; Patzer 2006; Saporta and Halpern 2002). As such, appearances are frequently converted to economic gain.

Thinking of beauty as cultural capital helps to explain Americans' propensity for physical alterations. In the United States, we are "lifted," "augmented," "tucked," "Botoxed," and liposuctioned more than any other country in the world. In 2006, for example, Americans had more than 1.9 million cosmetic surgeries (up 2% from the previous year) and more than 9.1 million nonsurgical procedures (up 8% from the previous year)—all of them performed for aesthetic reasons rather than reasons of necessity (American Society of Plastic Surgeons 2007a). Further, the patient in one out of every five of those cosmetic surgeries was between the ages of 13 and 29, indicating that our concerns with beauty start early (American Society of Plastic Surgeons 2007b). Some of us, of course, choose less drastic measures. National figures indicate that more than $112.2 billion is spent in the United States each year on cosmetics, perfumes, hair care, and health clubs. This figure has more than doubled in the past 10 years. And note that such "beauty spending" surpasses the dollar amounts Americans devote each year to other socially central concerns such as nursery, elementary, and secondary schools combined ($44.8 billion); dental visits (85.5 billion); books ($42.2 billion);

computers, peripherals, and software ($55.4 million); and financial invest-ment counseling ($90.5 million; *World Almanac* 2007:50). It also is worth noting that some impose their obsession with beauty on their pets! In 2003, controversy swirled through the prestigious Crufts Dog Show in England. It seems that Danny, a Pekingese who won the show, underwent facial surgery to improve his prospects of victory (Trebay 2003)!

"Buying" beauty is not strictly an American phenomenon. In many Asian and African cultures, for example, the increasing value placed on American facial and skin features has resulted in a dramatic upsurge in eyelid, nose, and facial reconstruction surgery as well as skin-lightening procedures. Reports also show massive increases in cosmetic sales throughout rural China and other Asian nations, and long lines in Moscow as Muscovites fight to purchase Estée Lauder and Christian Dior cosmetics (Branigan 2001; Doggett and Haddad 2000; Kovaleski 1999; Mok 1998; *New Zealand Herald* 2004; Parker-Pope 1997; Poblete 2000, 2001; Shaffer, Crepaz, and Sun 2000; *South China Morning Post* 2006). All in all, human behavior may confirm Aristotle's ancient claim: Beauty may be better than all the letters of recommendation in the world.

The effects of physical attractiveness go beyond our interactions with others. An individual's "attractiveness quotient" also proves to be one of the most powerful elements in the construction of one's self-identity. **Identity** refers to those essential characteristics that both link us and distinguish us from other social players and thus establish who we are.

Research suggests that physical attractiveness is critical to positive self-assessment. Physical attractiveness greatly boosts one's level of self-esteem and strengthens one's confidence. Unattractiveness, in contrast, appears to sow self-doubt and impede social interaction skills (Cash and Pruzinsky 1990; Figueroa 2003; Garcia 1998; Gergen et al. 2003; Patzer 2006; Phillips and Hill 1998; Sanderson, Darley, and Messinger 2002; Wood, Solomon, and Englis 2003). Some studies suggest, however, that this connection may be race specific. African Americans, for example, are far less likely than Whites to link their appearance to feelings of self-worth (Hebl and Heatherton 1998; Kelly et al. 2007; Lovejoy 2001; Milkie 1999; White et al. 2003).

When considering attractiveness and its impact on identity, body weight proves a particularly crucial factor. Each year, Americans spend more than $30 billion on weight loss programs, diet aids, and low-calorie foods in an effort to shed those extra pounds (American Obesity Association 2005). We trim down, pump up, tan, tattoo, and even surgically reshape our bodies, all in the hopes that a "new" and more beautiful body will boost our sense of self.

In theory, connections between body weight and identity should be quite straightforward. Throughout the socialization experience, we are exposed to what sociologists call appearance norms. **Socialization** refers to the process by which we learn the norms, values, and beliefs of a social group, as well as our place within that social group. **Appearance norms** refer to a society's generally accepted standards of appropriate body height, body weight, distribution or shape, bone structure, skin color, and so on.

When individuals conform to appearance norms, they enjoy positive feedback from intimates, peers, and social members at large. These reactions enable one to develop a "normal" body image and a heightened sense of self. In contrast, individuals who deviate from appearance norms are likely to be negatively sanctioned. As such, those who stray from average body weight or ableness may develop deviant or negative self-identities (Goffman 1963; Millman 1980; Schur 1984; for recent experimental work, see Abell and Richards 1996; Carr and Friedman 2005; Gergen et al. 2003; Gimlin 2002; Hurd 2000; Kent 2000; Kostanski and Gullone 1998; and Neumark-Sztainer et al. 2002).

The process sounds straightforward. Yet in the everyday world of experience, body weight and its connection to identity can be quite complex. For example, several studies, as well as testimony found on countless weight loss Web sites, show that when certain individuals move from thin to fat (in American society, a shift from a normal to a deviant body), such individuals nevertheless maintain a slim, and hence "normal," body image. This sense of normalcy often persists even in the face of objective evidence to the contrary, such as scale readings or clothing size (Berscheid 1981; Degher and Hughes 1992; Gettleman and Thompson 1993; Jenny Craig 2007; Kuchler and Variyam 2003; Millman 1980). Similarly, some individuals who achieve "normal" bodies via diet, eating habits, illness, or surgery continue to identify themselves as overweight, disproportioned, or disfigured (Altheimer 1994; Kuchler and Variyam 2003; Rubin, Shmilovitz, and Weiss 1993; Waskul and van der Riet 2002; WebMD 2007; Williamson et al. 2001).

What explains the failure to incorporate a "new" body into one's identity? Some believe the phenomenon is social in nature. This is because misperception of one's body varies with one's social location. Thus overweight men are more likely than overweight women to underestimate their weight. Average or underweight women are more likely than average or underweight men to overestimate their weight. And the elderly as well as those with low levels of education are more likely than other age and education groups to underestimate their weight (Kuchler and Variyam 2003).

But the misperception of one's body may also be a function of one's childhood years—in particular, the "first impressions" such individuals formed of their bodies during their primary socialization. Sociologists define **primary socialization** as the earliest phase of social "training," a period in which we learn basic social skills and form the core of our identities.

Children who develop "slim and trim" images of their bodies often succeed at maintaining that image as they build their adult identities. In essence, that skinny kid of an individual's past can cover her or his adult eyes and obscure the portly grown-up in the mirror (Laslett and Warren 1975; Millman 1980). In contrast, children who are labeled as "fat" or ridiculed during their early years seem never to fully embrace the notion of a normal or thin body, even when they achieve body weight within or below national weight guidelines (Altheimer 1994; Pierce and Wardle 1997; Rubin et al. 1993; Sands and Wardle 2003; Thompson and Stice 2001).

Can those affected by first impressions of their bodies ever synchronize their identities with their current physical condition? Research shows that certain rituals prove helpful in this regard. Sociologists define **rituals** as a set of actions that take on symbolic significance. When body transitions are marked by some sort of "rite of passage," individuals are more likely to adjust their identities to reflect their new weight. So, for instance, patients opting for surgical weight loss may request a "last meal," write a will, or burn old clothing and photographs. Such rituals prove quite powerful in signaling the death of one's "old" body. Similarly, dieters often engage in rituals such as clothing shopping sprees or body-boasting beach vacations to mark the achievement of a target weight. Dieters report the power of these rituals in signifying a physical "rebirth" (McCabe and Ricciardelli 2003; Rubin et al. 1993, 1994).

Intense social feedback also appears critical to synchronizing identity with body weight. Repeated reaction to one's actual weight can eventually alter faulty self-perceptions. Thus, although the overweight individual may be able to neutralize the numbers that appear during his or her morning weigh-in, that same individual proves unable to ignore repeated stares or blatant comments on weight gain by family, friends, or strangers. Similarly, the newly thin often report the wide-eyed gasps, exclamations, and smiles of those viewing their new bodies for the first time as the factors most significant to their adoption of a true sense of body size (Altheimer 1994; McCabe and Ricciardelli 2003; Rubin et al. 1993, 1994).

Note, however, that some sources of social feedback can hinder the synchronization process. For example, when individuals use TV images to measure their own appearance, they tend to overestimate their body weight. Such overestimations, in turn, have a negative impact on self-identity. Women appear particularly susceptible to such media influence. Although the media present the "acceptable" male in a variety of shapes and sizes, "acceptable" females rarely deviate from the thin standard (Dittmar 2005; Dohnt and Tiggemann 2006; Hargreaves and Tiggemann 2002; Harrison 2000; Harrison and Cantor 1997; Myers and Biocca 1992; Myers et al. 1999; Van den Buick 2000; Vartanian, Giant, and Passino 2001).

Work by communication researchers Philip Myers and Frank Biocca (1992; Myers et al. 1999) demonstrates that daily exposure to as little as 30 minutes of TV programming may contribute to the self-overestimation of body size typical among women. Furthermore, these same short periods of TV viewing may indirectly increase the incidence of anorexia nervosa and bulimia among women (see also Groesz, Levine, and Murnen 2002; Park 2006; Stice, Spangler, and Agras 2001; and Thomsen et al. 2002).

Before leaving this discussion of the ideal body, it is important to note that definitions of that ideal can change dramatically as one moves through history or across different racial and ethnic groups. As recently as the 1950s, for example, a Marilyn Monroe-ish figure—5'5" and 135 pounds—was forwarded as the American ideal. But just four decades later, the ideal body has slimmed down considerably. Images of the 1990s depict that same 5'5" female at under 100 pounds (Greenfield 2006; Killbourne 2000; Wolf 1991)! The movement toward thinness is also illustrated in longitudinal studies of beauty icons such as Miss America winners and Playboy centerfolds. Current figures suggest that these icons are approximately 20% thinner than a woman of average size. Indeed, an increasing number of these icons fall within the medically defined range of "undernourished" (Rubinstein and Caballero 2000; Wiseman et al. 1992). But note that such research projects illustrate race-specific standards of attractiveness. For example, African Americans— both men and women—associate fewer negative characteristics with overweight bodies than do Anglo-Americans. Furthermore, in cross-sex relationships, African American males are nearly twice as likely as Anglo-American males to express a preference for heavier females (Hawkins, Tuff, and Dudley 2006; Hebl and Heatherton 1998; Jackson and McGill 1996; Lovejoy 2001; Milkie 1999; Thompson, Sargent, and Kemper 1996).

Social feedback on weight and the use of such feedback in identity construction illustrate the utility of Charles Horton Cooley's concept, the looking-glass self. The **looking-glass self** refers to a process by which individuals use the reactions of other social members as mirrors by which to view themselves and develop an image of who they are. From Cooley's perspective, individuals who seem unable to "see" their current bodies may be using reactions of the past as their mirrors on the present. Similarly, the use of TV "mirrors" in the definition of self may lead to "fun house" type distortions. The key to accepting one's current body type is collecting appropriate contemporary mirrors and elevating them over those of the past.

Thus far, we have discussed the various effects exerted by an individual's physical appearance. But it is interesting to note that the influence of physical appearance goes beyond the realm of the person. Appearances influence our evaluation of objects as well. Often, we judge the value or goodness of things in accordance with the way they look. Some researchers have discovered, for example, that the architectural style of a home can affect the way in which others describe the atmosphere within the structure. Farmhouses, for instance, are generally identified with trustworthy atmospheres. Colonial-style homes are perceived to be the domains of "go-getters." And Tudor-style homes are associated with leadership (Freudenheim 1988). And, of course, the great chefs have taught us a similar lesson: Looks equal taste. Thus, great chefs underscore the beauty of food. For the connoisseur, the presentation of the food—the way it looks on the plate—is as important as the flavor.

Such links between an object's appearance and notions of quality or identity are at the heart of the marketing industry. Indeed, in the world of advertising and public relations, "packaging" a product so as to convey the right image is truly the name of the game. A product must be more than good. Its appearance and "story" must lure the consumer. The importance of packaging holds true even when the object is a living thing! Indeed, research shows that "good marketing" can change our perception of an animal's attractiveness, and thus its desirability. In one set of studies, labeling an animal as an endangered species increased subjects' perceptions of the animal's attractiveness. Once subjects learned that an animal was endangered, animals routinely thought to be ugly were reassessed as cute, majestic, or lovable. This shift in perception is important, because the same study showed that people are more sympathetic to campaigns designed to save physically attractive animals. Like people, being attractive affords an animal with more cultural capital (Gunnthorsdottir 2001).

Is beauty only skin deep? After reviewing research findings on physical attractiveness, we cannot help but view this conventional wisdom with some skepticism. When it comes to evaluating and reacting to others, ourselves, and even inanimate objects, beauty matters. The more attractive the proverbial "cover of the book," the more likely we are to value its story.

Learning More About It

For a collection of "state of the art" summary essays on physical appearance research, see *Body Image: A Handbook of Theory, Research, and Clinical Practice* edited by Thomas F. Cash and Thomas Pruzinsky (New York/London: Guilford Press, 2004). In *Interpreting Weight: The Social Management of Fatness and Thinness,* Jeffrey Sobal and Donna Maurer provide some compelling articles that use symbolic interactionism to examine the ways in which people deal with body image and construct, define, and sanction fatness and thinness (New York: Aldine de Gruyter, 1999).

In *Beauty Junkies: Inside Our $15 Billion Obsession With Cosmetic Surgery,* *New York Times* feature writer Alex Kuczynski offers an engaging "review" of plastic surgery and its growing importance in America (New York: Doubleday, 2006). Sander Gilman offers an engaging history of aesthetic plastic surgery in *Making the Body Beautiful: A Cultural History of Aesthetic Surgery* (Princeton, NJ: Princeton University Press, 1999).

In *Thin,* Lauren Greenfield explores the intersection of femaleness and weight in America. Her photographs are paired with extensive interviews and journal entries from twenty girls and women who are suffering from various weight-related afflictions (San Francisco: Chronicle Books, 2006). Leslie Goldman spent five years visiting locker rooms across the country talking with American women swept up in the search for perfection. See *Locker Room Diaries: The Naked Truth About Women, Body Image, and Re-Imagining the "Perfect" Body* (Boulder, CO: Da Capo Lifelong Books, 2007).

Want to see a visual timeline recounting changing images of the ideal female body? Visit Healthbolt.net at http://www.healthbolt.net/2006/12/27/a-short-history-of-the-ideal-female-body

The Renfrew Center provides information and educational resources on body image, self-esteem, and weight control. Visit its Web site at http://www.renfrew.org

Exercises

1. Choose approximately 10 bridal pictures from your local paper. Using conventional cultural standards, choose brides of varying attractiveness. Remove any identifying names and show the pictures you've selected to five "judges." Supply the judges with a 5-point scale, where 5 equals "just right" and 1 equals "inadequate," and have the judges rate the brides on the following standards:

attractive	sensual	good-humored	sophisticated	happy
successful	intelligent	trustworthy	pretty	wealthy

   Check the judges' ratings. Is there any relationship between the answers addressing physical attractiveness and those pertaining to personality characteristics? Now, repeat Exercise 1 using pictures of men from your local newspaper. In choosing your pictures, be sure to select men who are similarly dressed and of similar ages.

2. For this exercise, you will need to gather 20 to 30 ads that feature both products and people. In making your selections, choose ads for "glamorous" products (perfume, clothing, vacations, and the like), as well as ads for

nonglamorous products (antacids, cleansers, insecticides). Analyze the patterns you find (if any) between the type of product being marketed and the attractiveness of the people used in the product's ad.

3. Review the personal ads in three newspapers: the *Village Voice*, your local town newspaper, and your college newspaper. Content-analyze three days' worth of ads that feature people. Record all the information about their physical appearance—weight, height, facial characteristics, and so on. What do your data tell you about current appearance norms? Using your data, discuss the similarities and differences in the appearance norms that govern each of these three contexts. Now look at the personal descriptions offered on 10 MySpace or Facebook sites. Are the appearance norms for cyberspace different from those stressed in the print media?

Stratification

Essay 11

Conventional Wisdom Tells Us . . . The More We Pay, the More It's Worth

If so, our garbage collectors are worth more than our teachers, and baseball players are worth more than those searching for a cure to AIDS. This essay addresses the inconsistencies often found between what we pay for work and the value we place on it.

Price tags mean a lot to consumers. With time and experience, most consumers come to embrace the notion that "you get what you pay for." To be sure, many shoppers are frequently driven to find a good bargain. But on the whole, Americans seem to equate high price with quality.

Antonio Rangel and colleagues at the California Institute of Technology demonstrated this tendency quite dramatically. The researchers asked 20 people to sample wine while undergoing MRIs that would map their brain activity. The subjects were told they were tasting five different Cabernet Sauvignons, each selling for a different price. In reality, however, the "tasters" received only three wines. Two of those wines were offered twice—each time marked with a different price. For example, a $90 bottle of wine was presented with its real price, and then later as a wine costing only $10 a bottle. Similarly, a $5 bottle of wine was presented with its real price, and then later as a wine costing $45 a bottle. In each instance, tasters were drinking the same wine. But their brains showed more pleasure at the higher price than at the lower one (Schmid 2007).

In the "real world," Americans' willingness to equate high prices with quality has led to some ingenious marketing strategies. The founders of Häagen-Dazs ice cream, for example, readily admit to conscious price inflation in introducing their product on the market. Given consumer tendencies to gauge product value and attractiveness by price, the owners of Häagen-Dazs correctly perceived a high price tag as the best path to high sales (Cowe 1990). Thus business economists Michael J. Silverstein and Neil Fiske (2003) ask this question: Does that high-priced Starbucks coffee really taste that much better than its Dunkin' Donuts counterpart, or does Starbucks' "double-the-price" cost influence our taste buds?

The more we pay, the more it's worth. The art world has certainly embraced the conventional wisdom. Indeed, the willingness of Mexican financier David Martinez to pay more than $140 million for Jackson Pollock's "No. 5, 1948" (a record price at this writing) drastically changed the value, not only of that single painting but of master art works in general (Vogel 2006).

Conventional wisdom seems "on the money" with regard to patterns of product consumption. However, it is important to note that the adage falls short when we apply it to other economic arenas. For example, in the area of human effort or work, what we pay is not always a signal of the worth of people's work. Determining the social worth of work requires that we look far beyond an individual's paycheck.

We might begin our inquiry by asking these questions: What do we pay for work? What occupations draw the biggest paychecks in the United States?

Chief executive officers (CEOs) of large corporations earn the highest yearly wages in the United States. Analysis by the Corporate Library shows that, in 2006, the average CEO of a Standard & Poor's 500 company received $14.78 million in total compensation. (This represents a 9.4% increase in CEO pay over 2005; see AFL-CIO 2007.) What do these figures mean in relative terms? Currently, the CEOs of America's major corporations earn 71 times the salary of the Chief Justice of the Supreme Court, 303 times the average salary of a U.S. elementary schoolteacher, and 450 times the average construction worker's wage (*How Stuff Works* 2007; U.S. Bureau of Labor Statistics 2007a).

Close on the heels of the CEOs are major league baseball players. Along with long winter vacations and great adulation, the "boys of summer" enjoy an average yearly wage of $2.7 million (CBS Sportsline 2006).

Not surprisingly, physicians also fall near the top of the nation's pay scale. But note that within the profession, the distribution of salaries is somewhat varied. A family practitioner (average yearly salary: $142,516) or a psychiatrist (average yearly salary: $142,610), for example, earns significantly less than an anesthesiologist (average yearly salary: $265,753) or a radiologist (average yearly salary: $286,361; see Studentdoc.com 2007).

American lawyers also earn a hefty paycheck. But like physicians, attorneys' financial rewards vary across employment settings. The average salary for partners in a large law firm is nearly $600,000, whereas associates in the same firm average only about $126,000. And lawyers employed by manufacturing firms (median yearly salary: $126,250) earn nearly twice as much as those employed by state and local governments (median yearly salary: $70,280; see ClearLead Inc. 2007; U.S. Bureau of Labor Statistics 2007b).

We have reviewed some of the highest paid occupations in America. What occupations generate the smallest paychecks in the United States? The average yearly salaries of home health aides ($19,224), garment pressers ($18,578), child care workers ($18,126), teaching assistants ($17,205), fast-food cooks ($15,724), and farm workers ($15,561) make these some of the lowest paid occupations in the United States. And it is worth noting that those who care for our children earn more than 10% less than those who care for our pets! (Animal caretakers average $20,230 per year.) Those who care for our children fare even worse when compared to those who care for our appearance. Note that the average yearly salaries for manicurists ($21,280), hairdressers ($24,550), and skin care specialists ($29,550) are 15–60% higher than the salaries of child care workers (U.S. Bureau of Labor Statistics 2007c)!

Are members of highly paid occupations worth the paychecks they collect? Is income the true measure of worth in the United States? **Income** refers to the amount of money earned via an occupation or investments during a specific period of time. One theoretical position in sociology, the Davis-Moore thesis, supports the connection between income and worth. The **Davis-Moore thesis** asserts that social inequality is beneficial to the overall functioning of society. According to Davis and Moore, the high salaries and social rewards attached to certain occupations reflect the importance of these occupations to society. Furthermore, high salaries and social rewards ensure that talented and qualified individuals are well motivated to pursue a society's vital jobs. Inequality, then, is an important source of occupational motivation; income variation ultimately works to the benefit of society as a whole (Davis and Moore 1945; Jeffries and Ransford 1980).

The Davis-Moore thesis represents a functional analysis of society. A **functional analysis** focuses on the interrelationships among the various parts of a society. The approach is ultimately concerned with the ways in which such interrelationships contribute to social order. But not all sociologists share this functionalist view.

Proponents of conflict theory question the social benefits of salary discrepancies. **Conflict theorists** analyze social organization and social interactions by attending to the differential resources controlled by different sectors of a society. Conflict theorists note that certain occupational salaries far outweigh the occupation's contribution to society. Furthermore, negative attitudes and bias can prevent some people from occupying jobs for which they nonetheless are qualified. Thus, conflict theorists suggest that salary variations reflect discrepancies in wealth and power, discrepancies that allow a select group of individuals to determine the financial rewards of various occupations (Tumin 1967). **Wealth** refers to the totality of money and resources controlled by an individual (or a family). **Power** is the ability of groups and/or individuals to get what they want even in the face of resistance. Consider, for example, that in 2006, CEOs of Fortune 500 companies saw their salaries increase by 9.4%. These CEOs managed to award themselves these extra dollars while holding their workers to a modest 3.5% increase (AFL-CIO 2007; Labor Research Association 2006). The conflict perspective suggests that these salary increases are not reflective of the CEOs' social contributions. Rather, the increases occurred because the CEOs had the capacity, or the power, to command them.

Similar reasoning is used to explain the multimillion dollar salaries of some baseball stars. From the conflict perspective, these megasalaries do not reflect the contributions of these athletes. Rather, wealthy team owners pay the salaries because they are convinced that they will reap the financial benefits of such investments. Baseball stars can generate huge baseball revenues for club owners by attracting paying customers to the stadium gates and to home TV screens.

Note that income, wealth, and power do not tell the whole story when it comes to defining the social worth of one's work. Worth is also a function of occupational prestige. **Occupational prestige** refers to the respect or recognition one's occupational position commands. Occupational prestige is determined by a variety of job-related factors: the nature of the job, the educational requirements for the job, honors or titles associated with the job, the job's use of "brainpower" versus "brute strength," and the stature of the organizations and groups affiliated with the job.

Periodically, Americans give insight into the prestige factor by rating hundreds of U.S. occupations. Researchers then use such ratings to form an occupational prestige scale. The **occupational prestige scale** provides relative ratings of select occupations as collected from a representative national sample of Americans. In reviewing these ratings, we can quickly see that prestige complicates the road to worth. High income, power, and prestige do not always travel together (Gilbert 2003).

CEOs, for example, enjoy great wealth and can wield immense power. Yet the prestige associated with this occupation is comparatively weak: CEOs score only 72 when rated on the 100-point prestige scale. Doctors and dentists earn similar average salaries, yet doctors enjoy significantly more prestige for their work, earning a rating of 86 versus a 72 rating for dentists.

Bank tellers and secretaries find themselves near the bottom of the income scale. Yet their prestige ratings are more moderate in magnitude; these occupations receive rankings of 43 and 46, respectively. And a rating of 65 suggests that if prestige were currency or power, U.S. teachers would take home much larger paychecks.

Occupational prestige ratings also can take us beyond the workplace and into the realm of general American values. Often, such insight presents a disturbing commentary. Consider that the lifesaving acts of a firefighter (rated 53) are given no more social recognition than the cosmetic acts of a dental hygienist (rated 52). Similarly, police officers, our legally sanctioned agents of power (rated 59), appear only slightly more valued than the actors who entertain us (rated 58). The "information highway" seemingly has bulldozed the heartland, for the farmers who grow our food appear equal in prestige to the telephone operator who answers our information questions (both rated 40). Trades that played a central role in building the nation—carpenters, masons, and miners—no longer command our favor when it comes to prestige (their ratings are 39, 36, and 26, respectively). And, interestingly, the midwife who delivers a baby (rated 23) fares slightly worse than the waitress who delivers food (rated 28), the bellhop who delivers bags (rated 27), and the bartender who delivers drinks (rated 25; General Social Survey 1999).

When we note that income, power, and prestige are not always a "package deal," we come to realize the complexity of the U.S. stratification system. The **stratification system** ranks individuals hierarchically with regard to their control of a society's resources, privileges, and rewards.

Those on the highest rungs of the stratification ladder enjoy a critical combination of wealth, power, and prestige. Knowing this helps explain why electricians or plumbers are rarely considered members of the "upper crust." Their incomes may be high, but their prestige levels are relatively low because of a lack of higher education and title and the use of manual labor in their jobs. Similarly, major league baseball players rarely are classified among the elite. Although their incomes are high, their level of prestige is moderate (rated 65). Furthermore, the historic baseball strike of 1994–1995 suggests that the high income associated with this occupation does not always translate into power.

Individuals who enjoy high income and prestige but are barred from the inner circles of power will never gain full entry to the American upper class.

Indeed, many argue that it is this very condition that impedes the progress of political minorities—African Americans, Hispanics, women, youth, and so on—in our nation. Our public rhetoric suggests open access to advanced education, good jobs, and thus high incomes, but our behaviors often block members of minorities from entering the professional and social networks through which power is "brokered."

The more we pay, the more it's worth. Conventional wisdom needs some qualification here. When it comes to the value of certain objects, conventional wisdom may be accurate, but with regard to other aspects of the economy—such as human effort or work—research suggests that the more we pay simply means the more we pay.

Learning More About It

For a good review of occupations in the United States, see Irene Padavic and Barbara Reskin's *Women and Men at Work,* 2nd edition (Thousand Oaks, CA: Pine Forge Press, 2002).

The definitive work on the three dimensions of stratification—wealth, prestige, and power—can be found in Max Weber's classic work *Economy and Society* (New York: Bedminster 1968; original work published 1922).

For a classic review of the functionalist versus conflict perspectives on stratification, see Arthur Stinchcombe's article, "Some Empirical Consequences of the Davis-Moore Theory of Stratification" (*American Sociological Review* 28(5):805–808, 1963).

Visit the U.S. Bureau of Labor Statistics Web site and access the *Occupational Outlook Handbook.* Learn about hundreds of occupations and find information on training, earnings, working conditions, and job outlooks: http://stats.bls.gov/oco/

How many years would it take you to earn the same amount of money that either Coca-Cola's, Exxon's, or Walt Disney's CEO earns in a year? How much would you be earning if your salary increased at the rate of CEOs? *Executive Paywatch* allows you to compare your salary with that of more than 200 U.S. CEOs. Visit http://www.aflcio.org/corporatewatch/paywatch/

Exercises

1. Make a list of all the occupations mentioned in this essay. Classify each occupation with regard to the gender, race, and ethnicity of those typically associated with the occupation. What patterns can you determine with reference to income and prestige as the occupations vary by gender, race, and ethnicity?

2. Ask 10 of your relatives and/or friends to list their occupations. Then ask them to rate the prestige of the occupation on a 100-point scale. Compare the occupation ratings given by your "subjects" with the national ratings found in your library's copy of the General Social Survey. Did your subjects underestimate, overestimate, or pinpoint their prestige levels? If errors were made, were there any patterns to these errors that might be related to the age, ethnicity, gender, or race of your subjects?

Essay 12

Conventional Wisdom Tells Us . . . Money Is the Root of All Evil

This essay documents the impact of income on issues of mortality and life chances. Money, with all its alleged downfalls, can still mean the difference between life and death.

When it comes to issues of wealth and poverty, conventional wisdom spins a compelling tale. On the one hand, we are warned of money's ills. Money is touted as the "root of all evil," an intoxicating drug with the power to enslave us. (Charles Dickens's "Scrooge" could tell us something about that!) Biblical scripture contains similar cautions, noting that one "cannot serve God and money." And adages of popular culture warn that "money can't buy happiness or love."

In conjunction with admonitions regarding the perils of wealth, conventional wisdom often paints a rather comforting picture of poverty. From Shakespeare, one hears that "poor and content is rich, and rich enough." In the modern era, Gershwin promoted a similar sentiment, writing that "plenty o' nuttin" is plenty enough. These messages reflect a more general belief that poverty brings serenity and simplicity to one's life. The poor are lauded as free of the possessions that can cloud the mind and tempt the spirit. Indeed, the conventional wisdom on poverty suggests that it can breed great character. Such beliefs may explain why politicians—Abraham Lincoln, Richard Nixon, and Bill Clinton among them—love to remind us of their humble beginnings.

Is money the root of all evil, and poverty a blessing in disguise? The everyday world of wealth and poverty contradicts such conventional wisdom. Indeed, when we review the connections between one's wallet and one's well-being, it becomes quite clear that the difference between wealth and poverty can literally have life-and-death consequences.

Consider, for example, the issue of mortality. **Mortality rates** document the number of deaths per each 1,000 (or 10,000 or 100,000) members of the population. Such rates suggest that the length of one's life is greatly influenced by one's socioeconomic status. **Socioeconomic status** refers to a particular social location defined with reference to education, occupation, and financial resources.

Those in America who have the highest socioeconomic status live significantly longer than those who have the lowest status. In fact, some sources suggest that a privileged person's life-span can exceed that of a disadvantaged person by as much as three to seven years. Patterns of infant mortality paint a similar picture. **Infant mortality rates** gauge the number of deaths per 1,000 live births for children under one year of age. Rates of infant mortality are twice as high among the economically disadvantaged as they are among the privileged (Cockerham 2006; Deaton 2003; Houweling et al. 2005; Lindstrom and Lindstrom 2006; Mirowsky, Ross, and Reynolds 2000; National Center for Health Statistics 2006; Ram 2006; Robert and House 2000).

The link between poverty and mortality stems, in part, from issues of health care. The economically disadvantaged have less access to health care than do members of any other socioeconomic status. Furthermore, the quality of care received by the disadvantaged is significantly worse than that enjoyed by those with higher incomes. Thus, people at the bottom of the U.S. economic hierarchy face the greatest risk of contracting illness and disease. When the disadvantaged get sick, they are more likely to die from their ailments than those who are more economically privileged (Cockerham 2006; Deaton 2003; National Center for Health Statistics 2006).

Poor individuals, for example, are much more likely to suffer fatal heart attacks or fatal strokes or to die from cancer than members of any other socioeconomic status. Interestingly, these economic patterns of health hold true even for diseases nearly eradicated by modern medicine. Disadvantaged patients are several times more likely to die of tuberculosis, for example, than their more privileged counterparts. Similarly, the poor are more likely than are members of any other socioeconomic strata to die from generally nonfatal illnesses, such as influenza, stomach ulcers, and syphilis. These trends led former U.S. Surgeon General C. Everett Koop to remark, "When I look back on my years in office, the things I banged my head against were all poverty" (Cockerham 2006; Mirowsky et al. 2000; National Center for Health Statistics 2006; Robert and House 2000).

Poverty's relationship to life and death, to health and well-being, is a worldwide phenomenon. According to the World Health Organization, 1.2 billion people around the world—just over 20% of the world population—suffer from serious illnesses attributable to poverty (World Health Organization 2007a). Poor sanitation, unvaried diet, and malnutrition all set the stage for poor health. The lack of medical care also greatly contributes to the high rates of death and disease among the poor. Note that in the world's most disadvantaged nations—for example, Chad, Ethiopia, Malawi. Mozambique, Niger, Rwanda, Sierra Leone, or Somalia—there are fewer than five doctors for every 100,000 of the country's inhabitants! Nations with slightly more resources do not fare much better. Throughout Indonesia and approximately two-thirds of the African nations, there are fewer than 50 doctors for every 100,000 people (World Health Organization 2007b).

The effects of world poverty seem especially harsh when one considers the plight of children. Despite the technological advancements of the 20th century, 11 million children worldwide will never see their fifth birthdays. In the poorest nations of the world, such as Afghanistan, Liberia, or Sierra Leone, approximately 1 in 4 children face this sad plight. And it is important to note that 60% of those children who die before the age of five will not succumb to incurable diseases or tragic accidents. Rather, their deaths will be linked to malnutrition, a problem that is clearly solvable (Disease Control Priorities Project 2006; Dunphy 2005; World Health Organization 2007b).

Poverty also helps explain the short life expectancies of those living in the poor nations of the world. **Life expectancy** refers to the average number of years that a specified population can expect to live. For example, although a U.S. citizen can expect to live approximately 77 years, individuals in many African nations can only expect to live for roughly 50 years. For some nations, life expectancy is significantly lower. In Afghanistan, the average citizen lives for 42 years. In Angola, the average life-span is 40 years. And in Swaziland, average life expectancy is under 38 years (World Health Organization 2007b)! Clearly, for many parts of our world community, poverty can be viewed as the leading cause of death.

Poverty's link to mortality goes beyond issues of health and hygiene. Simple membership in a society's lower economic status, regardless of one's health, increases the risk of premature death. The sinking of the *Titanic* in 1912 offers a stark illustration of this phenomenon. Among passengers on that ill-fated ship, socioeconomic status was a major determinant of survival or death. When disaster strikes on the high seas, norms dictate that women and children should be the first evacuated. On the *Titanic,* however, that norm apparently applied only to wealthier passengers. Forty-five percent of the women in third class met their deaths in contrast to the 16% death rate of women in second class and the 3% death rate of women in first class. What explains the discrepancy? Historians tell us that first-class passengers (both male and female) were given the first opportunity to abandon ship, while those in third class were ordered—sometimes forced at gunpoint—to stay in their rooms. It was only when the wealthy had been safely evacuated from the ship that third-class passengers were permitted to leave. Thus, for many aboard the *Titanic,* mere membership in the ranks of the poor proved to be a fatal affiliation (Hall 1986; Lord 1981; Zeitlin, Lutterman, and Russell 1977).

Of course, we don't have to travel very far in time to see a repeat of the lessons learned from the *Titanic*. It was the poor in New Orleans and throughout Mississippi who bore the brunt of Hurricane Katrina's death and destruction. Homes in wealthier neighborhoods fared better than those in poor areas; injuries to those in wealthy neighborhoods were lower than those suffered by people in poor neighborhoods. Perhaps one statistic, more than any other, drives home the hopelessness of poverty. Nearly 134,000 of the people in Katrina's path simply could not evacuate before the storm because they could not afford transportation (Faw 2007).

The link between poverty and mortality, so dramatically witnessed on the decks of the *Titanic* and in the winds of Katrina, haunts every corner of American life. In the United States, poverty doubles one's chances of being murdered, raped, or assaulted. Similarly, members of the lower economic strata are more likely than others to die as a result of occupational hazards— that is, from diseases such as black lung, from machinery injuries, and the like. Among children, those of the lower class are more likely to drown, to die in fires, to be murdered, or to be killed in auto accidents than their more affluent counterparts. And during wars, the sons of the poor are most likely to serve in the military and therefore most likely to be casualties (Cockerham 2006; Dunne 1986; Kids Count 2003; Reiman 2006; U.S. Department of Justice 2007a, 2007b).

Physical health, life, and death—poverty influences all of these. But the negative effects of low socioeconomic status extend beyond physical well-being. Many studies document that poverty can also negatively influence mental and emotional states. For example, the poor are more likely than those in middle and upper economic groups to report worrying all or most of the time that their household incomes will be insufficient to meet their basic family expenses. Similarly, the poor are less likely to report feelings of happiness, hope, or satisfaction than their more wealthy counterparts. As a result, the poor are more likely to greet the day with trepidation, despair, and depression than with enthusiasm, drive, and stamina (Cockerham 2005, 2006; Cutrona et al. 2005; Luo and Waite 2005).

Negative life events also befall the disadvantaged more frequently than those of any other socioeconomic status. **Negative life events** refer to major and undesirable changes in one's day-to-day existence, such as the loss of a spouse, divorce, or unemployment. For example, divorce occurs most frequently among the poor, with rates steadily decreasing as one moves up the socioeconomic hierarchy. Similarly, job loss and unemployment are most common among those of the lower socioeconomic strata. The frequency with which the poor experience such events affects their mental and emotional well-being as well. Negative life events have been linked to increases in depression, low self-esteem, and use of drugs and alcohol (Cockerham 2005, 2006; Combs-Orme and Cain 2006; U.S. Department of Health and Human Services 2005).

Socioeconomic status can also influence the ability to cope effectively with life's struggles; the poor again appear at a disadvantage in this regard. Consider that family members typically constitute the support networks of the poor. This stands in contrast to the networks of the privileged, which typically are made up of friends, neighbors, colleagues, and Internet-based support networks. The restricted outlets of the poor are not without cost. Research indicates that the poor experience less security in social exchanges with nonfamily members and greater distrust and fear of the "outside world" than those in more privileged segments of the population (Cockerham 2005, 2006; Knowlton and Latkin 2007).

Poverty's links to premature death, physical disease, and poor mental and emotional health suggest that membership in the lowest socioeconomic strata can severely limit an individual's life chances. **Life chances** are the odds of one's obtaining desirable resources, positive experiences, and opportunities for a long and successful life.

Poverty damages the general quality of life. The condition also limits the ability to improve or change one's circumstances. In the face of disease, depression, unrest, or danger, it becomes hard to summon the motivation necessary for upward mobility.

Given the debilitating consequences of poverty, why have societies been so ineffective in combating it? Sociologist Herbert Gans (1971) suggests that poverty may serve some positive social functions for society. In this regard, he offers a functional analysis of poverty. A **functional analysis** focuses on the interrelationships among the various parts of a society. The approach is ultimately concerned with the ways in which such interrelationships contribute to social order.

Consider the economic benefits afforded by the existence of poverty. The poor constitute an accessible pool of cheap labor. They fill jobs that are highly undesirable yet completely necessary to a functioning society: garbage collector, janitor, poultry processor, and so on. The existence of poverty also generates jobs for those in other socioeconomic strata. Social workers, welfare agents, and public defenders, for example, occupy positions created either to service the poor or to isolate them from the rest of society. A society's poor also provide a ready market for imperfect or damaged goods. By consuming products that others would not consider, the poor help many manufacturers avoid financial loss.

At a social level, the poor provide a measuring rod against which those of other socioeconomic statuses gauge their performance. In this way, the continued existence of a poor class reassures the more privileged of their status and worth. Finally, the poor often function as social scapegoats, symbols by which the larger society reaffirms its laws and values. The poor are more likely to be arrested and convicted of crimes than are members of any other socioeconomic strata (Reiman 2006). By focusing the social audience on the "sins" of the poor, societies can effectively convey the message that crime doesn't pay.

Reviewing the realities of money and poverty and their place in a society casts serious doubt on conventional wisdom. Money may not guarantee happiness; it may not buy love. Money may trigger greed and, ultimately, personal pain. Yet the disadvantages of money pale in comparison to the absence of money and its effects. Poverty has clear, negative consequences for social actors. In fact, it can be argued that poverty has been a more destructive force in this nation than any medical disease or any international threat. Yet poverty also has clear, positive social functions for society as a whole. Perhaps this point best explains a harsh fact of our times: Despite society's "war on poverty," poverty has proven a tenacious opponent. The battle wages on, with casualties growing in number. Yet victory over poverty may come at a cost too high for the nonpoor to embrace.

Learning More About It

Two poignant accounts of the lives and conflicts faced by those near the bottom of the economic scale are offered in David Shipler's *The Working Poor: Invisible in America* (New York: Vintage, 2005) and Barbara Ehrenreich's *Nickel and Dimed: On (Not) Getting by in America* (New York: Henry Holt and Co., 2001).

Paul Krugman provides a very engaging look at the growing economic divide in America. See *The Conscience of a Liberal* (New York: W. W. Norton, 2007).

Jeffrey Reiman offers a highly readable look at the ways in which poverty influences justice in *The Rich Get Richer and the Poor Get Prison* (Boston: Allyn & Bacon, 2006).

The World Health Organization provides a wealth of information on global health patterns. Its Web site provides a variety of reports and surveys that fully document the effects of poverty on health and life chances: http://www.who.int/en/

Want to calculate your life expectancy based on your personal and social characteristics? Visit the Life Expectancy Calculator: http://moneycentral.msn.com/investor/calcs/n_expect/main.asp

The following organizations can help you learn more about poverty:

Center for Community Change
http://www.communitychange.org

National Center for Children in Poverty
http://www.nccp.org

National Coalition for the Homeless
http://www.nationalhomeless.org

Exercises

1. Essay 6, on aging, introduced the concept of master status. Consider the ways in which an individual's financial position can function as a master status in our society. What auxiliary traits or characteristics are presumed to accompany the status of rich? Of poor? Under what conditions does one's financial status fail to operate as a master status?

2. Consider the ways in which money affects the life chances of a college student. Being as systematic as possible, identify academic and nonacademic activities that increase one's chances of successfully negotiating a college career. How does the ready availability of cash facilitate or impede these various activities? What are the implications of your findings?

Essay 13

Conventional Wisdom Tells Us . . . You've Come a Long Way, Baby

In the past 40 years, women have made great strides toward equality with men, but have they journeyed far enough? Here, we focus on gender relations in the home, the schools, and the workplace, illustrating the gains and losses faced by women and men in the current era.

D rop in on any historical period—past or present—and chances are great that you will find a story filled with gender inequality:

- *Dateline, Preindustrial Europe:* Artisan guilds limit their apprenticeships to men, thereby ensuring the exclusion of women from the master crafts (Howell 1986).
- *The Shores of Colonial America:* Colonists adopt "the Doctrine of Coverture" from British common law, thus subsuming women's legal identities and rights to those of their husbands (Blackstone 1765–1769/1979).
- *United States, circa 1870:* The "conservation of energy" theme is used to support the argument that education is dangerous for women. The development of the mind is thought to occur at the expense of the reproductive organs (Clarke 1873).

- *The State of Virginia, 1894:* In reviewing a case on a Virginia state regulation, the U.S. Supreme Court rules that the word "person" is properly equated with "male," not "female." The decision upholds the state's decision to deny a law license to a "nonperson" female (Renzetti and Curran 1989).
- *Turn-of-the-century America:* Twenty-six U.S. states embrace the doctrine of "separate spheres" and pass laws prohibiting the employment of married women. The doctrine asserts that a woman's place is in the home, while a man's is in the public work sphere (Padavic and Reskin 2002; Skolnick 1991).
- *Sharpsburg, Maryland, 1989:* A female participant in a historical re-creation of the Civil War battle of Antietam is forced to leave the event. She was evicted by a park ranger who told her that women were not allowed to portray Civil War soldiers at reenactments.[1]
- *June 2007:* Former CBS news anchor Dan Rather criticized the network's 2006 hiring of Katie Couric. Rather contended that Couric's hiring was an attempt to "dumb down and tart up" the news to attract a younger audience.

"You've come a long way, baby." No doubt, you have heard this phrase used to acknowledge the dramatic change in women's social roles and achievements. Today, much has improved for women. Thousands of women have moved into traditionally male jobs. Marital status is no longer a legal barrier to the employment of women. Court rulings have struck down gender-based job restrictions. Women participate in higher education at rates equal to or greater than men, and the law has made concerted efforts to advance and protect the legal rights of women. Even the historical record is slowly but surely being corrected. Yet despite the long way that "baby" has traveled, a careful assessment of gender relations in the United States indicates that "baby" has a long haul ahead.

Obstacles to gender equality begin with gender socialization. **Gender socialization** refers to the process by which individuals learn the culturally approved expectations and behaviors for males and females. Even in a child's earliest moments of life, gender typing, with all its implications, proves to be a routine practice. **Gender typing** refers to gender-based expectations and behaviors. Several early studies documented parents' differential treatment of male and female infants. An observational study by Goldberg and Lewis (1969), for example, revealed mothers unconsciously rewarding and reinforcing passivity and dependency in girls while rewarding action and independence in boys. In another early study by Lake (1975), researchers asked 30 first-time parents to describe their newborn infants. The exercise revealed that parents' responses were heavily influenced by prominent gender stereotypes. **Stereotypes** are generalizations applied to all members of a group. Thus, daughters were most often described using such adjectives as "tiny," "soft," and "delicate." In contrast, boys were most frequently described with adjectives such as "strong," "alert," and "coordinated" (also see Karraker, Vogel, and Lake 1995; Rubin, Provenzano, and Luria 1974; and Sweeney and Bradbard 1988). Other studies on gender typing in infancy uncovered similar patterns. For example, when the infants were dressed in blue clothing and identified as boys, women participating in the study described the infant in masculine terms and engaged in more aggressive (bouncing and lifting) play. When the *very same* infants were dressed in pink and identified as girls, women participating in the study described the infants in feminine terms, handled them more tenderly, and offered the "girls" a doll (Bonner 1984; Will, Self, and Dalton 1976). Similarly, when asked to assess the crawling ability of their babies, mothers overestimated the ability of their sons and underestimated the ability of their daughters. In actual performance, infant boys and girls displayed identical levels of crawling ability (Mondschein, Adolph, and Tamis-LeMonda 2000). Gender typing in infancy is a widespread phenomenon. Even in Sweden, a society that actively promotes gender equality, there is nonetheless evidence of differential treatment of male and female infants by mothers (Heimann 2002).

Often, the gender typing of infants occurs in subtle ways. Several studies, for example, have focused on gender differences in vocalizations of both infants and parents. In one study, both mothers and fathers perceived their crying infant girls more negatively as the crying increased. Increased crying by sons, on the other hand, led their mothers to rate them as "more powerful" (Teichner, Ames, and Kerig 1997). Another study found that babies who "sounded" like boys (i.e., babies with less nasal vocalizations) received higher favorability ratings by adults (Bloom, Moore-Schoenmakers, and Masataka 1999)! And research has also documented that fathers sing more playfully and expressively to sons, while mothers do the same with daughters (Trehub, Hill, and Kamenetsky 1997). Gender typing can even occur in the realm of naming. In many traditional cultures (e.g., Iranian, Japanese, or Jewish), the naming of boys involves more elaborate public rituals than the naming of girls. These differences suggest that boys' identities are viewed as more central to the society's well-being. Following a similar logic, immigrant Hispanic couples are more likely to give sons Spanish names while giving daughters names with no Spanish referents, a practice that sends a very early message about the perceived keepers of family heritage (Sue and Telles 2007).

Gender typing is not restricted to the infancy period; it continues during the toddler years. Observation studies of parents and toddlers reveal that parents are rougher and more active with their sons than with their daughters. Studies also show that parents teach their toddlers different lessons about independence. For example, fathers teach boys to "fend for themselves," while encouraging daughters to "ask for help." These distinctions occur even among parents who claim to use identical child-rearing techniques with their sons and daughters (Basow 1992; Lindsey and Mize 2001; Lips, 1993; Lytton and Romny 1991; Richardson 1988; Ross and Taylor 1989; Witkin-Lanoil 1984). When toddlers play with other children, the gender typing continues. At the playground, for example, fathers' supervision of sons is more lax than their supervision of daughters, suggesting different expectations with regard to risk-taking and injury (Kindleberger Hagan and Kuebli 2007). And daughters seem to model their parents' fear and avoidance reactions to a greater degree than sons (Gerull and Rapee 2002). When it comes time to discipline a toddler, gender typing remains. Misbehaviors from sons elicit anger from mothers while misbehaviors from daughters elicit disappointment. This is because mothers expect more risk-taking behaviors from sons but think there is less they can do to prevent it. (You know the old saying: Boys will be boys!) On the other hand, mothers think they can modify risk-taking behaviors among daughters (Morrongiello and Hogg 2004).

Of course, not all gender typing is quite so blatant. Studies show that parents of young children engage in more implicit gender scripting as well. In storytelling about their own pasts, for example, studies show that fathers tell stories with stronger autonomy themes than do mothers, and sons hear these stories more than daughters (Fiese and Skillman 2000). Research also suggests that the very presence of sons versus daughters can influence general family dynamics. Fathers invest more and are more likely to stay married in families that have sons. Mothers report greater marital happiness if they are in families with sons (Raley et al. 2006).

To be sure, parents are not the only family members to contribute to the process. Siblings are also involved in gender typing. Studies show that boys with older brothers and girls with older sisters engage in more gender-typed behaviors than children whose older siblings are of the opposite sex (Rust et al. 2000). Indeed, having an older sibling of the opposite sex can lead to different dynamics. For example, boys with older sisters are significantly less likely than those with older brothers to engage in deviant behavior (Cattat Mayer, Farrell, and Barnes 2005).

Children appear to learn their gender lessons well and early. In one study, toddlers were shown photos of male and female adults engaged in gender-stereotyped activities and gender-neutral activities. Toddlers as young as two years of age were able to identify "men's work" and "women's work" (Serbin, Poulin-Dubois, and Eichstedt 2002). Indeed, well before their third birthdays, children display knowledge of the ways in which familiar family activities are gender stereotyped (Poulin-Dubois et al. 2002). That knowledge appears to get stronger with age. Preschool children prove quite aware of gender-typed competencies and occupations (Levy, Sadovsky, and Troseth 2000). In one study, children three to five years old predicted that their parents would be upset if they were to play with cross-gender toys. This finding was true even for children whose parents claimed to reject common gender stereotypes (Freeman 2007).

Of course, the gender typing of infants and toddlers is not confined to the family. From child care settings (Chick, Heilman-Houser, and Hunter 2002) to T-ball fields (Landers and Fine 2001), observation data document the prevalence of gender stereotyping. In peer play activities, girls are more likely to engage in pretend play, whereas boys are more likely to engage in physical play (Lindsey and Mize 2001). Young boys also seem particularly concerned about proper gender-typed behavior. When in the company of same-sex peers, boys are more likely than girls to present themselves as engaging in gender-appropriate play (Banerjee and Lintern 2000).

And, of course, no discussion of gender typing would be complete without a serious look at gender stereotypes in the media. The mass media contribute to gender inequality by prioritizing the male experience in explicit ways. While their numbers have grown over the years, women are still underrepresented in leading movie roles and in prime-time television programming. Indeed, nearly two-thirds of prime-time characters are men (Children Now 2004; Eschholz, Bufkin, and Long 2002; Signorielli and Bacue 1999). Popular prime-time programs (e.g., *Desperate Housewives,* the *Law and Order* series, etc.) and reality shows (e.g., *Survivor* or *The Apprentice*) frequently reinforce negative stereotypes of women (Cuklanz and Moorti 2006; Lauzen, Dozier, and Cleveland 2006; Merskin 2007). Music videos also deliver clear gender scripts that reinforce traditional gender views (Ward, Hansbrough, and Walker 2005). Even television coverage of Olympic-level athletes reveals a strong gender bias. When analyzing media coverage of the 2000 Sydney games, researchers found that male athletes were characterized as more athletic and committed (and received more air time) than their female counterparts (Billings and Tyler Eastman 2002).

Television commercials present more of the same—despite the fact that women do most of the purchasing for the home, male characters outnumber females and gender stereotypes still fill prime-time commercial spots (Ganahl, Prinsen, and Netzley 2003). When men are shown doing domestic chores in commercials, they are inept or unsuccessful, thus reinforcing traditional gender scripts about housework (Scharrer, Kim, Lin, and Liu 2006). Commercials depicting female athletes emphasize their sex appeal rather than their athletic achievements (Carty 2005). Even commercials directed at children continue to reinforce stereotypical gender roles. Both active characters and characters portrayed in occupational settings are more likely to be men (Davis 2003). The gender bias that fills the airwaves permeates other media venues as well. Ads in magazines geared toward women seem to be the worst offenders, overemphasizing female beauty products and presenting women in stereotypical roles (Lindner 2004; Smith 2006). And when magazines and marketers sell gender-neutral products such as computers or cell phones, they favor a hyper-feminine pitch: Don't use that phone for business—get it to keep in touch with the kids (Gannon 2007)!

The media give priority to males in subtle ways as well. One study challenged viewers to turn on their TV sets, close their eyes, flip through the channels, and note the gender of the first voice they heard on each station. With few exceptions, the voice turned out to be male, a trend suggesting that men are the appropriate gatekeepers of the airways (Atkin 1982; Courtney and Whipple 1983). A more recent study on commercial voice-over work suggests that this "flip and listen" challenge would yield similar results today. Although there has been an increase in female voice-overs in recent years, more than 70% are still male (Bartsch, Burnett, Diller, and Rankin-Williams 2000).

It is important to note that gender stereotypes seep beyond prime-time programming and adult-geared media. Even clip art presents characters in gender-stereotyped ways (Milburn, Carney, and Ramirez 2001). Children's programming also retains a clear male bias. Such programs as the *Teletubbies* and *Barney* do advance some change in gender messages. Nevertheless, these shows still reinforce gender stereotypes for girls (Powell and Abels 2002). Cartoons, likewise, reinforce traditional gender scripts. Studies find that males are overrepresented in cartoons, which also portray female characters in stereotypical ways—acting fearful, romantic, polite, emotional, or motherly or restricted to the home (Klein, Shiffman, and Welka 2000; Leaper, Breed, Hoffman, and Perlman 2002). And when children's programming gets "serious," gender typing does not. Studies focusing on educational science programs and educational software found that male characters outnumbered female characters two to one. When females did appear on the shows, they were seldom seen in the role of expert scientist. Rather, females were seen in supportive roles, such as apprentices, assistants, or pupils (Sheldon 2004; Steinke and Long 1996).

Network officials defend this imbalance in children's programming as a valid, indeed sensible, marketing call—nothing more. Marketing research shows that although girls will watch male-dominated shows, boys will not "cross over" to female-dominated programs. And because boys watch more TV than girls, networks bow to the preference of their male audience members (Carter 1991). Perhaps marketing considerations help explain the imbalance found in video games as well. Recent studies of Nintendo, Sony PlayStation, and Sega Genesis games found that female characters are missing from most of these video games. When females are present, they are often portrayed in ways that reinforce the idea of women as sex objects or as victims of violence (Beasley and Standley 2002; Dietz 1998).

Reviewing the places and ways in which gender typing occurs is important because such stereotypes have tangible and important outcomes. Gender stereotypes, for example, have resulted in strikingly different educational experiences for boys and for girls. Research documents that elementary and junior high school teachers give more attention and praise to male students. Furthermore, boys tend to dominate classroom communication and receive more support than girls do when working through intellectual problems (Chira 1992; Sadker and Sadker 1985, 1998; Thorne 1995). Social scientists contend that such differential treatment can have long-term consequences. Teacher response patterns send an implicit message that male efforts are more valuable than female efforts. More importantly, teachers' gender-driven responses also appear to perpetuate stereotypes of learning. Consider that gender stereotypes suggest that boys are more skilled at math and science than girls. Yet more than 100 studies document that during the elementary and middle school years, girls actually perform equal to or better than boys in math and science. Some suggest that the decline in girls' math skills and interest during the high school years occurs because teachers begin tracking boys and girls in drastically different directions. Teachers urge boys to value math and science skills, while girls are taught to devalue them (Feingold 1988; Hyde, Fennema, and Lamon 1990). Teacher bias appears to affect other subject areas as well. For example, research suggests that teacher bias may result in the overidentification of boys and the underidentification of girls with reading disabilities (Share and Silva 2003).

Of course, teachers are not the only factor here. Peer and family support also seem to influence boys' and girls' intellectual preferences and future aspirations. Girls with interests in the sciences, for example, enjoy less support from their friends than do their male counterparts. Yet such support appears to be essential for gifted female students contemplating a future in science (Stake and Nickens 2005). Parents contribute to the mix by perceiving sons as more competent in the sciences, and thus expecting more from them (Andre, Whigham, Hendrickson, and Chambers 1999; Bhanot and Jovanovic 2005; Brownlow, Jacobi, and Rogers 2000; Dai 2002). And students' own gender biases about their competencies influence their choice of education and career plans (Brownlow et al. 2000; Correll 2001; Guimond and Roussel 2001; Keller 2002).

Teachers,' parents,' and students' perceptions and actions have tangible costs. **Longitudinal data**—data collected at multiple points in time—show that 7th- and 10th-grade boys and girls have a similar liking for both math and science. But by the 12th grade, boys are more likely than girls to report enjoying math and science (U.S. Department of Education 1997). Gender differences in actual performance increase over time as well. A study of high-scoring male and female math students found that, despite a similar starting point in elementary school, the male students' math performance accelerated faster as years in school progressed (Freeman 2004; Leahey and Guo 2001). And to come full circle, such performance differences have been attributed to pedagogical approaches that are male-friendly rather than female-friendly (Strand and Mayfield 2000).

Given these dynamics, it should not surprise us to learn that junior high school students today express career interests that fall along traditional gender paths (Lupart and Cannon 2002). Furthermore, the lack of training in math and science also serves to keep females out of lucrative career paths in engineering and the sciences (Mitra 2002). While females earned 48% of all doctoral degrees in 2003–2004, they earned only 28% of the doctoral degrees in math and statistics, 28% of the degrees in the physical sciences, and 18% of the doctoral degrees in engineering (U.S. Department of Education 2006, Indicator 30). And consider some noteworthy developments in the area of computers. Male and female students appear equal in their access to and use of computers (Freeman 2004). Yet, in 2002, 86% of high school students who took the AP exam in computer science were males. In 2004, men earned 69% of the master's degrees and 78% of the doctoral degrees in computer/information sciences (U.S. Department of Education 2006, Table 30.2). Gender scripts and stereotypes surely play some role in this outcome.

Perhaps the most telling "lesson" regarding the relationship between gender and education, however, is that schooling leads to greater financial benefits for males than it does for females. For every level of educational attainment, median earnings for women are lower than those for men. In 2005, a male with a bachelor's degree or higher earned 23% more than a female with the same level of education (U.S. Department of Education 2007a, Indicator 20). In that same year, a female high school graduate's earnings were only slightly above the average earnings for a male with less than a ninth-grade education. Indeed, it takes a *college degree for a female worker* to exceed the average earnings of a *male with a high school diploma.* The gender gap in earnings grows still larger for those with graduate training. In 2005, American males (aged 25–64) with master's degrees had an average annual income of nearly $87,500 per year, whereas females with the same amount of graduate training averaged just over $50,600 per year.

Males (aged 25–64) with professional degrees had average earnings of more than $144,000, while their female counterparts averaged under $84,000 (U.S. Census Bureau 2006c, PINC-03). The lower financial returns of education for women are made more exasperating when one realizes that women are increasingly participating in advanced education. Since 1976, female enrollment in graduate schools has increased 112%. In 2005, 60% of those enrolled in graduate school were women (U.S. Department of Education 2007a, Indicator 9).

When boys and girls become men and women, they carry learned gender differences into the domestic sphere. Thus despite current rhetoric to the contrary, the division of labor on the domestic front is anything but equal. A recent Bureau of Labor study found that on an average day 84% of women and 64% of men report spending some time on household activities (cooking, cleaning, lawn care, etc). Women, however, regardless of marital status, spend more time on these activities: 2.7 hours a day for women versus 2.1 hours a day for men. If we restrict the focus exclusively to *housework*, then on an average day 52% of women versus 20% of men report doing some cleaning or laundry (U.S. Department of Labor 2007a). In recent years, there has been a narrowing of the gap between women's and men's contributions to housework. (In 2005, for example, women spent 2.27 hours on household activities versus 1.35 hours for men; U.S. Department of Labor 2006a). But this "advance" is attributed to the fact that women have been systematically cutting back on the number of hours they spend on housework (Bianchi, Milkie, Sayer, and Robinson 2000). Interestingly, even traditionally liberal arenas such as "academic" households can't escape the gender scripts of housework: Female college professors do considerably more household work than their male colleagues, especially when they are married and have children (Suitor, Mecom, and Feld 2001). Finally, in addition to doing about 70% of the household chores (Bianchi et al. 2000), women also bear the primary responsibility for purchasing goods and services and managing family organization and schedules (Daly 2001; U.S. Department of Labor 2006a; Zimmerman, Haddock, Ziemba, and Rust 2001).

Most sociologists agree that the greatest strides toward gender equality have been made within the workplace. Despite such strides, however, the old industrial practice of separating work along gender lines continues. Sex segregation is common practice in many workplaces and within many occupations. **Sex segregation** in the work sphere refers to the separation of male and female workers by job tasks or occupational categories.

When it comes to women and work, it is very clear that sex segregation still thrives. Indeed you might be surprised to see how many common occupations are still "nontraditional" for women. Take a look at Table 13.1.

Table 13.1   A Sampling of Nontraditional Occupations for Women, 2006

Occupation	Percent Female
Chefs and Head Cooks	24%
Chief Executives	23%
Chiropractors	23%
Dentists	23%
Architects	22%
Couriers/messengers	19%
Taxi drivers and chauffeurs	16%
Parts salesperson	16%
Clergy	13%
Police patrol officers	13%
Truck drivers	5%
Construction workers	4%
Firefighters	4%
Surveying and mapping technicians	3%
Aircraft pilots	2%

SOURCE: U.S. Department of Labor, Women's Bureau. "Quick Facts on Nontraditional Occupations for Women," http://www.dol.gov/wb/factsheets/nontra2006.htm

NOTE: *A nontraditional occupation is one in which women comprise 25% or less of total employment.*

One of every three female workers can be found in "sales and office occupations" (U.S. Department of Labor 2007b). Ninety-one percent of registered nurses, 93% of receptionists, 94% of child care workers, 97% of secretaries, 98% of preschool and kindergarten teachers, and 99% of dental hygienists are female (U.S. Department of Labor 2006b). Table 13.2 lists the ten most prevalent occupations for women in 2006.

The histories of many female-dominated occupations suggest an economic motive for such segregation: Employers used female workers to reduce their wage costs. Employers were able to pay female workers lower wages than males. Employers also thought that women were less likely to be susceptible to the organizational efforts of unions. Furthermore, by confining their hiring to young, single women, employers ensured a high worker turnover in their businesses (young, single women left their jobs to marry), and thus a continuous supply of inexperienced, low-wage workers (Padavic and Reskin 2002).

We may be tempted to think that sex segregation can lead to certain positive outcomes. For example, an abundance of women within certain occupations suggests arenas of power born from numbers. However, it is important to note that there is a negative relationship between the percentage of female workers within an occupation and that occupation's earnings.

Table 13.2   The Ten Most Prevalent Female Occupations, 2006

Occupation	Number (in thousands)
1. Secretaries and administrative assistants	3,348,000
2. Registered nurses	2,309,000
3. Cashiers	2,291,000
4. Elementary and middle school teachers	2,220,000
5. Retail salespersons	1,740,000
6. Nursing, psychiatric, and home health aides	1,694,000
7. First-line supervisors/managers of retail sales workers	1,436,000
8. Waitresses	1,401,000
9. Bookkeeping, accounting, and auditing clerks	1,364,000
10. Customer service representatives	1,349,000

SOURCE: U.S. Department of Labor, Women's Bureau. http://www.dol.gov/wb/factsheets/20lead2006.htm

NOTE: *These figures are for full-time wage and salary workers.*

Occupations dominated by women enjoy less pay, less prestige, and less power than occupations dominated by males. Female-dominated industries also fare less well on health insurance coverage than do male-dominated industries (Dewar 2000). Furthermore, once an occupation becomes female dominated, it is effectively abandoned by men.

The opposite trend—male displacement of female workers—is unusual (Padavic and Reskin 2002). Indeed, it is a trend typically limited to instances where immigrant men replaced native-born women, as they did in American textile mills or in the cigar-making industry (Hartman 1976; Kessler-Harris 2003). Men moving into female work has also occurred when there has been a compelling financial incentive. Title IX of the 1972 Higher Education Act, for instance, required salaries of college coaches of female teams to be brought in line with those for coaches of male teams. With this change, there was a marked increase in the number of men taking positions as coaches for women's collegiate programs (Padavic and Reskin 2002). Men in female-dominated professions (e.g., male librarians and nurses) can benefit from presumed leadership skills and careerist attitudes (Simpson 2004). In general, however, men have little motivation to enter lower paying, lower status, female-dominated occupations. Those who do are apt to encounter challenges to their masculinity and witness eventual wage erosion in the occupation (Catanzarite 2003; Cross and Bagilhole 2002; Simpson 2004).

In general, male workers dominate in relatively high-paying precision production, construction, repair, and protective service occupations. Only 6% of employed women are found in production, transportation, and material-moving occupations. Only 1% are found in natural resources, construction, and maintenance occupations (U.S. Department of Labor 2006b, 2007b). In addition, the most prestigious professions are primarily the domains of men. Only 13% of aerospace engineers, 22% of architects, 23% of dentists, 32% of physicians and surgeons, and 33% of lawyers are female (U.S. Department of Labor 2006b). Women who enter nontraditional occupations are likely to face gender segregation within the occupation. For example, females in medicine are most likely to specialize in pediatrics or obstetrics and gynecology, while anesthesiology and radiology remain the preserve of male physicians (American Medical Association 2006). And in the last decade medical specialties dominated by women are finding it more and more difficult to recruit new residents (Bienstock and Laube 2005).

Women who enter nontraditional occupations are also underrepresented in leadership positions. Among physicians, for example, women make up 49% of graduating medical students and 42% of residents and fellows. Yet, they constitute only 16% of full professors and 11% of medical school deans (Association of American Medical Colleges 2006). Similar patterns are found in the legal profession. A recent study of Massachusetts lawyers found that while men and women enter law firms in equal numbers, women leave law firm practice at much higher rates than men. The primary reason for the departure: the conflict between maximizing billable hours for firms and attending to family needs (Harrington and Hsi 2007). The female exodus from law firms means that fewer women "make partner" and fewer women lawyers become judges, law school professors, and business executives (Pfeiffer 2007).

In professional occupations, men are much more likely than women to be in the highest paying professions (e.g., engineers and mathematical and computer scientists). Women are more likely to work in lower paying occupations, such as teaching. They also tend to take jobs that allow them to move into and out of the labor force in order to accommodate family needs. Such jobs tend to offer lower compensation (Day and Downs 2007; U.S. Department of Labor 2006c). The picture fails to brighten in service-oriented work. In the realm of real estate, for example, women sell homes, while men sell commercial properties (Thomas and Reskin 1990). (Guess which is the more lucrative branch of the field?) In the world of waiting tables, gender segregation persists as well. Expensive restaurants tend to hire waiters; inexpensive eateries and diners hire waitresses (Padavic and Reskin 2002). Even in the "work of God," sex segregation rules the day. Women clergy are overrepresented in low-status, subordinate congregational positions (Sullins 2000).

The gender segregation of jobs and occupations takes a financial toll on women. For example, in 2006, the median weekly earnings for full-time male workers averaged $743; for female workers, weekly earnings averaged $600 (U.S. Department of Labor 2007b). This disparity means that women must work about 15 months to earn the 12-month wage of men. Such pay discrepancies are reflected in a statistic known as the **pay gap**. The pay gap refers to a ratio calculated when women's earnings are divided by men's earnings. Historically, a pay gap favoring men over women is a well-established tradition. Currently, the pay gap for the annual average of median weekly earnings is approximately 81—that is, for every $10,000 paid the average male worker, the average female worker is paid around $8,100. While the gap did narrow through the 1980s, it has been maintained over the last decade (Institute for Women's Policy Research 2007a). Furthermore, review of the Bureau of Labor statistics on weekly median earnings clearly shows the pay gap holds across virtually all occupations (U.S. Department of Labor 2006c, Table 18).

However, the pay gap can vary according to the age, race, and educational level of workers. For example, the gap increases when we compare the salaries of older female and male workers with those just entering the workforce. Females with professional degrees face a larger pay gap vis-à-vis their male counterparts (72%) than that found between female and male high school dropouts (75%; U.S. Department of Labor 2006c). Women hoping to improve their financial status should consider the jobs listed in Table 13.3. These jobs offered the highest median weekly earnings for full-time female workers in 2006.

Ironically, one area in which women do appear to be achieving equity is in the realm of disease and mortality. Traditionally, women have enjoyed a health advantage over men. Females display lower rates of infant mortality than males. Females enjoy longer life-spans than males. Male death rates

Table 13.3 Top Ten Occupations with Highest Median Weekly Earnings for Full-time Female Workers, 2006

Occupation	Median Weekly Earnings
1. Pharmacists	$1,564
2. Chief executives	$1,422
3. Lawyers	$1,333
4. Computer and information systems managers	$1,330
5. Physicians and surgeons	$1,329
6. Computer software engineers	$1,372
7. Physical therapists	$1,086
8. Management analysts	$1,069
9. Medical and health services managers	$1,064
10. Computer scientists and systems analysts	$1,039

SOURCE: U.S. Department of Labor, Women's Bureau, Quick Stats 2006. http://www.dol.gov/wb/stats/main.htm

generally are higher than female death rates within all age categories. But as women embrace more of the behaviors traditionally associated with the male role (such as alcohol consumption and smoking), and as they make inroads into male occupations, their health advantage may be waning.

Consider smoking. Currently, smoking is the leading cause of preventable death in the United States. In 2005, 24% of men and 18% of women were smokers (Centers for Disease Control 2006b). Since 1984, the incidence rate for lung cancer has been *decreasing* for men but *increasing* for women, although as of 2007, the rate appears to have reached a plateau for women (see American Cancer Society 2007). Today lung cancer accounts for the largest number of cancer-related deaths in both men and women. The Surgeon General reports that smoking causes 80% of lung cancer deaths in women, a figure closing in on the 90% rate for men. The Surgeon General also notes that women's risk of cervical cancer increases with the duration of their smoking habit (Centers for Disease Control 2004a). Since 1987, more women have died from lung cancer than from breast cancer (American Cancer Society 2007).

Similarly, women's increased representation in the workforce has been linked to increases in female heart disease. Heart disease is now the leading cause of death for both men and women. One in three adult *females and males* suffer from some form of cardiovascular disease—known as CVD. CVD kills more than 480,000 women a year (American Heart Association 2006). Since 1984, the number of CVD deaths for females has exceeded those for males (American Heart Association 2007b).

Despite women's increasing representation in cancer and heart disease rates, several studies show that the female experience receives only secondary consideration by medical researchers. There is still a common perception, for instance, that heart disease is not a significant problem for women. Indeed only 13% of women themselves view heart disease as a health threat (American Heart Association 2007b). And although heart disease is the leading cause of death for both men and women, their medical treatment varies greatly. Physicians are less likely to counsel women about key risk factors and lifestyle changes relevant to heart disease. After the first heart attack, women are less likely to receive diagnostic, therapeutic, and rehabilitative procedures. Consequently women are more likely to die or suffer a second heart attack (Agency for Healthcare Research and Quality 2005).

Clearly, the social and economic contexts of women's lives are related to their health and health care. During the 1990s, activists aggressively lobbied Congress to obtain a more equitable share of funding for women's health issues. A 2001 Institute of Medicine (IOM) report stressed the need for research on the biological and physiological differences between men and women with regard to disease and medical practice and therapies (Institute of Medicine 2001). A similar agenda was forwarded in 2007 when the Office of Research on Women's Health called for studies to examine the ways in which health and disease processes may differ between men and women (Office of Research on Women's Health 2007). There is increasing recognition that gender equity is an essential part of health care policy reform (Moss 2002; Strobino, Grason, and Mikovitz 2002).

In general, women's health care reflects many of the gender stereotypes and discrepancies documented throughout this essay. To make this point clear, consider the ways in which the experience of pain differs by gender. **Gender scripts**—the articulation of gender norms and biases—are useful in this exercise. The nurturing and empathic roles supported by female gender scripts make women more likely to see pain in others. As a result women are more likely to acknowledge and experience pain themselves. In contrast, male gender scripts emphasize courage and strength. Hence men are slow to acknowledge pain to themselves and even slower to report pain to their doctors. Gender scripts even influence medical protocols on pain treatment. Because women are viewed as overly sensitive, women's pain has been taken less seriously by the medical community. As such, women who complain of pain are too often discounted (Wartik 2002).

It is often said that the longest journey begins with the first step. Women have taken that step, but their journey is far from complete. Perhaps the greatest evidence of the distance yet to be covered is found in the area of politics. Governorships, Senate seats, and House seats are noteworthy for their near absence of women. Only nine women currently serve as governors, and note that this is an all-time high. Only 86 of 535 seats in the 110th Congress are held by women—16 in the Senate and 70 in the House of Representatives (Center for American Women and Politics 2007). Is it any wonder, then, that in the summer of 2007, only 58% of Americans thought that the United States was ready to elect a female president (Newsweek Poll 2007)? Social psychologist Sandra Lipsitz Bem (1993) contends that the male dominance of political power has created a male-centered culture and social structure. Such an environment works to the clear advantage of men. A male-centered perspective on the world dictates a set of social arrangements that systematically meets the needs of men, while leaving women's needs unmet or handled as "special cases."

Witness, for instance, the influence of the male perspective within the legal arena: A case in point is the area of no-fault divorce laws. Such laws treat parties to a divorce as equal players despite their unequal work and occupational histories. Present social arrangements are such that a husband's earning power is enhanced over the course of a marriage. Consequently, in the wake of no-fault divorce laws, ex-wives typically experience a decrease in their standard of living, while ex-husbands typically enjoy an increase (Peterson 1996). A male-centered perspective can also influence government labor policies and assistance programs. With regard to the unemployment insurance (UI) system, for example, note that many states exclude part-time workers from eligibility. Since women account for 70% of all part-time workers, such policies are particularly harsh on females (Institute for Women's Policy Research 2001). The Temporary Assistance to Needy Families (TANF) program has been criticized as well for forcing mothers to prioritize wage work (in low-paying female jobs) over child care responsibilities (Oliker 2000; Peterson 2002a). Indeed, family support and occupational segregation issues have been systematically neglected as critical elements to any welfare or workforce reform efforts (Jones-DeWeever, Peterson, and Song 2003). Finally, it is worth noting that women are disproportionately found in low-wage occupations. Such occupations are least likely to offer key employee benefits. Consider for instance that 57% of women in the ten largest low-wage occupations for women do not have any paid sick days; 47% of women working in the private sector also lack any paid sick days. Since women are still the primary caregivers in families, unpaid sick days put female workers in an untenable position when they have to meet their own or their families' health care needs (Institute for Women's Policy Research 2007b).

Male-centered social arrangements also permeate current disability policies. Such policies recognize nearly all "male" illnesses and medical procedures (circumcision, prostate surgery, and so on) as potentially eligible for compensation. In contrast, the female condition of pregnancy is defined as a "special condition" unique to women and therefore ineligible for coverage. In essence, models or standards of normalcy and behavior are male oriented, a situation that automatically puts women at a disadvantage (Bem 1993; Crocker 1985).

By increasing their numbers and voice in the political arena, women may achieve an effective "check" on social inequality. In recent years, women have made important strides in the area of voter turnout: In every presidential election since 1980, the percentage of female voters exceeded the percentage of male voters. Indeed in 2006 female votes were critical in shifting control of the U.S. Senate back to the Democrats (Center for American Women and Politics 2007). Without these kinds of developments, it will remain far too easy to sustain policies and practices that disadvantage women. Gender inequality will continue to be business as usual.

Learning More About It

For an extensive collection of articles on gender (as well as race and class) in the media, see Gail Dines and Jean Humez's edited volume, *Gender, Race and Class in Media: A Text-Reader* (Thousand Oaks: Sage Publications, 2003).

An interesting and provocative discussion of gender inequality is offered by social psychologist Sandra Lipsitz Bem in *The Lenses of Gender: Transforming the Debate on Sexual Inequality* (New Haven: Yale University Press, 1993).

In *Mismatch: The Growing Gulf Between Women and Men* (New York: Scribner, 2003a), Andrew Hacker examines the widening divide between men and women as evidenced in marriage patterns, divorce trends, career paths, politics, and so on.

A very readable and interesting discussion of the working woman's disproportional domestic duties is offered by Arlie Russell Hochschild (with Anne Machung) in *The Second Shift: Working Parents and the Revolution at Home* (New York: Penguin, 2003b).

Irene Padavic and Barbara Reskin have constructed a very readable review of gender and its relationship to work. Readers can consult *Women and Men at Work,* 2nd edition (Thousand Oaks, CA: Pine Forge Press, 2002).

Three recent *Annual Review of Sociology* articles should help the reader become well-grounded in individual and organizational-level approaches to understanding sex inequality in the workplace: Barbara Reskin, Debra McBrier, and Julie Kmec's "The Determinants and Consequences of Workplace Sex and Race Composition" (*Annual Review of Sociology* 25:335–361, 1999), Barbara Reskin's "Getting It Right: Sex and Race Inequality in Work Organizations" (*Annual Review of Sociology* 26:707–709, 2000), and Tanja van der Lippe and Liset van Dijk's "Comparative Research on Women's Employment" (*Annual Review of Sociology* 28:221–241, 2002).

The following organizations can also help you learn more about gender relations in society:

Center for American Women and Politics
http://www.cawp.rutgers.edu/

Institute for Women's Policy Research
http://www.iwpr.org
(Click the link for "The Status of Women in the States" to see how each of the 50 states ranks on indicators such as political participation, earnings, health and well-being, social autonomy, etc. FYI: The top three states [overall] for women are Vermont, Connecticut, and Minnesota. The single worst state for women is Mississippi.)

Society for Women's Health Research
http://www.womenshealthresearch.org/site/PageServer

Exercises

1. Using your own experiences and the experiences of friends and classmates, construct a list of paying jobs typically performed by adolescent boys and girls. Be sure to note the activities, duration, and rate of pay that normally characterize these jobs. Discuss the anticipatory socialization (see Essay 6) implications of your findings.

2. Using your college catalog, examine the gender distribution across the various academic departments and administrative levels. Note the total number and percentage of female faculty and administrators. Are women equally likely to appear in all fields and levels of work? Within specific fields and departments, is there any evidence of job-level segregation? (For example, are women more likely to occupy adjunct or assistant professor positions?) Review some recent course registration materials and see whether there is any pattern to the courses assigned to female faculty. Are your findings consistent with the image projected by your institution in its promotional materials?

3. Observe parents with small children in some public setting. Identify 5 to 10 gender lessons being provided by the nonverbal exchanges you observe.

4. Visit the Institute for Women's Policy Research Web site and review the information found via the "Status of Women in the States" link. Do you think that the indicators for assessing the status of women are reasonable ones? Are there areas or issues of life that are overlooked or slighted? Would the same indicators work for assessing the status of men?

Note

1. In fact, more than 250 women fought on both sides of the Civil War; 5 women died at the battle of Antietam (Marcus 2002).

Essay 14

Conventional Wisdom Tells Us . . . America Is the Land of Equal Opportunity

Is the United States a level playing field for all Americans despite race? In this essay, we review the many arenas of continued segregation and racism in America. Furthermore, we explore the basis for determining one's race, noting that with all of the implications the classification holds, categorizing race is, at best, a tenuous process.

In 2007, the Pulitzer Prize in History went to *The Race Beat*—a book documenting journalists' role in the civil rights movement. The book was 16 years in the making, and the authors, Gene Roberts and Hank Klibanoff, attribute that fact to the complexity of the story (Online Newshour 2007; Roberts and Klibanoff 2006). To be sure, issues of race in America are extraordinarily complex. Some recent news events drive this point home. Consider the 2007 controversy involving popular radio personality Don Imus. (Popular may be an understatement, as Imus was once listed among the 25 most influential people in America and remains a member of the National Broadcaster Hall of Fame.) On his April 4, 2007, broadcast, Imus bantered about the NCAA women's basketball championship. During his comments, he referred to players on the Rutgers women's basketball team as "nappy-headed hos."

Within 24 hours, the National Association of Black Journalists demanded that Imus be fired. A week later on April 12th, CBS did just that. Reactions to the CBS action were mixed. Supporters of the firing thought it an appropriate sanction of offensive racist (and sexist) speech. Imus defenders decried the firing as an assault on free speech. (Apparently convinced by that argument, Imus retained an attorney who specializes in First Amendment issues and filed a $40 million lawsuit against CBS for breach of contract; see CBS News 2007.) But reactions to the Imus affair were further complicated by race. An ABC/Washington Post Poll taken after the firing found that while 73% of Blacks agreed with the firing, only 47% of Whites thought it was the right response (PollingReport.com 2007).

Now consider another telling episode—Hurricane Katrina and its aftermath. Here, too, race greatly complicated the story. There was much written about the inadequacy of the government response to this disaster. But responses to government actions varied widely by race. A Pew public opinion poll found that only 17% of Whites thought the response would have been faster if the victims had been White. In contrast, 66% of Blacks held this view. Similarly, 32% of Whites felt that the disaster revealed the enduring problem of racial inequality in U.S. society. Contrast that figure with 71% of Blacks (Pew Research Center 2005).

The racial divide witnessed in these two incidents should not surprise us. This is because our race, as well as our other social statuses, greatly influences our perceptions of reality. **Social status** refers to the position or location of individuals vis-à-vis each other with reference to characteristics such as age, education, gender, income, race, religion, and so on. Indeed racial status is an extremely pertinent location in anyone's **status set**. A status set refers to the total collection of statuses that a social actor occupies.

In survey data, the links between race and perception come through loud and clear. In 2007, for example, 75% of Whites described race relations as good, whereas only 55% of Blacks felt this way. Indeed only 30% of Blacks (versus 71% of Whites) reported being satisfied with the way Blacks are treated in the United States (Saad 2007a). This low level of satisfaction among Blacks is no doubt driven by elements of the Black experience. About one-quarter of Blacks report being mistreated at work, about one-fifth report being mistreated by police, and just over one-fifth believe that racial minorities do not have job opportunities that are equal to Whites (Saad 2007a).

Blacks and Whites see educational opportunities in the United States very differently as well. When asked about the chances for Black children to get a good education, 80% of Whites but only 49% of Blacks believe that there is equal educational opportunity in the United States (Saad 2007b). Indeed when it comes to the issue of special treatment, the divide between Blacks and Whites is profound. A 2003 Gallup Poll found that 70% of Blacks and 63% of Hispanics favor affirmative action; only about half of White Americans share that position (PollingReport.com 2007). The significance of this divide is highlighted by a recent Supreme Court ruling that held public school admission policies *must* be colorblind. Chief Justice Roberts wrote that "the way to stop discrimination on the basis of race is to stop discriminating on the basis of race."

The Supreme Court ruling on school admissions is in line with a popular sentiment: Special treatment of minorities is no longer needed and does more harm than good. Many in the United States believe that racial inequality and discrimination are primarily things of the past. Progress has been made, and the nation is now a "level playing field." Are such claims accurate? Has racial equality been achieved in the United States? Furthermore, when inequalities do arise, are they rightfully attributable to race or racism?

Before answering these questions, it is important to define the terms we will be using in this essay. **Race** is typically defined as a group of individuals who share a common genetic heritage or obvious physical characteristics that are deemed socially significant. **Racism** refers to prejudice and discrimination based on the belief that one race is superior to another. **Prejudice** refers to an unfavorable prejudgment of an individual based on the individual's group membership. **Discrimination** refers to unfavorable treatment of individuals on the basis of their group membership.

Public opinion polls suggest that many aspects of race relations have improved in the past few years. According to a 2006 Associated Press Poll, 75% of all Americans believe that we have made progress in achieving Dr. Martin Luther King's dream of racial equality in the United States (PollingReport.com 2007). But despite these good feelings, racial divisions in America persist. And this division is most apparent in our local communities and neighborhoods.

Housing patterns in the United States clearly underscore America's racial divide. An ABC News/Washington Post poll found that only 46% of Blacks believe that they have as good a chance as Whites to obtain affordable housing. In contrast, 81% of Whites believe this to be true (ABC News/Washington Post 2003). In home-buying decisions, the neighborhood's racial composition matters to White buyers (Emerson, Yancey, and Chai 2001). Whites are less willing than Blacks to live in integrated neighborhoods. While Blacks are comfortable with a 50/50 racial divide, Whites are reluctant to move into areas where more than one-fifth of the residents are Black (Krysan 2002; Krysan and Farley 2002).

Attitudes on neighborhood living arrangements reflect actual residential patterns in the United States. Despite the civil rights movement, affirmative action programs, and other equality initiatives, housing segregation is still a fact of American life: A third of Blacks and more than half of Whites live on blocks that are racially homogeneous (*Economist* 2003). In its most recent report, the National Fair Housing Alliance charges that systematic racial discrimination in the United States has produced a "hyper-segregated" society. The Alliance estimates that the incidence of housing discrimination against minorities approaches 4 million violations each year (National Fair Housing Alliance 2007). These "hyper-segregated" residential patterns preclude the development of meaningful interactions and relations between racial groups and further promote segregated living arrangements (Bonilla-Silva, Goar, and Embrick 2006).

In a phenomenon referred to as "tipping," data show that White residents begin to relocate from neighborhoods when the African American population exceeds the 8% threshold. With African Americans constituting approximately 12% of the U.S. population, the tipping phenomenon makes full integration virtually impossible (Chideya 1995). On average, an urban White American lives in a neighborhood that is 80% White and only 7% Black. Furthermore, race, not income, is the single most important determinant of where people live (Iceland, Sharpe, and Steinmetz 2005; National Fair Housing Alliance 2007). The power of race over income is seen most clearly in the illegal but common practice of **racial steering**. In racial steering, real estate agents direct prospective buyers toward neighborhoods that largely match the buyer's race or national origin (National Fair Housing Alliance 2007).

Ironically, education may be another driving force behind segregated living arrangements. Higher-educated Whites are more likely to consider race when selecting schools for their children, and they are more likely to live in "whiter" neighborhoods (Emerson and Sikkink 2006). Childhood memories also have a hand in perpetuating segregated living. When making adult housing selections, Americans tend to reproduce the neighborhoods of their childhoods, thus keeping residential segregation alive (Dawkins 2005).

In buying a home, research documents that minorities often receive unequal treatment when trying to finance home purchases—they are often denied essential information about the loan process and products (Urban Institute 2003). Studies also show that home loan applications for Blacks and Hispanics are rejected at a higher rate than those for Whites, regardless of applicants' income levels (Brenner and Spayd 1993; Conner and Smith 1991; Dedman 1989; Institute on Race & Poverty 1998; *Progressive* 2000; Silverman 2005; U.S. Department of Housing and Urban Development 2005). When loans for Blacks are approved, they are often at less generous amounts and terms and at higher subprime lending rates (Andrews 2005; *Progressive* 2000). Even when minorities succeed in buying and financing homes, they may find it more difficult to insure their properties. **Linguistic profiling**—that is, identifying a person's race from the sound of their voice—occurs and negatively affects the insurance services offered to minorities (Squires and Chadwick 2006). In light of this information, it is not surprising to learn that Blacks and Hispanics are less likely to own their homes. Members of these minority groups also have lower equity in their homes than do Whites (Flippen, 2001, 2004; Institute on Race & Poverty 2002).

Discriminatory practices are still a part of the rental process as well. Web sites advertising apartments can use language that would be prohibited in newspaper classifieds (National Fair Housing Alliance 2007). And in e-mail exchanges, landlords can use tenant names as cues for racial/ethnic identity. In a recent experiment, White, Arab, and Black names were randomly attached to e-mails inquiring about advertised apartments. Across all rental categories, landlord responses were significantly different for the three groups—Blacks received fewer positive responses than either Arab or White names (Carpusor and Loges 2006).

The various inequities involved in U.S. residential patterns have had long-term effects on the landscape of America. Housing segregation practices have contributed to the creation of **concentrated-poverty neighborhoods**. This term refers to neighborhoods in which 40% or more of the population is at or below the poverty level. Poverty became more and more concentrated through the 1980s, before the trend was reversed during the 1990s. Still, the share of all high-poverty neighborhoods that are predominantly Black remains high: 39% (Kingsley and Pettit 2003).

Segregated living imposes other financial burdens on racial and ethnic minorities. Minorities living in central cities encounter a shrinking job market. Between 1993 and 1998, more than 14 million jobs were created in the United States, but only 13% of them were located in central cities. The picture becomes even bleaker when we consider entry-level jobs. While the entry-level labor *pool* resides in urban areas, the majority of entry-level *jobs* (70%) are located in White suburbs (Institute on Race & Poverty 2002). This mismatch between job skills and worker location is particularly acute for Blacks because of their greater residential segregation and their lower rates of car access (Stoll 2005). Ironically, those minorities who try to rectify this mismatch by buying cars for commuting to the suburbs may well find themselves the victims of racial bias in dealer-arranged car loans (Henriques 2000; *New York Times* 2003a).

Some sociologists contend that race segregation ultimately translates into knowledge segregation. The 2005 high school dropout rate for 16- to 24-year-old White students was 6.0%—a figure much lower than the 10.4% and 22.4% rates for Blacks and Hispanics, respectively (U.S. Department of

Education 2007a, Indicator 23). Approximately 28% of the White population earn a college degree in contrast to 18% of Blacks and 12% of Hispanics (U.S. Census Bureau 2007d, Table 214). Similar discrepancies exist in other education-related practices. For example, Whites have higher rates of computer usage at home than do Blacks and Hispanics (U.S. Department of Education 2006, Indicator 37). For students 15 years of age and older, 84.5% of Whites use computers at home versus 49.6% of Blacks and 55.7% of Hispanics. This "technology gap" continues into college. At the college level, 84.2% of White undergraduates use computers at home versus 65.2% of Black and 71.4% of Hispanic undergraduates. Further, 92.7% of White undergraduates use the Internet versus 80% of Black and 78.4% of Hispanic undergraduates (U.S. Department of Education 2005a, Tables 417 and 419).

Racial inequality in the educational sphere is an old story. America's public school system has battled the issue for decades. In 1954, the U.S. Supreme Court's *Brown v. Board of Education* decision ordered American schools to desegregate with all deliberate speed. Yet, more than 50 years later, full integration still eludes public schools. In many cases, White parents effectively circumvented the desegregation ruling by relocating to suburban school districts or by enrolling their children in private schools. In Mississippi, for instance, court-ordered desegregation was met with a dramatic increase in private segregationist academies (Andrews 2002). And the migration of White and middle-class families to suburban school districts continues to hold steady today (Carr 2007; NAACP 2005). In fact, in the 1990s, Supreme Court rulings put an end to many desegregation plans in school districts across the nation (Orfield and Eaton 2003). Our nation's courts, once champions of desegregation efforts, are declaring more and more school districts "unitary" and therefore released from desegregation plans (Baldas 2003; NAACP 2005). In June 2007, the Supreme Court delivered a blow to school diversity when it ruled against the use of race-based admission policies in public schools pursuing voluntary integration strategies.

Our public schools are becoming increasingly re-segregated along racial and economic lines. Minority students comprise more than 40% of all public school students in the United States today—nearly twice the number recorded in the 1960s. Nearly 40% of Black and Hispanic students attend schools in which the student body is at least 90% minority; only 1% of White students attend such schools (NAACP 2005). From 1972 to 2005, the percentage of White students in public schools dropped from 78% to 58% (U.S. Department of Education 2007a, Indicator 5). And only 14% of White students attend **multiracial schools**—schools in which at least three minorities each represent 10% or more of the school population (Frankenberg, Lee, and Orfield 2003a). The typical White public school student attends a school that is nearly 80% White (NAACP 2005). These developments mean that lower levels of interracial exposure—or what some are calling a "re-segregation trend"—are occurring in numerous school districts across the nation (Frankenberg and Lee 2002; Kozol 2005; NAACP 2005).

Charter schools, touted as solutions to failing public education, are as segregated or more segregated than public schools (Frankenberg, Lee, and Orfield 2003b; Renzulli and Evans 2005). And a re-segregation trend has emerged in private schools as well. Overall, 76% of students enrolled in private schools are White, while only 9% are Black and 9% are Hispanic. Within central cities, that figure improves somewhat—31% of students enrolled in private schools are minorities (U.S. Department of Education 2007a, Indicator 4). Residential patterns help explain this development, since more than 40% of private schools are located in central cities (Alt and Peter 2002).

Parents who can afford to send their children to private schools reap rewards for their financial investments. Parental satisfaction levels with teachers, academic standards, and a school's order and discipline are all higher for parents of private school children than for parents of public schoolers (U.S. Department of Education 2006, Indicator 38). Private schools also offer advantages over public schools in terms of student/teacher ratios and educational outcomes. And private schools exhibit higher rates of teacher satisfaction across a variety of measures, including class size, availability of educational materials, colleagues, parental support, and teaching (Alt and Peter 2002).

Sociologist Jonathan Kozol (1991, 1995, 2001) has long studied the vast resource differences that characterize White versus non-White schools. In his seminal work, *Savage Inequalities* (1991), Kozol found that the poor resources of one predominantly African American Chicago Southside school forced chemistry teachers to use popcorn poppers as Bunsen burners. In contrast, students in a nearby predominantly White suburban school were enjoying a facility that housed seven gyms, an Olympic-sized pool, and separate studios for fencing, dance instruction, and wrestling. Similarly, Kozol found that PS 261 in the South Bronx housed 400 more students than permitted by local fire codes. Just a few bus stops away in the wealthy Riverdale section of the Bronx, PS 24 touted class sizes well below the city average.

Because most public school budgets are tied to local economic resources, schools in wealthy, White neighborhoods fare better than schools in poor, non-White neighborhoods (Cummings 2003). Furthermore, state spending on public education *decreases* as racial/ethnic diversity *increases*. In a recent analysis, the Population Reference Bureau found that those states with the highest racial/ethnic diversity spent the lowest share of their gross state product on education (3.4%), whereas those states with the lowest racial/ethnic fragmentation spent the highest share on education (4.2%). While these percent differences may appear small, they translate into differences of billions of dollars for educational spending (Mather 2007).

The work of Kozol and others suggests that school segregation is especially destructive because of the powerful tie between highly segregated schools and concentrated poverty. Nationally, about half of Black and Hispanic students attend schools in which three-quarters of the students are poor. In schools where 90% or more of the students are poor, 80% of the students are Black and Hispanic (NAACP 2005). Research clearly demonstrates that economically disadvantaged students and schools perform less well than their more affluent counterparts (Frankenberg and Lee 2002; Orfield, Eaton, and the Harvard Project on Desegregation 1996; Orfield and Yun 1999). Segregated minority schools have weaker academic offerings, fewer resources, and less experienced teachers (NAACP 2005). The formal schooling experiences of poor and minority children reinforce and magnify the inequalities between disadvantaged and advantaged students (Lee and Burkam 2002). Not surprisingly, then, academic performance gaps (in reading, math, and science) between minority and White students stubbornly endure (U.S. Department of Education 2007a, Indicators 13 and 14).

In addition to the unequal distribution of resources, researchers note that the lessons taught in predominantly White versus predominantly non-White schools can differ dramatically. Students in predominantly White schools learn to be self-directed, inquisitive, and ambitious. In contrast, students in predominantly non-White schools are taught to obey rules and maintain the status quo (Bowles and Gintis 1976, 2002; Kozol 1991; Miron 1997; Polakow 1993). While it has been more than 15 years since Kozol wrote his stirring indictment of our segregated public schools, the inequality he found there still exists (Books and McAninch 2006; Feldman 2003). Indeed Kozol (2005) warns that the conditions have grown worse for inner-city youth as our schools revert to levels of segregation higher than they were in the late 1960s.

After graduation, former students find that racial boundaries are maintained within the workplace as well. White high school dropouts are twice as likely to find jobs as are Blacks. One-third of Black teenagers looking for work don't find it. And the Black unemployment rate is twice the national average (NAACP 2006). While employment rates for young Black women have been increasing since the onset of welfare reform, the rates for young Black males have been declining (Urban Institute 2006). In 2006, the Equal Employment Opportunity Commission received 27,000 race discrimination charges—the year's largest category of filings (EEOC 2007). Controlled **paired testing** hiring experiments—experiments in which two equally qualified candidates of different races each apply for the same job—reveal that hiring discrimination is pervasive, affecting approximately 20% of African American job applicants (Bendick, Jackson, and Reinoso 1999; Urban Institute 1999). Other research indicates that employers' perceptions of job candidates' merits are often biased by racial stereotypes (Moss and Tilly 2001). Such findings have prompted a call for a "national report card" on discrimination as well as an expanded "paired testing" program to promote public understanding of the prevalence of racial discrimination (Urban Institute 1999).

Once on the job, discrimination continues. Let's look at things on the wage front. In 2005, the median household income for non-Hispanic Whites, for Blacks, and for Hispanics was $50,784, $30,858, and $35,967, respectively (U.S. Census Bureau 2006d). Education doesn't eliminate such gaps. In 2004, the median annual earnings of full-time workers aged 25–34 with a college degree or higher was $44,600 for Whites, $39,200 for Blacks, and $40,100 for Hispanics (U.S. Department of Education 2006, Table 22.1). These gaps grow still larger when minority women enter the equation. Black women working full time earn only 67% of their White male counterparts' wages. For Hispanic women, that percentage falls to 56% (National Women's Law Center 2006). Such differences may help explain why Blacks and Hispanics have poverty rates that are approximately three times as high as the rates for Whites (U.S. Census Bureau 2006d).

Evidence of the racial divide makes its way into the entertainment sphere as well. Perhaps one of the most telling signs of racial inequality is found in children's books—a source regarded by some to be important primers for a society's culture. A recent content analysis of children's books found a dearth of Black characters. In addition, depictions of egalitarian interracial interactions were rare (Pescosolido, Grauerholz, and Milkie 1997). Put down the books and pick up the TV remote, and racial/ethnic inequities persist. Prime-time television shows little of the diversity that characterizes our society. Whites are overrepresented both in prime-time programs and in starring roles. Note too that the eight o'clock viewing hour, the one most likely to be watched by children, is the least racially diverse hour of prime-time programming. And sitcoms, the most popular programming among youth, represent the most segregated programming genre (Children Now 2004).

Commercials, like prime-time programs, teach. And the lessons they teach misinform us about minorities. For example, Hispanics are seriously underrepresented and are frequently depicted in ways that reinforce stereotypes. While Whites appear in ads for upscale products and home goods, minorities appear in ads for fast foods and soft drinks and for sports equipment and financial services (Jacobs Henderson and Baldasty 2003; Mastro and Stern 2003). Television news and sport broadcasts also tend to reinforce racial stereotypes (Rada and Wulfemeyer 2005; Schaffner and Gadson 2004). And while multiethnic TV series have increased in recent years, the number of shows that could be characterized as Black-character-dominant has declined (Freeman 2002).

Clearly, many inequalities still exist in the various sectors of U.S. society. Yet many contend that such inequalities are not the product of racism. Many continue to believe that race, as a biological attribute, indicates some inherent differences in individuals' ability to achieve.

At first glance, this argument may appear valid. Biology would appear to be the unequivocal determinant of racial group distinctions. Thus, different biologies could conceivably lead to different levels of ability. Yet a biological definition of race does not produce a simple or clear racial classification scheme. In fact, identifying groups who share obvious physical characteristics proves to be a less-than-obvious task.

Using a biological definition of race, biologists and physical anthropologists can "find" as few as 3 or as many as 200+ different races. These classifications are muddied further when we note that generations of intergroup marriage and breeding ensure that no "pure" races exist. Indeed, a remarkable similarity exists across the genes of all humans: Of the DNA molecules that account for racial categories, 95% to 99% are common across all humans (Shipman 1994). Thus, if the human essence is "all in the genes," then racial similarities, not distinctions, are most noteworthy. The genome project has offered consistent evidence that there is only one race: the human race (Angier 2000; Graves 2006).

From a biological perspective, "racial differences" are best understood as beneficial, adaptive changes for our human species (Molnar 1991). For instance, the dark skin of peoples living near the equator serves as vital protection against dangerous sun rays. Similarly, the longer, narrow noses found among those living in colder northern climates help warm the air before it reaches the temperature-sensitive lungs. If the earth were to shift on its axis so that the Northern Hemisphere moved into direct line with the sun, we would expect an adaptive change in the skin color and nose configurations of the northern population (Rensberger 1981). Geography, then, is central to the variations we so readily attribute to race (Diamond 2005; Jablonski 2005; Lehrman 2003; "Race: The Power of an Illusion" 2003).

A biological approach to the race issue is really insufficient for understanding the dynamics of racial categories. Noted biological anthropologist Alan Goodman has observed that race is not about biology, but rather about an *idea* we *ascribe* to biology ("Race: The Power of an Illusion" 2003). The respected *New England Journal of Medicine* has asserted that "race is biologically meaningless" (Kristof 2003). Indeed, the task of identifying discrete racial categories has largely been abandoned by many physical anthropologists. Sociologists suggest that race is more properly understood as a *social* rather than a biological phenomenon: Race is socially constructed. The **social construction of reality** occurs when individuals create images, ideas, and beliefs about society based on their social interactions.

The social constructionist approach suggests that racial categories emerge from social interaction, social perception, and social opinion. Historians, for instance, observe that the idea of biologically based races was advanced as a way to defend slavery in North America—that is, as a way to justify the unequal treatment of slaves in a land that promoted equality (Lee 2003; "Race: The Power of an Illusion" 2003; Smedley and Smedley 2005). Social encounters repeatedly expose individuals to specific definitions of race. If these definitions suggest clear and natural boundaries and rankings between various groups of people, the definitions can institutionalize racism as part of a society's stock of knowledge. Such definitions come to reify, or substantiate, racial distinctions that may not be supported in fact. **Reification** refers to the process by which the subjective or abstract erroneously comes to be treated as objective fact or reality. From such a perspective, we must view race as a characteristic that resides in the "eye of the beholder." Change the group doing the perceiving and defining—that is, change the eye of the beholder—and you will change the racial distinctions being made.

For example, it is estimated that more than 70% of Black Americans have some White ancestors (Kilker 1993; Roberts 1975). Yet this biological lineage does not alter public perception. Despite evidence of White ancestry, such individuals are still classified as Black. U.S. classification patterns resulted from a long-standing legal practice that mandated percentage or "one drop of blood" standards for determining racial classifications. Until 1983, for instance, the law of Louisiana dictated that individuals with 1/32 of "Negro blood" were properly classified as belonging to the Black race. In the 2000 census, respondents were able to identify themselves as bi- or multiracial by checking more than one race category. Interestingly, however, the "one drop of blood" rule seems to be making a comeback. The U.S. Office of Management and Budget guidelines dictated that anyone marking "White" plus any other non-White category be counted as non-White (Goldstein and Morning 2002). Were we to change the standards used for racial classification, however, very different designations of race would emerge. In Brazil, for example, any individual who has "some" White ancestry is classified as belonging to the White race. Consequently, by Brazilian standards, most Black Americans would be classified as White (Denton and Massey 1989).

At first glance, perceptual differences of race may not seem very significant. Such differences merely underscore a major premise of the sociological perspective: Social context is an important factor in understanding, explaining, or predicting human attitudes and behaviors (see the introductory essay). **Social context** refers to the broad social and historical circumstances surrounding an act or an event. But the intriguing nature of race as a social creation becomes clearer when we view it as a significant social status, or more specifically as a significant *ascribed* status. Some of the statuses we occupy are the result of our own personal efforts; these are achieved statuses. An **achieved status** is one earned or gained through personal effort. One's statuses as Red Cross volunteer, parent, or worker are all achieved statuses. In contrast, some of our statuses are "assigned" to us, independent of our personal efforts, desires, or preferences; these are ascribed statuses. An **ascribed status** is one assigned or given without regard to a person's efforts or desires. Age, gender, and racial status are all ascribed statuses.

The average reader of this book will occupy many of the following statuses (try classifying each as "achieved" or "ascribed"): son or daughter, student, friend, spouse, sibling, male or female, citizen, voter, consumer, employee. Often, however, one of our many statuses will dominate the rest. This dominant status forms a master status (see Essay 6). A **master status** is a single social status that overpowers all other social positions occupied by an individual. A master status directs the way in which others see, define, and relate to an individual.

If we consider race in light of these status distinctions, we begin to more fully appreciate the implications of race as a social creation. For although race is a social creation, it is also an ascribed status. As such, race is imposed on the individual; one's race is beyond one's control. Race also frequently serves as a master status. As a master status, race has the ability to influence the social identity and life chances of an individual. **Identity** refers to those essential characteristics that both link us and distinguish us from other social players and thus establish who we are. **Life chances** refer to one's odds of obtaining desirable resources, positive experiences, and opportunities for a long and successful life. For races classified as social minorities, this influence is often negative. A **social minority** is a group regarded as subordinate or inferior to a majority or dominant group. Social minorities are excluded from full participation in society; they experience inferior positions of prestige, wealth, and power.

Note the irony here. Ascribed master statuses are beyond the individual's control. They are assigned, yet they have a remarkable capacity to control the individual. Indeed, certain ascribed master statuses can prove more important to one's identity than personal efforts. The irony intensifies when we acknowledge that race, an assigned status, is nonetheless a social creation. Racial designations can change as audience perceptions change.

The significance of these last few points becomes more apparent when we reconsider the real-life consequences of racial designations:

- In 2005, the poverty rate was 8.3% for Whites, 24.9% for Blacks, and 21.8% for Hispanics (DeNavas-Walt, Proctor, and Hill-Lee 2006).
- In 2005, 93% of White children but only 87% of Black children and 78% of Hispanic children were covered by health insurance (DeNavas-Walt et al. 2006).
- Approximately 28% of the White population earns at least a college degree compared with only 17.6% of the African American population and approximately 12% of Hispanic Americans (U.S. Census Bureau 2007d: Table 214).
- The 2005 high school dropout rates for 16- to 24-year-olds were 6% for Whites, 10.4% for Blacks, and 22.4% for Hispanics (U.S. Department of Education 2007a, Indicator 23).
- The 2010 average life expectancy for newborns is projected to be 76 years for White males, 71 years for Black males, 82 years for White females, and 78 years for Black females (U.S. Census Bureau 2007d: Table 100).
- The infant mortality rate for White babies is under 6 deaths per 1,000 live births. The rate for African American babies is 14 deaths per 1,000 live births (U.S. Census Bureau 2007d: Table 106).

Indeed, take any set of statistics regarding life chances—health and illness rates, divorce rates, crime victimization rates, death rates, and so on—and you will undoubtedly come to the conclusion that race matters.

This essay suggests that racial distinctions cannot be equated with biological or genetic differences. Race is not a simple matter of physiology. Rather, racial distinctions are more properly understood as social creations. Skin color proves to be the primary marker of racial distinctions in U.S. society; other cultures have focused on such characteristics as height or hair and eye color. No matter what a society's marker, once certain characteristics are deemed worthier than others—that is, once racial categories are created—powerful social processes such as prejudice and discrimination are set into motion.

Still, race has proven itself a highly dynamic process; the human species has shown a remarkable capacity to adapt to environmental demands. The pressing question for today and the near future is whether our social definition of race will prove equally adaptive to changes in our social and cultural environments. It is presently projected that by the year 2050, the United States will be a country where Whites will be a numerical minority. One in five Americans are expected to self-identify as multiracial (Lee and Bean 2004). Given these projected demographic changes, rethinking the race issue may well be a social and cultural necessity. Perhaps by stressing the *social* nature and origins of racial distinctions, we will find that such distinctions are more amenable to change than conventional wisdom currently allows.

Learning More About It

To learn more about the continued presence of racial inequality in the United States, see the most recent edition of Andrew Hacker's *Two Nations: Black and White, Separate, Hostile, Unequal* (New York: Simon and Schuster, 2003b).

W. E. B. Du Bois offers a classic treatise on the dynamics of U.S. race relations in *The Souls of Black Folks* (New York: Penguin, 1903/1982). Cornel West thoughtfully grapples with issues of race in a more contemporary book entitled *Race Matters* (New York: Random House, 1994).

In *The Declining Significance of Race: Blacks and Changing American Institutions*, 2nd edition (Chicago: University of Chicago Press, 1980), William Julius Wilson posits the controversial thesis that social class is more significant than race in defining opportunities for African Americans.

New York Times correspondents offer a series of essays that capture how race is experienced in our day-to-day lives and relationships in *How Race Is Lived in America* (New York: Times Books, 2001).

David Roediger explores the social construction of race and the historical redrawing of racial lines in his book *Working Toward Whiteness: How America's Immigrants Became White* (New York: Basic Books, 2005).

In *Finding Oprah's Roots,* Henry-Louis Gates, Jr., provides a roadmap for using public documents and online databases for researching one's past. He also provides information on genetic testing resources currently available for tracing one's tribal roots (New York: Random House, 2007).

A thorough review of the literature on residential segregation can be found in Camille Charles's article, "The Dynamics of Racial Residential Segregation" (*Annual Review of Sociology* 29:167–207, 2003).

The transformation of the United States from a mainly biracial to a multiracial society and the "boundary" implications of these changes are considered in Jennifer Lee and Frank Bean's article, "America's Changing Color Lines: Immigration, Race/Ethnicity, and Multiracial Identification" (*Annual Review of Sociology* 30:221–242, 2004).

Shannon Harper and Barbara Reskin provide a review of the history and impact of affirmative action in the areas of education and employment in their article, "Affirmative Action at School and on the Job" (*Annual Review of Sociology* 31:357–380, 2005).

You can also consult the following organizations/sites to learn more about race and ethnic relations in America and abroad:

AntiRacismNet
http://www.antiracismnet.org/main.html

Equal Employment Opportunity Commission
http://www.eeoc.gov/

Institute on Race and Poverty
http://www.irpumn.org/website/

National Urban League
http://www.nul.org

Exercises

1. Imagine that height is a critical marker for social ranking in the United States: Shortness is valued, and tallness is devalued. Speculate on the ways in which the social structure of your hometown might change if residential, educational, and occupational patterns influenced by prejudice and discrimination were based on human height.

2. Racial categories are social creations that emerge from social interaction. Gather a sample of ads from two magazines that target different classes of readers. For instance, one magazine might be targeting an elite readership (for example, *Martha Stewart Living* or *Gourmet*), whereas the second might target a more general, less affluent readership (for example, *Family Circle* or *Good Housekeeping*). Are racial lessons delivered through these ads? Do the ads indicate any differences in life aspirations by race or ethnic group? Consider the data on life chances as presented in this essay. How does reality compare to the lifestyles projected in your sample ads?

3. Explore the impact of social structure *via* the Survey Documentation Analysis (SDA) Web page.
   - Access the SDA Web page: http://sda.berkeley.edu/
   - Click on the SDA archive link
     o Click on the GSS Quick Tables link

   - Explore the various social issues covered in the quick tables and create four to six tables that enable you to see the impact of race on American's attitudes and/or behaviors.
     o NOTE: Before doing your runs, look at the chart options box. Choose the option that you think offers the best visual display of the effects you are presenting. (No matter which option you choose, be sure to check the "show percents" box.)

Deviance, Crime, and Social Control

Essay 15

Conventional Wisdom Tells Us . . . Violence Is on the Rise in the United States—No One Is Safe

In recent decades, Americans have wrestled with a growing fear of violence. Is that fear justified? Here we review the state of violence in America, and we explore those instances in which the public's fears of violence are justified and those in which they are exaggerated. As such, the essay explores the many problems surrounding the detection and perception of danger and crime.

On April 16, 2007, the students, professors, and staff at "Virginia Tech" university began another routine day of classes. But as fate would have it, the day would be anything but routine. For on this day, 28 students and 5 of their professors would never return home.

At 7:15 AM, the busy motion of the campus was shattered by the sounds of gunfire. A disgruntled student, Cho Seung-Hui, stormed Ambler Johnston Hall. He killed two of the students inside. Two hours later, the rampage continued in Norris Hall, where Cho killed 30 people and then turned his gun on himself. "When it was over, even sidewalks were stained with blood" (Hauser and O'Connor 2007)—blood that signified the most deadly mass murder in U.S. history.

The Virginia Tech story is not the most famous of the decade; it is not the most unusual or the most brutal narrative of our time. Rather, this entire incident represents just one of many violent events—events that, some argue, have become a routine feature of modern life.

When Americans are asked to name the country's most troubling problems, they rank violent crime very high on the list (Gallup 1976–2003, 2004–2007). Drive-by shootings, gang warfare, metal detectors at the doors of our schools, yellow and orange terror alerts: In the "new" millennium, these images have become all too common, and they are images that can provoke a sense of fear and panic. Americans are now acting on their fears. Recent polls show that Americans are increasing the number of protective measures they take against murderers and other violent criminals. Record numbers are installing special locks or alarms in their homes, buying dogs or guns for protection, changing their nighttime walking patterns, and minimizing contact with strangers (Home Safety Channel 2006; Wirthlin Report 2001).

Is the rising fear of violence justified? Is conventional wisdom correct in suggesting that our streets have become more dangerous than ever before? Just how likely is it that any one of us will become the victim of a violent crime?

Americans do indeed face a greater risk of violence than the inhabitants of many nations in the world. Murder, for example, as well as violent crimes such as assault or rape, occur anywhere from 2 to 40 times more frequently in the United States than in the developed nations of the world. The United States also has higher rates of violent crime than nations suffering from intense poverty or political turmoil—places such as Costa Rica, Croatia, Greece, India, Indonesia, Yemen, and so on (Nationmaster 2007).

Rates of violence in the United States, when compared to rates found in other nations, suggest that violence is a serious problem for Americans. At first glance, such rates seem to support the conventional wisdom that violence is on the rise. However, recent statistics tell us that things in the United States may be changing. The tide of violence may be turning in Americans' favor.

Each year, the FBI provides statistics on crime in the **Uniform Crime Reports Index for Serious Crime** (hereafter referred to as the *UCRs*). According to the *UCRs*, violent crime in the United States reached an all-time high in 1991; that year, the nation experienced approximately 1.9 million violent crimes, including murder, rape, robbery, and aggravated assault. But recent statistics show that the number of violent crimes has dropped significantly. In 2005, the nation experienced approximately 1.39 million acts of violence. That number represents more than a 25% decrease in the violent crime rate. Many are hopeful that this trend will continue into the new century (U.S. Department of Justice 2006b, 2006c, 2006d).

To be sure, many will argue that official statistics such as found in the *UCRs* grossly underestimate violence in America. **Victimization studies—** that is, statistics based on victims' self-reports and not the reports of police— present a picture of violent crime that differs significantly from the one painted by the FBI. For example, statistics from the National Crime Victimization Survey estimate that just over 5 million Americans fell victim to violent crime in 2005 (U.S. Department of Justice 2005). Similarly, the Family Violence Prevention Fund (2007) argues that as many as 3 million women experience domestic abuse each year. And the U.S. Department of Health and Human Services, Administration on Children, Youth and Families (2007b), contends that nearly 900,000 incidents of child abuse occur in the United States each year.

Just as some researchers criticize the *UCRs* for underestimating violent crime, other researchers criticize victimization studies for overestimating the problem. Which statistics are correct? Experts in the field disagree, but the key point to remember is this: *All* statistics on violent crime—*UCRs* and victimization surveys alike—show a similar decrease in the violent crime rate from 1992 to the present.

If, as statistics suggest, violent crime is waning, then what explains Americans' persistent—even increasing—fear of violence? Even with decreasing rates, does violent crime occur with staggering frequency?

Violent crime cannot be described as a frequent event. Indeed, within the world of crime, violence is quite rare. FBI statistics show that, overall, property crimes (e.g., arson, auto theft, burglary, and larceny) occur 7.3 times more often than violent crimes (see Figure 15.1). (Victimization surveys suggest a similar relationship, with property crime rates 6.75 times higher than violent crime rates.) More specifically, the FBI notes that the typical American is 129 times more likely to be burglarized than murdered and 72 times more likely to be a victim of theft than of rape. Indeed, when it

Figure 15.1   FBI Time Clock, 2005

CRIME CLOCK 2005

One Violent Crime Occurs Every 22.7 Seconds

One Murder . . . . Every 31.5 minutes
One Forcible Rape . . . . Every 5.6 minutes
One Robbery . . . . Every 1.3 minutes
One Aggravated Assault . . . . Every 36.5 seconds

One Property Crime Occurs Every 3.1 Seconds

One Burglary . . . . Every 14.6 seconds
One Larceny-Theft . . . . Every 4.7 seconds
One Motor Vehicle Theft . . . . Every 25.5 seconds

SOURCE: U.S. Department of Justice 2006e.

comes to fatal victimization, statistics show that Americans are more likely to take their own lives than to be killed by violent criminals (U.S. Census Bureau 2007d: Table 116; U.S. Department of Justice 2006b, 2006c, 2006d, 2006e, 2007a, 2007b).

Given the relative rarity of violent crime, what other factors might explain Americans' growing fear of violence? Some suggest this fear may be linked to the perceived randomness of such crimes. Americans tend to view violence as an event that can strike anyone at any time. As conventional wisdom states, "No one is safe." Crime statistics, however, do not substantiate this image (Macmillan 2001). Consider the act of murder. Most Americans picture murder as an unpredictable attack that is likely to be perpetrated by a stranger. Yet "friendly murders"—that is, murders committed by relatives, friends, or acquaintances of the victim—are more than three times more common than murders perpetrated by strangers. Furthermore, far from being random, murder exhibits several striking social patterns. For example, murder is a crime of the young. An individual's risk of being murdered peaks at age 25, regardless of race or gender. (Recall from Essay 6 that senior citizens are most fearful of violent crime, yet crime statistics show that seniors are least likely to become murder victims.) Murder also is a "male" crime; more than 85% of all perpetrators and 70% of all victims are male. Note, too, that murder systematically varies by race; it is an overwhelmingly intraracial crime. Whites tend to murder other Whites, Blacks tend to murder other Blacks, and so on. The crime of murder also occurs disproportionately among the poor. In addition, socioeconomic status appears related to when and how a murder occurs. Members of the lower socioeconomic strata, for instance, are most likely to be murdered on a Saturday night, and the grisly event is likely to involve alcohol and passion. In contrast, members of the upper strata are murdered with equal frequency during all days and times of the week. In addition, murders among the "privileged" typically result from premeditation rather than passion (U.S. Department of Justice 2006b–e).

Statistics on other violent crimes dispel the myth of random violence as well. Rape, for example, is rarely the product of a surprise attack. Indeed, rapes by strangers account for only about a third of such crimes. Similarly, simple assault usually takes place between intimates, the result of a building animosity between two individuals. Intimacy is especially characteristic of assaults involving female victims. Women are twice as likely to be attacked by an intimate or an acquaintance than they are to be attacked by a stranger (U.S. Department of Justice 2007c).

Our visions of violence seem not to match the realities of the world around us (Altheide 2002, 2006; Glassner 2000). Contrary to perceptions of violence on the rise, its high frequency of occurrence, and the randomness of violent events, violent crimes are relatively rare, highly patterned, and decreasing in recent years. Given these facts, what else might explain Americans' persistent fears and misperceptions?

One might be tempted to explain these fears by referring to the high personal cost of violence—namely, serious injury or death. However, if the risk of injury or death alone stimulated such fears, we would find similar dread surrounding other high-injury and high-mortality settings. Consider the area of occupation-related injuries and deaths. Although fewer than 20,000 Americans are murdered each year, some studies estimate that more than 60,000 U.S. workers die annually due to occupational disease or unsafe working conditions. Similarly, while the FBI estimates that approximately 1.7 million Americans become victims of violent crime, some estimates suggest that nearly 4 million suffer physical harm on the job. Despite the staggering figures on occupational disease and death, Americans' fear of the work setting is negligible relative to their fear of violent crime (Reiman 2006; Smith 2007; U.S. Census Bureau 2007d: Table 639). Now consider life on American roads. Americans are more than twice as likely to die in automobile accidents as they are to be murdered, and nearly twice as likely to be injured in an automobile accident as they are to be injured by a violent criminal. However, few would cite a level of fear that precludes one's "taking to the roads" (National Highway Traffic Safety Administration 2007).

Considerations regarding the reality and cost of violent crime contribute little to our understanding of Americans' intense fear of violence. Violence in the United States is clearly a problem, but it does not appear to warrant the level of fear expressed by the American public. As a result, some sociologists contend that Americans' fear of violence may in part be socially constructed. The **social construction of reality** occurs when individuals create images, ideas, and beliefs about society based on their social interactions. The social constructionist approach suggests that certain social encounters expose individuals repeatedly to information on violence—information that suggests that violent crime is on the rise and that it occurs frequently, randomly, or at the hands of strangers. As a result, these data—even though they represent misinformation—come to form the public's "reality" of violence.

The mass media, especially television, are the greatest source of misinformation on violence. The National Television Violence Study (1996–1998) as well as longitudinal research conducted by scholars in both the United States and abroad (Browne and Hamilton-Giachritsis 2005; Diefenbach and West 2001; Gerbner et al. 2002; Mathews et al. 2005) provide a wealth of evidence on this point. Researchers involved in these projects have meticulously analyzed the content found in sample weeks of prime-time and daytime television. Their findings show that the rates of violent crime in "TV land" are disproportionately high compared with real-world figures.

Sixty-one percent of television programs contain some type of violence. During any weeknight, viewers see an average of three violent acts per hour. On Saturday mornings, a time period dominated by child viewers, the rate of violence increases to 18 violent acts per hour. Furthermore, some studies estimate that by the time most children leave high school, they have viewed approximately 13,000 murders on TV! The figures on TV violence are significant, for they suggest a world quite different from everyday reality. In the real world, fewer than 1% of all Americans become involved in violence. In TV land, 64% of all characters are involved in violence. Therefore, those who rely on television as their window on reality may come to view the world as a perilously dangerous place (Browne and Hamilton-Giachritsis 2005; Diefenbach and West 2001; Gerbner et al. 2002; Mathews et al. 2005; National Television Violence Study 1996–1998).

To substantiate this claim, the Annenberg research group regularly compares both heavy and light television viewers with regard to their perceptions of violence. Respondents participating in these studies are asked a series of questions requiring them to estimate rates of murder, rape, and assault. They are generally presented with two choices in making these estimates. One choice typically reflects real rates of violence in the United States, whereas the other choice better reflects rates of violence in TV land.

In each of the Annenberg studies, results consistently show that heavy television viewers are much more likely to overestimate rates of violence than those who watch little or no television. Heavy television viewers routinely favor TV-land estimates of violence over real-world estimates. Furthermore, heavy television viewers perceive the world to be a more dangerous place than those who watch little or no TV. Thus, heavy viewers are more likely than light viewers to take the protective measures mentioned earlier: installing special locks or alarms in their homes, buying dogs or guns for protection, or changing their nighttime walking patterns (Diefenbach and West 2001; Gerbner et al. 2002; Nabi and Sullivan 2001; Signorielli, Gerbner, and Morgan 1995).

Complementing the social constructionist view, some suggest that Americans' disproportionate fear of violent crime emerges from a long-standing cultural value that supports a fear of strangers. A **cultural value** is a general sentiment that people share regarding what is good or bad, right or wrong, desirable or undesirable. A **fear of strangers** refers to a dread or suspicion of those who look, behave, or speak differently from oneself. Such fears can ultimately make the world seem unfamiliar and dangerous.

In the United States, cultural values instill a sense of mistrust and foreboding toward those we do not know. Couple this phenomenon with the fact that most Americans view violent crime as "stranger crime," and the misinformation that links violence to an already feared social category—strangers—serves to exacerbate and perpetuate public fears of such crimes (McDonald 2003; President's Commission on Law Enforcement and Administration of Justice 1968).

The public's misplaced fears and misperceptions of violence are not without serious consequences. Such misconceptions sometimes result in an ineffective approach to crime. For example, high-profile murder cases such as the Rabbi Fred Neulander case in New Jersey, the Toni Riggs case in Detroit, or the Susan Smith case in South Carolina illustrate the danger of equating murder with strangers. In these cases, the murder victims were killed by immediate family members: Neulander and Riggs murdered their spouses, and Smith murdered her children. Yet in all cases, resistance to the notion of "friendly" murder initially led to the detention of innocent people. (The false leads in the Riggs and Smith cases also involved Black males; indeed, 35 Black males were questioned in the Smith case.) Such "mistakes" substantiate the power of socially constructed scripts—scripts that depict the "typical" nature of murder and the "probable" perpetrator of the crime (Brown 1994; McDonald 2003).

Misplaced fears and misperceptions of violence also can detract attention from the critical sites of violence in the United States. To be sure, Americans display greater concern for violent crimes on our nation's streets than they do for violence in the home. Yet sociologist Richard Gelles notes that, aside from the police and the military, the family is the single most violent institution in our society (Family Violence Prevention Fund 2007; Gelles and Loseke 1993; Gelles and Straus 1988; Mignon et al. 2002; Ruane 1993; Straus 2001; Straus and Gelles 1990; Straus, Gelles, and Steinmetz 1980).

Finally, some worry that the constant bombardment of violent media programming as well as the ways in which violent stories are told—for example, the vantage point of the viewer, the context of violence, the response of other characters to the perpetrator—will eventually desensitize readers and viewers to real-world violence. Constant media exposure may make readers and viewers more tolerant of violent acts in the real world (Cerulo 1998; Gerbner et al. 2002; Larson 2003; National Television Violence Study 1996–1998).

If Americans' fear of violence is socially constructed and our perceptions of violent crime are inaccurate, should society shift its attention from the issue of violence? We suggest nothing of the kind. To be sure, any instance of violence represents one death or one injury too many. In this sense, violence may indeed be all too common in the United States. As a nation, we appear to be making strides in reducing the incidence of violence. Can levels of violence in the United States be further reduced? It is difficult to say, but any solutions to the violence problem require us to adopt a more accurate picture of the scope and patterns that characterize violent crime in America.

Learning More About It

To keep track of yearly increases and decreases in violent crime, visit the FBI's Web site and read the FBI's *Uniform Crime Reports:* http://www.fbi.gov/ucr/ucr.htm. One can also follow results from the National Crime Victimization Survey at http://www.ojp.usdoj.gov/bjs/cvict.htm

The National Crime Prevention Council provides information on building safer, stronger communities: http://www.ncpc.org

Mary R. Jackman provides a wonderful summary of recent research on violence in her article, "Violence in Social Life" (*Annual Review of Sociology* 28:387–415, 2002).

Barry Glassner offers an engaging look at the culture of fear in America. See *The Culture of Fear: Why Americans Are Afraid of the Wrong Things* (New York: Basic Books, 2000). In *Creating Fear: News and the Construction of Crisis* (New York: Aldine de Gruyter, 2002) and in *Terrorism and the Politics of Fear* (New York: Alta Mira, 2006), David Altheide reflects on the ways that the fear of crime—especially terrorism—contributes to social policies that promote strict social control and threaten civil liberties.

Nancy Signorielli and Mildred Vasan offer a comprehensive review of the literature on media violence and its impact on viewers. See *Violence in the Media: A Reference Handbook* (Santa Barbara, CA: ABC-CLIO Publishers, 2005).

A classic essay by Georg Simmel, "The Stranger," offers an insightful exploration into our cultural beliefs about those we do not know; see *The Sociology of Georg Simmel,* edited by K. Wolff (pp. 402–408, New York: Free Press, 1950b).

Exercises

1. Interview from 10 to 15 people about their working "models" of crime. Be sure to obtain information on such things as the appearance of the typical criminal, the location of the typical crime, the typical criminal offense, and so on. Determine whether a general model emerges, and discuss how this model allows certain acts to escape the label "criminal."

2. This essay provides a detailed profile of the social patterns of murder: age, gender, site, and social class. Go to your local or university library and collect similar statistics for the crimes of burglary, larceny, and auto theft. Based on your data, speculate on the ways in which the "face" of murder differs from the "face" of property crimes.

3. Visit the FBI's Web page (<http://www.fbi.gov>) and find the most recent rates for murder, rape, assault, and robbery. Then create a "multiple-choice"

test designed to tap individuals' perceptions of violent crime rates. Your survey might include questions such as the following:

In the United States, _____ murders occur each year:

(a) 5,000 (b) 20,000 (c) 50,000 (d) 100,000

Administer your survey to 10 to 15 people you know to be avid TV watchers and to 10 to 15 people you know to be only occasional TV watchers. Compare the answers of heavy and light TV viewers. Which group better estimated the actual violent crime rate?

Essay 16

Conventional Wisdom Tells Us . . . There Ought to Be a Law

There's no social ill that the law can't fix . . . or at least that is what many Americans believe. In this essay, we review various social functions of the law. We also consider whether or not we are overly dependent on this tool of formal social control.

"There ought to be a law" . . . it's a phrase that expresses Americans' penchant for the law. In the United States, no social realm is exempt from the rule of law. Indeed, law is a pervasive feature of American society. Family, civic duties, education, business and commerce, religion, government, even birth and death are regulated by law. Leave this world without your legal pass (i.e., a will or a trust) and your "life" (as it were) will become the domain of probate courts and lawyers.

Americans pride themselves on being a land of laws. The U.S. Constitution, our most cherished legal document, is invoked by liberal and conservative, law-abiding and law-violating individuals alike. Americans trust in the law and symbolically display it as "blind" to status differences. The law, it is argued, renders all parties equal before the scales of justice. No one in the United States, not even the president, is considered above the law. A few years back, Kenneth Starr rather dramatically reminded Bill Clinton of this fact. More recently, a federal court rejected the argument that President Bush had been granted "inherent powers" to violate the laws of Congress and ruled that the Bush administration's warrantless spying on ordinary citizens is unconstitutional (American Civil Liberties Union 2006). (The Sixth Circuit Court of Appeals dismissed the case in July 2007, but refused to rule on the legality of the program.) Americans expect great things of the law and are quick to express their displeasure and disappointment when the law behaves badly. A decision by a Michigan judge to settle a holiday visitation conflict between parents by flipping a coin received national coverage in February 2002. One party to the conflict felt the judge's behavior made a mockery of the judicial process; even the judge's superiors agreed that the incident hurt the judicial process (Ashenfelter 2002).

Many sociologists contend that social control represents the dominant function of the law. **Social control** refers to the process of enforcing social norms. **Norms** are social rules or guidelines that direct behavior. Social control can be informal or formal. **Informal social control** can be initiated by any party; no special status or training is required. It includes such mechanisms as socialization, gossip, ridicule, shaming, praise, or rewards. **Formal social control** is state centered, i.e., enforced by the power of the state. The law as a tool of formal social control is legitimated and enforced by the power of the state.

In recognizing the law's social control function, we acknowledge it as a vehicle for achieving and maintaining social order and stability. The law steps in when informal social control tactics fail to get the job done. For the most part, people readily appreciate the social control function of the law. Most would agree that certain behaviors—murder, robbery, assault, burglary, arson—are clearly social wrongs deserving the law's attention. Few would question the need to regulate such norm violations. Indeed, most would rail at the dangers posed by the absence of law in response to these behaviors.

The law, however, serves other social functions—functions about which one finds less public consensus. In addition to operating as a tool of social control, the law can function as a tool of **social engineering**. In this capacity, the law is constructed to satisfy social wants and to bring about desired social change.

Law for the sake of social engineering poses dilemmas for societies. Whose wants and desires should such law promote? Whose ideas of right and wrong should the law encode? Can we rightfully enact law that pushes forward a specific moral agenda?

Despite the dilemmas posed by socially engineered law, there is no shortage of statutes and regulations that fit into this category. Indeed, the United States boasts a substantial historical record in which certain groups have legislated right and wrong—even amid the outcries of others. The "Roaring Twenties" provide perhaps the most notorious example of this process. In

1919, the National Prohibition Act (a.k.a. the Volstead Act) made the sale, manufacture, and transportation of liquor, beer, and wine illegal in the United States. In part, the Volstead Act resulted from efforts of middle-class groups to counteract the vices of newly arrived immigrants (Gusfield 1963). As is the case for many instances of social engineering law, however, not everyone agreed with the act's definition of right and wrong. As a result, the passage of the Volstead Act spurred several unintended consequences. For example, outlawed "saloons" were quickly replaced by newly devised "speakeasies." Hardware stores began to stock and sell portable stills. Libraries supplied instructional books and pamphlets needed for distilling homemade "hooch." California vintners (who actually expanded their acreage during Prohibition) introduced "Vine-glo," a grape juice that with proper care and time (60 days) could be turned into wine. Brewers followed suit, manufacturing and selling "wort," a half-brewed liquid that could be turned into beer with the simple addition of yeast. And since the Volstead Act allowed the sale of alcohol for medicinal purposes, doctors began writing alcohol prescriptions, and pharmacists began filling them in unprecedented numbers (Time-Life Books 1988). In short, Americans responded to the social-engineering nature of the Volstead Act by designing creative ways in which to avoid, evade, and ignore the law.

Americans' rebellious response to the Volstead Act was not an isolated incident. Many argue that certain drug laws have encouraged similar activities (Campos 1998). Here again, the actions of moral entrepreneurs have had unintended consequences. **Moral entrepreneurs** are individuals who seek to legally regulate behaviors that they consider morally reprehensible. Like Prohibition, efforts to criminalize certain drugs have created an extremely lucrative black market in illicit drugs. Drugs that have a negligible pharmaceutical value now command hundreds of dollars on the streets. Furthermore, the financial incentive associated with drug trafficking has provided an irresistible career option for certain individuals. Some would also argue that the legal prohibition of particular drugs ensures that increasingly potent and harmful forms of illicit drugs will continue to enter the illegal drug market. Former Baltimore Mayor Kurt Schmoke maintains that this scenario accurately describes the emergence of crack cocaine (Mills 1992).

The examples just cited illustrate the dangers posed when we use law as a tool of social engineering. Equating the law with general public sentiment is a tricky business. In modern, complex societies where there are multiple "publics," there is no simple relationship between public opinion and the law. Thus, the ability to translate social wants and desires into law involves social power more than social consensus. Why have anti-smoking campaigns and legislation been so successful? Some would argue that it's all about power and status politics—smoking is inversely related to social class and status (Tuggle and Holmes 1997). And why have anti-gun efforts failed? Again, we would have to cite power and status politics. The NRA (National Rifle Association) is a powerful organization that has been tremendously effective in its lobbying efforts to safeguard the rights of gun owners. No doubt our nation's response to the latest social issue to capture the public's attention, global warming, will reflect the input of various lobbying efforts. The number of *registered* lobbyists in our nation's capital has more than doubled since 2000. (The total number of lobbyists remains unknown since many do not register.) And if money talks, lobbyists will surely win something. In 2004, lobbyists spent an average of $177 million per month trying to promote/secure their interests (Purdum 2006)!

When special interests successfully mobilize resources on behalf of their own causes, the "law" can come to contradict the general public will. In such cases, Americans cling to a belief in equality before the law, but they also understand that lawmakers consider some people more equal than others. Consider these words about U.S. lawmakers penned by noted legal scholar Lawrence Friedman (1975):

> They know that 100 wealthy, powerful constituents passionately opposed to socialized medicine outweigh thousands of poor, weak constituents, mildly in favor of it. Most people . . . remain quiet and obscure . . . This is the "silent majority." (p. 164)

While these words were written more than a quarter of a century ago, they prove timely. Recent failed efforts to achieve health care reform by the U.S. Congress offer compelling evidence in this regard. A single, silent majority still encounters great difficulty when attempting to make its voice heard over that of a smaller but more powerful special interest group. Consider that from January 2005 to June 2006, drug companies spent $155 million on lobbying Congress and working to block any new legislation that would permit the federal government to negotiate lower prices for Medicare prescription drugs. Despite the fact that senior citizens, health activists, and some government officials support "open pharmaceutical markets," bills permitting such changes to the Medicare program have been consistently defeated (Ismail 2007).

Is it socially harmful when law becomes disconnected from general public opinion? Some maintain that laws contradicting public sentiment breed contempt and, more important, disregard. Consider the following examples. Unrealistic speed limits have invited many drivers to disregard traffic laws.

Sunday "blue laws" or laws prohibiting the sales of cigarettes and alcohol to minors have placed many merchants on the wrong side of the law. Many middle- and upper-class families procure child care providers, housekeepers, and landscapers as a means of making their busy lives easier, but some individuals do so at the cost of violating tax and immigration laws.

Social control or social engineering: Regardless of its social function, law is a dominant force in American society. One legal scholar observes that our devotion to reason leads us to legally regulate more and more of our social interactions. We use the law to satisfy our metaphysical anxieties (Campos 1998). As these formal rules come to dominate our lives, the potential for legal work grows and grows. Since the 1960s, the law represents the fastest-growing profession in the United States (Vago 2003). Paralegal and legal assistants make the Bureau of Labor Statistics' list of fastest growing occupations through the year 2014 (U.S. Department of Labor 2005a). A major staffing firm projected that first-year law associates would be in great demand and earning great salaries for 2007 (Robert Half International 2007). Our nation averages more lawyers per person than any other modern industrial society. And despite the high population density of lawyers, the law is still a popular career option for college graduates. During the 1990s and into the new century, close to 40,000 law degrees were conferred annually (U.S. Department of Education 2004: Table 257). The American Bar Association is the largest voluntary professional association in the world (American Bar Association 2007).

Against this backdrop of a legally saturated society, the United States has also acquired a reputation as a rather litigious society. Many argue that lawsuits have become Americans' favorite pastime. Have you ever lost an item at the dry cleaners? Sue! (In 2007, a D.C. administrative law judge was pursuing a $65 million lawsuit against a local dry cleaning business because the cleaners lost a pair of the judge's pants.) Has your child been injured playing Little League? Sue! (In 2007, a Long Island mother brought suit against a Little League coach for not teaching her son how to slide properly into a base.) Have you ever sustained a burn from an overly hot cup of coffee? Sue! (In 1992, a New Mexico woman sued McDonald's for compensatory and punitive damages after sustaining third-degree burns when a cup of McDonald's coffee spilled into her lap.) Has your favorite sports team been hurt by unpopular trades? Sue! (In 1997, fans of the Florida Marlins turned into plaintiffs when they filed a lawsuit over the breakup of the 1997 World Series title team.) Are you unhappy with the job your parents are doing? Sue! (In the early 1990s, a child sought and obtained a "divorce" from his biological parents; Tippet 1993.) Not pleased with the census-driven reapportionment of congressional seats? Sue! (In 2001, Utah sued the U.S. Census

Bureau in an effort to secure a House seat lost to North Carolina.) Are you an overweight fan of fast foods? Sue! (In 2002, several Americans filed lawsuits against McDonald's, Burger King, etc., arguing that the chains had not provided adequate warning about the dangers of overeating fast foods.) Not pleased that your high school wants you to share the valedictorian title with another student? Sue! (In the spring of 2003, a New Jersey high school student sued her Moorestown school district and won the right to be the solo class valedictorian.) Indeed each year, Americans address the wrongs they experience in life by filing civil lawsuits. **Civil lawsuits** are generally private legal proceedings for the enforcement of a right or the redressing of a wrong.

High-profile cases such as those just mentioned receive much popular press and prompt many to conclude that Americans are an excessively litigious group. Indeed, President Bush (as well as many others) believes that frivolous lawsuits are the cause of an emerging health care crisis in which physicians abandon their medical practices because of high malpractice insurance premiums. The issue became part of President Bush's domestic agenda and reelection campaign efforts (Stolberg 2003a). Some social observers expect the malpractice lawsuit reform effort to be a particularly interesting exchange since it pits two high-power interest groups against each other: doctors and lawyers (Stolberg 2003b). Indeed, it is worth noting that the American Medical Association had a large hand in creating the American Tort Reform Association, a group dedicated to reforming the civil justice system (American Tort Reform Association 2007).

The charge of excessive litigation is also made with regard to **class action suits.** Class action suits are litigation in which one or more persons bring a civil lawsuit on behalf of other similarly situated individuals. To be sure, some people regard malpractice suits and class action suits as threats to health care and to big business, and as negative manifestations of greedy plaintiffs and still greedier lawyers. Others, however, are less inclined to cast litigation in such a negative light. Ever-increasing malpractice insurance premiums may be attributed to the pecuniary interests of insurance companies who want to recover stiff Wall Street losses of the past few years. A recent report by Public Citizen, a nonprofit group representing consumer interests, found that the number and value of malpractice payouts have declined since 2001 (Schmitt 2005). Others argue that lawsuits are essential tools for achieving social justice and reform. What can't be achieved via legislation or regulation might nonetheless be accomplished via litigation (Hensler 2001). John Banzhaf, a key legal player in the recent efforts to sue the junk-food industry, believes that such action may help America come to grips with its increasing obesity problems and thereby serve the public interest (Gumbel 2002). Defenders of class action suits see them as offering solutions to the failure of government oversight of industry (RAND 2007). The idea of frivolous lawsuits is also challenged by a noteworthy statistic: Fully one-third of malpractice cases that resulted in payouts in 2004 involved patient deaths (Schmitt 2005).

While Americans may seem enamored with legal remedies, it is important to note that the law is not our most utilized social control tool. More than one-third of Americans will experience legal problems each year, but only about 10% of us will take the matter to an attorney (Vago 1997). Even after legal proceedings are initiated, it is unlikely that the matter will progress to trial: Either parties settle cases or judges decide them on legal motions. Consequently, there are those who argue that charges of a litigation explosion in the United States are unfounded, overstated, or public relations gimmicks (Abel 2002; Center for Justice and Democracy 2007; Chimerine and Eisenbrey 2005; Cochran 2005). Indeed, a widely utilized report on tort costs is produced by a paid (and highly criticized) consultant to the *insurance* industry: Tillinghast-Towers Perin.

For some, the most notable change in legal work has been the increase in work for corporations and the government, while work for individual clients has remained relatively stable (Heinz, Nelson, and Laumann 2001; National Association for Legal Professionals 2007a). In the last decade, there has been a marked increase in the percentage of lawyers working for the public interest (National Association for Legal Professionals 2007b). Similarly, while there is growing concern about the use of class action suits, in fact such suits constitute a very small percentage of the total civil caseload (Hensler 2001). Instead, much litigation is essentially a business matter; that is, businesses suing other businesses (Heinz et al. 2001). Furthermore, in recent years, more and more alternative dispute resolution (ADR) processes such as mediation and arbitration are being considered as reasonable alternatives to adjudication.

Contrary to the notion of a litigation explosion, some statistics suggest that America is a nation of legal restraint. For example, it is estimated that only 2% of victims of medical negligence file a claim (George 2006). Data from the National Center for State Courts indicate that tort filings in 35 key states (representing nearly 80% of the U.S. population) have declined by 4% between 1993 and 2002 (Chimerine and Eisenbrey 2005). Even at the highest level of our court system, there is no evidence of a litigation explosion. In the opening months of its 2006 term, the Supreme Court took 40% fewer cases than it did in the previous period. This is a continuation of a trend that started in the Rehnquist years. Within five years of Rehnquist becoming chief justice, the number of Supreme Court decisions dropped from 145 to 107. The number of cases with signed opinions for the 2005 term was 69, the lowest number since 1953. The decline in Supreme Court activity is tied in part to fewer appeals coming out of the lower courts and fewer laws being enacted by Congress (and needing judicial interpretation; Greenhouse 2006).

What explains the general legal restraint we see? One contributing factor is cost. The practice of law is expensive. Many Americans with legal problems cannot afford to resolve them via the law. It is estimated that less than one-fifth of the legal needs of the eligible poor are met by legal aid organizations. Similarly, many middle-class individuals, ineligible for government-funded legal aid, must forgo legal redress because of prohibitive costs (George 2006). (Indeed, the high cost of legal action is one reason that some persons resort to a class action suit—it can make the cost of litigation more affordable for persons suffering moderate financial loses.) This is true despite the fact that lawyers frequently accept cases on a contingency fee basis. In contingency fee cases, attorneys receive compensation (typically 33–50% of the client's post-cost financial recovery) only if they prevail in the case. While this arrangement can motivate attorneys to seek high damages, it also ensures that attorneys will refrain from taking meritless or weak cases. Pursuing no-win cases is a losing proposition. Thus, despite the rather common belief that contingency fee arrangements encourage litigation, the evidence does not support this view. The most recent study by the National Center for State Courts indicates that 62% of tort cases are motor vehicle trials with median awards of under $18,000. Punitive damages were awarded in less than 5% of tort cases (National Center for State Courts 2005). Even class action suits that many identify as contributing to our tort crisis rarely produce extraordinary monetary settlements. A recent RAND study of class action suits against insurance companies found that only 12% of cases resulted in a class settlement and the median benefit available to class members was $97. Attorneys for plaintiffs were awarded a median 30% of the common fund (RAND 2007).

The high cost of the law ensures that most of those facing social wrongs will react by adopting some informal, extralegal response. Some will avoid contact or refuse to cooperate with those who do them wrong. Others may resort to gossip or direct scorn against wrongdoers. Certain individuals elect to settle scores by seeking revenge. Indeed, many incidents of personal violence, as well as property crimes, can be attributed to such revenge seeking, or "self-help" behaviors (Black 1998). Most of us, however, are likely to respond to wrongs against us by "lumping" them; we will, in effect, turn the other cheek. Indeed, tolerance is "the most common response of aggrieved people everywhere" (Black 1998). **Tolerance** refers to inaction in the face of some offense.

The juxtaposition of tolerance vis-à-vis the law is a compelling reminder of the need to develop our sociological vision. The law is a social phenomenon, and as such it varies greatly within its social environment. To understand its availability, distribution, usage, nonusage, and even its suspension requires us to analyze the law in light of **social context**—the broad social and historical circumstances surrounding an act or event. The post-9/11 efforts of the Bush administration provide a timely illustration of this point. Immediately after the September 11, 2001, terrorist attacks on America, the president signed the *USA PATRIOT Act* in October 2001. This act strengthened federal investigations in several ways. It broadened the information-gathering, surveillance, and detention powers of the Justice Department; it also limited judicial oversight of these activities. Then-Attorney General John Ashcroft defended the act as an essential tool for fighting terrorism. But in the years since 9/11, critics of the act have come to see it as a serious threat to fundamental constitutional rights. Perhaps in an ironic twist, some of the most vocal opposition has come from the not so hushed voices of librarians. In 2005, the American Library Association challenged an FBI demand—one linked to arguments of national security. The FBI sought Connecticut library use records as well as the issuance of a Justice Department gag order to preclude the library system from discussing the case. (The gag order was needed because the FBI request came via a National Security Letter [NSL]; parties receiving such letters are forbidden by law to reveal requests made within.) A federal court subsequently ruled in favor of the librarians ("American Patriots" 2006).

While the PATRIOT Act was reauthorized by Congress in 2006, demands for reform of the act continue. In particular, critics continue to speak out against the NSL provision of the act. Data from the Justice Department's Office of Inspector General reveal that more than 143,000 NSL requests were made between 2003 and 2005. Perhaps that is why the American Civil Liberties Union continues to challenge the constitutionality of the act. In this case, Americans apparently agree with the ACLU's position. A recent ABC News Poll found that 60% of Americans favored extending the PATRIOT Act, but 68% were against allowing the FBI to demand records without court approval (ABC News 2005).

Despite its cultural importance, the law does not represent the whole story of social control in our society. Instead, we must view the law as one form of control among many. Pursuing such second thoughts about the law will help us see how it is that our very demand for the law and social control can contribute to much of the extralegal activity in our society.

Learning More About It

In *Supreme Conflict: The Inside Story of the Struggle for Control of the United States Supreme Court* (New York: Penguin, 2007), Jan Crawford Smith offers a detailed and dynamic account of conservatives' bid for control of the Supreme Court and the restriction of the Court's future role in government.

A thorough review of the theory and techniques of conflict management can be found in Donald Black's *The Social Structure of Right and Wrong* (San Diego: Academic Press, 1998).

For an analysis of how the law can be used as a tool of moral entrepreneurs, see Joseph Gusfield's classic work on prohibition, *Symbolic Crusade: Status Politics and the American Temperance Movement* (Urbana, IL: University of Illinois Press, 1963).

An interesting review of American's appetite for fast food, social change, and litigation is found in Andrew Gumbel's "Fast Food Nation: An Appetite for Litigation" (http://news.independent.co.uk/world/americas/article179042.ece).

More information about the PATRIOT Act can be found at the American Civil Liberties Union's Web site: http://www.aclu.org

The Center for Public Integrity is a useful source of information about the political process in the United States: http://www.publicintegrity.org

The following organizations can help you learn more about law in American society:

National Lawyers Guild
http://www.nlg.org

Public Justice
http://www.tlpj.org

Rand Institute for Civil Justice
http://www.rand.org/icj/

Exercises

1. Donald Black's (1976) theory of law asserts that social intimates (such as family members) are less likely to use the law against each other than are nonintimates. Identify and speculate as to alternate means of social control that might prove to be particularly effective in family settings. What are their implications for the legal process?

2. Consider the legal and extralegal ramifications of formally regulating our social relations in cyberspace. How have we tried to regulate cyberspace relations via the law? What do you see as some of the most likely extralegal responses to these legal rules?

Essay 17

Conventional Wisdom Tells Us . . . Honesty Is the Best Policy

. . . except, of course, when reporting your income, revealing your age, sparing the feelings of another—the list can go on and on. In this essay, we explore the conditions under which lying is viewed as normal. In so doing, we use lying as a case study that aptly demonstrates both the pervasiveness and the relative nature of deviance.

"Honesty is the best policy," wrote Ben Franklin. From an early age, parents and teachers urge us to embrace this sentiment. We learn cultural fables and tales that underscore the value of truthfulness—remember Pinocchio or George Washington and the cherry tree? Similarly, religious doctrines turn honesty into law with lessons such as "Thou shalt not lie." In civics class, individuals learn that perjury—lying while under oath—is an illegal act.

Prohibitions against lying are among the earliest norms to which individuals are socialized. **Norms** are social rules or guidelines that direct behavior. They are the "shoulds" and "should nots" of social action, feelings, and thought. As we grow older, we witness firsthand the ways in which dishonesty can lead to the downfall of individuals, families, careers, communities—even presidencies. Indeed, many social commentators identify the Watergate incident, and the high-level lying that accompanied it, as the basis for today's widespread public distrust of the U.S. government. The Iran Contra scandal and the Clinton-Lewinsky affair added fuel to the fire—so much so that recent polls suggest that fewer than 70% of Americans trust the federal government (Gallup Poll 2007a; Watson and Jones 2006; Zogby International 2006).

But if honesty is the best policy, how do we understand the findings of recent surveys that document widespread dishonesty in our high schools and colleges? Anywhere from 50% to 80% of high school and college students have admitted to cheating in their student careers. Cheating includes everything from stealing tests and carrying "cheat sheets" to giving assignments and test answers to others, buying term papers, or plagiarizing other people's work (Conradson and Hernández-Ramos 2004; *Washington Post* 2007).

If honesty is the best policy, how do we understand the deceit that is rampant in corporate America? Many Enron employees as well as countless investors had their financial futures destroyed because they believed the fraudulent bookkeeping practices tendered by J. P. Morgan, Chase, and Citigroup; the lies told by Enron's CEO, Ken Lay; and the cover-up instigated by Andersen Worldwide, the once highly respected auditing firm (Eichenwald and Atlas 2003). The Enron story is not unique. Media mogul Martha Stewart had no sooner completed her prison term issued for lying and obstruction of justice when Dennis Kozlowski, the former CEO of Tyco International, was sentenced 8 1/3 to 25 years behind bars for his dishonest business practices. In recent years, one major corporation after another— Apple, IBM, Microsoft, Xerox—has had to issue restatements of their financials to "get the numbers right." Corporate boards of directors are supposed to keep a watchful eye on CEOs, but in too many cases (like WorldCom and Tyco), the boards fail to keep anyone in check (Byrne, Arndt, Zellner, and McNamee 2002; Eichenwald 2003; Frankel 2005; Parloff 2007).

If honesty is the best policy, how do we understand the scandal that has rocked the Roman Catholic Church for the last few years? Hundreds of priests stand accused of sexually molesting young charges and parishioners. And the scope of the scandal has escalated as we slowly discovered the reactions of the church hierarchy. In the summer of 2003, the public learned of a 40-year-old Vatican document that instructed bishops to cover up sex crimes. The document was described by one defense attorney as a "blueprint for deception" (CBS News 2003). Bishops across the United States kept the illicit behaviors of clergy under wraps by reassigning errant priests and/or buying the silence of victims (Williams 2005).

Even now, as we struggle to make sense of our transformed "post–9/11" society, we repeatedly must come to terms with the honesty issue. Dishonest claims and fraudulent documents paved the way for the terrorists' sinister activities in the months and days before the deadly attacks. Since September 11, 2001, there has been increasing interest in and demand for research and technology that will improve our ability to uncover lies and deceptive behaviors (Adelson 2004; CBS News 2006). And perhaps coming full circle, Americans are learning more about the possibly deceitful practices of our own government in its efforts to manipulate public reaction and combat terrorism. An internal Environmental Protection Agency (EPA) report has acknowledged that the agency, under prompting by the White House, misled the public by declaring the "ground zero" area of New York City to be safe *before* any air testing results were obtained. Further, the White House has also been accused of politically manhandling the EPA by insisting that all EPA press releases regarding air quality at ground zero be cleared by the National Security Agency (Currie 2007; Preston 2006).

Political lying—the list goes on. Months after President Bush declared the "major fighting" in Iraq to be over, Americans were trying to discern the truth about the start of the war. Did the president deliberately lie to both Congress and the people when he described Iraq's weapons of mass destruction program and Saddam Hussein's ties to al-Qaeda? Were these statements merely a means to secure support for launching the invasion of Iraq? A June 2003 University of Maryland poll found that more than half of respondents believed President Bush "stretched the truth" when making the case for war (Yahoo News 2003). And in the fall of 2003, after weeks of discussing the claims and counterclaims regarding Saddam Hussein's connection to 9/11, social commentators warned that President Bush was teetering on the edge of being a "serial exaggerator." Commentators reminded him that "stark honesty" is the best weapon for maintaining public confidence in his leadership (*New York Times* 2003b; Simendinger 2003; Watson and Jones 2006).

Clearly, we would be lying to say that our culture firmly endorses honesty as the best policy. The conventional wisdom regarding the virtue of honesty is strong, yet we must also note that almost as early as we learn prohibitions against lying, we also learn how to rationalize the telling of lies. We learn that "little white lies" are not as serious as "real lies." We learn that context matters: Lying to strangers is not as serious as lying to friends; lying to peers is more excusable than lying to parents or authorities. We learn that lies don't count if we cross our fingers or wink while telling them. And we learn that lies told under duress are not as awful as premeditated or "barefaced lies" (Bussey 1999; Ekman 2002; Lawson 2000; Lee 2004; Schein 2004; Williams 2001).

Thus, despite conventional wisdom to the contrary, lying stands as a ubiquitous social practice. Children lie to parents, and parents lie to grandparents. Employees lie to employers, and employers lie to regulators. Confessors lie to clergy, and clergy lie to congregations. Presidents lie to Congress and the public, and governments lie to the people. Indeed, there may be no social sphere to which lying is a stranger (Associated Press 2006; DePaulo, Kashy, and Kirkendol 1996; Ekman 2002; Henig 2006; Lalwani, Shavitt, and Johnson 2006; Lerer 2007).

What explains the prevalence of lies when conventional wisdom so strongly supports honesty? What accounts for the discrepancies between what we say about lies and what we do? Is lying wrong? Is it deviant or not?

To start, we must first appreciate the role of cultural values in our often contradictory stance on honesty. A **cultural value** refers to a general sentiment regarding what is good or bad, right or wrong, desirable or undesirable. Cultural values can be powerful motivators that "drive" our behaviors. In reviewing the previous list of dishonest activities of students, corporate executives, clergy, and political leaders, it is easy to identify some overriding or motivating cultural values. Some students, for instance, cheat in the name of getting good grades or good jobs. Some CEOs engage in creative bookkeeping to achieve personal success and wealth. The church hierarchy is interested in preserving the integrity of that institution, and some bishops were willing to mislead parishioners about the conduct of priests in the hope of maintaining that integrity. And some of our political leaders might well be willing to engage in hyperbole and thus stretch the truth in the name of fighting terrorism. In short, for some, the pursuit of high and noble values can invite expedient behavior—we do whatever we must to achieve what we think is worthy or desirable. Unfortunately, however, expedient behavior often takes us into the realm of deviance (Merton 1938; Muftic 2006).

Deviance is typically defined as any act that violates a norm. Definitions of deviance are rarely "black and white." Rather, determining what is deviant is a relative process, because norms can vary with time, setting, or public consciousness. Thus, today's deviant behaviors may be tomorrow's convention. (Think of some "deviant behaviors" that subsequently entered the realm of conformity: long hair on men, jeans on students, living together before marriage, smoking among women.) *Ideally*, norms reflect or are consistent with our cultural values. A culture that promotes the value of family should direct people to marry and have children. A culture that promotes democracy should direct people to vote and participate in community affairs. Values and norms *should* coincide, but that doesn't always happen. They can get out of balance with each other. Frequently, values dominate; we are willing to do anything to accomplish our values or goals. When values dominate, expedient behavior rules, and the normative order can be compromised. If expedient behaviors violate social norms, we enter the realm of deviance. While honesty may be the best policy, dishonesty is often the most expedient way to achieve, succeed, manage, and win. Thus, if I am truly convinced that the grade is everything, I may find it easy to lie and claim the work of others as my own. Similarly, if financial success means everything to me, I might find it easy to lie about company profits if it will help boost stock prices. If protecting the church from scandal is my highest priority, I might find it easy to lie about the reason for reassigning priests. And if fighting terrorism is my goal, I might find it very easy to say what I must to get the job done.

Because lying, like all deviant acts, is variable, sociologists distinguish between two types of lies: deviant lies and normal lies. **Deviant lies** are falsehoods always judged to be wrong by a society; they represent a socially unacceptable practice, one that can devastate the trust that enables interaction within a complex society of strangers. **Normal lies** are a socially acceptable practice linked to productive social outcomes. Individuals rationalize and legitimate normal lies as the means to a noble end: the good of one's family, colleagues, or country. A lie's relative deviancy or normalcy depends on who tells it; when, where, and why it is told; to whom it is told; and the outcome of its telling (Barnes 1994; Blum 2005; Ericson and Doyle 2006; Lalwani et al. 2006; Lee 2004; Manning 1974, 1984; Ruane, Cerulo, and Gerson 1994; Ryan 1996; Seiter, Bruschke, and Bai 2002; Straughan and Lynn 2002; Zagorin 1996).

For example, withholding your AIDS diagnosis from your elderly mother may be viewed as an act of mercy. In contrast, withholding the diagnosis from a sex partner would probably be viewed as immoral or potentially criminal. Similarly, lying about one's age to engage a new romantic interest is likely to be defined as significantly less offensive than lying about one's age to secure Social Security benefits. As with all forms of deviance, lie classification is based on **social context**—the broad social and historical circumstances surrounding an event. We cannot classify a lie as deviant or normal on the basis of objectively stated criteria. In being slow to judge—be it President Clinton's response to charges of adultery, President Bush's stated reasons for going to war, or Alberto Gonzalez's testimony to Congress regarding the federal attorney firings, Americans try to carefully assess the context of any alleged misstatements.

Although deviant lies can destroy social relations, normal lies can function as a strategic tool in the maintenance of social order. Normal lies become a "lubricant" of social life; they allow both the user and receiver of lies to edit social reality. Normal lies can facilitate ongoing interaction (Associated Press 2006; Blum 2005; Goffman 1974; Goleman 1985; Lalwani et al. 2006; Lee 2004; Sacks 1975; Schein 2004).

If our boss misses a lunch date with us, we tell her or him it was "no big deal," even if the missed appointment led to considerable inconvenience in our day. Similarly, we tell a soldier's parents that their son or daughter died a painless death even if circumstances suggest otherwise. In both of these cases, the normal lie represents a crucial mechanism for preserving necessary social routines.

In the same way, normal lies also are important in maintaining civil social environments. Thus, when a truthful child announces someone's obesity, foul smell, or physical disability while on a shopping trip at the mall, parents are quick to instruct him or her in the polite albeit deceptive practices of less-than-honest tact. Similarly, the daily contact between neighbors inherent in most city and suburban layouts leads us to tell a rather bothersome neighbor that she or he is "really no trouble at all." In both of these cases, honesty would surely prove a socially destructive policy—the normal lie allows individuals to preserve the interaction environment.

What processes allow us to normalize an otherwise deviant behavior such as lying? In a classic article, sociologists Gresham Sykes and David Matza (1957) identify five specific techniques of neutralization that prove useful in this regard. **Techniques of neutralization** are methods of rationalizing deviant behavior. In essence, these techniques allow actors to suspend the control typically exerted by social norms. Freed from norms in this way, social actors can engage in deviance. Using the techniques of neutralization—denial of responsibility, denial of injury, denial of victim, condemning the condemner, and appealing to higher loyalties—individuals effectively explain away the deviant aspects of a behavior such as lying. Individuals convince themselves that their actions, even if norm violating, were justified given the circumstance. Once an individual has learned to use these techniques, she or he can apply them to any deviant arena, thereby facilitating an array of deviant behaviors: stealing, fraud, vandalism, personal violence, and so on.

Employing Sykes and Matza's techniques, then, one might *deny responsibility* for a lie, attributing the action to something beyond one's control: "My boss forced me to say he wasn't in." One might *deny injury* of the lie, arguing that the behavior caused no real harm: "Yes, I lied about my age. What's the harm?" One might *deny the victim* of the lie by arguing that the person harmed by the lie deserves such a fate: "I told her that her presentation was perfect. I can't wait for it to bomb; she deserves it." *Condemning one's condemner* allows an individual to neutralize a lie by shifting the focus to how often one's accuser lies: "Yes, I lied about where I was tonight, but how often have you lied to me about that very thing?" Finally, *appealing to higher loyalties* neutralizes lying by connecting it to some greater good: "I didn't tell my wife I was unfaithful because I didn't want to jeopardize our family."

Just as individuals learn to neutralize certain lies, they also learn appropriate reactions to normal lies. With time and experience, individuals learn that challenging normal lies can be counterproductive. Such challenges can disrupt the social scripts that make collective existence possible. **Social scripts** document the shared expectations that govern those interacting within a particular setting or context.

If the social audience wishes to maintain smooth social exchange, then each member must learn to tolerate certain lies. By doing so, individuals downplay deviations from the social script. Like actors on a stage, individuals ignore momentary lapses and faux pas so that the "performance" can continue (Goffman 1959, 1974).

The U.S. military policy of "Don't ask, don't tell," for example, is built on such logic. Military officials look the other way to avoid the potential disruption embodied in a truthful response to the question of homosexuality. Similarly, the spouse who fails to question a partner's change in routine or habit may do so in an effort to shield the marriage from the threat posed by potential truths.

A variety of social settings require that we take someone at her or his word or accept things at face value. We learn to listen with half an ear, to take things "with a grain of salt," or to recognize that people don't always "say what they mean or mean what they say." Paul Ekman, an eminent researcher on deceit, maintains that successful liars most often depend on willfully innocent dupes (Ekman 2002). In the end, these strategies or roles offer support and tolerance for the normal lie.

This discussion of lying raises important points about deviance in general. Despite norms forbidding it, deviance happens. Studies show that nearly every member of the U.S. population engages in some deviant behaviors during their lifetime (Associated Press 2006). Indeed, Emile Durkheim (1938/1966), a central figure in sociology, suggested that deviance would occur even in a society of saints.

Theorist Edwin Lemert contends that certain types of deviance are universal. Everyone, at one time or another, engages in such acts. Lemert refers to these universal occurrences of deviance as primary deviance. **Primary deviance** refers to isolated violations of norms. Such acts are not viewed as deviant by those committing them and often result in no social sanctions. Deviance remains primary in nature as long as such acts "are rationalized or otherwise dealt with as functions of a socially acceptable role" (Lemert 1951:75–76). (Note that normal lying fits easily within this category.)

Herein lies the importance of techniques of neutralization and social scripts of tolerance. The techniques and scripts can keep us and our behaviors within the confines of primary deviance. They can keep us from moving to a more significant type of deviance, which Lemert refers to as secondary deviance. **Secondary deviance** occurs when labeled individuals come to view themselves according to what they are called. The labeled individual incorporates the impression of others into her or his self-identity.

Although all of us engage in primary deviance, relatively few of us become ensnared by secondary deviance. The techniques of neutralization allow the social actor to rationalize periodic infractions of the rules. Social scripts of tolerance allow the social audience to accept such infractions as well. As such, social audiences refrain from publicly labeling the "neutralized" actor as deviant. By anchoring an individual in primary deviance, the techniques of neutralization ease the return to a conforming status. Understand, then, that when CEOs defend creative bookkeeping as a required part of their job or when bishops act in ways to "spare" the faithful unnecessary details about the reassignment of clergy, they are in effect working to maintain the primary status of their deviance.

When it comes to norms on lying, or any other social behavior, conformity may be, as conventional wisdom suggests, the best policy. However, when we understand the complexity involved in the workings of norm violations, we cannot help but note that deviating from the "best policy" may not be all that deviant after all.

Learning More About It

"The Lie," by Georg Simmel, is a classic sociological essay on the topic. See *The Sociology of Georg Simmel* (New York: Free Press, 1950a:312–316).

Paul Ekman's *Telling Lies* (New York: W.W. Norton, 2002) is a highly readable and comprehensive examination of social scientific experimental research on lying. Robin M. Henig offers a very readable discussion of neurological research on lying. See "Looking for the Lie" (*New York Times Magazine* [February 5], 2006:46–53; 76; 80; 83).

Carl Hausman examines lies in advertising, retail, politics, and the media and offers tips on how we might better equip ourselves to spot and stop falsehoods in *Lies We Live By: Defeating Double-Talk and Deception in Advertising, Politics and the Media* (New York: Routledge, 2000). In "Detecting the Effects of Deceptive Presidential Advertisements in the Spring of 2004," Kenneth Winneg, Kate Kenski, and Kathleen Hall Jamieson discuss the harm lies do in presidential elections (*American Behavioral Scientist* 49:1:114–129, 2005).

For a detailed consideration of normal lying in an occupational setting, consult Janet Ruane, Karen Cerulo, and Judith Gerson's 1994 article, "Professional Deceit: Normal Lying in an Occupational Setting" (*Sociological Focus* 27:2:91–109). For a look at how the normal lie operates in the world of students, see the 2007 *Washington Post* article, "At Least Half of Students Admit to Cheating."

For an explicit discussion on how corporate culture influences deceit in business practices, see Tamar Frankel's *Trust and Honesty: America's Business Culture at a Crossroad* (New York: Oxford University Press, 2005).

Gresham Sykes and David Matza's 1957 article, "Techniques of Neutralization: A Theory of Delinquency" (*American Sociological Review* 22:664–670), offers readers some insight into the dynamics that feed the legitimation process.

Exercises

1. Consider the normal lie as it exists in the world of advertising. Collect a sample of ads targeting different audiences: adults versus children, men versus women, yuppies versus the elderly. Is there any pattern in the ads' reliance on normal lying as a marketing technique? What would be the ramifications of unmasking the normal lie in advertising?

2. Consider the function of normal lying in the successful completion of the student role. Are there ways in which dishonesty has been institutionalized in the student role? What do your own experiences and the experiences of your friends suggest are the important sources of such deception?

3. Select and carefully follow the media coverage of a current "scandal." Discuss the relevance of the concepts of primary and secondary deviance. Identify and document the techniques of neutralization that are being used to control or limit the public's perception of deviance.

Social Institutions: Marriage and Family

Essay 18

Conventional Wisdom Tells Us . . . The Nuclear Family Is the Backbone of American Society

Mom, dad, and the kids—is this the unit on which American social life is built? This essay documents the history of family in America, showing that the nuclear family is a relatively recent phenomenon and one that soon may be replaced by other forms of family. In addition, the stability of the nuclear family is explored in light of idyllic stereotypes.

Hearing a speech by a major political figure, surfing the offerings of the vast array of cable stations, or listening to a Top 40 radio station—all show us to be a nation hooked on nostalgia. We yearn for the "good old days," a time when life was simpler, the nation was prosperous, and nuclear families prayed and stayed together.

A return to the family—this plea rests at the heart of current rhetoric. Today's popular culture touts the world of the Andersons (*Father Knows Best*), the Cleavers (*Leave It to Beaver*), the Cunninghams (*Happy Days*), the Huxtables (*The Cosby Show*), and most recently the Barones (*Everybody Loves Raymond*) as an American ideal. One social observer has speculated that the popularity of the television series *The Sopranos* may have been due to protagonist Tony's traditional "yearning for yesterday" views (Teachout

2002). Working dads, stay-at-home moms, and carefree yet respectful kids: Conventional wisdom promotes such units as the cornerstone of this nation.

Many believe that only a return to our nuclear "roots" can provide a cure for our ills. Only the rebirth of nuclear family dominance can restore the backbone of our floundering society. The **nuclear family** refers to a self-contained, self-satisfying unit composed of father, mother, and children. Are conventional sentiments correct? Will a return to this nation's nuclear roots bring stability to American society?

To answer these questions, we need some facts on what families really look like—both today and yesterday. We can start to get a feel for the current living arrangements in the United States by first considering household data. A **household** consists of all the people who occupy a housing unit. The Census Bureau recognizes two categories of households: family and nonfamily. In 2006, there were more than 114.3 million *households* in the United States. Just over half (51%) of all *households* consisted of married-couple families. Another 12% consisted of female-headed families (no husband present), 4% were male-headed families (no wife present), and 32% were nonfamily households (U.S. Census Bureau 2007e: Table H1).

Now let's narrow our focus to families rather than households. The Census Bureau defines a **family** as two or more people residing together and related by birth, marriage, or adoption. In 2006, there were 77.4 million family households in the United States and more specifically 58.1 million *married-couple families*. Of these married-couple families, 31.9 million had children while 26.2 million did not have any children (U.S. Census Bureau 2007e: Table F1). From the children's point of view, however, there is little that resembles the Cleaver or the Anderson families from 1950s TV land. Since the 1970s, the percentage of children living with both parents has been decreasing. In 1970, just over 85% of children lived in two-parent households. In 2005, only 67% of children lived with both parents, 23% lived with mothers only, 5% lived with fathers only, and nearly 5% lived in households with no parents present (U.S. Census Bureau 2005b). In 2005, of the 41.1 million children under 15 living in married-couple families, only 11.2 million had stay-at-home moms (U.S. Census Bureau 2007d: Table 63).

With such departures from the traditional nuclear family, are we charting new terrain? History suggests not. A macro-level analysis of family in America suggests that nonnuclear family forms are common in America's past. A **macro-level analysis** focuses on broad, large-scale social patterns as they exist across contexts or through time. The form of the "typical" American family has changed quite frequently throughout our nation's history. Indeed, historically speaking, the nuclear family is a fairly recent as well as a relatively rare phenomenon. Knowing this, it is difficult to identify the nuclear family as either *the* traditional family format or the rock upon which our nation was built. Furthermore, social history reveals that the nuclear family's effects on American society have often proved less positive than nostalgic images suggest.

Historically, American families have displayed a variety of forms. In preindustrial times, the word *family* conjured up an image quite different from the nuclear ideal. Preindustrial families were truly interdependent economic units. All members of the household—parents, children, and quite often boarders or lodgers—made some contribution to the family's economic livelihood. Work tasks overlapped gender and age groups. However, frequently parental contributions were ended by early mortality. In the preindustrial era, average life expectancy was only 45 years (Rubin 1996). One-third to one-half of colonial children had lost at least one parent by the time they reached 21 years of age (Greven 1970).

During the early stages of industrialization, the face of the family changed. Many families of the era began to approximate the "dad-mom-and-the-kids" model. Yet early industrialization also was a time when the number of extended families in the United States reached its historical high. An **extended family** is a unit containing parent(s), children, and other blood relatives such as grandparents or aunts and uncles. Although the extended family has never been a dominant form in U.S. society, 20% of this period's families contained grandparents, aunts, uncles, or cousins (Hareven 1978).

The stay-at-home mom, a mom who focused exclusively on social activities and household management, first appeared in America's middle-class Victorian families. This new role for Victorian women, however, came on the backs of working-class mothers and children. Many women and children of the working class were hired as domestics for middle-class families. In the early days of industrialization, such women and children were also frequently employed as factory workers. Only as industrialization advanced were working-class women relegated to the home sphere (Padavic and Reskin 2002). By the late 1800s, a typical family included a mother who worked exclusively at home.

Children, however, continued to work outside the home for wages. Indeed, in New England, an 1866 Massachusetts legislative report hailed child labor as a boon to society (TenBensel, Rheinberger, and Radbill 1997). Throughout the Northeast, children were regularly employed in industry or the mines (Bodnar 1987; Schneiderman 1967). In the South, children comprised nearly one-fourth of all textile workers employed at the turn of the century (Wertheimer 1977). Across the nation, approximately 20% of American children were relegated to orphanages because parents could not afford to raise them (Katz 1986).

The modern nuclear family that Americans so admire did not fully come into its own until the 1950s. A careful review of families emerging from this period suggests a unit that both confirms and contradicts conventional wisdom's idyllic models.

Historian Stephanie Coontz (2000) notes that the nuclear unit of the 1950s emerged as a product of the times. The family model of the era developed in response to a distinct set of socioeconomic factors. The post–World War II decade saw great industrial expansion in the United States. The nation enjoyed a tremendous increase in real wages. Furthermore, Americans experienced an all-time high in their personal savings, a condition that resulted largely from U.S. war efforts. The nuclear family became a salient symbol of our country's newfound prosperity.

Consumerism was a significant hallmark of 1950s nuclear families. Spending devoted to products that enhanced family life brought significant increases in our nation's GNP (gross national product). Indeed, the buying power of the 1950s family was phenomenal. During the postwar era, for example, home ownership increased dramatically. There were 6.5 million more homeowners in 1955 than in 1948 (Layman 1995). Federal subsidies enabled families to buy homes with minimal down payments and low-interest (2%–3%) guaranteed 30-year mortgages. It is estimated that half the suburban homes of the 1950s were financed in this way (Coontz 2000).

Consumerism added a new dimension to the American family. By 1950, 60% of all U.S. households owned a car (Layman 1995). Cars, cheap gas, and new highways made mobility a part of family life. The purchase of television sets converted the home into both an entertainment and consumer center. In 1950, there were 1.5 million TV sets in the United States. A year later, there were 15 million (Knauer 1998)! Indeed, 86% of the U.S. population owned TVs by the decade's end, bringing about a 50% decrease in movie theater attendance (Jones 1980). In 1954, Swanson Foods introduced a new food product to complement our fondness for the tube: the frozen TV dinner (Layman 1995). Advertisers took advantage of the new medium to sell their products to the American public like never before. By the end of the 1950s, 2 out of every 10 minutes of TV programming were devoted to advertising (Layman 1995).

Other new and improved tools and appliances (power mowers, electric floor polishers) made the home an efficient and comfortable place to live. Shopping malls appeared on the suburban landscape for ease of access by the growing suburban population (Layman 1995). The growth of the credit card industry strengthened the nuclear family's consumer patterns and encouraged a "buy now, pay later" mentality (Dizard and Gadlin 1990; Ritzer

1995). And pay later we did. Some would argue that the debt-laden 1990s were the legacy of the spend-and-grow mentality established in the 1950s.

The buying power of the 1950s nuclear family suggested a unit with the potential to fulfill all needs. At first glance, this development may seem to be a positive aspect of the era, but some argue that it marked the beginning of a harmful trend in our society—the decline of community commitment. Such critics contend that by emphasizing the "private" values of the individual and the family, the nuclear unit intensified individualism and weakened civic altruism (Bellah et al. 1985; Collier 1991; Sennett 1977). Thus, the seeds of our later decades of self-indulgence and excess may well have been planted in the nuclear family era of the 1950s. As historian Coontz (2000) observes, "The private family . . . was a halfway house on the road to modern 'me-first' individualism" (p. 98).

Consumerism, however, is only a part of the nuclear family's legacy. There were profound changes in domestic behavior patterns as well. In contrast to the ideal lives enjoyed by the Andersons, the Cleavers, or the Cunninghams, home life of the 1950s showed some problematic developments.

For example, couples married at younger ages than earlier generations had. The formation of a nuclear family was an integral part of "making it" in the United States. As a result, many people moved rapidly toward that goal. But the trend toward early marriage was not without cost. National polls showed that 20% of the period's married couples rated their marriages as unhappy—interestingly enough, this figure is higher than any displayed in recent General Social Surveys. In the heyday of the nuclear family, millions of couples resolved their marital differences by living apart (Komarovsky 1962; May 1988; Mintz and Kellogg 1988).

The 1950s also saw couples starting families at younger ages than their predecessors. In addition, families were larger and grew more quickly than families of previous decades. More than ever before or since, married couples faced enormous pressure to have children. Indeed, *Life* magazine declared children to be a built-in recession cure (Jones 1980). But the emphasis on childbearing had some unintended consequences. The period saw a substantial increase in fertility rates, largely due to teenage pregnancies. (Kids were having kids—sound familiar?) Half of all 1950s brides were teenagers who had children within 15 months of getting married (Ahlburg and DeVita 1992). The number of out-of-wedlock babies placed for adoption increased by 80% between 1944 and 1955, and the proportion of pregnant brides doubled during this era (Coontz 2000).

City living was largely abandoned by families in the 1950s. The new young families of the era put down roots in the suburbs, which seemed ideal for breaking with old traditions. The suburbs were well suited to the newly emerging idea of the family as a self-contained unit, a unit that would supplant the community as the center of emotional investment and satisfaction. Fully 83% of the population growth in the 1950s occurred in the suburbs. Indeed, *Fortune* magazine noted that more people arrived in the suburbs each year than had ever arrived at Ellis Island (Jones 1980).

Changing family lifestyles brought changes to the workplace as well. By 1952, 2 million more women were in the workforce than had been there during World War II. This time, however, female entry into the workplace was not fueled by patriotic duty. Rather, many women were entering the workforce to cover the rising costs and debts associated with the nuclear family's consumer mentality (Rubin 1996). Others went to work to help young husbands complete educational and career goals.

The working women of the 1950s faced a workplace less receptive to them than it had been to the "Rosie the Riveters" of the World War II era. The industries that had welcomed women during the war years now preferred to keep American women at home or in dead-end jobs. Popular magazines of the day ran articles examining the social menace and private dysfunction of working women.

The pressures and rejections faced by women in the workplace had important links to the amazing increase in production and use of newly developed tranquilizers: 462,000 pounds of tranquilizers were consumed in 1958, and 1.15 million pounds of tranquilizers were consumed in 1959! Consumers were overwhelmingly female (Coontz 2000).

In considering the realities of the nuclear family, it becomes clear that neither it nor any other family form can be a remedy for social ills. Debates on the virtue of the "good old days" or attempts to identify the "perfect family" form thus seem an exercise in futility. Each historical period, with its own combination of economic, political, and social forces, redefines perfection. Necessity is the mother of invention, and major social changes of our times (delayed and reduced fertility and increases in children born to unmarried mothers, or living in blended families, in gay families, and in single households) will no doubt force us to rethink our conceptions of families and their roles in society.

These thoughts may help us better appreciate the risk entailed in trying to build current social policy around institutions whose times may have come and gone. Perhaps the best course of action today is to resist nostalgic "retrofitting" and instead assist the family in making adaptive changes to our current social circumstances. Such changes may well be the new "traditions" that future generations will yearn to restore.

Learning More About It

Stephanie Coontz offers a detailed historical review of the American family from colonial times to the present in *The Way We Never Were: American Families and the Nostalgia Trap* (New York: Basic Books, 2000). In particular, the author systematically debunks many of our most cherished family myths.

For a picture of the changing face of nuclear families, see Karen V. Hansen's *Not-So-Nuclear Families: Class, Gender, and Networks of Care* (New Brunswick, NJ: Rutgers University Press, 2005).

For reflections on the current state of the American family, see Stephanie Coontz's *The Way We Really Are: Coming to Terms with America's Changing Families* (New York: Basic Books, 1998).

Expressing America: A Critique of the Global Credit Card Society, by George Ritzer (Thousand Oaks, CA: Pine Forge, 1995), presents a sociologically informed analysis of the growth of consumerism and the credit industry. *Explorations in the Sociology of Consumption: Fast Food, Credit Cards, and Casinos* by George Ritzer (Thousand Oaks, CA: Sage, 2001) examines the irrational consequences of consumption.

The Families and Work Institute offers an array of information on changes in the family and the workplace: http://www.familiesandwork.org/. The Child Trends Data Bank offers a collection of pertinent indicators for monitoring trends in child and family welfare: http://www.childtrendsdatabank.org/about.cfm

The following organizations and sites can also help you learn more about family life:

Children's Rights Council
http://www.gocrc.com

Research and Training Center on Family Support and Children's Mental Health
http://www.rtc.pdx.edu

Exercises

1. Use your sociological imagination to identify some key factors that prompt our present nostalgia for the past. For example, think in terms of historical and social developments that may help explain why the past looks so good to us now.

2. We noted in this essay that nuclear families were a product of specific historic and socioeconomic conditions. Consider a family type common to the 1990s,

the "blended family." Blended families are units that consist of previously married spouses and their children from former marriages. What are the current historic and socioeconomic conditions that explain the blended-family phenomenon? What social policy changes might enhance the success of this family form?

3. In the essay on climate (Essay 8), we introduced the reader to functional analysis. Try identifying the various functions (manifest, latent, positive, and negative) of the following trends:

- an increase in women electing to have babies outside of marriage
- a continued increase in the percentage of individuals electing to live alone
- an increase in gay couples having/raising children

Essay 19

Conventional Wisdom Tells Us . . . Marriage Is a Failing Institution

High divorce rates, couples living together, the need for "space," fear of commitment—have such trends doomed the institution of marriage? Here, we discuss research suggesting that the practice of marriage is alive and well despite conventional wisdom to the contrary. We also note the historical "popularity" of divorce in America and speculate on why such a trend marks our culture.

Politicians say it and social commentators lament it: Many of our current social and economic problems stem from deteriorating family values. The conventional wisdom on the matter suggests that high divorce rates are jeopardizing the future of marriage and the family. Many fear that "till death us do part" has become a promise of the past. Recent presidents (representing both political parties) and Congresses have endorsed legislation to protect and encourage marriage. Are our fears and legislative action well grounded? Is marriage really a failing institution?

Most research on the matter suggests little cause for such alarm. Indeed, a variety of indicators document that marriage remains one of society's most viable social institutions. **Marriage** refers to a socially approved economic and sexual union. A **social institution** consists of behavior patterns, social roles, and norms, all of which combine to form a system that ultimately fulfills an important need or function for a society.

The United States has the highest marriage rate of any modern industrial society (United Nations 2002). Most young adults plan to marry at some point in time, although the age of first marriage is increasing. A higher age for first marriage is itself a good sign for the institution, since it is associated with increased marital stability (National Marriage Project 2006). In 2006, only 25% of those 18 years of age and older had never been married. After age 30, the percentage of married women is at least four times higher than the percentage of those who never married (U.S. Census Bureau 2007e, Table A1).

In the United States, the marriage institution enjoys much "positive press." For Americans, marriage appears to be a key to happiness. The majority of married men (65%) and women (60%) in the United States indicate that they are *very* happy with their marriages. While these percentages are lower than those reported 30 years ago, they are trending once again in a positive direction (National Marriage Project 2006). To be sure, the link between marriage and happiness is not unique to the United States. Recent studies involving as many as 64 countries also document that married individuals reported higher levels of happiness (Doyle 2002; Stack and Eshleman 1998). Furthermore, marital bliss appears to have a halo effect and creates what is known as the **happiness gap**—that is, married individuals report higher levels of general happiness than the never-married (Lee and Bulanda 2005).

In addition to raising individuals' happiness quotient, marriage also makes us healthy and wealthy (if not wise). Marriage pays well, especially for those with long unions. Married couples live more economically and save and invest more for their futures than the nonmarried. The long-term effects of these economic benefits are noteworthy: Those who never marry and those who divorce and remain unmarried suffer 75% and 73% reductions in their overall wealth, respectively. The earning power of married men is greater than that of single men with similar education and work backgrounds (National Marriage Project 2006). In addition to boosting financial well-being, marriage is also associated with mental and physical health benefits as well as with the reduction of risky behaviors (Centers for Disease Control 2004b; Duncan, Wilkerson, and England 2006; Preidt 2007; Wilcox, Wait, and Roberts 2007). Perhaps the biggest benefit of pledging "till death us do part" is reducing our chances of death. There is evidence that marriage helps keep us alive: Both married men and women show significantly lower risks of dying than the unmarried, and the effect is not simply due to married individuals selecting healthy partners. The lower mortality benefit remains even after health status is controlled (Bramlett and

Mosher 2002; Lillard and Waite 1995). Having never been married is a strong predictor of premature mortality (Kaplan and Kronick 2006).

The benefits of marriage provide important insight into another recent development: the marriage movement among gays and lesbians. Many same-sex couples want their unions to have the same protection, benefits, and recognition as accorded to traditional marriages. Despite the 1996 Defense of Marriage Act, which defined marriage for federal purposes as being between one man and one woman, efforts are continuing for gender-neutral civil-marriage laws. Massachusetts was the first state to pass such a law, and other states may be moving in that direction. Such developments would appear to be in keeping with ancient practices. Newly uncovered historical evidence suggests that same-sex unions were legally sanctioned and accepted in medieval Europe (Bryner 2007).

Marriage in the United States occurs with great frequency and generates high overall satisfaction for those who enter the union. It is also a right embraced, desired, and defended by many. What, then, explains the alarm sounded by many regarding the institution's failure? Recent changes in the American household are a concern to some. In 2005, 51% of U.S. households were maintained by married couples—this figure is down from 55% in the 1990 census and from 71% in the 1970 census. The second most common type of household (at 26%) consists of people living alone—a figure that has steadily increased from 17% in 1970 (Fields and Casper 2001; Simmons and O'Neill 2001; U.S. Census Bureau 2007d: Table 59). In the past 40 years, we've also seen a 10-fold increase in the number of unmarried, cohabiting couples. It is estimated that today more than half of all first marriages are preceded by living together—a practice that was virtually nonexistent in earlier eras (National Marriage Project 2006). Typically, though, divorce is cited as the primary threat to the health of the marriage institution. While our divorce rate has been declining since the mid-1980s (the 2004 rate of 3.7 per 1,000 population is the lowest in the last quarter-century), the United States still has one of the highest divorce rates in the world (Blankenhorn 2003; United Nations 2004; U.S. Census Bureau 2007d: Table 119). Yet note that our propensity toward divorce is not a recent or modern phenomenon.

Divorce is a rather old and well-established practice in America. Indeed, from the late 1800s through the turn of the new century, the United States has been a world leader with regard to the divorce rate (although for the last few years, a handful of other nations have been posting rates on par with or higher than the U.S. rate) (United Nations 2004). The first American divorce was recorded in 1639 and occurred in Puritan Massachusetts (Riley 1991/1997). The Puritans viewed unsuccessful marriages as obstacles to the harmony deemed important to their society. Consequently, divorce was regarded as a necessary tool for the *safeguarding* of marriage, family, and community (Riley 1991/1997; Salmon 1986; Weisberg 1975).

By the Revolutionary War, divorce was a firmly established practice in the colonies, one defended via the revolutionary values and rhetoric of our newly formed nation. Thomas Jefferson, for example, in preparing notes for a divorce case in Virginia, defended the right to a divorce, using the principles of "independence" and "happiness" (Riley 1991/1997). In 1832, divorce entered the White House. Andrew Jackson was elected to the presidency despite a much publicized marriage to a divorced woman (Owsley 1977).

By the mid-1800s, divorce was characterized as a right of those whose freedom was compromised by an unsuccessful marriage. In the years following the Civil War, the U.S. divorce rate increased faster than the rates of both general population growth and married population growth (Riley 1991/1997). By World War I, this nation witnessed one divorce for every nine marriages (Glick and Sung-Ling 1986). For a short time after World War II, there was one divorce for every three marriages of women over 30! In 1960, the U.S. divorce rate began to increase annually, until the rate doubled and peaked in 1982. Today, it's thought that the lifetime probability of recent first-time marriages ending in divorce or separation is between 40 and 50% (National Marriage Project 2006). When viewed within its historical context, it is clear that divorce is an American tradition.

In considering high divorce rates in the United States, we must take care not to interpret these figures as an indictment of the marriage institution. Despite a lack of success in first-time marriages, most divorced individuals do remarry, and half do so within about three years (Kreider 2005). Fifty-four percent of divorced women remarry within 5 years, and 75% remarry within 10 years (Bramlett and Mosher 2002). High remarriage rates indicate that divorce is clearly a rejection of a specific partner and not a rejection of marriage itself. Indeed, these remarriage patterns have prompted some observers of the family to recognize a new variation on our standard practice of monogamy: namely, serial monogamy. **Monogamy** refers to an exclusive union: for example, one man married to one woman at one time. **Serial monogamy** refers to the practice of successive, multiple marriages—that is, over the course of a lifetime, a person enters into successive monogamous unions.

The prevalence of serial monogamy in the United States suggests that the old adage "Once burned, twice shy" does not seem to apply to people who have been divorced. Indeed, the inclination to remarry—even after one has been "burned"—may provide the greatest testimony to the importance of marriage as a social institution. Even those individuals with extremely costly failed marriages—the ultra rich with expensive prenuptial pacts—are committed to trying marriage again and again. Ronald Perelman (one of Forbes' richest men in America) has had four marriages to date. Donald Trump has been married three times (Zernike 2006).

Is there a positive side to divorce? Some research suggests that divorce does provide a latent function in U.S. society. A **latent function** is an unintended benefit or consequence of a social practice or pattern. Studies show that as divorce rates in the United States increase, so do rates of marital satisfaction. Considering high divorce rates in conjunction with increasing marital satisfaction suggests that, in the long run, divorce may make marriage a healthier institution (Veroff, Douvan, and Kulka 1981). There is also evidence that staying in an unhappy marriage can negatively affect one's self-esteem, life satisfaction, and overall health (Hawkins and Booth 2005). Divorce, then, can improve the well-being of some people. By dissolving unhappy unions, divorce frees individuals of distress and allows them to seek new and, it is hoped, happier unions. Within happy marriages, fear of divorce also may encourage continued dedication to maintaining a successful union. Since most divorces are followed by remarriages, divorce can also be seen as giving people opportunities for growth and second chances in life (Hetherington and Kelly 2002; Visher, Visher, and Pasley 2003).

Any latent functions aside, divorce certainly carries several manifest dysfunctions as well. A **manifest dysfunction** refers to an obvious negative consequence of a social practice or pattern. For example, divorce has highly negative effects on the emotional well-being of ex-spouses. Research documents that ex-spouses face an increased incidence of psychological distress, depression, loneliness, and alcohol use (Hope, Rodgers, and Power, 1999; Johnson and Wu 2002; Williams and Dunne-Bryant 2006). Divorced individuals may also suffer a permanent alteration of their original quality of life (Lucas 2007). Financial hardship also plagues victims of divorce—this is especially true for women. In 2006, the mean income for a married individual 18 years of age and older was $45,242; the mean income for divorced females was $34,941 (U.S. Census Bureau 2007f: Table PINC-02). (The mean income for divorced males 18 years of age and older was $44,630.) Studies show significant decreases in the standard of living for divorced women and their children (Bartfeld 2000; Peterson 1996; Sorenson 1990; Whitehead 1993). In 2005, 5% of married couples were poor in contrast to 29% of female-headed families (Institute for Research on Poverty 2007). Among economically disadvantaged women, poverty rates for divorced women exceed those of never-married women (Lichter, Graefe, and Brown 2003).

The percentage of children living with two married parents has been declining for the last several decades (see Figure 19.1). Each year, about 1 million children must deal with the aftermath of parental divorce (National

Marriage Project 2004). The children of a divorce often pay an undeniably high price for this breakup; they experience negative life outcomes at rates two to three times higher than those for children in married-parent families (National Marriage Project 2006). Children of divorce display greater emotional conflict than children from intact families, conflicts that can persist into adulthood (Amato 2000; Amato and Sobolewski 2001; Lauer and Lauer 1991; Orbuch, Thornton, and Cancio 2000; Wallerstein and Blakeslee 1990). Children of divorce also suffer in terms of their academic achievement, self-concepts, and social relations (Amato 2001a; Reifman et al. 2001). The effects of divorce can follow children into their adult relationships: Young adults from divorced families report less trust in or commitment to their own romantic relationships (Jacquet and Surra 2001). Experiencing a parental divorce at an early age also is associated with poor mental health in early and young adulthood (Chase-Lansdale, Cherlin, and Kiernan 1995; Cherlin, Chase-Lansdale, and McRae 1998).

Figure 19.1   Percentage of Children Under 18 Living With Both Parents: 1970–2005

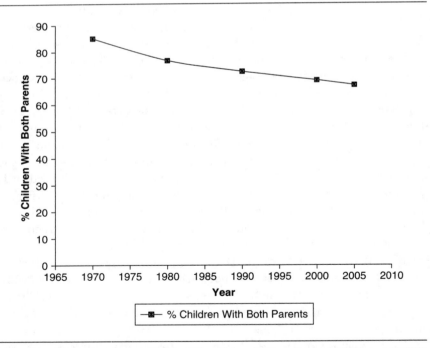

SOURCE: U.S. Census Bureau 2005b. "The Living Arrangements of Children in 2005" Population Profile of the United States: Dynamic Version http://www.census.gov/population/ pop-profile/dynamic/LivArrChildren.pdf

Divorce can erode bonds between parents and children, especially those between fathers and their children (Amato and Sobolewski 2001; Bulduc, Caron, and Logue 2007; Hallie 2007; Scott and Church 2001). These bonds are not necessarily replaced by step-parents. Research suggests that children in step-families fare no better than children in single-parent families (National Marriage Project 2006). Furthermore, the children of divorce are likely to "lose" one of their parents. Despite a growing trend toward joint parental custody of children, the number of fathers living apart from their children continues to grow (Leite and McKenry 2002). In 2006, of the 20.6 million children living with just one parent, 83% (17.1 million) lived with their mothers, and only 17% (3.4 million) lived with their fathers (U.S. Census Bureau 2007e: Table C2). While one-quarter of noncustodial fathers see their children at least once a week, approximately one-third have no contact at all over the course of the year (Family Strengthening Policy Center 2005; National Child Care Information Center 2004). In general, there is a gradual withdrawal of fathers from their children's lives. And as visits with noncustodial parents decrease, so does the receipt of child support payments (Family Strengthening Policy Center 2005). The most recent census data indicate that only 45.3% of custodial mothers receive full child support payments from fathers (Grall 2006). Lack of child support is not the only risk of "out of touch" fathers. Absent fathers can have a negative impact on a son's self-esteem and his ability to form intimate relationships (Balcom 2002). Having an absent father also may increase the risk of early sexual activity among daughters (Ellis et al. 2003; McLanahan 2002).

Although divorce clearly poses serious problems for a society, the practice appears firmly rooted in the United States. Ironically, some suggest that the prevalence of divorce in our nation may stem from the heightened health and longevity of Americans. Historian Lawrence Stone (1989) argues that divorce is the functional substitute for death. In earlier periods of our history, marriages—good and bad alike—were typically terminated by death. The high mortality rates that characterized colonial America, for example, guaranteed that most marriages lasted less than 12 years (Fox and Quit 1980). But as life-spans grew longer and longer, marriages faced new tests. In the current day, promises of "till death us do part" now constitute oaths that can traverse decades. Surely, such a profound demographic shift has had an effect on our divorce rates (Wells 1982).

In addition to increased life expectancy, some contend that the ready availability of divorce in the United States helps explain the prevalence of the practice. By 1970, every state in the union permitted divorce. In that same year, no-fault divorce was introduced in California, and many states quickly followed suit.

Yet although easy access may contribute to the high rate of divorce in the United States, history reveals that the "absence" of a divorce option does little to save bad marriages. For example, in states that were slow to recognize divorce as a legal option (typically, the southern states), marriages were far from indissoluble. In lieu of legal divorce, other adaptations were readily devised: annulments, desertion, migratory divorces (divorces sought after relocations to other states), premarital contracts, and separation agreements. Indeed, South Carolina's refusal to recognize divorce resulted in a curious development in the state's inheritance laws: Mistresses (another popular adaptation to troubled marriages) were legally precluded from inheriting *any more than 25%* of a husband's estate (Riley 1991/1997).

But longer life-spans and ease of access do not tell the whole story regarding divorce in America. Our high divorce rates must be examined in light of some core American values. Consider, for example, American values relating to romantic love. Americans have long identified romantic love as the most important dimension of marriage. Indeed, it is the power and passion of love that convinces us to separate from our **families of orientation** (the families into which we are born) and form new unions with others.

The principle of a love-based marriage guarantees excitement and euphoria for the individuals involved. But linking marriage to romantic love simultaneously introduces a high risk to the institution as a whole. Historian Stephanie Coontz argues that the origins of our modern divorce patterns are firmly rooted in the idea that marriage should be based on love (Coontz 2007). Love is a fickle enterprise. When the sparks of passion die, love can be fleeting. Love's fickle nature is exacerbated by the fact that people frequently fall in love with possibilities rather than realities—that is, they fall for what they *want* their future spouses to be rather than what they are (Berscheid and Hatfield 1983). Assumed similarity is common for married couples, but it is greatest for people who are dating (Schul and Vinokur 2000; Watson, Hubbard, and Wiese 2000). We also find ourselves juggling competing notions of love as we move through our lives. These competing views can make love an ambiguous basis for marriage and guarantee that individuals will have to work hard and compromise and change to keep love and marriages going (Swidler 2001). Consider also that a majority of men report seeking a "soul-mate" relationship when selecting a wife. Assuming that "soul-mate" has a romantic component, these men may well be willing to delay marriage while waiting to meet that perfect wife or to trade in one partner for a more satisfying other (National Marriage Project 2004). Indeed, professional "matchmakers" recognize the perils of matches based on romance and soul-mate searches and prefer using more rational strategies (Thernstrom 2005).

In short, love, especially passionate love, can and often does fade. And faded love can leave a marriage with *no raison d'être,* making it a union ripe for divorce. Indeed, some of the earliest U.S. divorce petitions—filed in the 1600s and 1700s—referenced lost affections and love as a justification for divorce (Riley 1991/1997). Knowing this, love may not be the strongest foundation for the marriage institution. Indeed, many other cultures of the world do not base marriages on love; some regard a loved-based marriage as a foolish endeavor (Jankowiak and Fischer 1992). Instead, marriages are arranged for practical, social, or economic reasons. There is some indication that these alternate factors result in more stable unions with higher survival rates than those motivated by love (Dion and Dion 1996; Levine 1993; Shaw 2006).

Romantic love is only one American value that may be linked to the nation's high divorce rates. The pursuit of personal freedom, self-actualization, and self-gratification—all values on which the establishment and expansion of our country were based—are also quite compatible with our well-exercised "right" to divorce. Consider that the westward expansion of this country was fueled, in part, by settlers who carried the spirit of rugged individualism. Many who migrated to the West did so without the support or company of recalcitrant spouses. Under such conditions, liberal divorce laws in western states and territories proved to be a valuable mechanism for resolving such migratory conflicts.

Liberal divorce policies also proved a boon to self-actualizing business entrepreneurs. For example, when social pressure from anti-divorce factions saw Nevada increase its divorce residency requirement from six months to a year, Nevada businesspeople vigorously protested the change. Such a change posed a threat to the valuable revenues typically generated by the "divorce trade." Thus, in the interest of capturing more and more of the dollars spent in pursuing a divorce, Nevada eventually dropped its residency requirement to six weeks (Riley 1991/1997).

If core American values contribute to high divorce rates, then a reversal of divorce trends in the United States may demand major cultural changes—changes that would be difficult to execute. For example, increasing marital stability may require that love give way to less romantic criteria in making marriage decisions. Yet that such a shift would be made seems highly unlikely. A cursory review of television programming, movie plots, literature, or music clearly demonstrates that Americans are "in love" with the notion of love. Viewers of romantic programming tend to have higher idealistic expectations of love (Segrin and Nabi 2002). Our romantic delusions may also explain the fact that long-distance dating relationships are found to be more stable than geographically close dating relationships. Idealized views of love appear to fuel this paradox: Absence makes the heart grow fonder.

Curiously enough, when long-distance relationships become close-distance ones, they become unstable (Stafford and Merolla 2007). Furthermore, surveys from the 1960s through the 1980s document an increase in Americans' commitment to love as the basis for marriage (Simpson, Campbell, and Berscheid 1986). More recently, an overwhelming majority of American college students indicated that they would not be willing to enter into a loveless marriage. Decidedly larger numbers of non-American students, however, were willing to entertain this possibility (Levine 1993).

Similarly, individualism's dire effects on many a happy marriage suggest that decreasing divorce rates may require an exchange of individualism for concerns of community. Again, however, such a change is unlikely. Individualism is arguably the "defining" American value. (Consider again, for instance, that single-person households are the second most common household type in the United States today.) Proposed solutions to other social problems, such as welfare, poverty, and homelessness, recommend a recommitment to individual accomplishment and responsibility. The "me-generation" of the 1980s, the decline in social connections, and the economic threats of the 1990s have put concerns for "Number 1" at the forefront of American attentions (Cerulo 2002, 2008a; Collier 1991; Etzioni 1994, 1996; Putnam 2000).

In contrast, many feel that concerns for community have gradually come to occupy the "back burner" of the American agenda. In recent years, national leaders such as former Speaker of the House Newt Gingrich have been known to fight community-minded programs (i.e., the National Youth Corp), arguing that volunteerism should be a "personal decision" rather than an institutionalized practice. Some social scientists contend that the average U.S. citizen may now share the Gingrich mentality. Robert Putnam, a political scientist who examines trends in community participation, notes a marked decline in civic involvement. He argues that few U.S. citizens are actively engaged in solving problems such as crime, drug abuse, homelessness, and unemployment—all threats to community stability (Putnam 1995, 2000).

As community loses its place on the American agenda, some speculate that family has come to fill the void. In many ways, family has become the substitute for community. In contrast to the America of the 1930s and 1940s, where "God, Home, and Country" were the rule, the America of recent decades finds religion and civic concerns overpowered by issues of family. Since 1995, "spending time with family" has been in the top three favorite leisure-time activities of Americans (Harris Poll 2004). A growing percentage of American youth report that having a good marriage and family life is extremely important to them (National Marriage Project 2006). As we move into young adulthood, our sense of family obligation increases

(Fuligni and Pedersen 2002). As we age, the emotional support we receive from our families is an important resource, one that increases our life expectancies (Ross and Mirowsky 2002). And the family is the backbone of supportive services for the aged and the disabled (American Association of Retired Persons 2003b).

Ironically, Americans' heavy investments in family may make this unit increasingly vulnerable to the practice of divorce. When family experiences fail to yield the expected emotional benefits, American cultural traditions and laws make it possible to "cut our losses" and invest anew. Oddly enough, our restricted family focus may render the family more, rather than less, vulnerable to disruption (Giddens 1992).

In considering the reasons for high divorce rates in the United States, some additional factors require attention. Certain social structural changes also mitigate the likelihood of waning divorce rates. For example, increased labor force participation of both married and unmarried women and high geographic mobility both create social contexts that increase the risk of marital dissolution (South 2001; South and Lloyd 1995). The practice of cohabiting before marriage is growing—about half of all first marriages are preceded by cohabitation. Yet there is a body of research that suggests that marriages preceded by cohabitation tend to have higher divorce rates (National Marriage Project 2006). Furthermore, it is estimated that 40% of children spend time in a cohabiting family (Bumpass and Lu 2000). Such arrangements as well as the reality of having divorced parents may offer children counterproductive lessons about commitment (Amato 2001b). The rise in single-person households over the last few decades may make it easier for some individuals to contemplate the prospect of "going it alone" after a divorce. Last, there has been a dramatic change in the relationship between marriage and having children. Not only are Americans desiring and having fewer children (six out of ten Americans think the ideal family size is two or fewer children), but children are also becoming less of a priority in marriages. By a margin of three to one, Americans see the main purpose of marriage as being personal fulfillment and happiness (68%) rather than having and raising children (21%; Pew Research Center 2007). Furthermore, more and more women are electing to have children outside of marriage. In 2004, 36% of all births were to unmarried women (Martin et al. 2006). These changes in attitudes and fertility patterns may mean that some unhappy spouses will perceive fewer obstacles to divorce.

Is marriage a failing institution? Hardly. But along with the health of marriage in America comes the health of divorce. Arguably, divorce is itself an established institution, one that facilitates the pursuit of some core American values. Without some changes to these values, we can well expect both marriage and divorce to be permanent features of society.

Learning More About It

Historian Stephanie Coontz explores the place of love and emotional commitment in the history of marriage in her book, *Marriage, a History: From Obedience to Intimacy, or How Love Conquered Marriage* (New York: Penguin, Reprint Edition 2006).

In *Alone Together: How Marriage in America Is Changing,* Paul Amato, Alan Booth, David Johnson, and Stacy Rogers examine recent adaptive changes (Cambridge, MA: Harvard University Press, 2007).

In *Same-Sex Marriage* (New York: Cambridge University Press, 2006) Kathleen Hull uses interview data from more than 70 people involved in same-sex relationships to explore the cultural practices and legal debates surrounding the issue of gay marriage.

The PBS documentary *Let's Get Married* (November 2002) provides a brief introduction to the new "marriage movement," its impact on government policies, and its reception by citizens and politicians alike: http://www.pbs.org/wgbh/pages/frontline/shows/marriage/

Sara McLanahan offers a very readable review of how children fare without fathers in "Life Without Father: What Happens to the Children?" (*Contexts* 1 (Spring):35–44).

Visit Public Agenda Online and click on the *Issue Guides* link. There, you'll find an overview of major family issues, competing perspectives on future policy, and public opinions on an assortment of family topics: http://www.publicagenda.org

Exercises

1. Trying to understand divorce in America provides a good opportunity for exercising our sociological imagination. Divorce, as it currently stands in our society, is not just a "private trouble"—a personal failing of the individual. Rather, it is a "public issue"—a phenomenon tied to myriad broader social, cultural, and historical events. Confusing public issues with private troubles results in misinformed social policy. Public issues cannot be remedied with individual-oriented solutions appropriate to private troubles. Instead, public issues require that we pay attention to changes in social forces that are larger than and transcend individuals. Recognizing divorce as a public issue, identify three appropriate targets for our reform efforts.

2. Go to your local or university library and collect recent statistics on national divorce rates, broken down by the following groups: African Americans, Asian Americans, Hispanics, and Whites of Western European origin. Attempt

to explain any differences you find using information on the cultural values held within each group.

3. Love is the basis on which current American marriages are built. Think of at least two other possible foundations for the institution of marriage. In each case, what are the likely ramifications of changing the "rules" of choosing a mate?

4. The Center for Marriage and Families at the Institute for American Values offers an index for tracking the health of marriage in the United States (http://center.americanvalues.org/?p=54). Take a look at the indicators used by the index. Are they reasonable? Are there any serious omissions?

Social Institutions:
The Economy

Essay 20

Conventional Wisdom Tells Us . . . Welfare Is Ruining This Country

A frequently expressed opinion when talk turns to welfare reform is that too many people are on the dole and too many recipients have other options. In this essay, we review some of the least understood dimensions of welfare and explore exactly where welfare moneys are going.

In conventional wisdom, charges against the U.S. welfare system abound. Welfare recipients are thought to be lazy people. They are accused of lacking the motivation to earn an honest living, preferring instead to take handouts from the government. Furthermore, many believe that the welfare rolls are continuously growing and riddled with fraud. Welfare is often discussed as a program plagued by able-bodied con artists—people with no financial need—who nonetheless manage to collect welfare checks.

Conventional wisdom also tells us that welfare fails to help those on the dole. Rather, it creates further dependency among its recipients. As such, many argue that welfare expenditures are ruining this nation. Welfare represents too great a burden for a government facing unsettled financial times.

Is the conventional wisdom regarding welfare accurate? Is welfare simply a tax on the economy, one destroying American initiative? A fair assessment of the system requires us to take a second look.

Many of the common and persistent beliefs about welfare are largely a product of the **Aid to Families with Dependent Children (AFDC)** era. The AFDC was a public assistance program rooted in the Social Security Act of 1935. Concerns about AFDC helped fuel the clamor for welfare reform. Reform materialized in 1996 with the passage of the Personal Responsibility and Work Opportunity Reconciliation Act (PRWORA), which abolished the AFDC program and replaced it with a new, time-limited program: **Temporary Assistance to Needy Families (TANF)**. TANF is a "welfare-to-work" program. It gives states much flexibility in structuring their welfare programs, but it imposes a restriction on federal funding: Families are subject to a lifetime limit of five years of support. TANF was implemented in all 50 states within 18 months of its 1996 passage (California was the last state to put TANF into effect). In this essay, we will look back at the AFDC era as well as at the current TANF program to see whether there is any basis for popular views about welfare.

Are welfare rolls spinning out of control? Data suggest that the answer to the question is no. A family is considered welfare dependent if more than 50% of its income is derived from welfare programs—for example, AFDC/TANF, food stamps, SSI (Supplemental Security Income). In 1996, 5.6% of the population was welfare dependent. In 2003, 3.4 million fewer Americans (or 3.6% of the population) were so classified. If we focus exclusively on AFDC/TANF caseloads, we see that in 2004, the average monthly number of TANF recipients was 5.4 million, a number that is 57% *lower* than the average monthly caseload for AFDC in 1996. While TANF is credited with these dramatic declines, the historical record also indicates that our welfare ranks have always been relatively small (U.S. Department of Health and Human Services 2006).

Do welfare recipients live "high on the hog" and have more and more kids just to keep the benefits flowing? In the pre-welfare reform period, the average monthly cash benefits to an AFDC family amounted to less than $500, an amount that was insufficient for lifting families out of poverty. Under the TANF program, cash benefits are even lower. The 2006 congressional report shows an average monthly cash payment of $360 for a program family. Also note that in both eras, AFDC and TANF, the typical welfare family has been small. In 1996, an AFDC family averaged 1.9 children; in 2004 a TANF family averaged 1.8 children (U.S. Department of Health and Human Services 2006).

Are welfare recipients simply lazy? No doubt some are. After all, laziness is a trait found in all social groups. However, it would be wrong to assume that the *typical* welfare recipient is a social loafer. The TANF program is essentially about assisting mothers with *dependent children*. (This was also true for the old AFDC program.) Today, fully 30% of adult TANF recipients are employed or in community service positions. Consider also that in 2004, nearly 41% of the TANF caseload consisted of "child-only" units—families in which there are no eligible adults in the assistance unit (U.S. Department of Health and Human Services 2006).

To be sure, the perceived positive value of work is the cornerstone of TANF: to receive temporary assistance, recipients *must* get job training or find work. At first glance, this would seem like a step in the right direction. TANF should provide some strong incentives that will move individuals from welfare to work. What could be wrong with this reasoning and policy? If you listen to the critics, there's plenty wrong.

Consider again the typical welfare family: mothers with dependent children. Critics of the "welfare-to-work" reform raise three key objections. First, TANF forces poor mothers to choose work *over* caring for their children. Eligibility requirements make full-time mothering, a choice for the economically advantaged, a nonoption for the poor (Boushey 2002; Jones-DeWeever et al. 2003; Oliker 2000). Perhaps this bind helps explain a newly emergent group: the no work, no welfare group. In an average month, there are roughly 1 million poor single mothers (with approximately 2 million children) who neither work nor collect TANF benefits (Parrott and Sherman 2006). Second, critics charge that TANF work requirements do little to combat the root cause of welfare: poverty. The disturbing truth is that many of the jobs currently available in our country—especially service sector jobs earmarked for women—simply pay too little to keep a family from the grips of poverty (Edin and Lein 1997a; Padavic and Reskin 2002; Rangarajan 1998). Nearly two-thirds of the projected fastest growing occupations for the next decade (many of which are female-dominated occupations like home health aides) will offer weekly median earnings that are below average earnings for all occupations (U.S. Department of Labor 2007b). Many single mothers who leave welfare for work still remain poor or near poor and see only modest income growth over time (Parrott and Sherman 2006). The **poverty threshold** is the federal government's designation of the total annual income a family requires to meet its basic needs; this figure is adjusted annually for inflation. Currently, the poverty threshold for a family of three (e.g., a mother and two children) is $16,242—that is, a family whose income is below this amount is designated as "poor" (U.S. Census Bureau 2007g). In 2005, 37 million people were below the poverty threshold (U.S. Census Bureau 2006d).

Approximately 2% of women over 16 years of age are full-time workers holding minimum wage jobs (i.e., $5.85 an hour in 2007). These women will earn approximately $12,000 a year. This amount would fail to put *any* working parent above the poverty threshold (U.S. Census Bureau 2007g).

Indeed, an analysis of Los Angeles County's welfare-to-work program found that 78% of current and former welfare recipients who entered the labor force since 1998 were nonetheless earning incomes below the poverty threshold (Rivera 2003). Even for those families who leave TANF, the average monthly income is close to the poverty threshold, with wages often in the $7–$8 an hour range (Parrott and Sherman 2006).

A third objection raised by critics of the welfare-to-work strategy is that the declines in caseloads achieved since the inception of TANF are occurring on the backs of the most vulnerable. Over the course of its first decade, TANF is serving fewer and fewer *eligible* families. Indeed fewer than half of families poor enough to qualify for TANF are actually receiving benefits. Between 2000 and 2004, the number of children living below half the poverty line has increased, yet the number of children getting assistance from TANF has declined! This decline delivers a double injury. These families miss out not only on cash benefits but also on noncash benefits for needy adults and children (Parrott and Sherman 2006).

As counterintuitive as it may seem, accepting a minimum- or low-wage job can actually prove a "costly" proposition for the poor. Employment can deprive former welfare recipients of other essential benefits, such as food stamps, housing assistance, and health care (Edin and Lein 1997a; Peterson 2002b; Rangarajan 1998). Follow-up studies find that many former TANF recipients are unaware that they may still be eligible for food stamps and Medicaid benefits after they leave the welfare rolls (Quint, Widom, and Moore 2001). Census data indicate that working actually hurts the chances of health care coverage for the poor: 54.5% of the working poor have health insurance, in contrast to 63.4% of the nonworking poor (Mills 2001). Other follow-up research on newly employed welfare recipients indicates a similar outcome—new workers experience a decline in access to employment-based health insurance post-TANF reforms (Jones-DeWeever et al. 2003). For some, "work first" employment has come at the cost of pursuing postsecondary education (Jones-DeWeever et al. 2003; Mazzeo, Rab, and Eachus 2003). Welfare-to-work programs also appear to have an adverse effect on participants' adolescent children who are experiencing increases in below-average school performances, repeating grades, and in receiving special education services (MDRC 2003).

Low-paying jobs also fail to provide a solution to a major obstacle facing poor female heads of households: child care. Research has shown that child care is central to improving employment outcomes and to families staying off welfare. Unfortunately, however, TANF child support assistance peaked in 2003 (Parrott and Sherman 2006). To be sure subsidies make a difference. In a national study of low-income families, subsidy payments reduced their child care costs by more than half (Layzer and Goodson 2006). In the major urban areas of 49 out of 50 states, it is more costly to provide a four-year-old with child care for a year than to pay a year's tuition for an older child at a public college (Schulman 2000). On average, working families devote 9% of their yearly earnings to child care. Child care, then, can easily be the second-largest expense (behind rent or mortgages) in a family budget (Giannerelli, Adelman, and Schmidt 2003). Ironically, as family income *decreases,* the proportion spent on child care *increases.* A family in poverty must be prepared to devote more than a third of its income to child care costs (Smith 2000). A recent report by the Children's Defense Fund charges that every state's child care subsidy system comes up short on quality and availability. Some states have unreasonably low income cutoffs (e.g., $25,000 for a family of three), others have excessively high co-payments, and still others are strapped for the resources to fund programs and as a result have long waiting lists (Children's Defense Fund 2001). At present, even when all federal funding is combined, only one in four eligible children are assisted with child care subsidies (National Council of Churches 2003). Without much-needed increases in TANF reauthorization funding, it is estimated that hundreds of thousands of children in working families will lose access to child care assistance in the near future (Fremstad 2003; Parrott and Mezey 2003).

The harsh truth is that hard work does not necessarily save one from the need for government assistance. In 2004, nearly 6% of those in the labor force were classified as "working poor"—that is, these individuals are employed but not making enough to get above the poverty threshold. Furthermore, the majority of the working poor (58%) are poor *despite holding full-time jobs* (U.S. Department of Labor 2006d). Homelessness—perhaps the most visible marker of poverty—offers additional evidence that work and poverty are not mutually exclusive. Recent surveys have found that about one-quarter of the urban homeless are employed. Their earnings, however, are *not* enough to pay for a place to live. In every state in the nation, above minimum wages are needed to secure one and two bedroom apartments at fair market value (National Coalition for the Homeless 2006).

The plight of the working poor is especially stark when we consider the effects on the family. For example, a family of four, with both parents working full-time at minimum wage jobs, will just barely keep their collective heads above the poverty line (using the current poverty threshold figures). Change the picture to a single-parent family—where only one parent's salary pays the bills—and the family will almost certainly fall into the clutches of poverty or near poverty. In 2005, the poverty rate for working-male-headed households with related children under 18 (no wife present) was 14%, while the rate for working-female-headed households with related children under 18 (no husband present) was 30%. When the children at home are under six years old, the poverty rate for these working fathers climbs to 20%, and the rate for these working mothers climbs to 42% The financial state of children in single-parent homes is quite precarious: Such children are much *more likely* to be poor than their counterparts in a two-parent family where both parents work (e.g., such families with children under six saw poverty rates of 3.3% in 2005; U.S. Census Bureau 2006a: Tables POV15, POV 16). With the development of unforeseen hardships such as illness, layoffs, home or car repairs, and so on, a hardworking, low-income family could quickly fall into official poverty. A hardworking family could all too easily find itself in need of welfare.

Do those who enter the welfare system become hopelessly dependent on it? The recent overhaul of the U.S. welfare program was tied to this assumption. Yet a large body of research proves that the assumption is false. Those who turn to the government for financial help tend not to seek that assistance for very long. Despite the rather prevalent belief that welfare is a chronic dependency condition (that is, a long-lasting condition assumed to destroy one's will to work), most people receive assistance for relatively short periods of time. Between 1992 and 1994, 30% of AFDC recipients spent only four months or less in the program. Between 2001 and 2003, half of TANF recipients spent only four months or less in the program. Between 1991 and 2000, fewer than 4% of AFDC/TANF participants received assistance for 9 to 10 years (U.S. Department of Health and Human Services 2006).

The welfare changes introduced by the TANF mandate relatively short assistance periods. In general, an adult-headed family is limited to 60 months of TANF-funded assistance *over its lifetime*. States are free to set shorter time limits if they so desire. Twenty states have done so (Schott 2000). Given the mandated time limits, many TANF recipients are motivated to leave welfare as soon as they begin working in order to "stop the clock" on their lifetime eligibility. Such findings would seem to confirm that welfare is not an enticing lifelong choice.

It is also important to note that most welfare stays are not the result of being born to poverty. Rather, ordinary life events such as unemployment, illness, or divorce can easily push one into poverty. A decrease in earnings was the single most common event prompting single mothers to seek TANF assistance according to a recent congressional report (U.S. Department of Health and Human Services 2006). Consider also that in 2005, 16% of Americans were without health care insurance. In the past, employment typically offered some health insurance benefits for workers, but this is no longer the case. The percentage of people with employment-based health coverage has dropped from 70% in 1987 to just under 60% in 2005. One-third of U.S. firms (and nearly two-thirds of small firms) did not offer health coverage in 2005 (National Coalition on Health Care 2007). Imagine, then, the potentially devastating financial consequences for those families facing a medical emergency. Given the relative ease with which one can slip into poverty, it is actually quite remarkable that only a very small percentage of American families remain permanently poor and therefore permanently tied to welfare programs.

Suppose we all agreed that most welfare recipients are hardworking, honest individuals who simply need some temporary help. Isn't it still the case that the welfare system represents too great a financial burden for our country? To answer this question accurately, we must carefully distinguish among the terms *poverty, public assistance programs* (a.k.a. *welfare programs*), and *social insurance programs* of the welfare state.

Poverty refers to an economic state in which one's annual income is below the threshold judged necessary to support a predetermined minimal standard of living. Between 2000 and 2005, the national poverty rate increased before dipping slightly in 2006 to just over 12% (DeNavas-Walt et al. 2007; U.S. Census Bureau 2006a: Table POV46). To be sure, we have experienced double-digit poverty rates in the United States for the last quarter of a century. Yet the percentage of families receiving AFDC/TANF over this same time period has never climbed out of the single digits. A few years prior to TANF reforms, just over 5% of the population received AFDC assistance. In 2004, 1.8% of the population were TANF recipients. Similarly, since TANF reform the number of children receiving benefits has been cut in half and is presently at an all-time low rate of less than 6%. Only a small percentage of the total population receives food stamps: 8% in 2004. For the past quarter-century, the percentage of all Americans who receive SSI (Supplemental Security Income for elderly, blind, or disabled individuals meeting income eligibility) has hovered around 2% (U.S. Department of Health and Human Services 2006). Clearly, only a small percentage of Americans participate in "traditional" welfare programs. More surprising, however, is the fact that only a portion of those living in poverty actually look to the government for help via some public assistance program.

Public assistance programs are those directed exclusively at the eligible poor—that is, recipients must meet income and, most recently, behavioral requirements. One might think that once determined to be eligible, families would rush to receive their due. This is hardly the case. Less than half of families eligible for TANF enroll and receive benefits (Parrott and Sherman 2006). In 2004, less than 30% of children in poverty were receiving TANF assistance. Similarly, only 64% of the poor participate in the food stamps program (U.S. Department of Health and Human Services 2006). These figures would suggest that public assistance is a safety net that many Americans would rather live without.

Underutilized or not, public assistance programs are costly. In 2006, Congress reauthorized funding for TANF with an annual cap of $16.5 billion. The total federal cost for the food stamp program was $27 billion in 2004. SSI expenditures totaled $37 billion in 2004 (U.S. Department of Health and Human Services 2006). But as expensive as these programs may seem, their costs wane in comparison to other government expenditures. Consider for instance that the 2007 federal outlays (estimated) for Social Security and Medicare were $582 and $367 billion, respectively. The 2008 budget allocates $481.5 billion for the Department of Defense base budget (Office of Management and Budget 2007). As these figures suggest, America's financial burdens lie not with antipoverty public assistance programs like TANF and food stamps, but elsewhere. More specifically, America's financial woes are located in broad social insurance programs (e.g., Social Security and Medicare) as well as in security spending. **Social insurance programs** are those that require payroll contributions from future beneficiaries. Neither eligibility for nor benefits from these programs are linked to financial need.

In reality, social insurance programs—not antipoverty public assistance programs—are our largest "welfare" expenditures. Indeed, these social insurance programs constitute the largest part of what we have come to define as America's "welfare state"—a state that transcends poverty per se and instead offers protection based on our more general rights of citizenship (Bowles and Gintis 1982). In 2006, only 9% of the federal budget was devoted to poverty-linked "safety net" programs while 19% was dedicated to Medicare/Medicaid, 21% to Social Security, 21% to Defense and Homeland Security, and 21% to paying for a variety of public services. The last 9% was earmarked for paying the interest on our national debt (Center on Budget and Policy Priorities 1998).

When we turn to facts and figures, we can quickly discredit the conventional wisdom on welfare. Yet we must also concede that year after year, conventional wisdom on this subject overpowers facts and figures. Why?

Some of our misconceptions regarding welfare no doubt are fueled by the profound changes occurring in the economic and occupational structure of our society. Americans today face a growing gap between the rich and poor—a gap that is setting all-time "highs" and "lows." Simply put, the rich are getting richer, and the poor are getting poorer (see Table 20.1). This long-standing trend makes the United States the most unequal democracy in the world (Boshara 2003). A recent Congressional Budget Office study found that over the last quarter-century, the top 1% of families saw their

Table 20.1   Average After-Tax Income by Income Groups—2004

	After Tax Income (2004)	Dollar Change Over 2003 (in 2004 dollars)	% Change
Top 1%	$867,800	$145,500	20.1%
Top one-fifth	$155,200	$11,600	8.1%
Next one-fifth	$67,600	$2,000	3.0%
Middle one-fifth	$48,400	$1,700	3.6%
Next one-fifth	$32,700	$900	2.8%
Bottom one-fifth	$14,700	$200	1.4%

SOURCES: Sherman and Aron-Dine (2007) and Center on Budget and Policy Priorities (2007): http://www.cbpp.org/1-23-07inc.htm#_ftn4

after-tax incomes rise 176%, the top fifth saw gains of 69%, and the middle fifth experienced a 21% gain (Sherman and Aron-Dine 2007). In 2005, the richest 1% of Americans (roughly those making more than $350,000) received 19% of the total national income. The poorest 20% received just 3.4% of the nation's income (Center for American Progress 2007). Tax cuts since 2001 have served to increase the concentration of income in the top income groups and exacerbate income inequality in the United States. In 2006, the bottom fifth of income groups received tax cuts that averaged $20 and raised after-tax income by 0.3%. The middle fifth received cuts that averaged $740 and raised after-tax income by 2.5%. The top 1 percent received tax cuts that averaged $44,200 and raised after-tax income by 5.4% (Sherman and Aron-Dine 2007).

Another telling way to understand the concentration of wealth in the hands of the few is by looking at the increases in millionaires and "decamillionaires" (individuals worth $10 million or more). In the past 25 years, the number of millionaires in the United States has more than doubled and in 2005 reached a record high of nearly 9 million (Sahadi 2006). During this same period, the number of "deca-millionaires" tripled, and they currently number approximately 250,000 (Boshara 2003; Northern Trust 2006).

In the face of present economic circumstances, intergenerational upward mobility is no longer a birthright for most Americans. **Intergenerational upward mobility** refers to social status gains by children vis-à-vis their parents. In the 1950s, the average male worker could expect a 50% increase in income over the course of his working lifetime. This expectation is no longer a safe bet for the average worker. Rather, present-day workers find themselves competing in a global economy. As a result of this turn of events, many American jobs have been lost to other countries, and wages for low-skill jobs have suffered a marked decline. Furthermore, present-day workers find themselves in an occupational landscape that is increasingly dominated by computer-related, health-related, and service industry jobs (U.S. Department of Labor 2007c). The fastest growing occupations are not necessarily routes to increase one's wealth quickly. For the projected top 10 fastest growing occupations in the United States, 4 promise low or very low earnings: a maximum of $28,570 a year (see Table 20.2) (U.S. Census Bureau 2008: Table 600). Looking ahead to 2014, generally the lowest paying occupations (all of which require some on-the-job training) will promise the greatest number of jobs (e.g., 974,000 home health aide jobs, 589,000 medical assistant jobs, and 988,000 personal and home care aide jobs). Consequently, many of those entering the labor force in the next few years will be faced with a serious challenge to upward mobility.

Shifts in the occupational and economic structure of our society have shaken the very core of American values. Americans invest heavily in the idea that they can and will work their way up the socioeconomic ladder; the economic shifts described here threaten that belief. The growing inability to achieve the "American Dream" has left many people frustrated and searching for someone to blame. In this regard, the poor—and welfare recipients in particular—are easy scapegoats. The logic of the welfare system is completely inconsistent with fundamental American values: individual effort, equal opportunity, success, and upward mobility. Rather than promoting hard work and achievement, welfare programs are thought to institutionalize

Table 20.2   Top 10 Fastest Growing Occupations, 2004–2014

Occupations	Earnings
1. Home health aides	Very Low
2. Network system and data communication analysts	Very High
3. Medical assistants	Low
4. Physician assistants	Very High
5. Computer software engineers: applications	Very High
6. Physical therapist assistants	High
7. Dental hygienists	Very High
8. Computer software engineers: systems software	Very High
9. Dental assistants	Low
10. Personal and home care aides	Very Low

Very High = $43,600 and over
High   = $28,580–43,590
Low   = $20,190–28,570
Very Low = up to $20,180

SOURCE: U.S. Census Bureau 2008d. *The 2008 Statistical Abstracts*. Table 600: "Employment Projects by Occupation: 2004–2014." http://www.census.gov/compendia/statab/tables/08s0600.xls

qualities that are directly opposite. In this way, welfare recipients come to constitute an out-group in our society (Feagin 1975; Lewis 1978). An **out-group** is considered undesirable and thought to hold values and beliefs foreign to one's own. An out-group is identified as such by an **in-group**, which holds itself in high esteem and demands loyalty from its members.

Individuals who can avoid public assistance, regardless of their exact income, can count themselves as members of the hardworking in-group. Indeed, it is the negative image of the welfare out-group that keeps many poor and near poor from accessing various forms of public assistance: "I may be poor, but I'm not on welfare."

The power of American values explains why we cling to conventional wisdom regarding welfare. This power also can help us better understand why relatively few Americans denigrate society's wealthy sector, even when that wealth is gained at the expense of the working and middle class. After all, a rising tide lifts all boats. The General Social Survey (GSS) has repeatedly found that fully 74% think that class differences are acceptable because they reflect what people have made of their opportunities; 59% of Americans agree that large income differences are needed to provide incentives for individual effort (General Social Survey 1999, 2000, 2004).

To be sure, those on the upper rungs of the U.S. stratification ladder are indeed accumulating wealth. Over the past 30 years, we have witnessed a 2,500% rise in CEO incomes (Krugman 2002). And the trend continues. In 2006 the average CEO received $14.78 million in total compensation, more than a 9% increase from 2005. At present, the average salary of top corporate executives is 411 times higher than that of the average hourly worker! And the accumulation of wealth continues even after the work is done. In 2006, the CEOs of Pfizer and Home Depot received *exit* packages of more than $200 million despite charges that both Pfizer and Home Depot underperformed during these CEOs' tenure (AFL-CIO 2007).

When we value individual effort and opportunity, tolerance of wealth must be expected. We embrace the old adage that "what's good for GM (or more recently GE) is good for America." (In his last full year running GE, CEO Jack Welch was paid $123 million; his retirement package included perks worth at least $2 million a year [Krugman 2002].) After his retirement, Welch went on to write a memoir sharing his secrets to success; it became a best-seller.) The wealthiest have already arrived where many of us would like to go. They are proof to us that individual efforts can pay off; they are proof that the American Dream, to which we are so committed, lives on.

To sustain the power of American values, we must lay the blame for poverty on the poor themselves. There is, of course, a certain irony and destructiveness to this process. Personalizing poverty deflects our attention from the social causes of poverty, such as the changing occupational structure and a lack of education. Such a stance lessens the likelihood that we will successfully reduce poverty. Indeed, without major social changes, social reproduction theory suggests that the American Dream will continue to elude the poor. **Social reproduction theory** maintains that existing social, cultural, and economic arrangements work to "reproduce" in future generations the social class divisions of the present generation. Princeton economist Paul Krugman identifies corporate culture and boardroom handshakes as the invisible force behind the recent explosion in CEO pay (Krugman 2002).

One proponent of social reproduction theory, Pierre Bourdieu (1977a, 1977b), maintains that the aspirations of lower class children are adversely affected by their class position. The lower class child is immersed in a social world hostile to the American Dream. The objective realities of the lower class environment deflate hopes of success; the restricted opportunity structure inherent in a lower class location leads to reduced life aspirations.

Social reproduction is not the only obstacle to poverty reduction. Structural functionalists remind us that the elimination of poverty is highly unlikely as long as the poor among us serve valuable social functions. **Structural functionalism** is a theoretical approach that stresses social order. Proponents contend that society is a collection of interdependent parts that function together to produce consensus and stability. **Social functions** refer to the intended and unintended social consequences of various behaviors and practices.

Personalizing poverty sustains a lower class. The lower class, in turn, fulfills many needs for those in other social locations. For example, the poor provide society with a cheap labor pool. They also create countless job opportunities for others: for those wishing to help them—social workers, policymakers, and so on—as well as for those wishing to control them—police and corrections officers. The poor even provide financial opportunities for those wishing to take advantage of them—loan sharks, for example, and corporations seeking tax breaks via the food discard market (Funiciello 1990; Gans 1971; Jacobs 1988). And sustaining the poverty out-group enables the social mainstream to better define and reaffirm some of its most fundamental values and beliefs.

In light of these functions, we must reexamine the notion that welfare is ruining this country. Welfare may breed dependency, but dependency for whom? Given the social functions of the poor, welfare may breed a social dependency of the masses on the few, as the poor ultimately serve as vehicles by which mainstream values are ensured.

Learning More About It

A comprehensive review of the impact of the economy on the living standards of Americans is offered by the Economic Policy Institute's *The State of Working America 2006/2007* (Ithaca: Cornell University Press, 2007).

In *The Working Poor* (New York: Vintage Books, 2005), David Shipler profiles some of those caught between poverty and prosperity and in so doing challenges many common misconceptions about those living in or near poverty in the United States.

If you want to learn more about the reality and challenges of working for poverty-level wages see Barbara Ehrenreich's best-selling *Nickle and Dimed: On (Not) Getting by in America* (New York: Owl Books, 2001).

To read more about the gender and racial base of poverty, see Kathryn Edin and Laura Lein's *Making Ends Meet: How Single Mothers Survive Welfare and Low-Wage Work* (New York: Russell Sage, 1997b).

In *Rachel and Her Children: Homeless Families in America* (New York: Crown, 2006), Jonathan Kozol uses both statistics and rich interview data to provide a compelling account of homelessness in America.

The classic work on the functions of poverty is Herbert Gans's "The Uses of Poverty: The Poor Pay for All" (*Social Policy*, Summer: 20–24, 1971).

To learn more about the growing inequality of wealth in America, you can access the study, "Pulling Apart a State-by-State Analysis of Income Trends" at the Economic Policy Institute's Web page: http://www.epinet.org/content.cfm/studies_pullingapart

The United States Conference of Catholic Bishops offers a short but insightful poverty "tour" at their Web page: http://www.usccb.org/cchd/povertyusa/index.htm

The Administration for Children and Families' Web page offers a link for information about TANF: http://www.acf.hhs.gov/acf_services.html#walia

The following organizations and sites can also help you learn more about welfare and related topics:

Information Resource Center of the Finance Project (resources for effective welfare policy)
http://www.financeproject.org/irc/win.asp

National Coalition for the Homeless
http://www.nationalhomeless.org

Exercises

1. American values are one explanation for the triumph of conventional wisdom over facts. Choose another concept from the material covered thus far in your course and provide an alternate explanation of why welfare gets such a "bum rap."

2. The cutoff level for official poverty is arbitrary. Identify five different consequences of setting the cutoff point higher; identify five consequences of setting the cutoff point lower. Are the consequences you identify primarily functional or dysfunctional for mainstream Americans?

Essay 21

Conventional Wisdom Tells Us ... Immigrants Are Ruining This Nation

"Why don't you go back where you came from?" This angry cry seems to be getting more and more familiar as the United States faces the highest levels of immigration in its history. Is immigration ruining this nation? This essay reviews the historical impact and future trends of immigration in the United States.

"Why don't you go back where you came from?" This is a familiar taunt that most of us have heard. Here in the United States, it is a question often born of ethnic and racial prejudice. And, increasingly, feelings of prejudice target members of immigrant groups. **Prejudice** refers to the prejudgment of individuals on the basis of their group membership. **Immigrant groups** contain individuals who have left their homelands in pursuit of new lives in new countries.

Immigration has always been a fact of American life. The earliest European settlers were immigrants to the 3 to 8 million Native Americans who already occupied the continent. In the first census, in 1790, approximately one in five Americans was an "immigrant" slave brought from Africa (U.S. Census Bureau 1993). Since the early 1800s, more than 72 million immigrants have arrived in the United States (Jeffreys 2007; U.S. Census

Bureau 2007d, Table 5). Undeniably, most Americans are truly indebted to their immigrant ancestors—all but 0.8% of us are descendants of immigrants (Schuman and Olufs 1995).

The U.S. immigration experience can be divided into four major waves. The earliest wave consisted mostly of English immigrants who arrived in the United States long before official entry records started to be recorded in 1820. This first group also consisted of immigrants from Scotland, Ireland, Germany, and other northern and western European nations. The second major wave occurred between 1820 and 1860 as many people who were being pushed out of Europe by forces of industrialization relocated to the United States and joined the westward expansion of the nation. About 40% of the immigrants who arrived during this period were from Ireland alone. The third wave occurred between 1880 and the outbreak of World War I. During this period more than 20 million immigrants from southern and eastern European nations arrived in the United States. Most of these immigrants moved to east coast and Midwest cities. By 1910, more than half of the workers in New York City, Chicago, and Detroit were immigrants. These three waves of activity were followed by an immigration lull (between 1915 and 1965) brought about by two world wars, the Great Depression in the United States, and the appearance of U.S. immigration quotas. We are currently in the midst of a fourth wave of immigration that started after 1965. This wave has a decidedly different look than previous waves and reflects a change in U.S. immigration policies that gives preference to family members of those already residing in the United States and to skilled workers in demand by U.S. employers. With this fourth wave, the predominant origins of immigrants shifted from European to Latin American and Asian countries. The current wave also is distinguished by an increase in the number of unauthorized immigrants entering the United States (Martin and Midgley 2006).

Immigrants account for at least one-third of recent U.S. population growth. While the current *percentage* of foreign born is around 12% (a figure lower than that for the early 1900s), the *number* of foreign-born residents today is at an all-time high—37 million in 2005. About 30% of this group are unauthorized residents—that is, **illegal aliens**. While more than half of these illegal immigrants evaded border controls when entering the United States, about 40% entered legally but overstayed the terms of their visas (Martin and Midgley 2006). Between 1990 and 2005, approximately 14.5 million immigrants became **legal permanent residents (LPRs or "green card recipients")** of the United States (an average of 1 million a year; see Box 21.1 for other immigration terms). Approximately 65% of legal permanent immigrants are family sponsored—that is, they are relatives of U.S.

citizens or of permanent immigrants. Despite our nation's immigration background, public opinion polls between the 1960s and 1990s indicated that a majority of Americans were in favor of reducing immigration levels in the United States. This restrictive sentiment abated somewhat during the economic good times of the late 1990s but after 2001 (and 9/11) the majority of Americans began expressing greater concern about immigration issues and asking political leaders for immigration reform (Martin and Midgley 2006).

BOX 21.1   Immigration Terms

Aliens: citizens of a foreign country. The United States distinguishes four legal statuses for aliens: legal immigrants, temporary legal migrants, refugees, and unauthorized migrants.

Legal immigrants (a.k.a. legal permanent residents [LPRs] or green card holders): foreigners granted a visa that allows them to live and work permanently in the United States. After five years, legal immigrants can apply to become **naturalized citizens**. There were over 1.1 million legal immigrants admitted to the United States in 2005.

Naturalized citizens: legal immigrants (at least 18 years of age) who have lived in the United States for at least five years, paid application fees ($675), undergone a background check, and passed English and civics tests.

Temporary legal migrants: foreigners in the United States for specific purposes (e.g., visiting, studying, or working). The United States issues 25 types of nonimmigrant visas, including B-visas for tourists, F-visas for foreign students, and H-visas for foreign workers. There were 32 million temporary legal migrants in the United States in 2005.

Refugees and asylees: foreigners allowed to stay in the United States because of fear of persecution in their home countries. Refugees may become legal permanent residents after living in the United States for a year.

Unauthorized migrants (a.k.a. illegal aliens): foreigners in the United States without valid visas (estimated at 11 million in 2005).

SOURCE: Martin and Midgley 2006.

Given America's immigration history, the current calls for reform seem somewhat ironic. We find ourselves casting doubt on the value of immigrants in a nation long considered the "land of immigrants." To be sure, our immigrant roots are well established (see Table 21.1). As evidenced by annual parades and festivals, a great many "hyphenated-Americans" take pride in their diverse ancestral roots. At the same time, our daily newspapers, television newscasts, and Internet blogs document a growing chorus of anti-immigration sentiments. Commentaries filled with fear, distrust, and hate are becoming a staple of talk-radio broadcasts. The Federation for American Immigration Reform (FAIR) has called for severe reductions in the number of U.S. immigrants to combat excessive population growth, environmental degradation, job loss, and low wages. FAIR works closely with talk radio to get its immigration reform message out to the American people. The tragic events of September 11, 2001, have prompted many Americans to rethink the wisdom of freely embracing foreigners. Building a 700-mile wall along the Mexican border, increasing the number of border patrol agents, assigning National Guard troops to border patrols, making illegal crossings a felony, and creating guest worker programs and amnesty programs are all part of the current immigration debate. Not surprisingly, immigration reform is a pledge heard from many presidential hopefuls. But the reform minded are not waiting for the federal government to act. Many critics maintain that immigrants place an unfair burden on state budgets. In the first six months of 2007, 171 immigration bills became law in 41 states (LeBlanc 2007).

Is the current conventional wisdom on immigration justified? Do these sentiments reflect a new anti-immigration trend? Or are these anti-immigration sentiments more common and long-standing than we realize?

Table 21.1   Total and Percentage Foreign Born for U.S. Population: 1900–2005 (Numbers in Thousands)

Year	Foreign-Born	
	Total	Percentage
1900	10,341	13.6
1910	13,516	14.7
1920	13,921	13.2
1930	14,204	11.6
1940	11,595	8.8
1950	10,347	6.9
1960	9,738	5.4
1970	9,619	4.7
1980	14,080	6.2
1990	19,767	7.9
2000	31,108	11.1
2005	37,000	12.0

SOURCE: U.S. Census Bureau 2000 and Martin and Midgley 2006.

The immigration history of the United States is nothing if not complex. Despite the message delivered by the "Lady in the Harbor," the United States has seldom greeted immigrants with totally open arms. Descendants of the first immigrant settlers, White Anglo-Saxon Protestants from England, were slow to welcome other newcomers. Rather, they expressed concern about "new" and undesirable immigrants and organized against those arriving from Germany, Ireland, Poland, Italy, and other White ethnic countries (Fallows 1983). The 1850s saw the rise of a political party—the Know-Nothings—whose unifying theme was decidedly anti-immigration. In the 1860s, James Blaine of Maine sought to curb Catholic immigration by seeking an amendment to the U.S. Constitution banning states from providing aid to schools controlled by religious groups. His efforts established the groundwork for restrictions on government aid to religious schools and the current school voucher debate (Cohen and Gray 2003). In the same decade that the Statue of Liberty first beckoned immigrants to our shores, a group of U.S. residents founded the first all-WASP (White Anglo-Saxon Protestant) country club; these residents also established the Social Register, a list identifying the exclusive "founding" families of the United States (Baltzell 1987). In the 1920s, President Hoover freely expressed clear anti-immigration sentiments when he encouraged New York City's mayor, Fiorello La Guardia, the son of immigrants, to go back where he belonged. The mass migration period of 1880 to 1924 saw nativists and politicians working hard to restrict immigration. Campaigns to impose literacy tests in order to hold the tide on immigration were repeatedly mounted in the late 1800s and early 1900s. And from 1921 to the mid-1960s, the government used a quota system to regulate and limit immigration. In 1965, Congress passed a new law that replaced quotas with a complex system that grants priorities to three categories: foreigners with relatives living in the United States, people needed to fill vacant jobs, and refugees. These changes produced a major shift in immigration patterns (more and more immigrants originating in Latin America and Asia) and renewed calls for immigration reform (Martin and Midgley 2006). These examples suggest that, although the United States proudly touts its immigration history, immigration in the United States has always been characterized by a love-hate relationship.

Americans' love-hate stance toward immigration may be the product of certain core cultural values. A **cultural value** is a general sentiment that people share regarding what is good or bad, right or wrong, desirable or undesirable.

We are a nation strongly committed to economic opportunity and advancement. At various times and to various parties, the labor of immigrants has provided one sure route to economic betterment. For example, estimates suggest that nearly half of colonial-era European immigrants came to America as indentured servants who were willing to work off their debts for a chance at a better life in the new land. Similarly, the forced immigration of African slaves provided cheap labor for the South's labor-intensive agricultural development (Daniels 1990). The construction of the transcontinental railroad and the economic development of the West depended on the willing and able labor of Chinese immigrants, and Japanese immigrants were welcomed as cheap, reliable labor for Hawaiian sugar plantations. By 1910, immigrants constituted 14% of our national population, yet they made up more than one-half of the industrial labor force (National Park Service 1998). During World Wars I and II, young Mexican men were invited into the United States as guest workers (via the Bracero program) to help fill the farm labor shortages that developed as American soldiers were shipped overseas for combat duty (Martin and Midgley 2006). In short, immigration has benefited many U.S. enterprises, industries, corporations, and war campaigns.

The ties that link immigrants to traditional American cultural values have not only benefited big business but also advanced the lives of countless immigrants. Indeed, the crush of immigrants in the mid-19th century was prompted by the immigrants' hopes that they could escape their own poverty via the economic expansion that was taking place in the United States. Such promises of economic betterment continue to attract immigrants to our shores, even amidst current trends toward economic globalization. The promise proves a potent one. Throughout the early 1990s, even the lowest paying jobs in the United States were an improvement over those most new immigrants left behind. Wages for unskilled labor in the United States, for example, were 7 times higher than wages in South Korea, 10 to 15 times higher than wages in Central America, and 35 times higher than wages in China (Baker, Smith, Weiner, and Harbrecht 1993; Bonacich et al. 1994; Braun 1991; Peterson 1992). Today, American workers continue to fare better than many other workers of the world. Witness the compensation figures for production workers listed in Table 21.2.

The cultural emphasis on economic advancement and opportunity helps explain the affinity between the United States and immigrants, but such emphasis also helps explain our long history of resisting immigrants. American tolerance for immigrants decreases whenever immigrants prove a threat to the economic well-being of "traditional" American workers. Indeed, the strongest support for immigration restrictions has often come from organized labor (Schuman and Olufs 1995).

Recall that Chinese immigrants played a critical role in the construction of the transcontinental railroad. However, the Chinese Exclusion Act of 1882 was passed when Chinese immigrants began to be viewed as a threat to the White labor force. Similarly, Mexicans were welcome immigrants to

Table 21.2   Hourly Compensation Costs for Manufacturing Production Workers in Select Locations, 2005 (in U.S. Dollars)

Country	Dollars per Hour
Mexico	2.63
Brazil	4.09
Poland	4.54
Hong Kong	5.65
Czech Republic	6.11
Taiwan	6.38
Singapore	7.66
Korea	13.56
United States	23.65

SOURCE: U.S. Department of Labor, Bureau of Labor Statistics, Nov. 2006. "International Comparisons of Hourly Compensation Costs for Production Workers in Manufacturing, 2005." http://www.bls.gov/news.release/pdf/ichcc.pdf

the United States during the labor shortages imposed by World Wars I and II and again during the farm labor shortages of the 1950s. However, in the 1960s and the 1980s, when traditionally White labor jobs were in jeopardy, attempts were made to stem the flow of Mexican immigrants (Martin and Midgley 2006; Schuman and Olufs 1995).

In the 1990s, economic changes created a double bind for the traditional American workforce. Specifically, many low-wage jobs left the United States for more profitable locations abroad. (Again, see Table 21.2 to understand the financial incentives that tempted employers to move their jobs out of the United States.) At the same time, more and more foreign workers entered America and offered direct competition for the low-wage jobs that remained. Add to the mix one other development emerging from the economic boom of the 1980s and the limited number of American students in the science and engineering fields: a growing demand for highly skilled migrant workers. College-educated immigrants are eligible for tens of thousands of work permits (H-1B visas) each year. These immigrants are very much in demand by American businesses, especially high-tech industries. The number of H-1B visas doubled during the 1990s and reached 400,000 in 2004. H-1B visa holders can stay in the United States if they are able to find employers willing to sponsor them. But opponents to this influx of highly skilled immigrants argue that the group only serves to undermine the working conditions and wages of their American counterparts (Caldwell 2006; Martin and Midgley 2006). Thus, the immigration squeeze on American workers is felt by those at both ends of the skills spectrum. Clearly, these economic realities play a significant role in fueling current anti-immigration sentiments.

Americans' avoidance attitude toward immigration is further explained by referring to the basic processes of group dynamics. We refer specifically to conventional patterns by which in-groups and out-groups develop. The people who constitute the group to which one belongs form an in-group. An **in-group** holds itself in high esteem and demands loyalty from its members. In-groups then define others as members of an out-group. An **out-group** is considered undesirable and thought to hold values and beliefs foreign to one's own. American society consists of a variety of ethnic groups. These groups are frequently ranked relative to their tenure in the country, but each wave of immigration to a country establishes new population configurations. In general, the most established immigrant groups cast themselves in the role of the in-group. Such groups define themselves as the "senior" and thus most valid representatives of a nation. These in-groups cast those that follow them in the role of out-groups. Recent arrivals are stigmatized as elements foreign to an established mold (Spain 1999).

Research demonstrates that members of an in-group carry unrealistically positive views of their group. At the same time, in-group members share unrealistically negative views of the out-group (Hewstone, Rubin, and Willis 2002; Tajfel 1982). As groups improve their status, they are more likely to display in-group bias (Guimond, Dif, and Aupy 2002). Threats to in-groups can increase the derogation of lower status out-groups (Cadinu and Reggiori 2002; Hopkins and Rae 2001). Low-status minorities are the most susceptible to in-group devaluation (Rudman, Feinberg, and Fairchild 2002). Exposure to prejudice about out-groups can increase the negative evaluations of those groups and hinder social ties with them, thus reinforcing destructive social dynamics (Levin, VanLaar, and Sidanius 2003; Tropp 2003). Because newcomers are viewed relative to those with earlier claims, the very process of immigration perpetuates social conflict. Indeed, the mechanics of immigration seem to guarantee a hostile boundary between the old and the new, between established ethnic groups versus recent arrivals.

In light of Americans' historical relationship with immigrants, should we simply dismiss current anti-immigration sentiments as "business as usual"? Perhaps not.

Figure 21.1 reveals the European background of earlier generations of immigrants to the United States. Indeed, these European origins are frequently credited with facilitating past immigrants' transition to U.S. culture. The many shared customs and characteristics and the spatial dispersion of various European ethnic groups facilitated the assimilation of each new European immigrant wave. **Assimilation** is the process by which immigrant groups come to adopt the dominant culture of their new homeland as their own.

Figure 21.1   Percentage of Legal Immigrants Reporting European Origins, 1820–2006

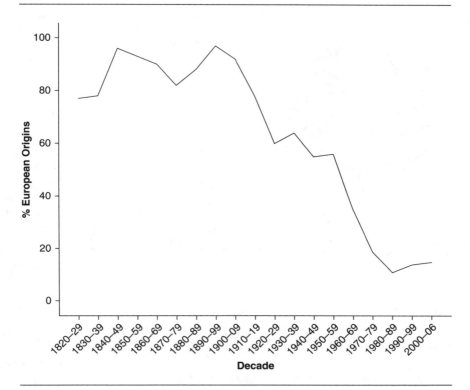

SOURCE: Department of Homeland Security, Yearbook of Immigration Statistics 2006. http:// www.dhs.gov/ximgtn/statistics/publications/yearbook.shtm

Today, the vast majority of immigrants are from Asian or Latin American nations. Table 21.3 lists the top 10 countries of origin for legally permanent immigrant residents in 2006. By the year 2050, most immigrants will hail from Latin America, Asia, Africa, the Middle East, or the Pacific Islands (Schmidley 2003). By 2050, Hispanics are expected to make up 25% and Asians 10% of the U.S. population (Martin and Midgley 2006). On the one hand, these shifts in immigration and population patterns should hardly be cause for concern. The immigration history of these new groups, like the history of previous immigrant groups, has largely been a story of success. Asian men and women, for example, have the highest median income of *any* single racial group (Webster and Bishaw 2006). In 2004, the median income for Asian households was about $8,000 higher than the median income for White households. For those 25 years of age and older, 48% of Asians

Table 21.3   Top 10 Countries of Origin for Legal Permanent Immigrants to the United States, 2006

Country	Percentage
1. Mexico	13.7%
2. China	6.9%
3. Philippines	5.9%
4. India	4.8%
5. Cuba	3.6%
6. Colombia	3.4%
7. Dominican Republic	3.0%
8. El Salvador	2.5%
9. Vietnam	2.4%
10. Jamaica	2.0%

SOURCE: Jeffreys 2007; U.S. Legally Permanent Residents: 2006. Annual Flow Report, Department of Homeland Security, Office of Immigration Statistics. http://www.dhs.gov/xlibrary/assets/statistics/publications/IS-4496_LPRFlowReport_04vaccessible.pdf

versus 30% of Whites have bachelor's degrees or higher. Approximately 46% of Asians aged 16 years and older work in management or professional occupations; 38% of Whites 16 and older are so employed. The median value of Asian owner-occupied homes is $300,000 or higher (about twice the median value for White owner-occupied homes; U.S. Census Bureau 2007h).

Hispanic immigrants to the United States can point to similar triumphs. Although it is true that the economic conditions of Hispanic Americans tend to lag behind national averages, the median income of Hispanic households reached nearly $38,000 in 2006 (U.S. Census Bureau 2007i). The percentage of Hispanic households with incomes over $100,000 has more than doubled since 1980 (U.S. Census Bureau 2007d, Table 671). There are more than 77,000 Hispanic CEOs, and in 2002 the revenue generated by Hispanic-owned businesses totaled more than $220 billion dollars (U.S. Census Bureau 2007i). The educational profile of Hispanics has improved greatly in recent years. Over the past two decades, the percentage of Hispanics obtaining high school degrees increased by 20% while the percentage receiving college degrees or higher increased by almost 50% (U.S. Census Bureau 2007d, Table 214). And during this same time period, Hispanics (along with Asians) have experienced the fastest growth in graduate and professional school enrollments (U.S. Department of Education 2003). Hispanic households also reaffirm important core American values. The family, for instance, is greatly respected in Hispanic culture. Seventy-seven percent of Hispanic households are family households (compared with 66% of White households). (Family households are those where one or more persons are related to the householder by marriage, birth, or adoption.) A smaller proportion of Hispanics than Whites are divorced (8% vs. 11%; U.S. Census Bureau 2007j). Hispanic American youth also report the strongest sense of family duty during young adulthood (Fuligni and Pedersen 2002). And in terms of politics, the Hispanic vote will surely receive more and more attention in local, state, and national elections as the number of Hispanic voters continues to grow.

While the faces of immigrants have changed in the past 50 years, intergenerational assimilation and upward mobility are still the norm (Card, DiNardo, and Estes 1998; Myers and Cranford 1998). Of the foreign-born who arrived in the United States before 1970, 81% have obtained citizenship. Of those who arrived in the United States between 1970 and 1979, nearly 70% have obtained citizenship. Citizenship rates for more recent arrivals are decidedly lower: 48% for those arriving during the 1980s and under 15% for those arriving since 1990 (Larsen 2004). Still these rates should increase as efforts to promote citizenship and accelerate the naturalization process continue. The 1990s saw an average of 500,000 naturalizations each year compared to annual averages of just over 200,000 in the 1980s. In 2006, 702,589 legally permanent immigrants became naturalized citizens. The naturalization numbers for 2007 will be even higher as more and more LPRs respond to the immigration debates by seeking the security of citizenship (Preston 2007). As recently as 2000, the median time lapse between the date of legal immigration to the United States and the date of naturalization was 10 years. For the 2006 cohort, the time gap was down to 7 years (Simanski 2007).

There also is a very clear association between length of time in the United States and both income and home ownership rates. While earnings of immigrants are initially lower than those of natives, the gap disappears over time. Immigrants also outpace native Americans in terms of entrepreneurial activity (Kauffman Foundation 2006; Martin and Midgley 2006). And the eventual mastery of the English language is another key to immigrants' economic success. Historically, the shift from speaking another language to speaking English has occurred over three generations. Among recent immigrants, however, the shift seems to be occurring within two generations (Martin and Midgley 2006; Portes 2002). This lower turnaround time may reflect the current reform mood of the country. A recent Gallup Poll reveals that 77% of Americans (and 59% of Hispanics) think that proficiency in English should be a condition for immigrants being allowed to stay in the United States (Carroll 2007).

In light of the general success rates posted by recent immigrants in general and by many Asian and Hispanic Americans, we must consider that current anti-immigration sentiments may be based on issues of race. Visible physical differences, as well as a lack of familiar cultural practices, make the assimilation of "new" immigrant groups more difficult than it was for earlier immigrants. New, non-European immigrants may lack the physical and cultural similarities necessary for eventual acceptance as part of society's in-group.

If immigration and population trends develop as predicted, anti-immigration sentiments fueled by issues of race may get worse before they get better. Demographers tell us that the dominant White population of U.S. society will be very close to becoming a numerical minority by the year 2050. By 2050, African Americans, Hispanics, Asian Americans, and Native Americans are expected to account for almost half the U.S. population (U.S. Census Bureau 2002, Table 16). If these projections are accurate, future immigration, in a very profound sense, will change the status quo. The practice of assimilation may necessarily give way to multiculturalism. **Multiculturalism** accentuates rather than dilutes ethnic and racial differences. Such an environment might strip in-groups of dominance and power. In contrast to the adversarial stance of the in-group/out-group design, a multicultural structure demands that all groups be viewed as equally valued contributors to the mainstream culture.

Immigration projections suggest that the United States is moving closer to being a microcosm of the world. Our nation will experience an increase in the diversity that already characterizes the younger generations of Americans. Such changes could bring us closer to fully realizing the motto that appears on all U.S. currency: *E Pluribus Unum,* one formed from many. Thus, current and future attitudes toward immigrants in America will hinge on our readiness to deal with fundamental population changes.

Certainly, some Americans will resist this development, arguing that it threatens our national identity and changes our national "face." Contemporary movements against bilingual education are evidence of such resistance. Nevertheless, others will view our changing population as a positive economic opportunity. Consider the fact that economists forecast a very different world for coming generations of Americans. More and more of us will be earning our livings in the service sector of an increasingly global, postindustrial economy. Postindustrial economies place a high premium on knowledge and information (Drucker 1993). Future job markets will demand and reward better educated and more literate workers (Hecker 2001; Sum, Kirsch, and Taggart 2002; U.S. Department of Labor 2005a). Immigration bodes well for educational advancement. Immigrant parents and children have higher education aspirations than native-born individuals. Immigrant students equal or exceed the educational attainment of their native-born counterparts (Kao and Thompson 2003; National Institutes of

Health 2004; Vernez and Abrahamse 1996). There is also a growing body of research that suggests that strong pro-education values as well as high valuation of close family ties found in some immigrant groups produce higher academic achievement (Kao and Thompson 2003). Some studies also indicate that bilingualism is positively associated with educational aspirations and achievements as well as self-esteem (Feliciano 2001; Portes 2002; St.-Hilaire 2002). Indeed, globalization makes multilingualism a way of life and a pathway to empowerment (UNESCO 2003). Multilingual workers will clearly occupy a position of advantage in an increasingly global economy and workplace (Portes 2002).

Framed in this way, new immigration patterns may help supply us with a new source of cultural capital (Archdeacon 1992). **Cultural capital** refers to attributes, knowledge, or ways of thinking that can be converted or used for economic advantage. Interestingly enough, as we witness various indicators attesting to the force of globalization, we also see more and more ethnic groups asserting their identities and pushing for political recognition and autonomy (Guillen 2001). By their familiarity with cultures now central to the world market, immigrants to the United States may well give our nation a competitive edge in a global playing field. Once again, immigrants to the United States may be the national resource that makes the United States a significant player in a new world economy.

Learning More About It

Aviva Chomsky explores the many misconceptions that distort our thinking and views on immigration in *"They Take Our Jobs!" and 20 Other Myths About Immigration* (Boston: Beacon Press, 2007).

David Roediger reviews the history of the intersection between immigrants' push for full rights and citizenship and racial issues in *Working Toward Whiteness: How America's Immigrants Became White* (New York: Basic Books, 2005).

In *Immigrant America: A Portrait*, 3rd edition (Berkeley, CA: University of California Press, 2006), Alejandro Portes and Ruben G. Rumbaut present a highly readable account of the complexities of immigration in America and mobilize data in the service of dismantling myths and misconceptions.

Richard Alba and Victor Nee offer an insightful review of assimilation of current immigrants in *Remaking the American Mainstream: Assimilation and Contemporary Immigration* (Cambridge, MA: Harvard University Press, 2005).

Mary Waters and Tomas Jimenez look at the degree to which recent immigrants are hitting the benchmarks of assimilation in their article "Assessing Immigrant Assimilation: New Empirical and Theoretical Challenges" (*Annual Review of Sociology*, 31:105–125, 2005).

The U.S. Citizenship and Immigration Services (formerly the INS) offers a wealth of information on immigration. Visit their Web site at http://www.uscis.gov/portal/site/uscis

You can test your immigration knowledge by taking an interactive pop quiz at the U.S. Census Bureau's foreign-born population page: http://www.census.gov/population/www/socdemo/foreign/graphics.html

Separate the fact from fiction about the 10 million plus undocumented immigrants in the United States by accessing the link "Undocumented Immigrants: Myths and Reality" at the Urban Institute's Web page: http://www.urban.org/publications/900898.html

Exercises

1. Visit a library that has back copies of local telephone directories. Examine the entries in the yellow pages for a variety of categories—beauty salons, physicians, restaurants, and so on. What insights about immigration patterns can be gleaned from your data as you move from year to year?

2. Conduct several in-depth interviews with people who were born in other countries and immigrated to the United States. Find out about the conditions of their immigration, the reception they received in their new communities, and, if appropriate, the reception they received at their new workplaces or their new schools. Try to vary the immigration background of your interview subjects; that is, choose individuals who came from different foreign countries. Consider whether one's status as an immigrant functions as a master status (see Essay 6 or 14).

3. Use your own college community to locate children of recent immigrants. Prepare an interview guide that will allow you to explore whether these individuals exist in two social worlds or cultures. (For example, how do language, food, fashion patterns, and so on vary from school to home?)

Social Institutions:
Media and Technology

Essay 22

Conventional Wisdom Tells Us . . . Technology Is Taking Over Our Lives

This essay examines new communication technologies and explores their role in contemporary social life. We begin by considering the ways in which technology has altered social inequality. We move on to examine technology's impact on the development of community and intimacy. And we conclude by exploring the impact of new technologies on our definitions of social relations, social actors, and the public and private spheres.

Look around. No matter where you are, you will see the signs. Technology rules the day. On the road? Electronic message boards and Amber Alert systems are sending immediate updates on road conditions, emergencies, or criminal matters. Now look at the drivers around you. Drive time has become talk time as more and more of us keep in touch with family and work via our cell phones. Check the scene at work or school. Everyone seems to have cell phones in their ears, iPods in their hands, and laptops on their shoulders. See something extraordinary in your travels? Grab the cell and send a picture! Hear a funny joke or a juicy piece of gossip? Share the wealth—text it to your best friend!

These days, it is easy to stay connected to family and friends. But the information boom is about much more than our social lives. Increasingly, governments, corporations, and law enforcement agencies are privy to our comings and goings. Surveillance cameras or electronic toll devices can record our physical whereabouts. "Cookies" can track our travels and tastes as we browse through cyberspace. Crime-fighting computers and medical data banks can verify our identities; they know us, right down to the chromosomes in our DNA. Even the mundane trip to the grocery store carries a technological flair. Computerized registers are able to "scan" our items and immediately deliver customized coupons that fit our tastes.

The **new communication technologies**—developments such as fiber optics, broadband, the Internet, rapid satellite transmissions, robotics, and virtual reality imaging—can take us to places that we've never been before. While sitting in front of our computer screens or while walking with our *iPhones*, we might participate in a virtual march on Washington; we might support our favorite cause via online volunteer work; we might participate in an online support group, or tour an art gallery, a historic site, or a home we are thinking about purchasing. Movies can be delivered on demand to our computers; the biggest concert tour of the year may be simulcast on the Internet. Opportunity is knocking . . . although for some it may not always be an easy door to open. Computer users really must become computer "techies" who can troubleshoot their way through various hardware and software problems. Luckily, this knowledge will serve the techie well in the future. Appliances, cars, and homes of tomorrow will all be "smart" and require consumers to be programming savvy. Downtime may be gone time. The Internet is never closed; technology whirls on, 24/7.

Conventional wisdom suggests that technological advancements are taking over our lives. Critics charge that we are slaves to our hi-tech toys, drowning in a sea of points, clicks, and wireless connections. Indeed, many believe we spend so much time with the new products of technology that we have forgotten or withdrawn from the "real" world. Is conventional wisdom correct in its anti-technology stance? Have we lost control of our lives . . . or merely learned a different way to live them? A number of sociologists are examining these issues in detail. Their research suggests that new communication technologies may be less "dangerous" than critics suggest.

What is it that people fear about the new communication technologies? One common concern involves the issue of inequality. Some researchers argue that new communication technologies are creating a digital divide. A **digital divide** refers to the formation of an information underclass—a portion of the population that cannot afford to access and capitalize on the things that new technologies have to offer. To be sure, *all* technological innovations result in a digital divide. Radios and televisions, telephones and automobiles—all seemed to be a luxury of the wealthy when first introduced.

But as these technologies were diffused within society at large, some of the access inequalities tended to disappear. New communication technologies are following this developmental pattern. For example, the racial and gender divides that once characterized computer access and usage have diminished considerably (although men and women use the Internet for different things). But in the areas of income and education, much work remains. It is still the case that the wealthier and more educated individuals are, the better the access they have to new technologies and the more technologically proficient they tend to be (Martin and Robinson 2007; Pew Foundation 2007; van Dijk 2005). It is important to note, however, that technology per se does not sustain or create inequalities between social groups. Rather, the structure of the contexts in which technology is used can either exacerbate or alleviate social inequality (Warschauer 2004).

Conventional wisdom also argues that new communication technologies are destroying people's involvement in civic and community life. Critics fear that individuals are substituting online activity for more traditional offline affiliations—an experience that critics contend is inferior to traditional modes of civic activity. Some fear that Internet users may be overwhelmed with available information. As a result, users may participate in selected interest groups that do little more than reinforce their existing beliefs. Others fear that users may encounter online activists who are much more extreme than their offline counterparts. Such encounters could be intimidating, resulting in users' complete withdrawal from the civic arena. Still others contend that users may decide that navigating the dense terrain of the Internet simply is not worth their effort (Calhoun 1998; Katz and Rice 2002:132). While such fears abound, recent studies on the Internet and community fail to lend them much credence. Current research suggests that online interactions tend to supplement, not replace, offline community involvements. In addition, heavy Internet use is actually associated with high levels of participation in offline voluntary organizations and politics. Thus, far from being overwhelmed or exceptionally selective, Internet users tend to be highly interested in a wide array of current events and highly involved in civic and political activities (Jensen, Danziger, and Venkatesh 2007; Katz and Rice 2002; Wellman 2004).

Note too that during the past few years there has been a remarkable growth in e-**philanthropy**—that is, online giving or "cyber giving." For example, Networkforgood.org has posted steady traffic and growth since its inception in 2001. Via the site, 430,000 people have donated more than $100 million to over 20,000 charities (Networkforgood.org 2007). The increasing popularity of e-philanthropy may be due to its complementary tie to our daily work patterns: 71% of all online donations are made at work. Since many of us are online during a normal working day, e-giving has become a quick and satisfying way to support our charitable causes (*Business Wire* 2002).

E-philanthropy has seen success in the area of online volunteering as well. The largest Web site for online volunteering is VolunteerMatch.org. This site connects potential volunteers with nonprofit groups. An individual simply submits a list of volunteering contingencies (i.e., the distance one is willing to travel, the time frame for one's volunteer work, and the type of cause or issue with which one wants to be associated). The site then searches for an organization that matches an individual's criteria. Since its launch in 1998, VolunteerMatch has generated well over 3,000,000 volunteer referrals—with the greatest growth in numbers occurring in the past five years (VolunteerMatch.org 2007).

E-philanthropy received a significant boost in the days following the September 11, 2001, terrorist attacks on America. On Sept 10th, there were but a few dozen donations to AOL's Networkforgood.org. On Sept 14th, there were 12,000 donations totaling more than $1.26 million. Indeed, in the first six months following 9/11, it is estimated that 10% of relief donations (or $150 million) came via the Internet. The Red Cross alone raised more than $63 million online after 9/11 (Larose and Wallace 2003). The "giving trends" initiated by the 9/11 disaster have grown with each passing year. In 2004, for example, a full 39% of donations for victims of the South Asian Tsunami came from online donations (Bhagat 2005). And in 2005, the Bush-Clinton Katrina Fund, established to benefit the survivors of Hurricane Katrina, took *less than 24 hours* to raise its first million dollars in online donations (Clinton Foundation 2005). Many believe that online donations will be the fuel of the 2008 presidential elections. Indeed, candidates are learning to use the fundraising power of the Internet in new and innovative ways. "John Edwards convinced more than 10,600 supporters to give from $6.10 to $54 in honor of his 54th birthday, in exchange for an emailed copy of his mother's pecan pie recipe. It took just two days for former Tennessee Senator Fred Thompson, a Republican, to collect more than $350,000 in donations on his Internet site. Mr. Obama, meanwhile, promised to have dinner with four randomly selected donors, who could give as little as $5" (Schatz 2007).

Beyond civic activity, critics of new communication technologies voice other concerns. Fears regarding the Internet and the destruction of community are matched by concerns for technology's effect on intimacy. In many ways, the intimacy debate centers on the difference between direct and mediated communication. According to conventional wisdom, intimacy demands **direct communication**, face-to-face or physically copresent exchange. For intimacy to grow, we must "be" with others, see, hear, and touch them.

Only then is a relationship "real." But online communication is **mediated communication**—an indirect connection funneled through a mechanical medium. Many feel that mediation makes communication impersonal, fleeting, and ingenuous. As such, it is an inappropriate means by which to establish deep and lasting connections.

The bias against mediated communication as a vehicle of intimacy is well established. Indeed, many would argue that those who build "technological ties" are really isolates and loners living fantasy lives and creating anonymous, meaningless worlds. To be sure, there are some well-executed studies that support these concerns. Certain works suggest that some Internet users become unduly drawn into cyberspace and thus neglect their offline relationships (see, e.g., Nie and Erbring 2000; Schroeder and Ledger 1998; Shapiro and Leone 1999). Other studies contend that the anonymity of Internet communication creates identity conflict and confusion (Turkle 1996, 1997). But in the final analysis, a greater number of studies forward a positive picture of technology's role in intimate relationships. Research shows that the Internet complements and enhances preexisting relationships. The Internet also facilitates new friendships and bonds that might not otherwise have been possible (Boase et al. 2006; Horrigan and Rainie 2006; Jensen et al. 2007; Wellman 2004). Researchers at UCLA, for example, have shown that, increasingly, the Internet is becoming people's medium of choice for connecting with significant others. Consider that more than 100 million Americans used the Internet to make emotional connections with friends and loved ones in response to the 9/11 attacks. These individuals consciously chose e-mail over telephone or letter writing as a method of linking to others (UCLA Internet Project 2002). Others have demonstrated that the Internet has become a central tool in coping with life's most serious problems. For example, about one-half of Americans say that the Internet played a central role in helping them cope with a family member's major illness or their own medical problems. Similar numbers reported reliance on the Internet for important career-related decisions (Boase et al. 2006; Horrigan and Rainie 2006). Thus, as Katz and Rice conclude, "The Internet is quite a social environment, inhabited by quite social folks" (Katz and Rice 2002:264).

Sociologists Karen A. Cerulo and Janet M. Ruane suggest that an accurate assessment of new communication technologies will require a more flexible way of conceptualizing social relations. **Social relations** refer to the types of connections and the patterns of interaction that structure the broader society. Traditionally, sociologists have argued that physical copresence is integral to important relationships—relationships that enable communities, friendships, and intimacy. Thus, physical copresence has become the standard by which to judge the quality and importance of interaction. Cerulo and Ruane suggest that "bodies" may not be the most important part of the intimacy equation. Rather, the cognitive context in which communication occurs may make certain forms of direct and mediated exchange equally valuable and "real." Frequent and balanced interaction among individuals with overlapping backgrounds, strong and long-term bonds, and the development of trust—these are the qualities that make us feel connected to others. When these things are present, in online or offline settings, individuals perceive the interaction to be central to their lives (Cerulo 1997; Cerulo and Ruane 1998; Cerulo, Ruane, and Chayko 1992; Chayko 2002).

The American courts have taken such ideas to heart. Indeed, over the past decade, the courts have substantially broadened their definition of intimacy. A New Jersey court, for example, entertained a divorce and adultery case in which the "third party" and the offending spouse never physically met. The courts considered an online romance, void of any physical contact, as sufficient grounds for divorce by reason of adultery. Similarly, in a Massachusetts custody battle, a probate judge granted a mother custody of her children and permitted her to leave the state and move to New York. The judge granted the children's father two weekend visits per month and two weekly visits—*virtual* visits made possible through Internet conferencing technology. The father's lawyers protested, arguing that "you can't hug a computer." But in the judge's estimation, the children's physical presence was not vital to a meaningful visit.

Embedded in concerns of intimacy is the notion that technology dehumanizes the species. Philosophers such as Adorno, Ellul, Heidegger, and Marcuse and dystopian works such as George Orwell's *1984* or Stanley Kubrick's *2001: A Space Odyssey* all promote a similarly frightening message: Technology has transformed our person-to-person world into a cold, anonymous person-to-machine existence. Technology "does to us" and "takes from us," all in the name of progress. Ultimately, it robs us of initiative, control, and basic human emotions. Supporters of this argument say that the "proof is in the pudding." Technology has made everyday USA into a surreal scene. Sociability is gone. We are lonely beings in a crowd, preferring our cell phones and PDAs to interactions with those around us.

Sociologist Clifford Nass is unconvinced by the dehumanization argument. In its place, Reeves and Nass forward an idea they call "the Media Equation." Don't let the mathematical term put you off. The equation is quite simple. The media equation states that "media equals real life" (Reeves and Nass 1996:5). In forwarding this notion, Nass presents us with an interesting proposition. He forces us to reconsider the very meaning of the term *social actor*.

Who is a social actor? Is the title restricted to another living, breathing human being . . . or can it be a television . . . a computer . . . a robot . . . a

Web site? Nass demonstrates that social actors respond to all of these entities in the same fundamentally social way. Rather than technology dehumanizing people, people humanize technology! To prove the point, Nass revisited a number of classic social science experiments designed to test person-to-person responses in social interaction. The researchers redid these experiments, making one critical change: Each experiment now tested person-to-computer interaction. In all cases, the results supported the media equation, demonstrating that people interact with media just as they interact with other humans. Indeed, even the most technologically sophisticated people treat boxes of circuitry as if they were other human beings. People are polite to computers; they respond to praise from them and view them as teammates. People like computers with personalities similar to their own. They find masculine-sounding computers extroverted, driven, and intelligent while they judge feminine-sounding computers knowledgeable about love and relationships. They alter their body posture and their moods according to the size and perspective of the images on the screens before them (Nass and Brave 2007; Nass and Moon 2000; Nass, Moon, and Carney 1999; Reeves and Nass 1996).

Sherry Turkle (2007), the founder of MIT's "Initiative on Technology and the Self," reports similar results. Turkle observed and interviewed both the elderly and children as they interacted with robots such as Sony's robotic dog AIBO, Hasbro's My Real Baby and Furby, and the Japanese robots Paro and Healing Partners. She chose these robots because they can recognize their owners, obey their commands, and adjust their personalities in accord with owners' utterances and actions. When faced with the robots, human users respond in social ways, according to Turkle. Among the elderly, interacting with robots diminished anxiety (especially in those suffering from dementia), and brought a sense of real companionship to mentally stable individuals. (For example, users of Healing Partners reported that "the robots are like having grandchildren around all the time"; Litke 2006.) Similarly, children perceived and related to the robots as "an autonomous and almost alive self," who, while clearly not human, were fully capable of a meaningful relationship.

Both Nass's and Turkle's work suggests that new technologies have blurred the boundaries between people and objects, allowing both to operate as viable actors in the social terrain. We are witnessing similar changes with reference to the boundaries that distinguish people from animals or the living from the dead. Via virtual imaging and advanced robotics, new communication technologies create a reality in which seemingly anything can happen—be it talking to your dog and having him or her answer back . . . experiencing a passionate romance with the man or woman of your dreams . . . or engaging in a conversation with a spouse, friend, or parent who is no longer alive. Just make-believe? On the one hand, yes. However, technology's projection of animals, fantasies, and spirits as viable social actors has had tangible consequences. In the past 10 years, we have witnessed increases in behaviors that confirm the reality of such images. Americans are, for example, spending more time with their pets—buying them clothes and furniture; taking them to spas, to psychotherapists, and to psychics; bringing them to work; and sending them to vacation resorts. Similarly, Americans are spending more time and money on mediums and other activities designed to contact spirits and angels. Mediums such as John Edwards and James Van Praugh have become media stars! (Indeed, the waiting time for a private reading with John Edwards is nearly three years!) Furthermore, Americans are gobbling up technological products that merge sounds and images of past and present. CDs and videos that bring us duets between the living and the dead are now hot properties. So . . . who is a social actor? Is the title reserved for a living, breathing human being? New technologies make the question a complicated one to answer (Cerulo 2009; Cerulo and Ruane 1997).

Technology does offer a potentially frightening "Big Brother" scenario when we consider the issue of privacy. The popularity and growth of electronic surveillance have had a chilling effect on many social observers. In a world of ever-increasing anonymity, we must rely on alternate ways of facilitating trust and maintaining social order. Surely, this is the very idea behind electronic satellite "boxes" used to keep track of an increasing number of parolees. These devices allow the government to monitor convicted felons as they move about in local communities (Lee 2002). But surveillance has also entered the world of ordinary, law-abiding citizens. The never-blinking security camera has become a mainstay of social control in our stranger-based and now terrorist-threatened society. Technology experts tell us that, each year, we are witnessing a 25% growth in video surveillance. By 2009, most major cities will support on-street surveillance cameras and one-third of American households will contain security systems (Lee 2006; Holtzman 2006).

Surveillance tapes, of course, know no distinction between the private and public realms. Behaviors that social actors may intend as private backstage exchanges (a furtive kiss in a parking deck) may very well play as front-stage performances on security video screens. Surveillance also occurs on less obvious levels. Our movements over the course of a day can be traced via electronic toll and parking passes, phone records, and credit card activity. And as many people have haplessly discovered, our travels on the Internet can be far too public an affair. Computer cookies can reveal our interests and decision making.

While opportunities for the misuse of surveillance tools abound, it is nonetheless true that technology clearly enhances our privacy. Our ability to live a totally anonymous or secluded existence is supported by technology that enables us to work, play, and conduct all of our social and business affairs without ever going public (Nock 1993). With this view, electronic surveillance is not an ogre, but rather a response to the social changes of modern, urban living. Clearly, technology offers a solution to the social control dilemma posed by the fact that we desire and lead increasingly private lives.

Since 9/11, Americans appear to be more tolerant of governmental surveillance and seemingly more willing to regard any opposition to the government's watchful eye as unpatriotic. Indeed, with the passing of the USA PATRIOT Act (2001), the terrorism Surveillance Act (2006), and the Protect America Act (2007), the government, in the name of fighting terrorism, is able to collect a staggering array of private information about individuals. To date, the response of Americans to this expansion of invasive government power has been remarkably tame (Carlson 2005), especially when we consider just how opposed we are to any commercial intrusions (Liptak 2002). Consider, for instance, that in the first four days of its availability, more than 10 million Americans registered their phone numbers with the national "Do Not Call" list in order to stop telemarketing calls. At this writing, that number has grown to 132 million (Federal Trade Commission [FTC] 2007a)! Similarly, we consider SPAM to be the bane of the Internet—an affront to our online privacy (although experts acknowledge that it is much more than this). On an average day, Americans use the Internet to forward more than 300,000 examples of SPAM to the FTC, all in a concerted effort to help that agency fight these unwanted electronic intrusions (FTC 2007b). Clearly, we value our privacy, but we also, for now, appear willing to draw distinctions between governmental and commercial intrusions and between what we think are invasions by law-abiding versus law-violating individuals (Liptak 2002). Our discerning response suggests that high tech itself isn't viewed as the culprit. Rather, we are willing to judge technology by the "cause" it serves.

Technology—new-fangled, oppressive devices or new, essential tools of social life? If history proves informative, we will likely find some truth in both views. We can also be confident about a few other things. Just as we get comfortable with the latest innovations, still more advanced bells and whistles will arrive to push our buttons and sound new alarms. New technologies will prompt new debates about the pros and cons of high-tech living. And society will take it all in its technological stride.

Learning More About It

For a very thorough and balanced treatment of new communication technologies, both the pros and cons, see James E. Katz and Ronald E. Rice's *Social Consequences of Internet Use: Access, Involvement and Interaction* (Cambridge, MA: MIT Press, 2002). For some interesting ideas on closing the digital divide, see Jan van Dijk's book, *The Deepening Divide: Inequality in the Information Society* (Thousand Oaks, CA: Sage, 2005).

For up-to-date articles exploring the role of new communication technologies in community and intimacy formation, visit the Pew Internet and American Life Project at http://www.pewinternet.org

To read Clifford Nass's fascinating work on the humanization of technology, see either *The Media Equation* (with Byron Reeves, New York: Cambridge University Press, 1996) or *Wired for Speech: How Voice Activates and Advances the Human-Computer Relationship* (Cambridge, MA: MIT Press, 2007). Sherry Turkle's work on robots as social actors can be found in *Evocative Objects: Things We Think With* (Cambridge, MA: MIT Press, 2007). Karen A. Cerulo reviews technology and its impact on the definition of the social actor in her article, "New Ideas on the Social Actor" (*Annual Review of Sociology* 35:2009).

For a fascinating excursion into privacy and the Internet, see David Holtzman's book *Privacy Lost: How Technology Is Endangering Your Privacy* (San Francisco: Jossey-Bass, 2006).

Exercises

1. Visit an online chat group. You can participate or just watch. However,
   - visit the same group three times, and
   - spend at least 30 minutes during each visit.

   How did your chat group visits compare to face-to-face interactions? Is intimacy possible in these forums? Did you feel more vulnerable to other interactants in the online forums . . . less vulnerable? Were you less honest in your online discussions . . . more honest? Is online communication more useful for some tasks than others?

2. Select five charity mailings (from different organizations) that you have received in the recent past. Access each organization's Web site. Do a systematic comparison of the "snail mail" pitch versus online presentations and appeals. What similarities and differences do you find, especially with regard to each organization's ability to personalize its message and requests?

Social Institutions:
Education

Essay 23

Conventional Wisdom Tells Us . . . Education Is the Great Equalizer

Conventional wisdom tells us that educating the masses will bring equal opportunities to people of all races, ethnicities, and genders. In this essay, we explore the truth of this claim and review the progress we have made in bringing quality education to all.

The United States has earned a reputation as the land of opportunity, and the opportunity that so many of us desire is the improvement of our socioeconomic lot. Intergenerational upward mobility is a key dimension of the American Dream. **Intergenerational upward mobility** refers to social status gains by children vis-à-vis their parents.

Historically, education has been offered as the route by which such mobility can best be realized. Our free common public school system, established just prior to the Civil War, was founded on the principle that everyone, regardless of social background, should be educated. Lester Ward, a prominent sociologist of the late 1800s, thought that universal education would eliminate the inequalities associated with social class, race, and gender. Similarly, educational reformer Horace Mann promoted an expanded educational system as the antidote to poverty (Katz 1971).

Such sentiments have survived the test of time. We are a nation fueled by the belief that education will lead to equal opportunity for individual achievement and success. Former "education president" George Bush (the elder) aptly captured this cultural value, characterizing education as the "great lifting mechanism of an egalitarian society. It represents our most proven pathway to a better life."

The conventional wisdom on education reflects a structural functionalist view of society. **Structural functionalism** is a theoretical approach that stresses social order. Proponents contend that society is a collection of inter-dependent parts that function together to produce consensus and stability. This perspective links education to social stability in two ways. First, in taking their place in the education system, students learn the key norms, values, and beliefs of American culture. Second, by affording all students a chance to develop their skills and talents, education can channel the "best and the brightest" to key social positions.

Does the conventional view of education paint an accurate portrait? Is America's education system really the great equalizer?

To be sure, the American education system has grown dramatically over the past century. At the turn of the last century, only 10% of U.S. youth earned high school degrees, and only 2% earned college degrees (Vinorskis 1992). By World War I, primary education became compulsory in every state; by World War II, the same was true for secondary education. Now fast forward about 100 years. In 2005, 86% of Americans (aged 25–29) had earned a high school degree, and about 29% had earned a bachelor's degree or higher (U.S. Department of Education 2006, Indicator 31). Higher education is also seen as a possibility for more and more Americans. The percentage of high school graduates who immediately enroll in college is taken as an indicator of the *accessibility* of higher education. In 1972, only 49% of high school graduates immediately enrolled in college. But in 2004, that figure increased to 67% (U.S. Department of Education 2006, Indicator 29).

The face of our nation's college population has become more socially diverse as well. At the turn of the 20th century, college students were primarily the sons of White upper-class professionals. In contrast, today's college population includes the sons and daughters of all social classes and all racial and ethnic groups. Currently, minority students account for approximately 30% of students enrolled in degree-granting institutions (U.S. Department of Education 2005a). In 2005, just under half of Blacks 25–29 years old and one-third of Hispanics in this age group had completed some college (U.S. Department of Education 2006, Indicator 31).

In support of conventional wisdom, one must note a strong and positive association between income and education. In 2004, for example, the median yearly income for those with advanced degrees was $43,500. Contrast that figure with the median yearly income of those lacking a high school degree: only $21,800. The differences are even more pronounced among males. Males with a bachelor's degree or higher earned 67% more than males with only a high school degree (U.S. Department of Education 2006, Tables 22.1, 22.2). As educational levels increase, the poverty rate decreases—22% of those without a high school degree are below poverty level compared to 4% of those with a college degree or higher (U.S. Census Bureau 2006a, POV29). Table 23.1 illustrates this connection; the table shows the poverty rates for the working poor—that is, individuals who have spent at least 27 weeks in the labor force. Again the positive benefit of education is apparent (U.S. Department of Labor 2005a).

Furthermore, there is a strong positive relationship between education and health, one that holds across various measures of social class (Lleras-Muney 2004). As education levels increase, so too does the percent of people meeting recommended physical activity levels (U.S. Census Bureau 2007d: Table 199). The world over, increased education translates into better nutrition, higher immunization rates, and lower mortality rates (World Bank 2005). And as educational achievement increases, so does individuals' civic involvement: Both voter registration and turnout increase with education (U.S. Department of Education 2005b). The benefits of education seem to touch even those who detour from life's conventional path: Prisoners' exposure to educational programs while incarcerated is associated with lower rates of recidivism (National Institute for Literacy 2007b).

The statistics just quoted suggest that education's links to "the good life" are right on target. However, on closer examination, one finds several situations that can weaken the strength of that bond. Education's "lifting mechanism" may not be fully functional for all social groups. Research verifies that the economically disadvantaged fail to reap the benefits of higher education. The pattern is very clear: As income decreases, so does the percentage of students who both expect to attend and who enroll in college. Only

Table 23.1   Poverty Rates of Working Poor by Education Levels, 2003

Education level	Poverty rates
Less than high school diploma	14.1%
High school degree, no college	6.2%
Some college, no degree	5.1%
Associate degree	3.2%
College degree	1.7%

SOURCE: U.S. Department of Labor 2005c: "Profile of Working Poor: 2003."

29% of students with the lowest socioeconomic status (SES) background expect to get a college degree, and only 22% expect to earn a graduate or professional degree. But among students with the highest SES background, 33% expect to earn a college degree, and 53% expect to earn a graduate or professional degree. Consider another important difference from data collected in 2004. While only 50% of students from low-income families immediately transitioned to college, a full 79% of students from high-income families did so (U.S. Department of Education 2006: Table 29.1). In short, family income remains the best predictor of both who will go to college and what college students will attend (Callan 2007). The pattern is in part explained by the preparation of students. Lower income high school graduates are less academically qualified for college than are their wealthier counterparts. Yet even when we look only at those students who are qualified for admission to a four-year college, the relationship between income and enrollment stubbornly persists: The higher the income, the higher the enrollment rate (McSwain and Davis 2007; U.S. Department of Education 2002).

The cost of a college degree has become increasingly less affordable since the 1990s. In 2006, tuition and fees for four-year public colleges were up 35% from 2001 *after* adjusting for inflation (College Board 2006a). According to our national report card on higher education, 43 states received flunking grades with regard to various indicators of affordability. Several states saw increases in the percentage of family income needed to pay the net costs of a four-year college—only one state (Louisiana) showed improvement on this indicator (National Center for Public Policy and Higher Education 2006). The financial burden of increasing college costs hits lower income families hardest. Compared to the early 1990s, the lowest income families today need an additional 16% of their income to pay for the increases in college costs. Highest income families only need an additional 1% (Callan 2007).

In recent years, student loans (which must be repaid) have supplanted grants as the primary means for financing college. And federal grant aid has failed to keep pace with inflation (College Board 2006b). It is estimated that between 1 and 1.6 million qualified high school graduates did not go onto college largely due to the lack of financial aid; we are likely to see another 1.4 to 2.4 million more high school graduates suffer the same fate in the next decade (Advisory Committee on Student Financial Assistance 2006). In 2004, two-thirds of all graduates of four-year colleges left school with a debt of just under $20,000 (Swarthout 2007; U.S. PIRG 2007). And even after receiving financial assistance via grants and loans, the 2004 low-income family still needed to pay $6,000 for a child to attend one year of a two- or four-year public college and more than $10,000 per year for access to a four-year private college (U.S. Department of Education 2006: Table 49.1).

Unfortunately, federal and state financial aid has not allowed middle- and lower income families to keep pace with the increasing costs of higher education. In the early 1990s, the average Pell Grant (the largest source of federal aid for financially needy students) covered 76% of tuition costs at public four-year colleges. In 2005, the average Pell Grants covered only 48% of those tuition expenses (Callan 2007). In 2006, we witnessed an unprecedented cut to federal student aid, a cut that took $12 billion from the federal student loan program to help finance a tax cut for the wealthiest Americans (U.S. PIRG 2007). The average Pell Grant in 2006 fell by $120 per recipient (College Board 2006b).

Today, colleges and universities provide the largest amount of student financial aid. And while one might expect that this institutional aid might be highest for those in the greatest financial need, this is *not* the case. The average institutional grant is larger for students from high- and middle-income families. This "anomaly" reflects colleges and universities' concern with their competitive ranking—a standing that benefits from admitting students with the best college prep backgrounds (see Table 23.2) (Callan 2007).

For some students, the answer to the high cost of a college education is the community college. Approximately 43% of undergraduates attend two-year institutions. The enrollment rate for two-year colleges grew significantly during the 1970s, and total enrollments are expected to reach new highs through 2016 (U.S. Department of Education 2007a). Two-year community colleges have been described as the "safety net" for a state's educational system. They have played a particularly important role for first-generation college students as well as for low-income and minority students (Callan 2003; Kao and Thompson 2003). They are seen by many financially strapped students as a practical and reasonable alternative to the escalating costs of four-year colleges (Evelyn 2004).

Table 23.2   Institutional Grant Support for Full-time Dependent Students by Parental Income, 2003–2004

Parental Income	Institutional Grant Award (Average)
Below $20,000	$4,700
$20,000–39,999	$5,000
$40,000–59,999	$5,500
$60,000–79,999	$5,700
$80,000–99,999	$6,100
$100,000 or more	$6,200

SOURCE: Callan 2007; http://measuringup.highereducation.org/commentary/collegeaffordability.cfm

As valuable a role as community colleges play, however, it is important to note some caveats of pursuing a college career via this route. Like four-year public colleges, community college costs have been increasing above inflation rates (College Board 2006a). At the same time, budgetary support for these institutions has grown more and more problematic. State and local support has decreased in recent years, forcing more community colleges to engage in private fundraising as well as to look to Washington for federal grants. These budgetary constraints have meant that many two-year colleges have had to turn away hundreds of thousands of students in recent years (Evelyn 2004). And despite their place in the higher-education landscape, community colleges simply don't yield the same long-term dividends of four-year institutions. Only half of community college students who enter with the goal of obtaining a bachelor's degree actually transfer to four-year institutions. And transfer students are still less likely than those who started at four-year institutions to actually complete a bachelor's degree: 44% versus 63% (U.S. Department of Education 2003). The implications of terminating college with an associate's versus a bachelor's degree are striking when we focus on the financial payoff of higher education. In 2005, median annual earnings for an associate versus a bachelor's degree were $41,200 and $54,800, respectively. Seventeen percent of bachelor's degree recipients earned $100,000 or more compared with 4% of associate degree recipients. Only 27% of associate degree holders earned more than the median annual income of those with bachelor's degrees (College Board 2006c).

The greatest financial return on a college degree is reserved for graduates of elite or selective private colleges (Coleman and Rainwater 1978; Hoxby 2001; Useem and Karabel 1986). Harvard economist Caroline Hoxby has determined that students attending the top-ranked selective colleges earn back their educational investments many times over during their working careers. Indeed, the ultimate value of attending an elite school is reflected in one of her more telling findings: Choosing a "free ride" at a highly competitive third-tier college (e.g., Georgetown or University of Virginia) is not as smart as *paying* for an education at a top-tier institution (e.g., Harvard or Johns Hopkins), since the lifetime return on the latter investment is so very lucrative (Hoxby 2001).[1] "Selective" colleges, however, are very selective about their student bodies. Despite years of affirmative action efforts, Black and Hispanic students are nonetheless underrepresented at selective colleges and universities (Harper and Reskin 2005). Gatekeeping practices (used to control students' educational progress), escalating costs, and increasing use of merit- rather than need-based financial aid packages by elite universities ensure that access to such institutions is restricted largely to members of the most privileged social classes. Educational ability proves less important than family background in gaining admission into top-tier or Ivy League institutions (Kao and Thompson 2003; Karen 1990; Persell and Cookson 1990).

Education's equalizing mechanism often seems to fail ethnic and racial minorities as well. The 2005 high school dropout rate for 16- to 24-year-old White students was 6.0%—a figure much lower than the 10.4% and 22.4% rates for Blacks and Hispanics, respectively (U.S. Department of Education 2007b, Indicator 23). In 2005, for the 25- to 29-year-old age group, 93% of Whites, 87% of Blacks, and 63% of Hispanics had completed high school. And in 2005 for the same age group, 34% of Whites but only 17.5% of Blacks and 11.2% of Hispanics had completed a college degree or higher (U.S. Department of Education 2006a, Indicator 31). In terms of the perceived accessibility of higher education, minority students face a more difficult transition path than White students: In 2004, 69% of White high school graduates immediately went on to college compared with 62% of African American high school graduates and 62% of Hispanic high school graduates (U.S. Department of Education 2006a, Indicator 29). When minority students go on to college, they frequently enter two-year colleges: About half of Black and Hispanic college students attend community colleges (Evelyn 2003). And while minority enrollments in graduate programs increased 269% since 1976, minorities made up just 23% of total graduate school enrollments in 2005 (U.S. Department of Education 2007b, Indicator 9). The financial burden of financing higher education is also particularly harsh on minority students: 55% of African American students and 58% of Hispanic students carry unmanageable debt burdens after college graduation, compared with 40% of all subsidized student loan borrowers (PIRG 2002).

Low educational achievement does more than deprive people of degrees and earnings. Low educational achievement imposes heavy costs on literacy. **Literacy** refers to the ability to use printed and written information to function in society and is assessed in three areas: prose, document, and quantitative. Across all three areas, as educational attainment increases, so too do literacy scores. The percentage judged proficient—that is, possessing the skills necessary for complex and challenging literacy activities—also increases with educational attainment (see Table 23.3) (U.S. Department of Education 2007a, Indicator 18). Our adult reading habits are also fueled by education—the higher the education level, the more likely we are to report reading newspapers, magazines, and books on a daily basis (U.S. Department of Education 2006, Indicator 20).

Table 23.3   Percentage of Adults (16+) Proficient in Prose, Document, and Quantitative Literacy by Education Level: 2003

Education Level	Adults Proficient in Various Types of Literacy		
	Prose	Document	Quantitative
Less than high school	1%	2%	1%
High school graduate	4%	5%	5%
Some college	11%	10%	11%
Associate's degree	19%	16%	18%
College degree	31%	25%	31%
Graduate study/degree	41%	31%	36%

SOURCE: U.S. Department of Education, 2007a, Table 18.2. http://nces.ed.gov/programs/COE/2007/section2/table.asp?tableID=693

The cycle of low educational achievement is hard to break: Parental involvement in the educational lives of their children—attending school meetings or teacher conferences or volunteering at school—is inversely related to parental education (U.S. Department of Education 2005a, Table 23). Dropout rates of students from the bottom 20% of incomes are six times higher than rates of students from the top 20% of incomes (U.S. Department of Education 2004, Indicator 16). While 86% of high school graduates whose parents have college degrees immediately transition to college, only 40% of graduates whose parents have less than a high school degree do so (U.S. Department of Education 2006, Table 29.3). Students whose parents have only a high school degree are less likely than their peers to enroll in a four-year college, and if they do enroll, they are less likely to graduate (U.S. Department of Education 2002). The lower the parents' levels of education, the more time it takes for their children to complete their college degrees (U.S. Department of Education 2003). To be sure, a college education is an expensive investment, one that takes careful planning and financial preparation. Even on this front, however, there are dynamics that hinder equal educational opportunity for all. Families with the lowest incomes and the least educated parents face the greatest uncertainty and know the least about the costs of attending college (Horn, Chen, and Chapman 2003; U.S. Department of Education 2001).

Perhaps the most dramatic failure of education's equalizing powers is witnessed in the area of gender. Although women are clearly "present" in the classroom today—they constitute 57% of college enrollments and 60% of graduate enrollments (U.S. Department of Education 2007a, Indicators 8 and 9)—this is a noteworthy break with the past. The educational history of women in the United States bespeaks little in the way of equal opportunity or achievement. In the 1900s, the doors to high schools and subsequently colleges were opened to women. Indeed, in 1907, there were 110 women's colleges in the United States. However, only 32% of these women's colleges met even the most basic standards of a true higher education program. Rather, most women's colleges were engaged in the task of preparing women for their "place" in society—that is, as homemakers. Government aid policies of the era reinforced this traditional tracking. Vocational training such as cooking, sewing, and home economics qualified for federal subsidies; commercial training did not (Stock 1978).

Women who wanted a "real" higher education were limited by restrictive college admission policies. Most elite schools of the East simply refused to accept women. Western institutions had more liberal policies, but such policies were generally driven by financial motives: They admitted women in an effort to ward off financial disaster. The most blatant example of this practice, however, occurred at the University of Chicago. Faced with bankruptcy in 1873, the university decided to admit women. When the financial situation of the university improved, the institution's stance toward female admissions changed dramatically. Women were immediately relegated to a separate junior college (Stock 1978).

The post–World War II era further compromised women's access to education. Prior to World War II, the percentage of women attending college had been increasing steadily. However, postwar college admissions gave absolute priority to war veterans. Such policies forced women back into the home, despite the work they had done during the war to keep America productive (Stock 1978). Furthermore, the postwar policy signaled the beginning of a long-term trend. Even today, despite their heavy investment in higher education, women do not enjoy returns equal to those of men; the financial benefits of education are significantly lower for women than for men at every level of educational achievement (see Essay 13).

Instances of class, racial, ethnic, and gender inequality lead many to doubt the conventional wisdom on education. Indeed, conflict theorists question education's ability to equalize. **Conflict theorists** analyze social organization and social interactions by attending to the differential resources controlled by different sectors of a society. Conflict theorists suggest that the U.S. education system actually transmits inequality from one generation to the next (Bidwell and Friedkin 1988; Bowles and Gintis 1976, 2002; Collins 2001; Kozol 1991, 1995, 2005; Swartz 2003).

The conflict view of education parallels structural functionalism in acknowledging the role of education within the socialization process.

Socialization refers to the process by which we learn the norms, values, and beliefs of a social group, as well as our place within that social group. But in contrast to structural functionalists, conflict theorists argue that the goals of socialization vary according to the social class of students.

In Essay 14, we noted Jonathan Kozol's observations regarding racial inequalities in U.S. schools. Kozol argued that Whites and non-Whites often learn different lessons within American schools. Kozol notes similar inequalities in comparisons of various social classes. (Indeed, Kozol argues that much racial inequality in the United States is fueled by factors that link minority racial status to low economic status.)

Through their elementary and high school education, lower- and working-class students are taught attitudes and skills that best prepare them for supervised or labor-intensive occupations. These include respect for authority, passivity, the willingness to obey orders, and so on (Kozol 2005; Solomon, Battistich, and Hom 1996). In contrast, middle- and upper-class children are taught skills essential to management-level jobs and professional careers—that is, responsibility and dependability. College and post-college education offer privileged students continued training in management and professional skills. The underrepresentation of lower- and working-class students at the college level and beyond excludes such students from similar training and, ostensibly, from upward career mobility (Kozol 1991, 2005).

Beyond socialization, the funding and delivery of education can also maintain and reinforce class divisions. Consider, for instance, the fact that local revenues provide more than 40% of the total funding for public school budgets (U.S. Department of Education 2007a). Affluent school districts (with fewer than 5% of students living in poverty) receive local revenues that are three times the amount of those received by impoverished districts (35% of students living in poverty) or approximately $6,000 of local revenues per student versus $2,000 per student (U.S. Department of Education 2003). State governments do try to close this gap by directing more state general revenues to poor school districts, but they do so without total success. In 2000, for instance, school districts with the lowest levels of poverty received 6% less, but districts with intermediate levels of poverty received up to 18% less in state revenue per student than districts with the highest poverty levels (U.S. Department of Education 2003). While the Bush administration's No Child Left Behind Act of 2001 drew praise for focusing attention on the educational needs of low-income and minority students, it has since been criticized as being largely an unfunded and therefore empty mandate (Rentner et al. 2003).

Remarkable progress has been made with regard to computer technology in our schools. As of 2005, 94% of public school instructional rooms had

Internet access; this figure is up from 3% in 1994. And the majority of schools with access reported broadband Internet connections. Still some remnants of a digital divide remain. Schools with the lowest levels of minority enrollments had a lower ratio of students to instructional computers (3.0) than did schools with higher minority enrollments (4.1). Nine percent of schools with the lowest minority enrollments provided handheld computers to their students and 15% loaned laptops to students. The figures for high minority schools were 6% and 7%, respectively (Wells and Lewis 2006).

The gaps become much wider as we follow students home from school. In 2003, 52% of students from families with incomes less than $10,000 used the Internet compared with 80% of students from families with incomes of $75,000 or more. For all age groups and for all education levels, Whites have higher rates of computer usage at home and higher rates of Internet usage than do Black and Hispanic students (U.S. Department of Education 2005a, Indicator 37, Tables 417 & 419; see Table 23.4).

Research also indicates that the size of schools and the number of students in classrooms can also make for very unequal educational experiences. Mid-sized schools offer the most positive environments for learning. Large schools (900+ students), however, dominate central city school districts. Four of the five largest school districts in the United States have student poverty rates in excess of 23% (U.S. Department of Education 2005a, Table 90). Student-teacher ratios are highest in our largest elementary and secondary public schools (U.S. Department of Education 2007a, Indicator 30). As the size of school increases, so does the reporting of serious student problems such as apathy, dropping out, and drug use (U.S. Department of Education 2003).

Overcrowding is another problem that diminishes the educational experience for students. Approximately 8% of our public schools are severely overcrowded—that is operating at 25% above their student capacity. Another 10% of public schools are overenrolled at 6–25% above capacity. Overenrollment is more likely in schools with more than 50% minority

Table 23.4   Computer/Internet Usage by White, Black, and Hispanic Youth and College Students

	Whites	Blacks	Hispanics
Computers used at home:			
15 years old +	85%	50%	56%
Internet usage:			
College students	93%	80%	78%

SOURCE: U.S. Department of Education 2005a, Tables 417 and 419.

enrollments, in large schools, and in urban schools. A common response to overcrowding is to increase class size (reported by 44% of public school principals). In 2005, 30% of students in public schools attended schools that were overenrolled (Chaney and Lewis 2007).

Teachers themselves may also play a role in transmitting educational inequality (Brophy 1983). Public schools with high minority enrollments are more likely to employ teachers lacking experience (U.S. Department of Education 2003). Students in high minority and high poverty high schools are more likely to be taught English, science, and math by "out of field" teachers—that is, teachers who did not major or are not certified in the subject they teach (U.S. Department of Education 2004, Indicator 24). Studies also show that the social characteristics of students often affect teacher expectations of student performance. Low expectations are most likely to be found in the most disadvantaged schools—inner-city schools with large enrollments of poor and minority students (Hallinan and Sorensen 1985; Kozol 1991, 2005; Lumsden 1997; Solomon et al. 1996).

Teachers' social characteristics can also influence their expectations of student performance. High-status teachers frequently display rather low expectations for their poor and minority students (Alexander, Entwisle, and Thompson 1987). But in this regard, there is also some encouraging news. Teachers who hold positive performance expectations appear to motivate positive results in their students. Indeed, high expectations and demands for academic excellence appear to offset the otherwise negative effects associated with class, race, and ethnicity (Bamburg 1994; Hoffer, Greeley, and Coleman 1987; Mehan, Hubbard, Lintz, and Villanueva 1994; Omotani and Omotani 1996; Raffini 1993).

Finally, conflict theorists cite tracking as an important source of educational inequality. **Tracking** is a practice by which students are divided into groups or classes based on perceived ability. Although tracking is meant to group students in terms of academic ability, in reality it tends to create economic, racial, and ethnic clusters. Since the 1980s, the *form* of tracking has been modified from total program (e.g., college prep tracks vs. vocational tracks) to course-level distinctions (e.g., honors courses in English, history, math, etc.), yet the inequality of the system remains. Studies that compare the performance of low-, medium-, and high-ability tracks show that tracking benefits only the high-ability groups (French and Rothman 1990; Kao and Thompson 2003; Lucas 1999; Shavit and Featherman 1988; Stockard and Mayberry 1992). And while theoretically, students should be able to achieve mobility within the system, downward movement is much more likely than upward (Lucas 1999). Thus, critics of tracking argue that the practice does little to equalize opportunity; its most ardent opponents argue that tracking creates de jure (legally sanctioned) segregation in our schools (Nelson 2001).

There is evidence that tracking fosters a self-fulfilling prophecy (Eder 1981; Lucas 1999; Nelson 2001). A **self-fulfilling prophecy** is a phenomenon whereby that which we believe to be true, in some sense, becomes true for us. Within the tracking system, students do as well or as poorly as they are expected (or given the opportunity) to do (Alexander and Cook 1982; Goodlad 1984; Hochschild 2001; Nelson 2001; Stockard and Mayberry 1992; Strum 1993; Vanfossen, Jones, and Spade 1987; Williams 2002).

The inequalities found in the U.S. education system are likely to grow worse in the near future. Our last recession took a hard toll on education. Across the nation, state budget crises were laid at the feet of students and their families. Since the early 1980s, the median family income has increased by 127%, but college tuition and fees have increased by 375%. Parents worry more about the rising costs of college than other essential expenditures and perhaps with good cause. The costs of a college education have greatly out-distanced cost increases in medical care, housing, energy, transportation, food, and the like (Callan 2007). This development is especially worrisome given the short- and long-range forecasts for higher education enrollments. By the end of the decade, we should see the largest high school graduating class in history. Our nation's demographics indicate that low-income and minority students will abound among these graduates (Callan 2003). Blocking their access to higher education would have ramifications for generations to come.

American youth must be ready to compete in an increasingly global and information-driven economy. Forecasted changes in the job market indicate an increasing demand for better educated and more literate workers (Hecker 2001; Sum et al. 2002). Twelve of the 20 fastest growing occupations require college or associate degrees (U.S. Department of Labor 2005b). The Employment Policy Foundation estimates that American jobs requiring college degrees will increase by 20 million over the next several years. The Foundation also estimates that, given our present college graduation rates, there will be a 33% shortfall in the number of educationally qualified workers (Employment Policy Foundation 2002). Clearly, an education system that fails to offer quality public education and restricts access to college and postcollege training assures a bleak future for the "undereducated." Students who are absent from these settings will also be chronically absent from the jobs of tomorrow and upward mobility. But there are larger implications as well. Consider the much anticipated aging of the baby boomers. The retirement of this cohort—the most educated generation in U.S. history—is anticipated to cause a decrease in the average education level in the United States. Such a change is predicted to result in decreasing personal incomes and decreasing tax revenues. The chances for such declines will certainly increase if we fail to improve the educational prospects of the fastest growing segments of the youth population: racial and ethnic minorities (Policy Alert 2005).

The inequalities found in the U.S. education system present an unavoidable irony. Education can indeed be a great equalizer, but at present, it is not. This tool of upward mobility is most likely to be placed in the hands of those who are already located in advantaged positions. Thus, rather than creating opportunity, the current educational system more accurately sustains the status quo. Our greatest educational challenge, then, may be to devise an ideology that can resolve such contradictions within the system.

Learning More About It

Samuel Bowles and Herbert Gintis offer a classic critique of the American educational system in *Schooling in Capitalist America: Educational Reform and the Contradictions of Economic Life* (New York: Basic Books, 1976). A more recent analysis can be found in Jonathan Kozol's books, *Savage Inequalities* (New York: Crown, 1991) and *Amazing Grace: The Lives of Children and the Conscience of a Nation* (New York: Crown, 1995). Kozol examines the growing resegregation of our public schools in *The Shame of the Nation: The Restoration of Apartheid Schooling in America* (New York: Crown, 2005). You can read an interview with Kozol about this recent work at Campusprogress.org (http://www.campus progress.org/features/552/five-minutes-with-jonathan-kozol).

In *Race in the Schools: Perpetuating White Dominance?*, Judith Blau offers a compelling case for the value of pluralism in American schools (Boulder: Lynne Rienner Publishers, 2003).

For an interesting history of the links between education and credentials, see Randall Collins's *The Credential Society: An Historical Sociology of Education* (New York: Academic Press, 1979).

Shannon Harper and Barbara Reskin review the history and impact of affirmative action in the areas of education and employment in their 2005 article, "Affirmative Action at School and on the Job" (*Annual Review of Sociology*, 31:357–380).

To learn the educational requirements for specific occupations see the Department of Labor's Occupational Outlook Handbook: http://stats.bls.gov/oco/home.htm

The following organizations and sites can help you learn more about various issues in education:

Institute for Higher Education (dedicated to improving access to and success in secondary education)
http://www.ihep.org

National Center for Public Policy and Higher Education
http://www.highereducation.org

(Once at the site, you might want to look at a report comparing states on higher education: "Measuring Up 2006: The State-by-State Report Card for Higher Education." Or access the report directly at http://measuringup.highereducation.org/)

National Assessment Governing Board (Responsible for issuing the "Nation's Report Card")
http://www.nagb.org

National Institute for Literacy
http://www.nifl.gov

U.S. Department of Education
http://www.ed.gov

Exercises

1. Obtain a college catalog from each of the following categories: (a) an Ivy League college, (b) a four-year state college, and (c) a local community college. Compare the mission statement contained in each school's catalog. Also compare each school's programs of study and the types of courses it offers. Use your data to prepare a discussion regarding the equal opportunity philosophy of U.S. colleges and universities.

2. Access the most recent edition of the *World Almanac*. Obtain information on the following four items: high school graduation rate by state, student-teacher ratio per state, per capita personal income per state, and state revenues for the public schools. Identify those states that represent the top five and the bottom five of each data category. Is there any overlap in these top five and bottom five groups? Speculate on your findings.

3. Imagine that you and your spouse and two small children are currently residing in New Jersey. You have just received two job offers. One would require a move to California, the other a move to New Mexico. Assume that education prospects for your children are a major consideration for you. Access the Web page for the National Center for Public Policy and Higher Education (http://www.highereducation.org/).

    *   Click on the link for the latest edition of *Measuring Up* (The National Report Card on Education).
    *   Use the Compare States link to access data that will help you decide whether you should remain in New Jersey or move west to California or New Mexico. Share and defend your decision.

Note

1. Hoxby used *Barron's Profile of American Colleges* to establish her tier rankings.

Social Institutions:
Religion

Essay 24

Conventional Wisdom Tells Us . . . We Are One Nation Under God

God bless America . . . it's an invocation frequently heard across the United States. Yet, in light of our country's long-standing commitment to the separation of church and state, God bless America is also a prayer that can make some uncomfortable. Are we united or divided with regard to the place of God in our nation? This essay explores the issue.

One nation under God . . . most recognize these words as part of the U.S. Pledge of Allegiance. For well over 100 years, American school-children have recited the pledge as part of their daily school ritual. The earliest version of the pledge, penned in 1892, was quite simple: I pledge allegiance to my Flag, and to the Republic for which it stands: one Nation indivisible, With Liberty and Justice for all.

The first significant change to the pledge was made in 1923. The place: the first National Flag Conference in Washington, D.C. At this time, "my flag" was changed to "the flag of the United States." (The change was designed to avoid potential confusion among members of the growing immigrant population in the United States.) A year later, the target of the pledge was further specified as "the flag of the United States of America." Finally, the addition of the words "under God" was authorized in 1954. The campaign to add these two words was led by the Knights of Columbus and was a byproduct of our national fear of communism. President Eisenhower authorized the change, arguing that it highlighted religion's significant place in American history and culture:

> In this way we are reaffirming the transcendence of religious faith in America's heritage and future; in this way we shall constantly strengthen those spiritual weapons which forever will be our country's most powerful resource in peace and war. (UnderGodProCon, 2006)

To be sure, religion and the American way form a natural pairing. The Pilgrims' arrival in the New World was motivated by the pursuit of religious freedom. The Puritans too actively sought to establish strong ties between politics and the tenets of Protestantism. In fact in some colonies, the Puritans successfully established official religions. And, of course, many credit the very spirit and growth of U.S. capitalism to the strong influence of Protestantism—especially its core value of the work ethic.

Many of our Founding Fathers supported the overlap between government and religion. George Washington asserted that it was impossible to govern without God and the Bible. Ben Franklin contended that no nation could rise without the aid of God. And for centuries, our secular government has peacefully coexisted with the sacred. Presidents invoke God's help as they are sworn into office, a practice started by George Washington (Davis 1990). Witnesses in our courts swear on bibles to tell the truth. Public ceremonies and congressional sessions start with religious invocations. Our national currency and motto both attest to our trust in God.

Of course, there are limits to the secular-sacred relationship. Despite early efforts by the Puritans, the United States has no official religion. Indeed, the Constitution mandates the separation of church and state. While some Founding Fathers supported the infusion of religion into politics, others opposed this development. President James Madison warned that failing to honor the separation between church and state would make us vulnerable to the religious conflicts that had plagued European nations. Jefferson advocated for a "wall of separation" between church and state. Every ten years, the U.S. government conducts a census of the entire population, yet Public Law 94–521 *prohibits* questions about religion. To be sure, we are a nation of believers, making us, in sociological terms, high in **religiosity**. Religiosity refers to our beliefs as opposed to our active participation in a religious groups. More than 90% of Americans report believing in God or a higher power (CBS News Poll 2006; Gallup Poll 2007b). Yet, many Americans are nonetheless diligent about preventing any real or apparent government promotion of religion. (Note, for example, that every holiday season seems to bring renewed efforts by some groups to keep the "sacred" out of official public displays and decorations.) So while we may pledge our allegiance to one nation under God, we remain vigilant about any religious undermining of our civil rights.

The 2004 presidential election spotlighted Americans' conflicted stance on the mixing of religion and politics. Recall that in his reelection campaign, George Bush promoted a "faith-based" presidency. According to many political analysts, Bush's open relationship with religion effectively mobilized the religious right. Without such support, many believe Bush could not have won reelection. A recent Pew Research poll on religion and politics suggests that the pundits may be right. For example, 56% of Evangelical Protestants identified themselves as affiliated with the Republican party. (Evangelical Protestants account for about one-quarter of the U.S. adult population and consist of individuals affiliated with historically white denominations like the Southern Baptist convention, the Assemblies of God, and the Presbyterian Church.) The figure increases to 70% among Traditionalist Evangelicals (i.e., Evangelicals characterized by high levels of orthodox beliefs and religious engagement; see Green 2004). Critics, both within and outside of the Republican Party fear the fallout expected from social policy informed more by faith than by facts. Bush's low approval ratings in his second term may indicate that these fears are well founded. Still it is clear that a powerful alliance has been formed by putting faith in politics. Some credit our recent welfare reform policies, tax cut policies, and attacks on the U.S. judiciary as evidence of the muscle of right-wing religious groups (Hough 2005).

Our approach-avoidance stance on religion may more accurately be characterized as ambivalence with *organized* religion than with an Almighty deity. Sociologists distinguish among several different kinds of religious groups that vary along their level of *social organization* and *social integration*. A **church** is a long-standing religious organization with a formalized social structure and routinized interactions. Churches typically enjoy strong ties to society. When some members of churches are dissatisfied with the established beliefs or practices, they might leave to form denominations and sects. **Denominations** are groups that break away from their "mother" churches and establish their own unique identities via their specific beliefs, traditions, and rituals. United Methodists, Presbyterians, and Episcopalians are all examples of Protestant denominations. **Sects** can be seen as the product of more conflictual breakaways; sects establish themselves as independent rival religious organizations. **Cults** are new and relatively small and unorganized religious groups whose beliefs set them apart from more established or mainstream groups. Cults are frequently met with suspicion by mainstream society. Yet note that many major religious groups of today started as cults (e.g., the Catholic Church and the Mormon Church).

A variety of polls consistently document that the overwhelming majority of Americans believe in God and an afterlife and hold a religious outlook on life (American Religious Identity Survey 2001; CBS News Poll 2006; Gallup Poll 2007b). But our *religious practices* are not so uniform. Not surprising in a culture that values personal freedom and autonomy, religious identification does not automatically translate into "belonging" or what sociologists call **religious affiliation**—formal group membership in a religious community. Across many religions, there is a gap between self-identification and actual membership, a gap that increased during the 1990s. For example, only 45% of those who identify themselves as Protestant report church membership. The membership rate for Catholics is 59%; and for those who self-identify as Jewish, it is 53%. Overall, among those who identify with a specific religion, nearly 40% indicate that neither they nor anyone in their household belongs to a religious institution (American Religious Identity Survey 2001). The percentage of Americans reporting no religious affiliation at all has also been increasing—from 9% in 1993 to 14% in 2002 (Smith 2004). Fully 41 of the states see more than 10% of their populations reporting no religious affiliation. In six states (Colorado, Nevada, Oregon, Vermont, Washington, and Wyoming) the percentage reporting no religion is 20% or higher (American Religious Identity Survey 2001).

The aging of our population may also forecast some challenges for organized religions. A recent AARP study suggests that Baby Boomers are extremely skeptical of *institutionalized* religion. The survey of more than 1,600 Americans aged 45 to 79 found that 40% of the respondents reported deriving their religious satisfaction from helping others; only 20% found that satisfaction in attending religious services. For those expressing dissatisfaction with their religion or church, many attributed it to conflict over official views (70%), to the behavior of church leaders (57%), or to the hypocrisy of church members (58%) (Montenegro 2004). These findings may help us understand a well-documented trend reported in ongoing Gallup polls. Over the last decade, only about one-third of Americans report attending weekly worship services (Gallup Poll 2007b). One third of the population may seem strikingly low. But some researchers maintain that this figure is unrealistically high, the effect of a **social desirability bias** in survey research (i.e., answering questions in a way that makes respondents look good). When researchers "count" people in attendance at a sample of churches, weekly attendance rates are found to be around 20% (Hartford Institute for Religion Research 2006).

Americans' skepticism toward organized religion may be well placed. Recent revelations of sexual misbehaviors and cover-ups by religious leaders have surely challenged the faith of some in organized religion. Additionally, more traditional and established religious groups like churches tend to be highly bureaucratic structures. **Bureaucracies** strive to achieve rationality and efficiency via a hierarchical authority structure, a clear division of labor, reliance on written rules/procedures, and impersonal interaction. As such, the bureaucratic structure contradicts the emotionally rich experiences many hope to achieve via their spiritual pursuits.

The desire for spiritually moving religious experiences is fueling the fast-growing Pentecostal movement. **Pentecostals** engage in "spirit-filled" worship (speaking in tongues, faith healing) and are found in most Christian traditions (Goodstein 2005). Pentecostalists are the fastest growing religious groups in the world (Phillips 2007). In the United States, Pentecostals account for 2.1% of the population, a figure that represents a 38% increase since 1990 (Adherents.com 2005a). Indeed, the largest church in the world is a Pentecostal one—the Yoido Full Gospel Church in Seoul, South Korea (Goodstein 2005).

Another source of American's cautious stance on organized religion may be the political activist stance associated with evangelical and fundamentalist religious groups in the United States. There are more than 70 million evangelical Christians in the United States today—this translates to roughly 23% of the population (Greenberg and Berktold 2004). **Evangelicals** don't share a common religious group or church; rather they share a style or approach to faith that transcends any one denomination. Consequently, it is possible to speak of evangelical Methodists, evangelical Lutherans, and even evangelical Catholics. Evangelicals view the Holy Scriptures as authoritative and infallible; they are the only path to salvation. A core evangelical belief is that we must be born again—that is, we must have our hearts changed by Jesus. Evangelicals are also committed to evangelizing—spreading the word and bringing others to Christ (Frontline 2004). Evangelicals tend to see themselves as an embattled subgroup in American society, one that must fight back against a hostile popular culture and media (Greenberg and Berktold 2004). Their "under siege" mentality has spurred evangelicals to develop and flex their political muscle; they are credited with having a significant hand in the elections of our most recent Republican presidents: Ronald Reagan, George H. W. Bush, and his son George W. Bush (Frontline 2004).

The general population does not share the perception of evangelicals as an embattled subgroup, however. For some Americans, the political mobilization of evangelicals (or of any religious group) is an affront to the ideal of the separation of church and state. Indeed, the IRS is increasingly monitoring the political activities of religious groups. Preaching politics from the pulpit is inconsistent with the tax-exempt status of churches (Kaye 2006).

Fundamentalists constitute a significant subset of evangelicals. About one-quarter of evangelicals identify themselves as fundamentalists (Greenberg and Berktold 2004). They differ from evangelicals on several fronts: They insist that the Bible must be read literally, they tend to be intolerant of alternate religious views, and they advocate separatism from those who don't share their views (Frontline 2004). These characteristics can be particularly troublesome in a nation that prides itself on religious freedom and tolerance. Indeed fundamentalists of any faith—Christian and non-Christian alike—appear to be falling out of favor worldwide. The decline in fundamentalism is attributed to its association with extremism, violence, and political agendas (Goodstein 2005). Since 9/11, the world has become more aware of certain fundamentalist groups like the Taliban and, more importantly, more aware of such groups' reliance on various terrorism campaigns to forward their political and religious causes.

Many of the Founding Fathers argued that the separation of church and state was the only way for religion to flourish in America. On this point they seem correct. Our legal and cultural tradition of separation of church and state has created a favorable environment for religious diversity. Table 24.1 lists the top 20 religious groups in America as of 2001.

The United States has the greatest number of religious groups of any nation of the world (Adherents 2005b). The Hartford Institute estimates that there are 335,000 religious congregations in the United States. Estimates suggest that there are more Muslims in the United States than there are Presbyterians or Episcopalians. (Since the U.S. Census is prohibited from asking questions about religious affiliation, data about the religious affiliations of Americans must be estimated from various sources.) Mormons are one of the fastest growing religious groups in the country today and may well be the third largest religious group in the United States by the end of the decade (Hough 2005). **Ecclesias**, official state religions, are simply not part of the U.S. landscape.

Still, despite the diversity of religions found here, America has long been regarded as a Christian and more specifically a Protestant nation. Indeed, as indicated in Table 24.1, Christians are the largest religious group in the United States today. The World Christian Database lists 635 Christian denominations in the United States (World Christian Database 2004). Protestants, the largest subgroup of Christians, constituted 52% of the population in 2004 (Smith 2004).[1] Furthermore, while many religious groups are found in America, the religious landscape of the United States is

Table 24.1   Top Twenty Religions in the United States, 2001

Religion	% of U.S. Population, 2000
1. Christianity	76.5
2. Nonreligious/Secular	13.2
3. Judaism	1.3
4. Islam	0.5
5. Buddhism	0.5
6. Agnostic	0.5
7. Atheist	0.4
8. Hinduism	0.4
9. Unitarian Universalist	0.3
10. Wiccan/Pagan/Druid	0.1
11. Spiritualist	0.05
12. Native American	0.05
13. Baha'I	0.04
14. New Age	0.03
15. Sikhism	0.03
16. Scientology	0.02
17. Humanist	0.02
18. Deity (Deist)	0.02
19. Taoist	0.02
20. Eckankar	0.01

SOURCE: Adherents.com 2005b: Self-identification, American Religious Identity Survey. http://www.adherents.com/rel_USA.html#religions

nonetheless dominated by a handful of traditional, mainstream Christian churches. If we were to list the largest churches in each of the 50 states, we would only need to list five: the Catholic Church, Southern Baptist Convention, Church of Jesus Christ of Latter-Day Saints, Evangelical Lutheran Church, and the United Methodist Church.

Many believed that the terrorist attacks on September 11 strengthened America's strong Christian ties. The event, it was said, promoted an "us against Islam" mentality. Yet, since 9/11, research shows that there has been a growing interest in *interfaith* worship and cooperation (FACT 2006). This development sees Christian and non-Christian religious groups engaging each other in dialogue to promote mutual fellowship and understanding. This interfaith movement can be seen as the latest manifestation of the United States's long-standing commitment to religious freedom and tolerance. It also bodes well in light of the changing face of religion in the United States. Since 1990, the percentage of the U.S. population self-identfying as adherents of non-Christian faiths (e.g., Islam, Buddhism, Hinduism) has increased at rates exceeding 100% (American Religious Identity Survey 2001).

One final point bears mentioning. Despite its conventional association with tradition, the real hallmark of religion is change. The variety of religious groups both in the United States and worldwide is powerful testimony of religion's capacity for responsive adaptation. Above all else, religion is functional—it serves basic human and social needs. Two important functions of religion are providing answers to the meaning of our existence and offering comfort to those in need. The inherent diversity of people—the diversity of their life issues and needs—guarantees that one religion will not fit all. Consistent with this dynamic face of religion, 16% of Americans are **"switchers"**—those who change their religious preferences or affiliation over time (American Religious Identity Survey 2001). It is estimated that "switchers" account for approximately half of the membership in an average Protestant church (Lawton 2002). This shopping for churches is consistent with American consumerism (Hough 2005). The search for a church that "fits" also accounts for the remarkable growth of megachurches. **Megachurches** are Protestant congregations with at least 2,000 members in weekly attendance. Currently, there are over 1,200 megachurches in America (Lampman 2006). Some argue that megachurches are mega-businesses that use entrepreneurial approaches to growing congregations (Kroll 2003). Indeed their innovative use of technology (visual presentations, podcasts, and Internet communications) makes megachurches powerful rivals to smaller, more traditional church groups.

To be sure, humans are active seekers of religious truths and meaningful existences. Cults form in response to changing times and newly emerging ideas and beliefs. Sects develop when groups grow dissatisfied with the status quo or when they desire greater exclusivity. Denominations offer new variations on established themes. Megachurches grow as individuals are more interested in finding a church that "works" for them and less interested in maintaining loyalty to a particular faith or denomination (*NewsHour* 2006). We may be one nation under God, but diversity is the insignia of religion in America.

Learning More About It

Michael Emerson and David Hartman offer an informative review of religious fundamentalism in their 2006 article "The Rise of Religious Fundamentalism" (*Annual Review of Sociology* 32:127–144).

A very informative review of the faith-based presidency of George W. Bush can be found at the PBS Frontline series (2004), "The Jesus Factor": http://www .pbs.org/wgbh/pages/frontline/shows/jesus/

The Hartford Institute for Religion Research provides a list of denominational Web sites at http://hirr.hartsem.edu/denom/homepages.html

Maps of the major religious groups in the United States can be seen at the Glenmary Research Center Web page: http://www.glenmary.org/grc/RCMS_2000/maps.htm

For further specification and clarification of various classifications of religious groups visit the following site: http://www.adherents.com/classify.html

A major recent survey on religion in the U.S. can be found at http://religions.pew forum.org/

Exercises

1. Use a "convenience sample" (people close at hand or easily accessed) to conduct an informal survey in which you ask your respondents to (a) self-describe their religious identification and (b) identify the top 10 religions in America. Compare the results you get with those found in the latest edition of the *Statistical Abstracts* ("Self-Described Religious Identification," http://www.census.gov/compendia/statab/tables/08s0074.pdf) as well as in Table 24.1 of this essay. What insights about religion or religious awareness in the United States are offered by this exercise?

2. Conduct another informal survey (see above) where you ask your respondents to reflect on the relative importance of their religious versus national identity when making important life decisions: for example, serving in the military, raising children, getting married, or endorsing candidates in local, state, or national elections.

Note

1. Still, the percentage of Protestants has been dropping in recent years (from 63% Protestant in 1993 to 52% in 2004), reflecting immigration patterns as well as increases in the number of people adhering to other or no religions at all. From 1993 to 2004, the percentage of people reporting that they had no religion has increased from 9 to 14% (Smith 2004).

Conclusion

Why Do Conventional Wisdoms Persist?

L ove knows no reason. . . . Beauty is only skin deep. . . . Honesty is the best policy. . . . Education is the great equalizer. These statements represent just a few of the conventional wisdoms that we so often hear throughout our lives.

In the introduction to this book, we noted that many of these adages contain some elements of truth. Within certain settings or under certain conditions, conventional wisdom can prove accurate. Yet throughout *Second Thoughts,* we have also noted that social reality is generally much more involved and much more complex than conventional wisdom would have us believe. Traditional adages and popular sayings rarely provide us with a complete picture of the broader social world. Knowing this, one might ask why individuals continue to embrace conventional wisdom. Given the limited usefulness of such assertions and tenets, why do such adages persist?

The Positive Functions of Conventional Wisdom

Conventional wisdom represents a people's attempt at "knowing." Such adages promise some insight into what is actually occurring. In this way, a culture's conventional wisdom comes to serve a variety of positive social functions; such adages can induce many productive outcomes for those who invoke them. Here, we speak specifically to five positive social functions served by conventional wisdom.

First, by providing an explanation for an unexpected or mysterious occurrence, *conventional wisdom helps social members confront the unknown and dispel the fear the unknown can generate.* When conventional wisdom proclaims that "immigrants are ruining this country," it provides members of a society with a tangible explanation for their increasing inability to "make ends meet." Similarly, when conventional wisdom advises us to "fear strangers," it offers up the usual suspects for the perennial and always frightening problems of crime, violence, loneliness, and chaos.

By identifying the causes of looming social problems, conventional wisdom not only dispels fear but also implies a hopeful resolution. As we noted in Essay 8, naming a problem's cause can increase our sense of control and encourage us to believe that a solution cannot be far away. Furthermore, identifying the cause of frightening social conditions offers a protective shield to the broader population. For example, consider a frequently heard bit of wisdom of the 1980s and 1990s: "Homeless people are mentally ill." Here, conventional wisdom cites a reason for a phenomenon most Americans find foreign and frightening. In addition, identifying mental illness as the instigator of the homeless condition gives most "sane" people a secure guarantee—homelessness could never happen to them. This piece of wisdom, like so many other adages, locates the source of a problem within the individual. Thus, as long as other social members distinguish themselves from the "problemmed" individual, they can protect themselves from the problem itself.

Second, *conventional wisdom also can function to maintain social stability.* Consider the common belief, "Every dog has its day." This adage urges people to be patient, to keep striving, or to leave revenge to fate—all attributes necessary for peaceful coexistence. Similarly, consider the adage, "Education is the great equalizer." This belief provides an incentive for citizen commitment to an institution whose greatest social contribution may be the consignment to the population of national customs, norms, and values. In the same way, conventional wisdom that warns that "united we stand, divided we fall" can effectively squelch protest or disagreement. Such a sentiment can enhance cooperation and dedication to a particular group or goal.

In these examples, and others like them, conventional wisdom "steers" a population toward behaviors that maintain smooth social operations. It keeps societies balanced by making constructive effort a matter of "common knowledge."

Third, under certain conditions, *conventional wisdom can function to legitimate the actions of those who invoke it.* Often, speakers will create or tap popular adages with a specific goal in mind. In such cases, conventional wisdom takes on the guise of political, religious, or social rhetoric. "Wisdom" emerges as strategically selected and stylized speech delivered to influence an individual or group.

As rhetoric, conventional wisdom proves effective in instituting policy or law because it promotes a vision of sound "common sense." For example, we witness politically conservative members of the U.S. Congress forwarding wisdom such as "Welfare is ruining this country" or "Welfare breeds dependency." They do so because such rhetoric projects a prudent justification for shaving federal contributions to this cause. Similarly, politicians often espouse wisdom that claims that "capital punishment deters murderers" or "affirmative action programs favor unqualified minorities." They offer these claims, despite factual evidence to the contrary, because such rhetoric effectively employs popular assumptions in the service of the speaker's special interests.

Fourth, at yet another level, *conventional wisdom can strengthen or solidify a social group's identity.* Conventional wisdom often underscores shared values or attributes. In so doing, such beliefs can enhance collective identity. Adages such as "Great minds think alike" or "Like father, like son" and sayings such as "The apple doesn't fall far from the tree" or "Birds of a feather flock together" bond individuals by accentuating their similarities. Such wisdom unites individuals by underscoring the common ground they share.

In some cases, however, note that conventional wisdom supports solidarity by creating a "them-versus-us" milieu. Such approaches may unite the members of one group by accentuating the group's hatred or fear of others. For example, Whites who feel threatened by the influx of non-White immigrants to the United States may readily espouse wisdom that advises individuals to "stick with their own kind." As like-minded individuals rally around such wisdom, White group solidarity can be heightened. Similarly, males who find it difficult to accept growing numbers of females in the workplace may rally around the traditional adage, "A woman's place is in the home." Using conventional wisdom to legitimate their fears, the threatened group can comfortably join in opposition.

Fifth, it is important to note that *conventional wisdom is often created or tapped as a tool for power maintenance.* When certain religious traditions defined "the love of money as the root of all evil," such wisdom effectively maintained the divide between the "haves" and the "have-nots." Dissuading the masses from engaging in the struggle for material goods allows those in power to maintain their control over limited resources. (Note that such reasoning led social philosopher Karl Marx to refer to religion as "the opiate of the people." Marx argued that religion promoted a passive acceptance among the poor of an unfair economic structure.) Similarly, adages such as "You've come a long way baby" or "Good things come to those who wait" serve to dampen efforts toward gender, racial, or ethnic equality. If common consensus suggests that minority group goals have been satisfactorily achieved or addressed, then the continued struggle toward true equality becomes difficult to sustain.

Conventional Wisdom as Knowledge

Whatever its functions, conventional wisdom appears to offer individuals an intelligence boost—a phenomenon social psychologist David Myers (2002:16) refers to as the "I-knew-it-all-along" effect. No matter what happens, there exists a conventional wisdom to cover or explain social behaviors; there always exists a saying or belief that predicts all outcomes. Herein lies conventional wisdom's most troubling feature: A society's "common knowledge" simultaneously proclaims contradictory "facts." For example, conventional wisdom assures us that "haste makes waste," while at the same time warning us that "he who hesitates is lost." Whereas one adage suggests that "too many cooks spoil the broth," another claims that "many hands make light work."

All in all, conventional wisdoms abound for every possible behavior and outcome. Such claims form a stockpile of knowledge to which socialization affords us access. Once introduced to a culture's conventional wisdom, social actors draw on this stockpile of ancient and contemporary adages to make almost any discovery seem like common sense. Thus, when I discover that separation intensifies my romantic attraction, I confirm the phenomenon by saying, "Absence makes the heart grow fonder." If, instead, separation dampens the fires of my romance, I confirm my experiences by noting, "Out of sight is out of mind." Indeed, conventional wisdom allows me to confirm any of my impressions and experiences—whatever they might be—and thereby frames those experiences as if they constitute a general norm or the ultimate truth.

The drawbacks of conventional wisdom are heightened by the fact that once introduced, these wisdoms take on lives of their own. Such adages become a "taken-for-granted" part of our culture; they state what is known, implicitly suggesting that such topics need not be further considered. In this way, conventional wisdom constitutes tenacious knowledge—information that endures even if there's no empirical evidence to support it. The mere passing of time, the longevity of an idea or belief, becomes a sufficient indicator of a tenet's veracity. Facts or observations that contradict the adage lose out to the test of time.

The "staying power" of conventional wisdom may be tied to dimensions of wisdom per se. Indeed, equating conventional adages with wisdom may help accentuate their appeal. Wisdom is a highly valued commodity in our society. It is born of good judgment and experience. Furthermore, it can offer us a sense of inner peace—an ability to live with what we know. Wisdom cannot be taught; courses in wisdom are not part of the college curriculum. Indeed, our formal education experiences often convince us that wisdom is not to be found in books or in research. Rather, wisdom emerges from the ordinary, the common, the everyday. In the final analysis, the wise person is one who has "lived."

In turning to our experiences for wisdom, however, we return to a problem cited earlier and explored at some length in this book's introduction—namely, the limitations of experientially based knowledge. If we base our wisdom solely on personal experiences, we will probably build dubious knowledge. Although our speculations about various social topics typically start with personal experiences, such experiences may not offer us the best empirical evidence for verification.

Our experiences are subjective and therefore vulnerable to distortion and personal bias. They require a "correction" factor, one that can control for distortions emerging from personal prejudices or sloppy thinking. Social scientific inquiry offers one such correction factor. The sociological approach to knowledge follows a set of standardized rules and procedures that can maximize our chances of obtaining valid and reliable knowledge. Although sociology may start with what we already know, good sociology does not end there. Rather, good sociology explores commonsense notions about the social world by collecting and comparing varied reports and observations in the interest of building an all-encompassing picture of reality.

In Closing

Joseph Story, an early Associate Justice of the U.S. Supreme Court, is quoted as saying: "Human wisdom is the aggregate of all human experience, constantly accumulating, selecting and reorganizing its own materials." Story's statement suggests that true wisdom requires a wealth of experience. It is in that spirit that we prepared *Second Thoughts*. In each essay, we proposed a wisdom that requires us to consider myriad experiences and facts. We advocated an approach to knowledge that remains open-ended, a stance that treats new information as an opportunity to rethink what we know. In this way, we cast all social actors as perpetual students of their environment—students who regularly question assumptions and who seek to see beyond themselves.

Learning More About It

The flaws inherent in relying on conventional wisdom for knowledge are effectively portrayed in a 1949 classic by sociologist Paul Lazarsfeld, entitled "The American Soldier: An Expository Review" (*Public Opinion Quarterly* 13(3):378–380). A similarly striking demonstration comes from social psychologist Karl Halvor Teigen in his 1986 article, "Old Truths or Fresh Insights? A Study of Students' Evaluations of Proverbs" (*Journal of British Social Psychology* 25(1):43–50).

In a related vein, anthropologist Claude Levi-Strauss explores the origins of myth in his book, *The Raw and the Cooked: Introduction to a Science of Mythology* (New York: Harper & Row, 1964).

Howard Kahane and Nancy Cavender provide a detailed exploration of both the tools and pitfalls of everyday reasoning and problem solving in *Logic and Contemporary Rhetoric: The Use of Reason in Everyday Life,* 9th edition (Belmont, CA: Wadsworth, 2002).

References

ABC News. 2005. "Poll: Support Seen for Patriot Act." (June 9). http://abcnews.go.com/US/PollVault/story?id=833703

ABC News/Washington Post. 2003. "Race Relations." (January 20). http://abcnews.go.com/sections/us/DailyNews/poll_race030123.html

Abel, R. 2002. "Judges Write the Darndest Things: Judicial Mystification of Limitations on Tort Liability." *Texas Law Review* 80:1547–1548.

Abell, S. C., and Richards, M. H. 1996. "The Relationship Between Body Shape Satisfaction and Self-Esteem: An Investigation of Gender and Class Differences." *Journal of Youth and Adolescence* 25(October):691–703.

Abramson, A., and Silverstein, M. 2006. *Images of Aging in America, 2004*. AARP and the University of Southern California. http://assets.aarp.org/rgcenter/general/images_aging.pdf

Abwender, D. A., and Hough, K. 2001. "Interactive Effects of Characteristics of Defendant and Mock Juror on U.S. Participants' Judgment and Sentencing Recommendations." *Journal of Social Psychology* 141(5):603–615.

Achenreiner, G. B., and John, D. R. 2003. "The Meaning of Brand Names to Children: A Developmental Investigation." *Journal of Consumer Psychology* 13(3):205–219.

Adams, R. G., and Allan, G. (Eds.). 1998. *Placing Friendship in Context*. Cambridge: Cambridge University Press.

Adelson, R. 2004. "Detecting Deception." *Monitor on Psychology* 35(7):70.

Adherents.com. 2005a. "Largest Denominational Families in the U.S., 2001." http://www.adherents.com/rel_USA.html#families

———. 2005b. "Largest Religious Groups in the U.S. of America." http://www.adherents.com/rel_USA.html#religions

Administration on Aging. 2007. "A Profile of Older Americans: 2006." Department of Health and Human Services. http://www.aoa.gov/prof/Statistics/profile/2006/10.asp

Administration for Children and Families. 2002. *Temporary Assistance for Needy Families Program (TANF) Fourth Annual Report to Congress*. http://www.acf.hhs.gov/programs/ofa/opreweb/ar2001/indexar.htm

———. 2005. *Child Maltreatment 2005*. http://www.acf.dhhs.gov/programs/cb/pubs/cm05/chapterthree.htm#child

Advisory Committee on Student Financial Assistance. 2006. "Mortgaging Our Future: How Financial Barriers to College Undercut America's Global Competitiveness." http://www.ed.gov/about/bdscomm/list/acsfa/mof.pdf

Affleck, G., Tennen, H., and Apter, A. 2000. "Optimism, Pessimism and Daily Life with Chronic Illness." In E. C. Chang (Ed.), *Optimism and Pessimism* (pp. 580–602). Washington, DC: APA Books.

AFL-CIO. 2007. "2006 Trends in CEO Pay." http://www.aflcio.org/corporate watch/paywatch/pay/index.cfm

Agency for Healthcare Research and Quality. 2005. "Women's Health Care in the United States: Selected Findings from the 2004 National Healthcare Quality and Disparities Reports." Fact Sheet. AHRQ Publication No. 05-P021. http://www .ahrq.gov/qual/nhqrwomen/nhqrwomen.htm

Ahlburg, D., and DeVita, C. 1992. "New Realities of the American Family." *Population Bulletin* 47(2): Washington, DC: Population Reference Bureau.

Alba, R., and Nee, V. 2005. *Remaking the American Mainstream: Assimilation and Contemporary Immigration.* Cambridge, MA: Harvard University Press.

Alcoff, L. M. 2005. "A Response to Garcia." *Philosophy and Social Criticism* 31(4):419–422.

Alexander, K., and Cook, M. 1982. "Curricula and Coursework: A Surprise Ending to a Familiar Story." *American Sociological Review* 47:626–640.

Alexander, K., Entwisle, D., and Thompson, M. 1987. "School Performance, Status Relations, and the Structure of Sentiment: Bringing the Teachers Back In." *American Sociological Review* 52(5):665–682.

Allan, G. 1989. *Friendship: Developing a Sociological Perspective.* Boulder, CO: Westview.

———. 1998a. "Friendship, Sociology and Social Structure." *Journal of Social and Personal Relationships* 15(5):685–702.

———. 1998b. "Reflections on Context." In R. G. Adams and G. Allan (Eds.), *Placing Friendship in Context* (pp. 183–194*).* Cambridge: Cambridge University Press.

Allsopp, J. 2006. "Heat Wave." *Weather Currents. National Weather Service, Chicago* 4(2). http://www.crh.noaa.gov/lot/?n=currents_summer2006

Alper, S., Tjosvold, D., and Law, K. S. 2000. "Conflict Management, Efficacy, and Performance in Organizational Teams." *Personnel Psychology* 53(3):625–642.

Alt, M., and Peter, K. 2002. "Private Schools: A Brief Portrait" (NCES 2002–013). Washington, DC: U.S. Department of Education.

Altheide, D. 2002. *Creating Fear: News and the Construction of Crisis.* New York: Aldine de Gruyter.

———. 2006. *Terrorism and the Politics of Fear.* New York: Alta Mira.

Altheimer, E. 1994. *Weight Loss and the Distortion of Body Image.* Henry Rutgers Scholars Thesis, Rutgers University, New Brunswick, NJ.

Amabile, T. M., and Kabat, L. G. 1982. "When Self-Descriptions Contradict Behavior." *Social Cognition* 1:311–335.

Amato, P. 2000. "The Consequences of Divorce for Adults and Children." *Journal of Marriage and the Family* 62(4):1269–1287.

———. 2001a. "Children of Divorce in the 1990s: An Update of the Amato and Keith (1991) Meta-Analysis." *Journal of Family Psychology* 15(3):355–370.

———. 2001b. "What Children Learn from Divorce." *Population Today* (January).

Amato, P., Booth, A., Johnson, D., and Rogers, S. 2007. *Alone Together: How Marriage in America Is Changing*. Cambridge, MA: Harvard University Press.

Amato, P. R., and Fowler, F. 2002. "Parenting Practices, Child Adjustment and Family Diversity." *Journal of Marriage and the Family* 64(3):703–716.

Amato, P., and Sobolewski, J. 2001. "The Effects of Divorce and Marital Discord on Adult Children's Psychological Well-Being." *American Sociological Review* 66(6):900–921.

American Association of Retired Persons (AARP). 2003a. *These Four Walls . . . Americans 45+ Talk About Home and Community*. http://research.aarp.org

———. 2003b. *Beyond 50.03: A Report to the Nation on Independent Living and Disability*. http://research.aarp.org

———. 2004. *Baby Boomers Envision Retirement II—Key Findings*. Prepared for AARP by RoperASW. http://assets.aarp.org/rgcenter/econ/boomers_envision_1.pdf

———. 2007. *The State of 50+ America*. http://assets.aarp.org/rgcenter/econ/fifty_plus_2007.pdf

American Bar Association. 2007. "About the ABA." http://www.abanet.org/about/

American Cancer Society. 2007. "Cancer Facts & Figures: 2007." http://www.cancer.org/downloads/STT/CAFF2007PWSecured.pdf

American Civil Liberties Union. 2006. "Federal Court Strikes Down NSA Warrantless Surveillance Program. http://www.aclu.org/safefree/nsaspying/26489prs20060817.html

———. 2007. "National Security Letters Gag Patriot Act Debate." http://www.aclu.org/safefree/nationalsecurityletters/index.html

American Enterprise. 1992. *Women, Men, Marriages and Ministers*. January/February:106.

American Heart Association. 2006. "Statistics." http://www.goredforwomen.org/newsroom/statistics.html

———. 2007a. "Stress Management at the Worksite." http://www.americanheart.org/presenter.jhtml?identifier=3045247

———. 2007b. "Women and Cardiovascular Diseases." http://www.americanheart.org/downloadable/heart/1168614043234WOMEN07.pdf

American Institute of Stress. 2007. "The Role of Stress in Health and Illness." http://www.stress.org/

American Medical Association. 2006. "Table 4: Women Residents by Specialty 2005." http://www.ama-assn.org/ama/pub/category/12915.html

American Obesity Association. 2005. "AOA Fact Sheet." http://obesity1.tempdomainname.com/subs/fastfacts/aoafactsheets.shtml

"American Patriots." 2006. *The Nation*. July 2. http://www.thenation.com/doc/20060717/editors

American Psychological Association. 2004. "The Different Kinds of Stress." http://apahelpcenter.org/articles/article.php?id=21

———. 2005. "Emotional Fitness in Aging: Older Is Happier." *Psychology Matters*. APA Online. http://www.psychologymatters.org/fitness.html

American Religious Identity Survey. 2001. "Key Findings." http://www.gc.cuny.edu/faculty/research_briefs/aris/key_findings.htm

American Society of Plastic Surgeons. 2007a. "11 Million Cosmetic Plastic Surgery Procedures in 2006—up 7%" http://www.plasticsurgery.org/media/press_releases/2006-Stats-Overall-Release.cfm

———. 2007b. "2007 Plastic Surgery Statistics." http://www.plasticsurgery.org/media/statistics/2006-Statistics.cfm

American Tort Reform Association. 2007. "ATRA at a Glance." http://www.atra.org/about/

Ameriprise Financial. 2006. "The Five Stages of Retirement." *Corporate Training and Development Advisor* 11(3):5.

Amodeo, N. P. 2001. "Be More Cooperative to Be More Competitive." *Journal of Rural Cooperation* 29(2):115–124.

Andre, T., Whigham, M., Hendrickson, A., and Chambers, S. 1999. "Competency Beliefs, Positive Affect and Gender Stereotypes of Elementary Students and Their Parents About Science Versus Other School Subjects." *Journal of Research in Science Teaching* 36(6):719–747.

Andreoletti, C., Zebrowitz, L. A., Leslie, A., and Lachman, M. E. 2001. "Physical Appearance and Control Beliefs in Young, Middle-Aged, and Older Adults." *Personality and Social Psychology Bulletin* 27(8):969–981.

Andrews, E. 2005. "Blacks Hit Hardest By Costlier Mortgages." *New York Times* (September 14) 154(53337):C1–C17.

Andrews, K. 2002. "Movement-Countermovement Dynamics and the Emergence of New Institutions: The Case of 'White Flight' Schools in Mississippi." *Social Forces* 80(3):911–936.

Aneshensel, C. 1992. "Social Stress: Theory and Research." *Annual Review of Sociology* 18:15–38.

Angier, N. 2000. "Do Races Differ? Not Really, Genes Show." *New York Times.* http://www.nytimes.com/library/national/science/082200sci-genetics-race.html

Archdeacon, T. 1992. "Reflections on Immigration to Europe in Light of U.S. Immigration History." *International Migration Review* 26(Summer):524–548.

Arichi, M. 1999. "Is It Radical? Women's Right to Keep Their Own Surnames After Marriage." *Women's Studies International Forum* 22(4):411–415.

Aries, P. 1962. *Centuries of Childhood: A Social History of Family Life.* R. Baldick, Trans. New York: Knopf.

Aronson, E. 1980. *The Social Animal.* San Francisco: Freeman.

Aronson, E., and Cope, V. 1968. "My Enemy's Enemy Is My Friend." *Journal of Personality and Social Psychology* 8:8–12.

Aronson, E., and Thibodeau, R. 1992. "The Jigsaw Classroom: A Cooperative Strategy for Reducing Prejudice." In J. Lynch, C. Modgil, and S. Modgil (Eds.), *Cultural Diversity in the Schools.* London: Falmer.

Ashenfelter, D. 2002. "Judge Criticized for Coin-Toss Custody Ruling; The Grandparents Who Lost Are Calling It 'A Mockery of the Judicial Process.'" *Philadelphia Inquirer* (February 10).

Associated Press. 2006. "If Surveys Tell the Truth, White Lies Are Necessary Evil." (July 12). http://www.boston.com/news/nation/articles/2006/07/12/if_surveys_tell_the_truth_white_lies_are_necessary_evil/

Association for Children for Enforcement of Support. 2008. "Child Support Statistics." http://childsupport-aces.org/index.php?option=com_content&task=view&id=7&Itemid=30

Association of American Medical Colleges. 2006. "An Overview of Women in U.S. Academic Medicine, 2005–2006." *Analysis in Brief* 6(7). http://www.aamc.org/data/aib/aibissues/aibvol6_no7.pdf

Atkin, C. 1982. "Changing Male and Female Roles." In M. Schwartz (Ed.), *TV and Teens: Experts Look at the Issues.* Reading, MA: Addison-Wesley.

Auerbach, J. A. 2003. "Passing Father's Surname on to Child Questioned." *Family Law* 228(71):10.

Axelrod, R. 2006. *The Evolution of Cooperation.* New York: Penguin.

Azaryahu, M., and Kook, R. 2002. "Mapping the Nation: Street Names and Arab-Palestinian Identity: Three Case Studies." *Nations and Nationalism* 8(2):195–213.

Babbie, E. 1994. *What Is Society? Reflections on Freedom, Order, and Change.* Thousand Oaks, CA: Pine Forge.

———. 1998. *Observing Ourselves: Essays in Social Research.* Prospect Heights, IL: Waveland.

———. 2006. *The Practice of Social Research,* 11th ed. Belmont, CA: Wadsworth.

Badr, L. K., and Abdallah, B. 2001. "Physical Attractiveness of Premature Infants Affects Outcome at Discharge from NICU." *Infant Behavior and Development* 24(1):129–133.

Baker, M. 2006. "2005 Vies for Hottest Year on Record." http://www.ucsusa.org/global_warming/science/recordtemp2005.html

Baker, S., Smith, G., Weiner, E., and Harbrecht, D. 1993. "The Mexican Worker." *Business Week* (April 19):84–92.

Balcom, D. 2002. "Absent Fathers: Effects on Abandoned Sons." In A. Hunter and C. Forden (Eds.), *Readings in the Psychology of Gender: Exploring Our Differences and Commonalities* (pp. 100–110). Needham Heights, MA: Allyn & Bacon.

Baldas, T. 2003. "Saying Goodbye to Desegregation Plans." *National Law Journal* 25:85.

Baltzell, E. D. 1987. *The Protestant Establishment: Aristocracy and Caste in America.* New Haven, CT: Yale University Press.

Bamburg, J. 1994. *Raising Expectations to Improve Student Learning.* Oak Brook, IL: North Central Regional Educational Laboratory.

Banerjee, R., and Lintern, V. 2000. "Boys Will Be Boys: The Effect of Social Evaluation Concerns on Gender-Typing." *Social Development* 9(3):397–408.

Banse, R. 1999. "Autonomic Evaluation of Self and Significant Others: Affective Priming in Close Relationships." *Journal of Social and Personal Relationships* 16(6):803–821.

Barnes, J. A. 1994. *A Pack of Lies: Toward a Sociology of Lying.* New York: Cambridge University Press.

Bartfeld, J. 2000. "Child Support and the Postdivorce Economic Well-Being of Mothers, Fathers, and Children." *Demography* 37(2):203–213.

Bartsch, R., Burnett, T., Diller, T., and Rankin-Williams, E. 2000. "Gender Representation in Television Commercials: Updating an Update." *Sex Roles* 43(9–10):735–743.

Basow, S. 1992. *Gender: Stereotypes and Roles.* 3rd ed. Monterey, CA: Brooks/Cole.

Beasley, B., and Standley, T. 2002. "Shirts vs Skins: Clothing as an Indicator of Gender Role Stereotyping in Video Games." *Mass Communication and Society* 5(3):279–293.

Becker, H. 1963. *The Outsiders.* Glencoe, IL: Free Press.

Bell, M. M. 2007. *An Invitation to Environmental Sociology.* Thousand Oaks, CA: Sage.

Bellah, R., Madssen, R., Sullivan, W., Swidler, A., and Tipton, S. 1985. *Habits of the Heart: Individualism and Commitment in American Life.* Berkeley: University of California Press.

Bem, S. L. 1993. *The Lenses of Gender: Transforming the Debate on Sexual Inequality.* New Haven, CT: Yale University Press.

Bendick, M., Jackson, C., and Reinoso, V. 1999. In F. Pincus and H. Ehrlich (Eds.), *Race and Ethnic Conflict: Contending Views on Prejudice, Discrimination, and Ethnoviolence* (pp. 140–151). 2d ed. Boulder, CO: Westview.

Bendor, J., and Swistak, P. 1997. "The Evolutionary Stability of Cooperation." *American Political Science Review* 91(June):290–307.

Bennett, N. G., Bloom, D. E., and Craig, P. H. 1992. "American Marriage Patterns in Transition." In S. J. South and S. E. Tolnay (Eds.), *The Changing American Family: Sociological and Demographic Perspectives.* Boulder, CO: Westview.

Benokraitis, N. 2007. *Marriages and Families: Changes, Choices, and Constraints* Upper Saddle River, NJ: Prentice Hall.

Berger, P. 1963. *Invitation to Sociology.* New York: Anchor Books.

Berscheid, E. 1981. "An Overview of the Psychological Effects of Physical Attractiveness and Some Comments upon the Psychological Effects of Knowledge on the Effects of Physical Attractiveness." In W. Lucker, K. Ribbens, and J. A. McNamera (Eds.), *Logical Aspects of Facial Form.* Ann Arbor: University of Michigan Press.

———. 1982. "America's Obsession with Beautiful People." *U.S. News and World Report* (January 11):59–61.

Berscheid, E., and Hatfield, E. 1983. *Interpersonal Attraction.* 2d ed. Reading, MA: Addison-Wesley.

Besnard, P., and Desplanques, G. 1993. *La Cote des Prénoms en 1994.* Paris: Balland.

Best, J. 2001. *Damned Lies and Statistics: Untangling Numbers from the Media, Politicians, and Activists.* Berkeley: University of California Press.

———. 2004. *More Damned Lies and Statistics.* Berkeley: University of California Press.

Bhagat, V. 2005. "The State of e-Philanthropy." http://www.pnnonline.org/article.php?sid=6104

Bhanot, R., and Jovanovic, J. 2005. "Do Parents' Academic Gender Stereotypes Influence Whether They Intrude on Their Children's Homework?" *Sex Roles* 52(9–10):597–607.

Bianchi, S., Milkie, M., Sayer, L., and Robinson, J. 2000. "Is Anyone Doing the Housework? Trends in the Gender Division of Household Labor." *Social Forces* 79(1):191–229.

Bidwell, C., and Friedkin, N. 1988."The Sociology of Education." In N. Smelser (Ed.), *Handbook of Sociology* (pp. 449–471). Newbury Park, CA: Sage.

Bienstock, J. L., and Laube, D. 2005. "The Recruitment Phoenix: Strategies for Attracting Medical Students into Obstetrics and Gynecology." *Obstetrics & Gynecology,* Part 1 of 2, 105(5):1125–1127.

Billings, A. C., and Tyler Eastman, S. 2002. "Selective Representation of Gender, Ethnicity, and Nationality in American Television Coverage of the 2000 Summer Olympics." *International Review for the Sociology of Sport* 37(3/4): 351–370.

Bishop, J. E. 1986. "'All for One . . . One for All?' Don't Bet on It." *Wall Street Journal* (December 4):31.

Bisin, A., Topa, G., and Verdier, T. 2002. "Religious Intermarriage and Socialization in the U.S." *Journal of Political Economy* 112(3):615-664.

Black, D. 1976. *The Behavior of Law.* New York: Academic Press.

———. 1998. *The Social Structure of Right and Wrong.* San Diego, CA: Academic Press.

Blackstone, W. [1765–1769] 1979. *Commentaries on the Laws of England.* Chicago: University of Chicago Press.

Blackwell, D. L., and Lichter, D. T. 2004. "Homogamy Among Dating, Cohabiting and Married Couples." *Sociological Quarterly* 45(4):719–737.

Blake, R. R., and Moulton, J. S. 1979. "Intergroup Problem Solving in Organizations: From Theory to Practice." In W. G. Austin and S. Worschel (Eds.), *The Social Psychology of Intergroup Relations.* Monterey, CA: Brooks/Cole.

Blankenhorn, D. 2003. "The Marriage Problem." *American Experiment Quarterly* 6(1):61–71.

Blau, J. 2003. *Race in the Schools: Perpetuating White Dominance.* Boulder: Lynne Rienner Publishers.

Bleiszner, R., and Adams, R. C. 1992. *Adult Friendships.* Newbury Park, CA: Sage.

Bloom, K., Moore-Schoenmakers, K., and Masataka, N. 1999. "Nasality of Infant Vocalizations Determines Gender Bias in Adult Favorability Ratings." *Journal of Nonverbal Behavior* 23(3):219–236.

Blum, S. D. 2005. "Five Approaches to Explaining 'Truth' and 'Deception' in Human Communication." *Journal of Anthropological Research* 61(3):289–315.

Boardman, J. 2004. "Stress and Physical Health: The Role of Neighborhoods as Mediating and Moderating Mechanisms." *Social Science and Medicine* 58:2473–2483.

Boase, J., Horrigan, J. B., Wellman, B., and Rainie, L. 2006. "The Strength of Internet Ties." http://www.pewinternet.org/pdfs/PIP_Internet_ties.pdf

Bodnar, J. 1987. "Socialization and Adaptation: Immigrant Families in Scranton." In H. Graff (Ed.), *Growing Up in America: Historical Experiences*. Detroit: Wayne State University Press.

Bonacich, E., Cheng, L., Chinchilla, N., Hamilton, N., and Ong, P. (Eds.). 1994. *Global Production: The Apparel Industry in the Pacific Rim*. Philadelphia: Temple University Press.

Bonilla-Silva, E., Goar, C., and Embrick, D. 2006. "When Whites Flock Together: The Social Psychology of White Habitus." *Critical Sociology* 32(2/3):229–253.

Bonner, J. 1984. *Research Presented in "The Two Brains."* Public Broadcasting System Telecast.

Books, S., and McAninch, A. 2006. "Jonathan Kozol's *Savage Inequalities*: A 15-Year Reconsideration." *Educational Studies* 40(1).

Boshara, R. 2003. "The $6,000 Solution." *Atlantic Monthly* (January/February):91–95.

Bourdieu, P. 1977a. "Cultural Reproduction and Social Reproduction." In J. Karabel and A. H. Halsey (Eds.), *Power and Ideology in Education*. New York: Oxford University Press.

———. 1977b. *Outline of a Theory of Practice*. Cambridge: Cambridge University Press.

———. 1984. *Distinction: A Social Critique of the Judgment of Taste*. Cambridge, MA: Harvard University Press.

Boushey, H. 2002. "'This Country Is Not Woman-Friendly or Child-Friendly': Talking About the Challenge of Moving from Welfare-to-Work." *Journal of Poverty* 6(2):81–115.

Bowles, S., and Gintis, H. 1976. *Schooling in Capitalist America: Educational Reform and the Contradictions of Economic Life*. New York: Basic Books.

———. 1982. "The Crisis of Liberal Democratic Capitalism: The Case of the U.S." *Politics and Society* 11:51–59.

———. 2002. "Schooling in Capitalist America Revisited." *Sociology of Education* 75(1):1–18.

Boyatzis, C. J., and Baloff, P. 1998. "Effects of Perceived Attractiveness and Academic Success on Early Adolescent Peer Popularity." *Journal of Genetic Psychology* 159(3):337–345.

Bramlett, M. D., and Mosher, W. D., 2002. "Cohabitation, Marriage, Divorce, and Remarriage in the United States. National Center for Health Statistics." *Vital Health Statistics* 23(22).

Brandenburger, A. M., and Nalebuff, B. J. 1996. *Co-Opetition*. New York: Doubleday.

Branigan, T. 2001. "Women: In the Eye of the Beholder: Black and Asian Women Are Spending Thousands on Plastic Surgery—to Look More Caucasian." *Guardian* 2:10.

Braun, D. D. 1991. *The Rich Get Richer*. Chicago: Nelson Hall.

Brenner, J. G., and Spayd, L. 1993. "A Pattern of Bias in Mortgage Loans." *Washington Post* (July 8).

Brinkman, I. 2004. "Language, Names and War: The Case of Angola." *African Studies Review* 47(3):143–163.

Brophy, J. 1983. "Research on the Self-Fulfilling Prophecy and Teacher Expectations." *Journal of Educational Psychology* 75:631–661.

Brown, J. F. 1994. "35 Black Men Quizzed in Union, S.C." *Afro-American* (November 12):A1.

Brown, M. 2007. "40: The New 30 in Major League Baseball." *Associated Press* (April 9).

Browne, K., and Hamilton-Giachritsis, C. 2005. "The Influence of Violent Media on Children and Adolescents: A Public Health Approach." *Lancet* 365:702–710.

Browne, M. W. 1997. "Naming of 6 Elements to End Long Disputes." *New York Times* (March 4):C5.

Brownlow, S., Jacobi, T., and Rogers, M. 2000. "Science Anxiety as a Function of Gender and Experience." *Sex Roles* 42(1–2):119–131.

Brunet, G., and Bideau, A. 2000. "Surnames: History of the Family and History of Populations." *History of the Family* 5(2):153–161.

Bruning, J. L., Polinko, N. K., Zerbst, J. I., and Buckingham, J. T. 2000. "The Effect on Expected Job Success of the Connotative Meanings of Names and Nicknames." *Journal of Social Psychology* 140(2):197–201.

Bryan, J. H., and Walbek, N. H. 1970. "Preaching and Practicing Generosity." *Child Development* 41:329–353.

Bryner, J. 2007. "Gay Unions Sanctioned in Medieval Europe." *Livescience.com.* August 27.

Bulduc, J., Caron, S., and Logue, M. E. 2007. "The Effects of Parental Divorce on College Students." *Journal of Divorce & Remarriage* 46(3/4):83–104.

Bumpass, L., and Lu, H. 2000. "Trends in Cohabitation and Implications for Children's Family Contexts in the United States." *Population Studies* 54(1): 29–41.

Burnard, T. 2001. "Slave Naming Patterns: Onomastics and the Taxonomy of Race in Eighteenth-Century Jamaica." *Journal of Interdisciplinary History* 31(3):325–346.

Burton, R. P. D. 1998. "Global Integrative Meaning as a Mediating Factor in the Relationship Between Social Roles and Psychological Distress." *Journal of Health and Social Behavior* 39:201–215.

Business Wire. 2002. "71% of Online Donors Give Weekdays from 9 a.m. to 6 p.m., Kintera Study Reports; Workplace Giving Important Factor in Rise of e-Philanthropy." *Business Wire* (November 14).

Buss, D. M., Shackelford, T. K., Kirkpatrick, L. A., and Larsen, R. J. 2001. "A Half Century of Mate Preferences: The Cultural Evolution of Values." *Journal of Marriage and the Family* 63(2):491–503.

Bussey, K. 1999. "Children's Categorization and Evaluation of Different Types of Lies and Truths." *Child Development* 70(6):1338–1347.

Button, J., and Rosenbaum, W. 1990. "Gray Power, Gray Peril or Gray Myth? The Political Impact of the Aging in Local Sunbelt Politics." *Social Science Quarterly* 71(1):25–38.

Byrne, J., Arndt, M., Zellner, W., and McNamee, M. 2002. "Restoring Trust in Corporate America." *Business Week* (June 24):30–36.

Cadinu, M., and Reggiori, C. 2002. "Discrimination of a Low-Status Outgroup: The Role of Ingroup Threat." *European Journal of Social Psychology* 32(4):501–515.

Caldwell, C. 2006. "The Other Immigration." *New York Times Magazine* (May 7).

Calhoun, C. 1998. "Community Without Propinquity Revisited: Communications Technology and the Transformation of the Urban Public Sphere." *Sociological Inquiry* 68(3):373–397.

Calhoun, L. G., and Tedeschi, R. G. 2001. "Posttraumatic Growth: The Positive Lessons of Loss." In R. A. Neimeyer (Ed.), *Meaning, Construction, and the Experience of Loss* (pp. 157–172). Washington, DC: American Psychological Association.

Callan, P. 2003. "A Different Kind of Recession." *National Crosstalk* (Winter).

———. 2007. "College Affordability: Colleges, States Increase Financial Burden on Students and Families." *Measuring Up. The National Report Card on Higher Education.* http://measuringup.highereducation.org/commentary/collegeafford ability.cfm

Campos, P. 1998. *Jurismania: The Madness of American Law.* New York: Oxford University Press.

Caplan, L. J., and Schooler, C. 2007. "Socioeconomic Status and Financial Coping Strategies: The Mediating Role of Perceived Control." *Social Psychology Quarterly* 70(1):43–58.

Card, D., DiNardo, J., and Estes, E. 1998. "The More Things Change: Immigrants and Children of Immigrants in the 1940's, the 1970's and the 1990's." Joint Center on Poverty Research. http://www. jcpr.org

Carley, K. M., and Krackhardt, D. 1996. "Cognitive Inconsistencies and Non-Symmetric Friendship." *Social Networks* 18(1):1–27.

Carlson, D. K. 2005. "Liberty vs. Security: Public Mixed on PATRIOT Act." http://www.gallup.com/poll/17392/Liberty-vs-Security-Public-Mixed-Patriot-Act.aspx

Carpusor, A., and Loges, W. 2006. "Rental Discrimination and Ethnicity in Names." *Journal of Applied Social Psychology* 36(4):934–952.

Carr, D., and Friedman, M. A. 2005. "Is Obesity Stigmatizing? Body Weight, Perceived Discrimination, and Psychological Well-Being in the United States." *Journal of Health and Social Behavior* 3(2):244–259.

Carr, N. 2007. "Courting Middle-Class Parents to Use Public Schools." *Education Digest* 72(6):35–41.

Carroll, J. 2007. "Hispanics Support Requiring English Proficiency for Immigrants." *Gallup Brain* (July 5). http://brain.gallup.com/content/default.aspx?ci=28048

Carter, B. 1991. "Children's T.V., Where Boys Are King." *New York Times* (May 1):A1.

Carty, V. 2005. "Textual Portrayals of Female Athletes." *Frontiers: A Journal of Women Studies* 26(2):132–155.

Cash, T. F., and Janda, L. H. 1984. "The Eye of the Beholder." *Psychology Today* (December):46–52.

Cash, T. F., and Pruzinsky, T. 1990. "The Psychology of Physical Appearance: Aesthetics, Attributes, and Images." In T. F. Cash and T. Pruzinsky (Eds.), *Body Images: Development, Deviance, and Change.* New York: Guilford.

———. (Eds.). 2002. *Body Image: A Handbook of Theory, Research, and Clinical Practice.* New York/London: Guilford.

Catanzarite, L. 2003. "Race-Gender Composition and Occupational Pay Degradation." *Social Problems* 50(1):14–37.

Cattat Mayer, K. A., Farrell, M. P., and Barnes, G. M. 2005. "Younger Sibling Modeling of Older Sibling Deviant Behavior: Does Gender Matter?" *Society for the Study of Social Problems,* Annual Meeting, Philadelphia.

Cavanagh, G. F. 2005. *American Business Values: A Global Perspective.* Englewood, NJ: Prentice Hall.

CBS News. 2003. "Sex Crimes Cover-Up by Vatican." CBS Evening News (August 6). http://www.cbsnews.com/storeis/2003/08/06/eveningnews/main566978.shtml

———. 2006. "Weeding Out Terrorism." http://www.cbsnews.com/stories/2006/08/15/eveningnews/main1898106.shtml

———. 2007. "Imus Reportedly Plans to Sue CBS." (May 3) http://www.cbsnews.com/stories/2007/05/03/national/main2757139.shtml?source=search_story

CBS News Poll. 2006. "Religion in America" (April 6–9).

CBS Sportsline. 2006. "Baseball Salary Average Soars 9% This Year." http://cbs.sportsline.com/mlb/story/9883043/rss

Center for American Progress. 2007. "From Poverty to Prosperity: A National Strategy to Cut Poverty in Half." Domestic & Economy. Center for American Progress. http://www.americanprogress.org/issues/2007/04/poverty_report.html

Center for American Women and Politics. 2007. "Facts and Findings." http://www.cawp.rutgers.edu/

Center for Justice and Democracy. 2007. "Mythbuster: Debunking Myths About Tort System Costs." http://www.centerjd.org/MB_2007costs.htm

Center for Law and Social Policy. 2007. "Child Support Substantially Increases Economic Well-Being of Low- and Moderate Income Families." Research Fact Sheet. http://www.clasp.org/publications/CS_Economic_FS.pdf

Center on Budget and Policy Priorities. 1998. "Strengths of the Safety Net: How the EITC, Social Security, and Other Government Programs Affect Poverty." http://www.cbpp .org/pubs/povinc.htm

———. 2003. "The New Definitive CBO Data on Income and Tax Trends." Table 2 and Appendix Table 2 (Sept 23). http://www.cbpp.org/9-23-03tax.htm

———. 2007. "Federal Budget Outlook." http://www.cbpp.org/budget-slideshow.htm

Centers for Disease Control and Prevention. 2002. *Web-based Injury Statistics Query and Reporting System (WISQARS).* http://www.cdc.gov/ncipc/wisqars

———. 2004a. "Surgeon General's Report—The Health Consequences of Smoking Among Adults in the United States: Cancer." http://www.cdc.gov/tobacco/data_statistics/sgr/sgr_2004/highlights/2.htm

———. 2004b. "Married Adults Are Healthiest." http://www.cdc.gov/nchs/pressroom/04facts/marriedadults.htm

————. 2006a. "Youth Risk Behavior Surveillance—United States, 2005." *Surveillance Summaries*. June 9, 2006. *MMWR 2006:55* (NO SS-5).

————. 2006b. "Fact Sheet Adult Cigarette Smoking in the United States: Current Estimates" (Updated November 2006). http://www.cdc.gov/tobacco/data_statistics/Factsheets/adult_cig_smoking.htm

————. 2007a. "Child Passenger Safety: Fact Sheet." http://www.cdc.gov/ncipc/factsheets/childpas.htm

————. 2007b. "Suicide: Fact Sheet." http://www.cdc.gov/ncipc/factsheets/suifacts.htm

————. 2007c. "Trends in Health and Aging." http://www.cdc.gov/nchs/agingact.htm

Cerulo, K. A. 1997. "Re-framing Sociological Concepts for a Brave New (Virtual?) World." *Sociological Inquiry* 67(1):48–58.

————. 1998. *Deciphering Violence: The Cognitive Structure of Right and Wrong*. New York: Routledge.

————. 2002. "Individualism . . . Pro Tem: Reconsidering U.S. Social Relations." In K. A. Cerulo (Ed.), *Culture in Mind: Toward a Sociology of Culture and Cognition* (pp. 135–171). New York: Routledge.

————. 2006. *Never Saw It Coming: Cultural Challenges to Envisioning the Worst*. Chicago: University of Chicago Press.

————. 2008. "Social Relations, Core Values and the Polyphony of the American Experience: Robin Williams Got It Right." *Sociological Forum* 23(2).

————. 2009. "Re-examining the Social Actor." *Annual Review of Sociology* 35.

Cerulo, K. A., and Ruane, J. M. 1997. "Death Comes Alive: Technology and the Re-conception of Death." *Science as Culture* 6(28):444–466.

————. 1998. "Coming Together: New Taxonomies for the Analysis of Social Relations." *Sociological Inquiry* 68(3):398–425.

Cerulo, K. A., Ruane, J. M., and Chayko, M. 1992."Technological Ties That Bind: Media-Centered Primary Groups." *Communication Research* 19(1):109–129.

Chan, K. B. 2002. "Coping with Work Stress, Work Satisfaction, and Social Support: An Interpretive Study of Life Insurance Agents." *Southeast Asian Journal of Social Science* 30(3):657–685.

Chaney, B., and Lewis, L. 2007. "Public School Principals Report on Their School Facilities: Fall 2005." U.S. Department of Education. Washington, DC: National Center for Education Statistics. (NCES 2007–007).

Charles, C. 2003. "The Dynamics of Racial Residential Segregation." *Annual Review of Sociology* 29:167–207.

Chase-Lansdale, P., Cherlin, A., and Kiernan, K. 1995. "The Long-Term Effects of Parental Divorce on the Mental Health of Young Adults: A Developmental Perspective." *Child Development* 66:1614–1634.

Chayko, M. 2002. *Connecting: How We Form Social Bonds and Community in the Internet Age*. Albany: SUNY Press.

Cherlin, A. 1999. "I'm OK, You're Selfish." *New York Times* (October 17)A:44–45.

Cherlin, A., Chase-Lansdale, P., and McRae, C. 1998. "Effects of Parental Divorce on Mental Health Throughout the Life Course." *American Sociological Review* 63(2):239–249.

Chia, R. C., and Alfred, L. J. 1998. "Effects of Attractiveness and Gender on the Perception of Achievement Related Variables." *Journal of Social Psychology* 138(4):471–478.

Chick, K., Heilman-Houser, R., and Hunter, M. 2002. "The Impact of Child Care on Gender Role Development and Gender Stereotypes." *Early Childhood Education Journal* 29(3):149–154.

Chideya, F. 1995. *Don't Believe the Hype: Fighting Cultural Misinformation About African-Americans.* New York: Plume.

Children's Defense Fund. 2001. "A Fragile Foundation: State Child Care Assistance Policies." http://campaign.childrensdefense.org/earlychildhood/childcare/fragile_foundation_exec_summary.pdf

———. 2005a. "Child Abuse and Neglect Fact Sheet." http://www.childrensdefense.org/site/DocServer/factsheet0805.pdf?docID=397

———. 2005b. *The State of America's Children 2005.* http://www.childrensdefense.org/site/DocServer/Greenbook_2005.pdf?docID=1741

———. 2006. "Child Health—Immunizations." http://www.childrensdefense.org/site/PageServer?pagename=childhealth_immunizations_default

———. 2007. "Each Day in America." http://www.childrensdefense.org/site/PageServer?pagename=research_national_data_each_day

Children's Monitor. 2003. "Hill Highlights: FY 2004 Bush Budget and Children." *Children's Monitor* 16(2):2–9.

Children Now. 2004. *Fall Colors: Prime Time Diversity Report 2003–2004.* http://publications.childrennow.org/assets/pdf/cmp/fall-colors-03/fall-colors-03-v5.pdf

Chimerine, L., and Eisenbrey, R. 2005. "The Frivolous Case for Tort Law Changes." Briefing Paper #157. Washington, DC: Economic Policy Institute.

Chira, S. 1992. "Bias Against Girls Is Found Rife in Schools, with Lasting Damage." *New York Times* (February 12):A1.

Chomsky, A. 2007. *"They Take Our Jobs!" and 20 Other Myths About Immigration* Boston: Beacon Press.

Christopher, A. N. 1998. "The Psychology of Names: An Empirical Examination." *Journal of Applied Social Psychology* 28(13):1173–1195.

Clarke, E. H. 1873. *Sex in Education: Or a Fair Chance for Girls.* Boston: J.R. Osgood.

ClearLead Inc. 2007. "American Lawyer Information." http://www.clearleadinc.com/site/lawyer-information.html

Clifford, M. M., and Walster, E. H. 1973. "The Effects of Physical Attractiveness on Teacher Expectation." *Sociology of Education* 46:245–258.

Clinton Foundation. 2005. "Bush-Clinton Katrina Fund Passes $1 Million in Online Donations." http://www.clintonfoundation.org/090605-nr-cf-ee-hur-usa-pr-bush-clinton-katrina-fund-passes-one-million-dollars-in-online-donations.htm

Cochran, J. 2005. "A Simple Case of Complexity." *CQ Weekly* (January 31).

Cockerham, W. 1997. *This Aging Society.* 2d ed. Englewood Cliffs, NJ: Prentice Hall.

———. 2005. *Sociology of Mental Disorder.* 7th ed. Upper Saddle River, NJ: Prentice Hall.

————. 2006. *Medical Sociology*. 10th ed. Upper Saddle River, NJ: Prentice Hall.

Cohen, L., and Gray, C. B. 2003. "The Blaine Game: School Vouchers and State Constitutions." *The Taubman Center Report—Our 15th Anniversary*. John F. Kennedy School of Government, Harvard University, Cambridge, MA.

Cohen, S. 2004. "Social Relationships and Health." *American Psychologist* 59:676–684.

Colantonio, S. E., Fuster, V., Ferreyras, M., and Lascano, J. G. 2006. "Isonymic Relationships in Ethno-Social Categories (Argentinian Colonial Period) Including Illegitimate Reproduction." *Journal of Biosocial Science* 38(3):381–389.

Coleman, R., and Rainwater, L. 1978. *Social Standing in America: New Dimensions of Class*. New York: Basic Books.

College Board. 2006a. "Trends in College Pricing 2006." *The College Board*. http://www.collegeboard.com/prod_downloads/press/cost06/trends_college_pricing_06.pdf

————. 2006b. "Trends in Student Aid 2006." *The College Board*. http://www.collegeboard.com/prod_downloads/press/cost06/trends_aid_06.pdf

————. 2006c. "Education Pays, Second Update 2006." *The College Board*. http://www.collegeboard.com/prod_downloads/press/cost06/education_pays_06.pdf

Collier, J. L. 1991. *The Rise of Selfishness in America*. New York: Oxford University Press.

Collier, R. 2005. "State Bypasses Kyoto, Fights Global Warming, California Tries to Cut Emissions on Its Own." *San Francisco Chronicle* (February 17). http://www.sfgate.com/cgi-bin/article.cgi?f=/c/a/2005/02/17/MNG1IBCSUS1.DTL

Collins, P. H. 1990. *Black Feminist Thought*. New York: Routledge.

Collins, R. 1979. *The Credential Society: An Historical Sociology of Education*. New York: Academic Press.

————. 2001. "Conflict Theory of Educational Stratification." In J. Ballantine and J. Spade (Eds.), *Schools and Society: A Sociological Approach*. Belmont, CA: Wadsworth/Thomson.

Combs, A. (Ed.). 1992. *Cooperation: Beyond the Age of Competition*. Philadelphia: Gordon and Breach.

Combs-Orme, T., and Cain, D. S. 2006. "Poverty and the Daily Lives of Infants: Consistent Disadvantage." *Journal of Children & Poverty* 12(1):1–20.

Congressional Budget Office. 2003. "The U.S. Retirement System and the Baby-Boom Generation." *Baby Boomers' Retirement Prospects: An Overview*. http://www.cbo.gov/ftpdoc.cfm?index=4863&type=0&sequence=2

Conner, G., and Smith, D. 1991. "Home Mortgage Disclosure Act: Expanded Data on Residential Lending." *Federal Reserve Bulletin* (November).

Conradson, S., and Hernández-Ramos, P. 2004. "Computers, the Internet, and Cheating Among Secondary School Students: Some Implications for Educators. *Practical Assessment, Research & Evaluation* 9(9). http://PAREonline.net/getvn.asp?v=9&n=9

Cooley, C. H. 1902. *Human Nature and Social Order*. New York: Scribner.

————. 1909. *Social Organization*. New York: Charles Scribner.

Coontz, S. 1998. *The Way We Really Are: Coming to Terms with America's Changing Families.* New York: Basic Books.

———. 2000. *The Way We Never Were: American Families and the Nostalgia Trap.* New York: Basic Books.

———. 2006. *Marriage, a History: From Obedience to Intimacy, or How Love Conquered Marriage.* New York: Penguin.

———. 2007. "The Origins of Modern Divorce." *Family Process* 46(1):7–16.

Cooper, M. 2002. "Poverty Increases in the United States, U.S. Census Bureau Reports." National Council of Churches. http://www.ncccusa.org/publicwitness/povertyincreases.html

Coopersmith, S. 1967. *Antecedents of Self-Esteem.* San Francisco: Freeman.

Correll, S. 2001. "Gender and the Career Choice Process: The Role of Biased Self-Assessments." *American Journal of Sociology* 106(6):1691–1730.

Cosaro, W. 2005. *The Sociology of Childhood.* Thousand Oaks: Sage.

Coser, L. 1956. *The Functions of Social Conflict.* Glencoe, IL: Free Press.

———. 1963. *Sociology Through Literature: An Introductory Reader.* Englewood Cliffs, NJ: Prentice Hall.

Courtney, A., and Whipple, T. 1983. *Sex Stereotyping in Advertising.* Lexington, MA: D.C. Heath.

Cowe, R. 1990. "New Ice Cream Plans to Lick Rivals." *Guardian II* (April 2):3.

Crane, D. R., and Heaton, T. B. 2007. *Handbook of Families and Poverty.* Thousand Oaks, CA: Sage.

Critser, G. 2003. *Fat Land: How Americans Became the Fattest People in the World.* Boston: Houghton Mifflin.

Crocker, P. 1985. "The Meaning of Equality for Battered Women Who Kill Men in Self-Defense." *Harvard Women's Law Journal* 8:121–153.

Cross, S., and Bagilhole, B. 2002. "Girls' Jobs for the Boys? Men, Masculinity and Non-Traditional Occupations." *Gender, Work and Organization* 9(2):204–226.

Cross, S. E., and Vick, N. V. 2001. "The Interdependent Self-Construal and Social Support: The Case of Persistence in Engineering." *Personality and Social Psychology Bulletin* 27(7):820–832.

Cuklanz, L. M., and Moorti, S. 2006. "Television's 'New' Feminism: Prime-Time Representations of Women and Victimization." *Critical Studies in Media Communication* 23(4):302–321.

Cummings, J. 2003. "When Poverty Cripples." *NEA Today* 21(4):22.

Currie, D. 2007. "Clearing the Air." *Weekly Standard* 12:41. http//www.theweekly standard.com

Cutrona, C. E., Russell, D. W., Brown, P. A., Clarkm, L. A., Hessling, R. M., and Gardner, K. A. 2005. "Neighborhood Context, Personality and Stressful Life Events as Predictors of Depression Among African American Women." *Journal of Abnormal Psychology* 114(1):3–15.

Dai, D. 2002. "Incorporating Parent Perceptions: A Replication and Extension Study of the Internal-External Frame of Reference Model of Self-Concept Development." *Journal of Adolescent Research* 17(6):617–645.

Dalphonse, S. 1997. "Choosing to Be Childfree: Broadening the Definition of Family." *The Population Connection Reporter* (May/June).

Daly, K. 2001. "Controlling Time in Families: Patterns That Sustain Gendered Work in the Home." *Contemporary Perspectives in Family Research* 3:227–249.

Daniels, R. 1990. *A History of Immigration and Ethnicity in American Life*. New York: Harper Perennial.

Danner, D. D., Snowden, D. A., and Friesen, W. V. 2001. "Positive Emotions in Early Life and Longevity: Findings from the Nun Study." *Journal of Personality and Social Psychology* 80:804–813.

Davis, K. 1990. *Don't Know Much About History*. New York: Harper Collins.

Davis, K., and Moore, W. 1945. "Some Principles of Stratification." *American Sociological Review* 27(1):5–19.

Davis, S. 2003. "Sex Stereotypes in Commercials Targeted Toward Children: A Content Analysis." *Sociological Spectrum* 23(4):407–425.

Dawkins, C. 2005. "Evidence on the Intergenerational Persistence of Residential Segregation by Race." *Urban Studies* 42(3):545–555.

Day, J., and Downs, B. 2007. "Examining the Gender Earnings Gap: Occupational Differences and the Life Course." Population Association of America 2007 Annual Meeting, New York, N.Y. http://paa2007.princeton.edu/

Deaton, A. 2003. "Health, Income, and Inequality." *National Bureau of Economic Research*. http://www.nber.org/reporter/spring03/health.html

De Cremer, D. 2001. "Relations of Self-Esteem Concerns, Group Identification, and Self-Stereotyping to In-Group Favoritism." *Journal of Social Psychology* 14(3):389–400.

Dedman, B. 1989. "Blacks Turned Down for Home Loans from S&L's Twice as Often as Whites." *Atlanta Constitution* (January 22):A1.

De Dreu, C. K. W., Weingart, L. R., and Kwon, S. 2000. "Influence of Social Motives on Integrative Negotiation: A Meta-Analytic Review and Test of Two Theories." *Journal of Personality and Social Psychology* 78(5):889–905.

Degher, D., and Hughes, G. 1992. "The Identity Change Process: A Field Study of Obesity." *Deviant Behavior* 2:385–401.

DeNavas-Walt, C., Proctor, B., and Hill-Lee, C. 2006. "Income, Poverty, and Health Insurance Coverage in the United States: 2005." U.S. Census Bureau. *Current Population Reports*, P60–231. http://www.census.gov/prod/2006pubs/p60-231.pdf

DeNavas-Walt, C., Proctor, B., and Smith, J. 2007. "Income, Poverty, and Health Insurance Coverage in the United States: 2006." U.S. Census Bureau. *Current Population Reports*, P60–233. http://www.census.gov/prod/2007pubs/p60-233.pdf

Denton, N., and Massey, D. 1989. "Racial Identity Among Caribbean Hispanics: The Effect of Double Minority Status on Residential Segregation." *American Sociological Review* 54:790–808.

DePaulo, B. M., Kashy, D. A., and Kirkendol, S. E. 1996. "Lying in Everyday Life." *Journal of Personality and Social Psychology* 70 (May):979–995.

DeSantis, A., and Kayson, W. 1997. "Defendants' Characteristics of Attractiveness, Race, Sex, and Sentencing Decisions." *Psychological Reports* 81 (October): 679–683.

De Schipper, S., Hirschberg, C., and Sinha, G. 2002. "Blame the Name." *Popular Science* 261(1):36.

Deutsch, M. 2000. "Cooperation and Competition." In M. Deutsch and P. T. Coleman (Eds.), *The Handbook of Conflict Resolution: Theory and Practice* (pp. 21–40). San Francisco: Jossey-Bass.

Deutsch, M., Coleman, P. T., and Marcus, E. C. (Eds.). 2006. *The Handbook of Conflict Resolution: Theory and Practice*, 2d ed. San Francisco: Jossey-Bass.

Deutsch, M., and Krauss, R. M. 1960. "The Effect of Threat on Interpersonal Bargaining." *Journal of Abnormal and Social Psychology* 1:629–636.

Deutscher, E., and Messner, D. 2005. "Europe's Response to World Politics." *Society* 42(6):59–63.

Dewar, D. 2000. "Gender Impacts on Health Insurance Coverage: Findings for Unmarried Full-Time Employees." *Women's Health Issues* 10(5):268–277.

Diamond, J. 2005. "Evolutionary Biology, Geography and Skin Colour." *Nature* 435(7040):283–284.

Diamond, L. M., and Dube, E. M. 2002. "Friendship and Attachment Among Heterosexual and Sexual-Minority Youths: Does the Gender of Your Friend Matter?" *Journal of Youth and Adolescence* 31(2):155–166.

Diefenbach, D. L., and West, M. D. 2001. "Violent Crime and Poisson Regression: A Measure and Method for Cultivation Analysis." *Journal of Broadcasting and Electronic Media* 45(3):432–445.

Dietz, T. 1998. "An Examination of Violence and Gender Role Portrayals in Video Games: Implications for Gender Socialization and Aggressive Behavior." *Sex Roles* 38(5–6):425–442.

Dines, G., and Humez, J. (Eds.). 2003. *Gender, Race and Class in Media: A Text-Reader*. Thousand Oaks, CA: Sage.

Dinger, E. 2006. "Legislative Issues in Maryland: A Survey of Self-Identified Registered Voters 50 Plus." AARP. Knowledge Management. http://assets.aarp .org/rgcenter/general/md_leg_2006.pdf

Dion, K. K. 1979. "Physical Attractiveness and Interpersonal Attraction." In M. Cook and G. Wilson (Eds.), *Love and Attraction*. New York: Pergamon.

———. 2001. "Cultural Perspectives on Facial Attractiveness." In G. Rhodes and L. A. Zebrowitz (Eds.), *Facial Attractiveness: Evolutionary, Cognitive, and Social Perspectives* (pp. 239–259). Greenwich, CT: Ablex.

Dion, K. K., and Berscheid, E. 1974. "Physical Attractiveness and Peer Perception Among Children." *Sociometry* 37:1–12.

Dion, K. K., Berscheid, E., and Walster, E. 1972. "What Is Beautiful Is Good." *Journal of Personality and Social Psychology* 24:285–290.

Dion, K. K., and Dion, K. 1996. "Cultural Perspectives on Romantic Love." *Personal Relationships* 3:5–17.

Dion, K. L. 1979. "Intergroup Conflict and Intragroup Cohesiveness." In W. G. Austin and S. Worschel (Eds.), *The Social Psychology of Intergroup Relations*. Monterey, CA: Brooks/Cole.

Disease Control Priorities Project. 2006. "Halting the Global Epidemic of Neonatal Death and Malnutrition." http://www.dcp2.org/features/10

Dittmar, H. 2005. "Vulnerability Factors and Processes Linking Sociocultural Pressures and Body Dissatisfaction." *Journal of Social and Clinical Psychology* 24(8):1081–1087.

Dizard, J. E., and Gadlin, H. 1990. *The Minimal Family*. Amherst: University of Massachusetts Press.

Doggett, S., and Haddad, A. 2000. "Global Savvy: Cosmetics Maker Is All Smiles as Sales Blossom in Overseas Markets." *Los Angeles Times* (March 27):C2.

Dohnt, H. K., and Tiggemann, M. 2006. "Body Image Concerns in Young Girls: The Role of Peers and Media Prior to Adolescence." *Journal of Youth and Adolescence* 35(2):141–151.

Dolgin, K. G., and Minowa, N. 1997. "Gender Differences in Self-Presentation: A Comparison of the Roles of Flatteringness and Intimacy in Self-Disclosure to Friends." *Sex Roles* 36(5–6):371–380.

Donohue, B. 2002. "Their Own Names Are What They Fear." *Star Ledger* (March 3):A1.

Doyle, R. 2002. "Calculus of Happiness." *Scientific American* 287(5):32–33.

Driskell, J. E., Johnston, J. H., and Salas, E. 2001. "Does Stress Training Generate to Novel Settings?" *Human Factors* 43(1):99–110.

Drucker, P. 1993. "The Rise of the Knowledge Society." *Wilson Quarterly* (Spring):52–71.

Du Bois, W. E. B. [1903] 1982. *The Souls of Black Folks*. New York: Penguin.

Dubois, N., and Beauvois, J. 2005. "Normativeness and Individualism." *European Journal of Social Psychology* 35(1):123–146.

Dudley, D. 2002. "Forever Cool." *AARP Modern Maturity*. http://www.globalaging .org/health/us/forevercool.htm

Duncan, G., Wilkerson, B., and England, P. 2006. "Cleaning Up Their Act: The Effects of Marriage and Cohabitation on Licit and Illicit Drug Use." *Demography* 43(4):691–710.

Dunne, J. G. 1986. "The War That Won't Go Away." *New York Review of Books* (September 25):25–29.

Dunphy, H. 2005. "11 Million in Developing Nations Die Before Age 5." *Associated Press* (April 18). http://deseretnews.com/dn/view/0,1249,600127104,00.html

Durkheim, E. [1938] 1966. *The Rules of Sociological Method*. 8th ed. S. A. Solovay and J. H. Mueller, Trans. New York: Free Press.

Dye, J. 2005. "Fertility of American Women: June 2004." *Current Population Reports*, P20–555. U.S. Census Bureau, Washington, DC.

Economic Policy Institute. 2005. "Facts and Figures: State of Working America 2004/2005, U.S. and the World." http://www.epinet.org/books/swa2004/news/ swafacts_international.pdf

———. 2007. *The State of Working America 2006/2007*. Ithaca, NY: Cornell University Press.

Economist. 2003. "Take It Block by Block." *Economist* 366(8308):35.

Eder, D. 1981. "Ability Grouping as a Self-Fulfilling Prophecy: A Micro-Analysis of Teacher Student Interaction." *Sociology of Education* 54(3):151–162.

Edin, K., and Lein, L. 1997a. "Work, Welfare, and Single Mothers' Economic Strategies." *American Sociological Review* 62(2):253–266.

———. 1997b. *Making Ends Meet: How Single Mothers Survive Welfare and Low-Wage Work*. New York: Russell Sage.

Ehrenreich, B. 2001. *Nickel and Dimed: On (Not) Getting by in America*. New York: Owl Books.

Eichenwald, K. 2003. "In String of Corporate Troubles, Critics Focus on Boards' Failings." *New York Times* (September 21):1.

Eichenwald, K., and Atlas, R. 2003. "2 Banks Settle Accusations They Aided in Enron Fraud." *New York Times* (July 29).

Ekman, P. 2002. *Telling Lies: Clues to Deceit in the Marketplace, Politics, and Marriage*. San Francisco: University of California.

Ekman, P., and Frank, M. G. 1993. "Lies That Fail." In M. Lewis and C. Saarni (Eds.), *Lying and Deception in Everyday Life* (pp. 184–200). New York: Guilford.

Ekman, P., O'Sullivan, M., Friesen, W. V., and Scherer, K. R. 1991. "Face, Voice and Body in Detecting Deceit." *Journal of Nonverbal Behavior* 15(2):125–135.

Eliasoph, N. 1998. *Avoiding Politics: How Americans Produce Apathy in Everyday Life*. Cambridge: Cambridge University Press.

Elles, L. 1993. *Social Stratification and Socioeconomic Inequality*. Westport, CT: Praeger.

Ellis, B., Bates, J., Dodge, K., Fergusson, D., Horwood, L., Pettit, G., and Woodward, L. 2003. "Does Father Absence Place Daughters at Special Risk for Early Sexual Activity and Teenage Pregnancy?" *Child Development* 74(3):801–821.

Ellis, H. C. 1972. "Motor Skills in Learning." In *Fundamentals of Human Learning and Cognition*. Dubuque, IA: Wm. C. Brown.

Emerson, M., and Hartman, D. 2006. "The Rise of Religious Fundamentalism." *Annual Review of Sociology* 32:127–144.

Emerson, M., and Sikkink, D. 2006. "School Choice and Residential Segregation in U.S. Schools: The Role of Parents' Education." *Ethnic and Racial Studies*.

Emerson, M., Yancey, G., and Chai, K. 2001. "Does Race Matter in Residential Segregation? Exploring the Preferences of White Americans." *American Sociological Review* 66(6):922–935.

Employment Policy Foundation. 2002. "Where Are Tomorrow's Workers?" News Release (August 14).

Enns, M. 2005. "'Now I Know in Part': Holistic and Analytic Reasoning and Their Contribution to Fuller Knowing in Theological Education." *Evangelical Review of Theology* 29(3):251–269.

Environmental Protection Agency. 2004. "Climate's Come a Long Way." http://www.epa.gov/globalwarming/kids/history.html

Equal Employment Opportunity Commission. 2003. "EEOC Reports Discrimination Charge Filings Up." http://www.eeoc.gov/press/2-6-03.html

———. 2007. "Race-Based Charges FY 1997–FY 2006." U.S. Equal Employment Opportunity Commission. http://www.eeoc.gov/stats/race.html

Erian, M., Lin, C., Patel, N., Neal, A., and Geiselman, R. E. 1998. "Juror Verdicts as a Function of Victim and Defendant Attractiveness in Sexual Assault Cases." *American Journal of Forensic Psychology* 16(3):25–40.

Ericson, R. V., and Doyle, A. 2006. "The Institutionalization of Deceptive Sales in Life Insurance: Five Sources of Moral Risk." *British Journal of Criminology* 46:6:993–1010.

Eschholz, S., Bufkin, J., and Long, J. 2002. "Symbolic Reality Bites: Women and Racial/Ethnic Minorities in Modern Film." *Sociological Spectrum* 22(3):299–334.

Espino, R., and Franz, M. M. 2002. "Latino Phenotypic Discrimination Revisited: The Impact of Skin Color on Occupational Status." *Social Science Quarterly* 83(2):612–623.

Etaugh, C. E., Bridges, J. S., Cummings-Hill, M., and Cohen, J. 1999. "Names Can Never Hurt Me? The Effects of Surname Use on Perceptions of Married Women." *Psychology of Women Quarterly* 23(4):819–823.

Etzioni, A. 1994. *The Spirit of Community: The Reinvention of American Society.* New York: Touchstone Books.

———. 1996. *The New Golden Rule.* New York: Basic Books.

———. 2003. *Monochrome Society.* New York: New Forum Books.

Evelyn, J. 2003. "The Silent Killer of Minority Enrollments." *Chronicle of Higher Education* (June 20). http://chronicle.com/free/v49/i41/41a01701.htm

———. 2004. "Community Colleges at a Crossroads." *Chronicle of Higher Education* (April 30). http://chronicle.com/free/v50/i34/34a02701.htm

FACT. 2006. "Interfaith Worship and Interfaith Cooperation Among Congregations Has Increased Significantly." *Faith Communities Today* (May 4).

Fallows, J. 1983. "Immigration: How It Is Affecting Us." *Atlantic Monthly* 252(5):45–48.

Family Strengthening Policy Center. 2005. "Sustaining and Growing Father Involvement for Low-Income Children." National Human Services Assembly. http://www.nassembly.org/fspc/practice/documents/Fathersbrief.pdf

Family Violence Prevention Fund. 2007. "Domestic Violence Is a Serious, Widespread Social Problem in America: The Facts." http://www.endabuse.org/resources/facts/

Fass, S., and Cauthen, N. 2006. "Who Are America's Poor Children? The Official Story." National Center for Children in Poverty. http://www.nccp.org/publications/pub_684.html

Faw, B. 2007. "Katrina Exposes New Orleans' Deep Poverty." MSNBC News. http://www.msnbc.msn.com/id/9163091

Feagin, J. R. 1975. *Subordinating the Poor.* Englewood Cliffs, NJ: Prentice Hall.

Federal Interagency Forum on Aging-Related Statistics. 2006. "Older Americans Update 2006: Key Indicators on Wellness." Federal Interagency Forum on Aging-Related Statistics. Washington, DC: U.S. Government Printing Office. http://pubdb3.census.gov/macro/032006/pov/new01_100_01.htm

Federal Interagency Forum on Child and Family Statistics. 2006. "America's Children in Brief: Key National Indicators of Well-Being, 2006." Forum on Child and Family Statistics. U.S. Government Printing Office. http://www.childstats.gov/americaschildren

Federal Trade Commission. 2007a. "Annual Report to Congress for FY 2006: The National Do Not Call Registry." http://www.ftc.gov/os/2007/04/P034305FY2006RptOnDNC.pdf

———. 2007b. "Spam." http://www.ftc.gov/bcp/conline/edcams/spam/report.html

Feeley, T. H. 2002. "Evidence of Halo Effects in Student Evaluations of Communication Instruction." *Communication Education* 51(3):225–236.

Feingold, A. 1988. "Cognitive Gender Differences Are Disappearing." *American Psychologist* 43:95–103.

Feinson, R. 2004. *The Secret Universe of Names.* New York: Overlook.

Feldman, B. 2003. "'Savage Inequalities' Revisited." *Dollars and Sense* (January/February). http://www.thirdworldtraveler.com/Education/SavageInequal_Revisited.html

Feliciano, C. 2001. "The Benefits of Biculturalism: Exposure to Immigrant Culture and Dropping out of School Among Asian and Latino Youths." *Social Science Quarterly* 82(4):865–879.

Felson, R. B., and Reed, M. 1986. "Reference Groups and Self-Appraisals of Academic Ability and Performance." *Social Psychology Quarterly* 49:103–109.

———. 1987. "The Effect of Parents on the Self-Appraisals of Children." *Social Psychology Quarterly* 49:302–308.

Festinger, L., Schachter, S., and Back, K. 1950. *Social Pressures in Informal Groups: A Study of Human Factors in Housing.* New York: Harper and Brothers.

Fields, J., and Casper, L. 2001. "America's Families and Living Arrangements: March 2000." *Current Population Reports* (P20–537). Washington, DC: U.S. Census Bureau.

Fiese, B., and Skillman, G. 2000. "Gender Differences in Family Stories: Moderating Influence of Parent Gender Role and Child Gender." *Sex Roles* 43(5–6):267–283.

Figueroa, C. 2003. "Self-Esteem and Cosmetic Surgery: Is There a Relationship Between the Two?" *Plastic Surgical Nursing* 23(1):21–25.

Finlinson, A. R., Austin, A. M. B., and Pfister, R. 2000. "Cooperative Games and Children's Positive Behaviors." *Early Child Development and Care* 164:29–40.

Fischer, C. 1982. *To Dwell Among Friends: Personal Networks in Town and City.* Chicago: University of Chicago Press.

Fischer, D. H. 1977. *Growing Old in America.* New York: Oxford University Press.

Fitzpatrick, M. 2006. "Human Fingerprints." http://www.ucsusa.org/global_warming/science/Fingerprints.html

Flashpoints. 2003. "The PATRIOT Act." PBS Broadcast (July 15). http://www.pbs.org/flashpointsusa/20030715/infocus/topic_03/

Flippen, C. 2001. "Racial and Ethnic Inequality in Home Ownership and Housing Equity." *Sociological Quarterly* 42(2):121–150.

———. 2004. "Unequal Returns to Housing Investments? A Study of Real Housing Appreciation Among Black, White, and Hispanic Households." *Social Forces* 82(4):1523–1551.

Foucault, M. 1971. *The Order of Things: An Archeology of Human Sciences.* New York: Pantheon.

Fox, V., and Quit, M. 1980. *Loving, Parenting, and Dying: The Family Cycle in England and America, Past and Present.* New York: Psychohistory Press.

Frank, J. B. 2002. *The Paradox of Aging in Place in Assisted Living.* Westport, CT: Bergin and Garvey.

Frankel, T. 2005. *Trust and Honesty: America's Business Culture at a Crossroad.* New York: Oxford University Press.

Frankenberg, E., and Lee, C. 2002. "Race in American Public Schools: Rapidly Resegregating School Districts." The Civil Rights Project, Harvard University, Cambridge, MA. http://www.civilrightsproject.harvard.edu

Frankenberg, E., Lee, C., and Orfield, G. 2003a. "A Multiracial Society with Segregated Schools: Are We Losing the Dream?" The Civil Rights Project, Harvard University, Cambridge, MA. http://www.civilrightsproject.harvard.edu

———. 2003b. "Charter Schools and Race: A Lost Opportunity for Integrated Education." The Civil Rights Project, Harvard University, Cambridge, MA. http://www.civilrightsproject.harvard.edu

Frazier, P. A., Tix, A. P., Klein, C. D., and Arikian, N. J. 2000. "Testing Theoretical Models of the Relations Between Social Support, Coping, and Adjustments to Stressful Life Events." *Journal of Social and Clinical Psychology* 19:314–335.

Freeman, C. 2004. "Trends in Educational Equity of Girls and Women: 2004." *Education Statistics Quarterly* 6(4). http://nces.ed.gov/programs/quarterly/vol_6/6_4/8_1.asp#2

Freeman, M. 2002. "Fewer Series Feature Black-Dominant Casts." *Electronic Media* 21(15):3–5.

Freeman, N. 2007. "Preschoolers' Perceptions of Gender Appropriate Toys and Their Parents' Beliefs About Genderized Behaviors: Miscommunication, Mixed Messages, or Hidden Truths?" *Early Childhood Education Journal* 34(5):357–366.

Fremstad, S. 2003. "State Fiscal Relief Funds Do Not Address the Need for Substantial Increases in Child Care Funding." Center on Budget and Policy Priorities. www.cbpp.org/pubs/welfare03.htm

French, D., and Rothman, S. 1990. *Structuring Schools for Student Success: A Focus on Ability Grouping*. Quincy, MA: Massachusetts State Department of Education, Bureau of Research, Planning, and Evaluation.

Freudenheim, B. 1988. "Who Lives Here, Go-Getter or Grouch?" *New York Times* (March 31):15–16.

Friedman, L. 1975. *The Legal System: A Social Science Perspective*. New York: Russell Sage.

Frontline. 2004. "The Jesus Factor; Evangelical: What It Means." http://www.pbs.org/wgbh/pages/frontline/shows/jesus/evangelicals/whatitmeans.html

Fukuoka, Y. 1998. "Japanese Alias vs. Real Ethnic Name: On Naming Practices Among Young Koreans in Japan." Paper Presented at the Annual Meeting of the International Sociological Association.

Fuligni, A., and Pedersen, S. 2002. "Family Obligation and the Transition to Young Adulthood." *Developmental Psychology* 38(5):856–868.

Funiciello, T. 1990. "The Poverty of Industry." *Ms.* (November/December): 32–40.

Furstenburg, F. Jr. 1979. "Pre-Marital Pregnancy and Marital Instability." In G. Levinger and O. C. Moles (Eds.), *Divorce and Separation*. New York: Basic Books.

Furstenburg, F. F. Jr., and Talvitie, K. G. 1980. "Children's Names and Parental Claims: Bonds Between Unmarried Fathers and Their Children." *Journal of Family Issues* 1:31–57.

Gallup, G. Jr. 1976–2003. *The Gallup Poll: Public Opinion*. Wilmington, DE: Scholarly Resources.

————. 2004–2007. *The Gallup Poll: Public Opinion.* Wilmington, DE: Scholarly Resources.

Gallup Poll. 2007a. "Gallup's Pulse of Democracy: Fixing Government." http://www .galluppoll.com

————. 2007b. "Religion." http://www.galluppoll.com/content/?ci=1690&pg=1

Ganahl, D., Prinsen, T., and Netzley, S. B. 2003. "A Content Analysis of Prime Time Commercials: A Contextual Framework of Gender Representation." *Sex Roles* 49(9/10):545–551.

Gannon, S. 2007. "Laptops and Lipsticks: Feminising Technology." *Learning, Media, & Technology* 32(1):53–67.

Gans, H. 1971. "The Uses of Poverty: The Poor Pay for All." *Social Policy* (Summer):20–24.

Garcia, S. D. 1998. "Appearance Anxiety, Health Practices, Metaperspectives and Self-Perception of Physical Attractiveness." *Journal of Social Behavior and Personality* 13(2):12–15.

Gardyn, R. 2002. "The Mating Game." *American Demographics* (July/August): 33–37.

Gates, H.-L., Jr. 2007. *Finding Oprah's Roots.* New York: Random House.

Gelles, R. J., and Loseke, D. R. (Eds.). 1993. *Current Controversies on Family Violence.* Newbury Park, CA: Sage.

Gelles, R., and Straus, M. 1988. *Intimate Violence.* New York: Simon and Schuster.

General Social Survey. 1999. *Cumulative Codebook. 1972–1998.* Chicago: National Opinion Research Center. http://www.norc.uchicago.edu/

————. 2000. *Cumulative Codebook. 1972–2000.* http://www.icpsr.umich.edu: 8080/GSS

————. 2004. *Cumulative File 1972–2004.* http://sda.berkeley.edu/cgi-bin/hsda? harcsda+gss04

George, J. 2006. "Access to Justice, Costs, and Legal Aid." *American Journal of Comparative Law* Supplement 54(Fall):293.

Gerbner, G., Gross, L., Morgan, M., Signorielli, N., and Shanahan, J. 2002. "Growing Up with Television: Cultivation Processes." In J. Bryant and D. Zillmann (Eds.), *Media Effects: Advances in Theory and Research* (pp. 43–67). 2d ed. Mahwah, NJ: Lawrence Erlbaum.

Gergen, K. 1971. *The Concept of Self.* New York: Holt, Rinehart and Winston.

Gergen, M. M., Gergen, K. J., March, K., and Ellis, C. 2003. "The Body and the Physical Self." In J. A. Holstein and J. F. Gubrium (Eds.), *Inner Lives and Social Worlds: Readings in Social Psychology* (pp. 301–340). London: Oxford University Press.

Gerull, F., and Rapee, R. 2002. "Mother Knows Best: The Effects of Maternal Modeling on the Acquisition of Fear and Avoidance Behavior in Toddlers." *Behavior Research and Therapy* 40(3):279–287.

Gettleman, T. E., and Thompson, J. K. 1993. "Actual Differences and Stereotypical Perceptions in Body Image and Eating Disturbance: A Comparison of Male and Female Heterosexual and Homosexual Sample." *Sex Roles* 29(7/8):545–562.

Giannerelli, L., Adelman, S., and Schmidt, S. 2003. "Getting Help with Child Care Expenses." *Assessing the New Federalism* (Occasional Paper No. #62).

Washington, DC: Urban Institute. http://www.urban.org/UploadedPDF/310615_OP62.pdf

Giddens, A. 1992. *The Transformation of Intimacy, Sexuality, Love and Eroticism in Modern Societies*. Stanford, CA: Stanford University Press.

Gilbert, D. 2003. *The American Class Structure in an Age of Growing Inequality*. Belmont, CA: Wadsworth/Thompson.

Gilman, S. 1999. *Making the Body Beautiful: A Cultural History of Aesthetic Surgery*. Princeton, NJ: Princeton University Press.

Gimlin, D. 2002. *Body Work: Beauty and Self-Image in American Culture*. Berkeley: University of California Press.

Giordano, P. 2003. "Relationships in Adolescence." *Annual Review of Sociology* 29:257–281.

Glassman, M. 2000. "Mutual Aid Theory and Human Development: Sociability as Primary." *Journal for the Theory of Social Behavior* 30(4):391–412.

Glassner, B. 2000. *The Culture of Fear: Why Americans Are Afraid of the Wrong Things*. New York: Basic Books.

Glenn, N. D., and Supancic, M. 1984. "The Social and Demographic Correlates of Divorce and Separation in the United States." *Journal of Marriage and the Family* 46:563–575.

Glick, P., and Sung-Ling, L. 1986. "Recent Changes in Divorce and Remarriage." *Journal of Marriage and Family* 48:737–747.

Goffman, E. 1959. *The Presentation of Self in Everyday Life*. New York: Anchor.

———. 1963. *Stigma: Notes on the Management of Spoiled Identity*. Englewood Cliffs, NJ: Prentice Hall.

———. 1974. *Frame Analysis*. Cambridge: Harvard University Press.

Goldberg, S., and Lewis, M. 1969. "Play Behavior in the Year-Old Infant: Early Sex Differences." *Child Development* 40:21–31.

Goldiner, D. 2001. "What's in a Name? At Least 500G Couple Hopes." *New York Daily News* (July 27).

Goldman, L. 2007. *Locker Room Diaries: The Naked Truth About Women, Body Image, and Re-Imagining the "Perfect" Body*. Boulder, CO: Da Capo Lifelong Books.

Goldstein, J., and Morning, A. 2002. "Back in the Box: The Dilemma of Using Multiple-Race Data for Single-Race Laws. In J. Perlman and M. Waters (Eds.), *The New Race Question: How the Census Counts Multiracial Individuals* (pp. 119–136). New York: Russell Sage.

Goleman, D. 1985. *Vital Lies, Simple Truths*. New York: Simon and Schuster.

Gonzalez Faraco, J. C., and Murphy, M. D. 1997. "Street Names and Political Regimes in an Andalusian Town (Almonte, Spain)." *Ethnology* 36 (Spring):123–148.

Goodlad, J. 1984. *A Place Called School: Prospects for the Future*. New York: McGraw-Hill.

Goodstein, L. 2005. "More Religion, but Not the Old-Time Kind." *New York Times*. Sunday (Jan 9) 4:1,4.

Gouldner, H., and Strong, M. S. 1987. *Speaking of Friendship: Middle-Class Women and Their Friends*. New York: Greenwood.

Goyer, A. 2006. "Intergenerational Relationships. Grandparents Raising Grandchildren." AARP Policy and Research. http://www.aarp.org/research/family/grandparenting/nov_05_grandparents.html

Graham, R. 2002. "The Science of Gray Hair." InteliHealth. www.intelihealth.com/IH/ihtIH/WSIHW000/9023/24253/348513.html?d=dmtContent

Grall, T. 2006. "Custodial Mothers and Fathers and Their Child Support: 2003." *Current Population Reports.* U.S. Census Bureau. www.census.gov/prod/2006pubs/p60-230.pdf

Grant, M. J., Button, C. M., Hannah, T. E., and Ross, A. S. 2002. "Uncovering the Multidimensional Nature of Stereotype Inferences: A Within-Participants Study of Gender, Age, and Physical Attractiveness." *Current Research in Social Psychology* 8(2):19–38.

Grassl, W. 1999. "The Reality of Brands: Towards an Ontology of Marketing." *American Journal of Economics and Sociology* 58(2):313–359.

Graves, J. 2006. "What We Know and What We Don't Know: Human Genetic Variation and the Social Construction of Race:" Is Race "Real"? Social Science Research Council. http://raceandgenomics.ssrc.org/Graves/

Green, J. 2004. "The American Religious Landscape and Political Attitudes: A Baseline for 2004." Pew Forum on Religion and Public Life. http://pewforum.org/publications/surveys/green-full.pdf

Greenberg, A., and Berktold, J. 2004. "Evangelicals in America." Greenbert, Quinlan, Rosner Research Inc. http://www.pbs.org/wnet/religionandethics/week733/results.pdf

Greenfield, L. 2006. *Thin.* San Francisco: Chronicle Books.

Greenhouse, L. 2006. "Dwindling Docket Mystified Supreme Court." *New York Times* (December 7).

Greenhouse, S. 2003. "Going for the Look, but Risking Discrimination." *New York Times* (July 12):A12.

Greimel, H. 2007. "Japan Changes Name of Iwo Jima." Associated Press, June 20. asp.usatoday.com/community/utils/idmap/29075632.story

Greven, P. J. 1970. *Four Generations: Population, Land, and Family in Colonial Andover.* Ithaca, NY: Cornell University Press.

Groesz, L. M., Levine, M. P., and Murnen, S. K. 2002. "The Effects of Experimental Presentation of Thin Media Images on Body Satisfaction: A Meta-Analytic Review." *International Journal of Eating Disorders* 31(1):1–16.

Grover, K. J., Russell, C. S., and Schumm, W. 1985. "Mate Selection Processes and Marital Satisfaction." *Family Relations* 34:383–386.

Gueguen, N., Dufourcq-Brana, M., and Pascual, A. 2005. "The First Name: An Attribute of Self-Identity That Affects One's Evaluation of Oneself and That of Others." *Cahiers Internationoux de Psychologie Sociale* 65:1:33–44.

Guillen, M. 2001. "Is Globalization Civilizing, Destructive or Feeble? A Critique of Five Key Debates in the Social Science Literature." *Annual Review of Sociology* 27:235–260.

Guimond, S., Dif, S., and Aupy, A. 2002. "Social Identity, Relative Group Status and Intergroup Attitudes: When Favorable Outcomes Change Intergroup Relations . . . for the Worse." *European Journal of Social Psychology* 32(6):739–760.

Guimond, S., and Roussel, L. 2001. "Bragging About One's School Grades: Gender Stereotyping and Students' Perceptions of Their Abilities in Science, Mathematics, and Language." *Social Psychology of Education* 4(3–4):275–293.

Gumbel, A. 2002. "Fast Food Nation: An Appetite for Litigation." *Independent. co.uk.* (June 4). http://www.commondreams.org/headlines02/0604-01.htm

Gunnthorsdottir, A. 2001. "Physical Attractiveness of an Animal Species as a Decision Factor for Its Preservation." *Anthrozoos* 14(4):204–215.

Gusdek, E. 1998. "Parental Rights Are Fundamental Human Rights." Family Research Council. http://www.frc.org/papers/insight/index.cfm

Gusfield, J. 1963. *Symbolic Crusade: Status Politics and the American Temperance Movement.* Urbana, IL: University of Illinois Press.

Haas, A., and Gregory Jr., S. W. 2005. "The Impact of Physical Attractiveness on Women's Social Status and Interactional Power." *Sociological Forum* 20(3):449–471.

Hacker, A. 2003a. *Mismatch: The Growing Gulf Between Women and Men.* New York: Scribner.

———. 2003b. *Two Nations: Black and White, Separate, Hostile, Unequal.* New York: Scribner.

Hacking, I. 1995. "The Looping Effect of Human Kinds." In D. Sperber, D. Premack, A. J. Premack, and J. Premack (Eds.), *Causal Cognition: A Multidisciplinary Debate* (pp. 351–394). New York: Oxford University Press.

———. 1999. *The Social Construction of What?* Cambridge, MA: Harvard University Press.

Hagan, J., MacMillan, R., and Wheaton, B. 1996. "New Kid in Town: Social Capital and the Life Course Effects of Family Migration on Children." *American Sociological Review* 61(3):368–385.

Halbert, D. J. 2002. "Citizenship, Pluralism, and Modern Public Sphere." *Innovation* 15(1):33–42.

Hall, W. 1986. "Social Class and Survival on the S.S. *Titanic.*" *Social Science and Medicine* 22:687–690.

Hallie, F. 2007. "Young Adults' Relationship with Parents and Siblings: The Role of Marital Status, Conflict and Post-Divorce Predictors." *Journal of Divorce & Remarriage* 46(3/4):105–124.

Hallinan, M., and Sorensen, A. 1985. "Ability Grouping and Student Friendships." *American Educational Research Journal* 22:485–499.

Hansen, K. 2005. *Not-So-Nuclear Families: Class, Gender, and Networks of Care.* New Brunswick, NJ: Rutgers University Press.

Hareven, T. 1978. "The Dynamics of Kin in an Industrial Community." In John Demos and Sarane Boocock (Eds.), *Turning Points: Historical and Sociological Essays on the Family.* Chicago: University of Chicago Press.

Hargreaves, D., and Tiggemann, M. 2002. "The Effect of Television Commercials on Mood and Body Dissatisfaction: The Role of Appearance-Schema Activation." *Journal of Social and Clinical Psychology* 21(3):287–308.

Hargreaves-Heap, S. P., and Varoufakis, Y. 2005. *Game Theory: A Critical Text.* London: Routledge.

Harper, S., and Reskin, B. 2005. "Affirmative Action at School and on the Job." *Annual Review of Sociology* 31:357–380.

Harrington, M., and Hsi, H. 2007. "Women Lawyers and Obstacles to Leadership." MIT Workplace Center. Spring. http://web.mit.edu/workplacecenter/docs/law-report_4-07.pdf

Harris Poll. 2004. "Different Leisure Activities' Popularity Rise and Fall, but Reading, TV Watching and Family Time Still Top the List of Favorites." #97 (December 8). http://www.harrisinteractive.com/harris_poll/index.asp?PID=526

Harris, T. G. 1978. *Introduction to E. H. Walster and G. W. Walster, a New Look at Love*. Reading, MA: Addison-Wesley.

Harrison, K. 2000. "Television Viewing, Fat Stereotyping, Body Shape Standards, and Eating Disorder Symptomatology in Grade School Children." *Communication Research* 27(5):617–640.

Harrison, K., and Cantor, J. 1997. "The Relationship Between Media Consumption and Eating Disorders." *Journal of Communication* 47(1):40–67.

Hartford Institute for Religion Research. 2006. "Fast Facts: How Many People Go to Church Each Sunday?" http://hirr.hartsem.edu/research/fastfacts/fast_facts.html

Hartman, H. 1976. "Capitalism, Patriarchy, and Job Segregation by Sex." *Signs* 1(3):137–170.

Haub, C. 2003. "The U.S. Birth Rate Falls Further." *Population Reference Bureau*. http://www.prb.org/Articles/2003/TheUSBirthRateFallsFurther.aspx

———. 2007. "Is Fertility Rising in Countries with Low Birth Rates?" *Population Reference Bureau*. http://www.prb.org/Articles/2007/IsFertilityRisinginLowBirthRateCountries.aspx

Hauser, C., and O'Connor, A. 2007. "Virginia Tech Shooting Leaves 33 Dead." *New York Times* (April 16).

Hausman, C. 2000. *Lies We Live By: Defeating Double-Talk and Deception in Advertising, Politics, and the Media*. New York: Routledge.

Hawkins, B., Tuff, R. A., and Dudley, G. 2006. "African American Women, Body Composition, and Physical Activity." *Journal of African American Studies* 10(1):44–56.

Hawkins, D., and Booth, A. 2005. "Unhappily Ever After: Effects of Long-Term, Low-Quality Marriages on Well-Being." *Social Forces* 84(1):445–465.

Healey, J. F. 2005. *Statistics: A Tool for Social Research*, 7th ed. Belmont, CA: Wadsworth.

Health and Medicine Work. 2002. "Aging: A Dilemma for Parents and Kids." (October 7):16.

Hebl, M. R., and Heatherton, T. F. 1998. "The Stigma of Obesity in Women: The Difference Is Black and White." *Personality and Social Psychology* 24(4):417–426.

Hecker, D. 2001."Occupational Employment Projections to 2010." *Monthly Labor Review* (November):57–84.

Heeren, J. W.1999. "Emotional Simultaneity and the Construction of Victim Unity." *Symbolic Interaction* 22(2):163–179.

Heimann, L. B. 2002. "Social Proximity in Swedish Mother-Daughter and Mother-Son Interactions in Infancy." *Journal of Reproductive and Infant Psychology* 20(1):37–43.

Heinz, J., Nelson, R., and Laumann, E. 2001."The Scale of Justice: Observations on the Transformation of Urban Law Practice." *Annual Review of Sociology* 27:337–362.

Henig, R. M. 2006. "Looking for the Lie." *New York Times Magazine* 46–53, 76, 80, 83 (February 5).

Henriques, D. 2000. "New Front Opens in Effort to Fight Race Bias in Loans." *New York Times* 150 (October 22).

Hensler, D. 2001. "Revisiting the Monster: New Myths and Realities of Class Action and Other Large Scale Litigation." *Duke Journal of Comparative and International Law* 11:179–213.

Hetherington, E. M., and Kelly, J. 2002. *For Better or for Worse: Divorce Reconsidered.* New York: W.W. Norton.

Hewstone, M., Rubin, M., and Willis, H. 2002. "Intergroup Bias." *Annual Review of Psychology* 53:575–604.

Hochschild, A. R. 2001 [1997]. *The Time Bind: When Work Becomes Home and Home Becomes Work.* New York: Owl Books.

———. 2003a. *The Commercialization of Intimate Life: Notes from Home and Work.* Berkeley: University of California Press.

———. 2003b. *The Second Shift: Working Parents and the Revolution at Home.* New York: Penguin.

Hoffer, T., Greeley, A., and Coleman, J. 1987. "Catholic High School Effects on Achievement Growth." In E. Haertel, T. James, and H. Levin (Eds.), *Comparing Public and Private Schools. Vol. 2: Student Achievement* (pp. 67–88). New York: Falmer.

Holman, T. B., Larson, J. H., and Olsen, J. A. 2001. *Premarital Predictors of Marital Quality or Breakup: Research, Theory and Practice.* New York/London: Kluwer Academic/Plenum.

Holtz, R., and Miller, N. 2001. "Intergroup Competition, Attitudinal Projection, and Opinion Certainty: Capitalizing on Conflict." *Group Processes and Intergroup Relations* 4(1):61–73.

Holtzman, D. H. 2006. *Privacy Lost: How Technology Is Endangering Your Privacy.* San Francisco: Jossey Bass.

Home Safety Channel. 2006. "Protect Your Home: Install a Home Burglar Alarm." http://homesafetychannel.com/protect-your-home-install-a-home-burglar-alarm

Hope, S., Rodgers, B., and Power, C. 1999. "Marital Status Transitions and Psychological Distress: Longitudinal Evidence from a National Population Sample." *Psychological Medicine* 29(2):381–389.

Hopkins, N., and Rae, C. 2001. "Intergroup Differentiation: Stereotyping as a Function of Status Hierarchy." *Journal of Social Psychology* 141(3):323–333.

Horn, L., Chen, X., and Chapman, C. 2003. "Getting Ready to Pay for College" (NCES 2003–0300). Washington, DC: U.S. Department of Education.

Horrigan, J., and Rainie, L. 2006. "The Internet's Growing Role in Life's Major Moments." Pew Internet and American Life Project. http://www.pewinternet.org/PPF/r/181/report_display.asp

Hough, J. 2005. "The Religious Situation in America." International Committee for the Peace Council. http://www.peacecouncil.org/hough.html

House, J. S. 2002. "Understanding Social Factors and Inequality in Health: 20th Century Progress and 21st Century Prospects." *Journal of Health and Social Behavior* 43:25–142.

House, J. S., Strecher, V., Metzner, H. L., and Robbins, C. A. 1986. "Occupational Stress and Health Among Men and Women in the Tecumseh Community Health Study." *Journal of Health and Social Behavior* 31(2):123–140.

Houser, A. 2007. "Women & Long Term Care: Research Report." AARP Policy and Research. http://www.aarp.org/research/housing-mobility/caregiving/fs77r_ltc.html

Houser, A., Fox-George, W., and Gibson, M. J. 2006. "Across the States 2006: Profiles of Long-Term Care and Independent Living." AARP Public Policy Institute. http://assets.aarp.org/rgcenter/health/d18763_2006_ats.pdf

Houston, J. M., Kinnie, J., Lupo, B., Terry, C., and Ho, S. S. 2000. "Competitiveness and Conflict Behavior in Simulation of a Social Dilemma." *Psychological Reports* 86 (3, Pt. 2):1219–1225.

Hout, M. 1982. "The Association Between Husbands' and Wives' Occupations in Two-Earner Families." *American Journal of Sociology* 88 (September):397–409.

Houweling, T. A., Caspar, A. E., Looman, W. N., and Mackenbach, J. P. 2005. "Determinants of Under-5 Mortality Among the Poor and the Rich: A Cross-national Analysis of 43 Developing Countries." *International Journal of Epidemiology* 34(6):1257–1265.

How Stuff Works. 2007. "How Much Does the U.S. President Get Paid?" http://people.howstuffworks.com/question449.htm

Howell, M. 1986. "Women, the Family Economy, and Market Production." In B. Hanawalt (Ed.), *Women and Work in Pre-Industrial Europe.* Bloomington: Indiana University Press.

Hoxby, C. 2001. "The Return to Attending a Highly Selective College: 1960 to the Present." In M. Devlin and J. Meyerson (Eds.), *Forum Future: Exploring the Future of Higher Education, 2000 Papers. Forum Strategy Series* (Vol. 3). http://www.educause.edu/ir/library/pdf/ffp0002.pdf

Hughes, E. C. 1945. "Dilemmas and Contradictions of Status." *American Journal of Sociology* 50(5):353–359.

Hull, K. 2006. *Same-Sex Marriage.* New York: Cambridge University Press.

Hunt, S. 2000. "'Winning Ways': Globalization and the Impact of the Health and Wealth Gospel." *Journal of Contemporary Religion* 15(3):331–347.

Hunter, M. L. 2002. "If You're Light You're Alright: Light Skin Color as Social Capital for Women of Color." *Gender and Society* 16(2):175–193.

Hurd, L. C. 2000. "Older Women's Body Image and Embodied Experience: An Exploration." *Journal of Women and Aging* 12(3–4):77–97.

Hyde, J. S., Fennema, E., and Lamon, S. J. 1990. "Gender Differences in Mathematics Performance." *Psychological Bulletin* 107:139–155.

Iceland, J., Sharpe, C., and Steinmetz, E. 2005. "Class Differences in African American Residential Patterns in US Metropolitan Areas: 1990–2000." *Social Science Research* 34(1): 252–266.

Information Please Almanac. 1997. O. Johnson (Ed.). Boston: Houghton Mifflin.

Insaf, S. 2002. "Not the Same by Any Other Name." *Journal of the American Academy of Psychoanalysis* 31(3):463–473.

Institute for Research on Poverty. 2007. "Who Is Poor?" Institute for Research on Poverty. University of Wisconsin-Madison. http://www.irp.wisc.edu/faqs/faq3.htm

Institute of Medicine. 2001. "Exploring the Biological Contribution to Human Health: Does Sex Matter?" Institute of Medicine of the National Academies (April 24). http://www.iom.edu/ reports.asp

Institute on Race & Poverty. 1998. "Examining the Relationship Between Housing, Education, and Persistent Segregation." http://www1.umn.edu/irp/publications/McKnightfinal.pdf

———. 2002. "Racism and Metropolitan Dynamics: The Civil Rights Challenge of the 21st Century." http://www1.umn.edu/irp/publications/racismandmetrodynamics.pdf

Institute for Women's Policy Research. 2001. "Today's Women Workers: Shut Out of Yesterday's Unemployment Insurance System" (IWPR Publication # A127). http://www.iwpr.org

———. 2007a. "The Gender Wage Ratio: Women's and Men's Earnings." Fact Sheet. IWPR # C350. http://www.iwpr.org/pdf/C350.pdf

———. 2007b. "Women and Paid Sick Days: Crucial for Family Well-Being." Fact Sheet. IWPR #B254a. http://www.iwpr.org/pdf/B254_paidsickdaysFS.pdf

Isaacs, H. 1975. *Idols of the Tribe.* Cambridge, MA: Harvard University Press.

Ismail, M. A. 2007. "Spending on Lobbying Thrives." Center for Public Integrity. http://www.publicintegrity.org/rx/report.aspx?aid=823

Jablonski, N. 2005. "The Evolution of Human Skin and Skin Color." *Annual Review of Anthropology* 33:585–623.

Jackman, M. R. 2002. "Violence in Social Life." *Annual Review of Sociology* 28:387–415.

Jackson, L. A. 1992. *Physical Appearance and Gender: A Sociobiological and Sociocultural Perspective.* Albany: SUNY Press.

Jackson, L. A., Hunter, J. E., and Hodge, C. N. 1995. "Physical Attractiveness and Intellectual Competence: A Meta-Analytic Review." *Social Psychology Quarterly* 58(2):108–122.

Jackson, L. A., and McGill, O. D. 1996. "Body Type Preferences and Body Type Characteristics Associated with Attractive and Unattractive Bodies by African Americans and Anglo Americans." *Sex Roles* 35 (September):295–307.

Jacobs, P. 1988. "Keeping the Poor, Poor." In J. H. Skolnick and E. Currie (Eds.), *Crisis in American Institutions.* Glenview, IL: Scott, Foresman.

Jacobs Henderson, J., and Baldasty, G. 2003. "Race, Advertising and Prime-Time Television." *Howard Journal of Communications* 14(2):97–113.

Jacobson, D. 1989. "Context and the Sociological Study of Stress." *Journal of Health and Social Behavior* 30(3):257–260.

Jacquet, S., and Surra, C. 2001. "Parental Divorce and Premarital Couples: Commitment and Other Relationship Characteristics." *Journal of Marriage and the Family* 63(3):627–638.

Jankowiak, W., and Fischer, E. 1992. "A Cross-cultural Perspective on Romantic Love." *Journal of Ethnology* 31:149–156.

Jaret, C., Reitzes, D. C., and Shapkina, N. 2005. "Reflected Appraisals and Self-Esteem." *Sociological Perspectives* 48:3:403–419.

Jeffreys, K. 2007 *U.S. Legal Permanent Residents: 2006. Annual Flow Report.* DHS Office of Immigration Statistics. http://www.dhs.gov/xlibrary/assets/statistics/publications/IS-4496_LPRFlowReport_04vaccessible.pdf

Jeffries, V., and Ransford, E. 1980. *Social Stratification: A Multiple Hierarchy Approach.* Boston: Allyn & Bacon.

Jehn, K. A., and Shah, P. P. 1997. "Interpersonal Relationships and Task Performance: An Examination of Mediating Processes in Friendship and Acquaintance Groups." *Journal of Personality and Social Psychology* 72 (April):775–790.

Jenny Craig. 2007. "Success Stories." http://www.jennycraig.com/success/story.asp?SID=140

Jensen, M. J., Danziger, J. N., and Venkatesh, A. 2007. "Civil Society and Cyber Society: The Role of the Internet in Community Associations and Democratic Politics." *Information Society* 23:(1):39–50.

Jensen, M., Johnson, D. W., and Johnson, R. T. 2002. "Impact of Positive Interdependence During Electronic Quizzes on Discourse and Achievement." *Journal of Educational Research* 95(3):161–166.

Johnson, C. 2000. "Perspective on American Kinship in the Later 1990s." *Journal of Marriage and the Family* 62(November):623–639.

Johnson, D., and Wu, J. 2002. "An Empirical Test of Crisis, Social Selection, and Role Explanations of the Relationship Between Marital Disruption and Psychological Distress: A Pooled Time-Series Analysis of Four-Wave Panel Data." *Journal of Marriage & the Family* 64(1):211–224.

Johnson, D. R., and Scheuble, L. K. 2002. "What Should We Call Our Kids? Choosing Children's Surnames When Parents' Last Names Differ." *Social Science Journal* 39(3):419–429.

Johnson, D. W., and Johnson, R. T. 1989. *Cooperation and Competition: Theory and Research.* Edina, MN: Interaction Books.

———. 2000. "The Three Cs of Reducing Prejudice and Discrimination." In S. Oskamp (Ed.), *Reducing Prejudice and Discrimination: The Claremont Symposium on Applied Social Psychology* (pp. 239–268). Mahwah, NJ: Lawrence Erlbaum.

———. 2002. "Social Interdependence Theory and University Instruction: Theory into Practice." *Swiss Journal of Psychology* 61(3):119–129.

———. 2005. *Joining Together: Group Theory and Group Skills.* Boston: Allyn and Bacon.

Johnson, J. L., McAndrew, F. T., and Harris, P. B. 1991. "Sociobiology and the Naming of Adopted and Natural Children." *Etiology and Sociobiology* 12:365–375.

Johnson, R., Toohey, D., and Wiener, J. M. 2007. "Meeting the Long-Term Care Needs of the Baby Boomers." Discussion Paper 07–04 in the Retirement Project Series, Urban Institute. http://www.urban.org/url.cfm?ID=311451

Jones, L. 1980. *Great Expectations.* New York: Ballantine Books.

Jones, W., Hansson, R. O., and Phillips, A. L. 1978. "Physical Attractiveness and Judgments of Psychopathology." *Journal of Social Psychology* 105:79–84.

Jones-DeWeever, A., Peterson, J., and Song, X. 2003. "Before and After Welfare Reform: The Work and Well-Being of Low-Income Single Parent Families." Institute for Women's Policy Research. http://www.iwpr.org.

Joubert, C. E. 1994. "Relation of Name Frequency to the Perception of Social Class in Given Names." *Perceptual and Motor Skills* 79(2):623–626.

Jurd, E. 2005. "Helping George Feel Valued." *Times Educational Supplement* (4/22) 4631:18–19.

Kahane, H., and Cavender, N. 2002. *Logic and Contemporary Rhetoric: The Use of Reason in Everyday Life.* 9th ed. Belmont, CA: Wadsworth.

Kalick, S. M., and Hamilton, T. E. 1986. "The Matching Hypothesis Re-Examined." *Journal of Personality and Social Psychology* 51(4):673–682.

Kalmijn, M. 1991. "Shifting Boundaries: Trends in Religious and Educational Homogamy." *American Sociological Review* 56(6):786–800.

———. 1994. "Assortive Mating by Cultural and Economic Occupational Status." *American Journal of Sociology* 100(2):422–452.

———. 1998. "Intermarriage and Homogamy." *Annual Review of Sociology* 24:395–421.

Kalmijn, M., and Flap, H. 2001. "Assortive Meeting and Mating: Unintended Consequences of Organized Settings for Partner Choices." *Social Forces* 79(4):1289–1312.

Kao, G., and Thompson, J. 2003. "Racial and Ethnic Stratification in Educational Achievement and Attainment." *Annual Review of Sociology* 29:417–442.

Kaplan, R., and Kronick, R. G. 2006. "Marital Status and Longevity in the United States Population." *Journal of Epidemiology & Community Health* 60(9):760–765.

Karen, D. 1990. "Toward a Political Organizational Model of Gatekeeping: The Case of Elite Colleges." *Sociology of Education* 63:227–240.

Karraker, K., Vogel, D., and Lake, M. 1995. "Parents' Gender-Stereotyped Perceptions of Newborns: The Eye of the Beholder Revisited." *Sex Roles* 33(9–10):687–701.

Karylowski, J. J., Motes, M. A., Wallace, H. M., Harckom, H. A., Hewlett, E. M., Maclean, S. L., Paretta, J. L., and Vaswani, C. L. 2001. "Spontaneous Gender-Stereotypical Categorization of Trait Labels and Job Labels." *Current Research in Social Psychology* 6(6):77–90.

Katz, J. E., and Rice, R. E. 2002. *Social Consequences of Internet Use: Access, Involvement and Interaction.* Cambridge, MA: MIT Press.

Katz, M. (Ed.). 1971. *School Reform Past and Present.* Boston: Little, Brown.

———. 1986. *In the Shadow of the Poorhouse: A Social History of Welfare in America.* New York: Basic Books.

Kauffman Foundation. 2006. "Entrepreneurship." http://www.kauffman.org/items .cfm?itemID=703

Kaufman, P., Chen, X., Choy, S. P., Peter, K., Ruddy, S. A., Miller, A. K., Fleury, J. K., Chandler, K. A., Planty, M. G., and Rand, M. R. 2001. *Indicators of School*

Crime and Safety: 2001 (NCES 2002–113/NCJ 190075). Washington, DC: U.S. Departments of Education and Justice.

Kaye, J. 2006. "Reassessing Tax-Free Churches." *Online NewsHour* (April 14). http://www.pbs.org/newshour/bb/religion/jan-june06/taxing_4-14.html

Keefe, K., and Berndt, T. 1996. "Relations of Friendship Quality to Self-Esteem in Early Adolescence." *Journal of Early Adolescence* 16(1):110–129.

Keller, J. 2002. "Blatant Stereotype Threat and Women's Math Performance: Self-Handicapping as a Strategic Means to Cope with Obtrusive Negative Performance Expectations." *Sex Roles* 47(3–4):193–198.

Keller, M. C., and Young, R. K. 1996. "Mate Assortment in Dating and Married Couples." *Personality and Individual Differences* 21(2):217–221.

Kelley, H. H., and Stahelski, A. J. 1970. "Errors in Perception of Intentions in a Mixed-Motive Game." *Journal of Experimental Social Psychology* 6:379–400.

Kelly, A. M., Wall, M., Eisenberg, M. E., Story, M., and Neumark-Sztainer, D. 2007. "Adolescent Girls with High Body Satisfaction: Who Are They and What Can They Teach Us?" *Journal of Adolescent Health* 37:5:391–396.

Kenealy, P., Frude, N., and Shaw, W. 1988. "Influences of Children's Physical Attractiveness on Teacher Expectations." *Journal of Social Psychology* 128(3):373–383.

Kennedy, Q., Mather, M., and Carstensen, L. L. 2004. "The Role of Motivation in the Age-Related Positivity Effect in Autobiographical Memory." *Psychological Science* 15(3).

Kent, G. 2000. "Understanding the Experiences of People with Disfigurements: An Integration of Four Models of Social and Psychological Functioning." *Psychology, Health, and Medicine* 5(2):117–129.

Kessler, R. C., Price, R. H., and Wortman, C. B. 1985. "Social Factors in Psychopathology: Stress, Social Support, and Coping Processes." *Annual Review of Psychology* 36:531–572.

Kessler-Harris, A. 2003. *Out to Work: A History of Wage-Earning Women in the United States*. New York: Oxford University Press.

Kids Count. 2003. "The High Cost of Being Poor." http://www.kidscount.org

Kifner, J. 1994. "Pollster Finds Error on Holocaust Doubts." *New York Times* (May 20):A12.

Kilker, E. 1993. "Black and White in America: The Culture and Politics of Racial Classification." *International Journal of Politics, Culture, and Society* 7:229–258.

Killbourne, J. 2000. *Can't Buy Me Love: How Advertising Changes the Way We Think and Feel*. New York: Touchstone.

Kindleberger Hagan, L., and Kuebli, J. 2007. "Mothers' and Fathers' Socialization of Preschoolers' Physical Risk Taking." *Journal of Applied Developmental Psychology* 28(1):2–14.

Kingsley, T., and Pettit, K. 2003. "Concentrated Poverty: A Change in Course" (Pub ID# 310790). *Urban Institute* 2 (May) http://www.urban.org/nnip

Kitson, G. C., Babri, K. B., and Roach, M. J. 1985. "Who Divorces and Why?" *Journal of Family Issues* 6:285–293.

Klein, H., Shiffman, K., and Welka, D. 2000. "Gender-Related Content of Animated Cartoons, 1930 to the Present." *Advances in Gender Research* 4:291–317.

Klein, L., and Knitzer, J. 2007. "Promoting Effective Early Learning." National Center for Children in Poverty. http://www.nccp.org

Knauer, K. (Ed.). 1998. *Time 75th Anniversary Celebration*. New York: Time, Inc.

Knowlton, A. R., and Latkin, C. A. 2007. "Network Financial Support and Conflict as Predictors of Depressive Symptoms Among a Highly Disadvantaged Population." *Journal of Community Psychology* 35:1:13–28.

Kochera, A., and Guterbock, T. 2005. *Beyond 50.05: A Report to the Nation on Liveable Communities Creating Environments for Successful Aging*. Washington, DC: AARP Public Policy Institute.

Koernig, S. K., and Page, A. L. 2001."What If Your Dentist Looks Like Tom Cruise? Applying the Match-Up Hypothesis to a Service Encounter." *Psychology and Marketing* 19(1):91–110.

Kohn, A. 1986. *No Contest: The Case Against Competition*. Boston: Houghton Mifflin.

Kollock, P. 1998. "Social Dilemmas: The Anatomy of Cooperation." *Annual Review of Sociology* 24:183–214.

Komarovsky, M. 1962. *Blue-Collar Marriage*. New Haven, CT: Vintage.

Kostanski, M., and Gullone, E. 1998. "Adolescent Body Image Dissatisfaction: Relationships with Self-Esteem, Anxiety, and Depression Controlling for Body Mass." *Journal of Child Psychology and Psychiatry and Allied Disciplines* 39 (February):255–262.

Kovaleski, S. F. 1999. "In Jamaica, Shades of an Identity Crisis: Ignoring Health Risks, Blacks Increase Use of Skin Lighteners." *Washington Post* (August 5):A15.

Kozol, J. 1991. *Savage Inequalities*. New York: Crown.

———. 1995. *Amazing Grace: The Lives of Children and the Conscience of a Nation*. New York: Crown.

———. 2001. *Ordinary Resurrections: Children in the Years of Hope*. New York: HarperCollins.

———. 2005. *The Shame of the Nation: The Restoration of Apartheid Schooling in America*. New York: Crown.

———. 2006. *Rachel and Her Children: Homeless Families in America*. New York: Crown.

Kreider, R. 2005. "Number, Timing, and Duration of Marriages and Divorces: 2001." *Current Population Reports*. Household Economic Studies. http://www.census.gov/prod/2005pubs/p70–97.pdf

Kristenson, M., Eriksenm, H. R., Sluiter, J. K., Starke, D., and Ursin, H. 2004. "Psychobiological Mechanisms of Socioeconomic Differences in Health." *Social Science and Medicine* 58(8):1511–1522.

Kristof, N. 2003. "Is Race Real?" *New York Times* (July 11):A17.

Kroll, L. 2003. "Megachurches, Megabusinesses." Forbes.com. http://www.forbes.com/2003/09/17/cz_lk_0917megachurch.html

Krugman, P. 2002. "For Richer." *New York Times Magazine* (October 20):62–67.

———. 2007. *The Conscience of a Liberal*. New York: W. W. Norton.

Krysan, M. 2002. "Community Undesirability in Black and White: Examining Racial Residential Preferences Through Community Perceptions." *Social Problems* 49(4):521–543.

Krysan, M., and Farley, R. 2002. "The Residential Preferences of Blacks: Do They Explain Persistent Segregation?" *Social Forces* 80(3):937–980.

Kuchler, F., and Variyam, J. N. 2003. "Mistakes Were Made: Misperception as a Barrier to Reducing Overweight." *International Journal of Obesity* 27:7:856–861.

Kulik, J. A., and Mahler, H. I. 1990. "Stress and Affiliation Research: On Taking the Laboratory to Health Field Settings." *Annals of Behavioral Medicine* 12(3):106–111.

Kulik, J. A., Mahler, H. I. M., and Moore, P. J. 1996. "Social Comparison and Affiliation Under Threat: Effects on Recovery from Major Surgery." *Journal of Personality and Social Psychology* 71:967–979.

Kutner, M., Greenberg, E., Jin, Y., Boyle, B., Hsu, Y., and Dunleavy, E. (2007). *Literacy in Everyday Life: Results from the 2003 National Assessment of Adult Literacy* (NCES 2007–480). National Center for Education Statistics. U.S. Department of Education. Washington, DC.

Labor Research Association. 2006. "Lower Wages, Higher Profits." http://www.labor research.org/print.php?id=415

Lake, A. 1975. "Are We Born into Our Sex Roles or Programmed into Them?" *Woman's Day* (January):25–35.

Lalwani, A. K., Shavitt, S., and Johnson, T. 2006. "What Is the Relationship Between Cultural Orientation and Socially Desirable Responding?" *Journal of Personality and Social Psychology* 90:1:165–178.

Lambton Health. 2002. "Ten Steps to a Healthy Body Image." http://www.lambton health.on.ca/youth/bodyimage.asp

Lampman, J. 2006. "Megachurches' Way of Worship Is on the Rise." *Christian Science Monitor* (February). http://www.csmonitor.com/2006/0206/p13s01-lire.html

Landers, M., and Fine, G. A. 2001. "Learning Life's Lessons in Tee-Ball: The Reinforcement of Gender and Status in Kindergarten Sport." In A. Yiannakis and M. Melnick (Eds.), *Contemporary Issues in Sociology of Sport* (pp. 73–77). Champaign, IL: Human Kinetics.

Langlois, J. H., Kalakanis, L., Rubenstein, A. J., Larson, A., Hallam, M., and Smoot, M. 2000. "Maxims or Myths of Beauty? A Meta-Analytic and Theoretical Review." *Psychological Bulletin* 126(3):390–423.

Langlois, J. H., and Stephan, C. W. 1981. "Beauty and the Beast: The Role of Physical Attractiveness in the Development of Peer Relations and Social Behavior." In S. S. Brehm, S. M. Kassin, and F. X. Gibbons (Eds.), *Developmental Social Psychology*. New York: Oxford University Press.

Lantz, P., House, J. S., Mero, R. P., and Williams, D. R. 2005. "Stress, Life Events, and Socioeconomic Disparities in Health: Results from the Americans' Changing Lives Study." *Journal of Health and Social Behavior* 3:274–288.

Lanzetta, J. T. 1955. "Group Behavior Under Stress." *Human Relations* 8:29–53.

Larose, M., and Wallace, N. 2003. "Online Giving Rose at Many Big Charities." *Chronicle of Philanthropy* (June 12).

Larsen, L. 2004. "The Foreign-Born Population in the United States: 2003." *Current Population Reports*. http://www.census.gov/prod/2004pubs/p20–551.pdf

Larson, M. S. 2003. "Gender, Race, and Aggression in Television Commercials That Feature Children" *Sex Roles* 48(1–2):67–75.

Lasch, C. 1979. *The Culture of Narcissism: American Life in an Age of Diminishing Expectations*. New York: W.W. Norton.

Laslett, B., and Warren, C. B. 1975. "Losing Weight: The Organizational Promotion of Behavior Change." *Social Problems* 23(1):69–80.

Latané, B., and Glass, D. C. 1968. "Social and Nonsocial Attraction in Rats." *Journal of Personality and Social Psychology* 9:142–146.

Lauderdale, D. 2006. "Birth Outcomes for Arabic-Named Women in California Before and After September 11." *Demography* 43:1:185–201.

Lauer, R., and Lauer, J. 1991. "The Long-Term Relational Consequences of Problematic Family Backgrounds." *Family Relations* 40:286–290.

Lauzen, M., Dozier, D., and Cleveland, E. 2006. "Genre Matters: An Examination of Women Working Behind the Scenes and On-Screen Portrayals in Reality and Scripted Prime-Time Programming." *Sex Roles* 55(7/8):445–455.

Lawson, T. 2000. "Are Kind Lies Better Than Unkind Truths? Effects of Perspective and Closeness of Relationship." *Representative Research in Social Psychology* 24:11–19.

Lawton, K. 2002. "Interview with Nancy Ammerman." *Religion and Ethics Newsweekly*. Episode #535 (May 3). http://www.pbs.org/wnet/religionandethics/week535/nammerman.html#right

Layman, R. (Ed.). 1995. *American Decades 1950–59*. Detroit, MI: Gale.

Layzer, J., and Goodson, B. 2006. "National Study of Child Care for Low-Income Families: Care in the Home: A Description of Family Child Care and the Experience of the Families and Children Who Use It. Wave 1 Report." U.S. Department of Health and Human Services, Administration for Children and Families. http://www.researchconnections.org/SendPdf?resourceId=11568

Lazarsfeld, P. 1949. "The American Soldier: An Expository Review." *Public Opinion Quarterly* 13(3):376–404.

Leahey, E., and Guo, G. 2001. "Gender Differences in Mathematical Trajectories." *Social Forces* 80(2):713–732.

Leaper, C., Breed, L., Hoffman, L., and Perlman, C. 2002. "Variations in the Gender-Stereotyped Content of Children's Television Cartoons Across Genres." *Journal of Applied Social Psychology* 32(8):1653–1662.

LeBlanc, S. 2007. "States Step into Void on Immigration Law." ABC News (August 6). http://abcnews.go.com/US/wireStory?id=3450397

Lee, D. A. 2006. "Dear Criminal: Smile for My Camera." *St. Petersburg Times* (September 12). http://www.sptimes.com/2006/09/12/Northpinellas/More_charges_filed_ag.shtml

Lee, G., and Bulanda, J. 2005. "Change and Consistency in the Relation of Marital Status to Personal Happiness." *Marriage & Family Review* 38(1):69–84.

Lee, J. 2002. "Some States Track Parolees by Satellite." *New York Times on the Web* (January 31). www.gyre.org/news/author/Jennifer+8.+Lee/

Lee, J., and Bean, F. 2004. "America's Changing Color Lines: Immigration, Race/Ethnicity and Multiracial Identification." *Annual Review of Sociology* 30:221–242.

Lee, S. 2003. "The Genetics of Differences: What Genetic Discovery and the Modern Biology of 'Race' Mean for Communities of Color Fighting Health Inequities." *ColorLines* 6(2):25–27.

Lee, S. T. 2004. "Lying to Tell the Truth: Journalists and the Social Context of Deception." *Mass Communication and Society* 7:1:97–120.

Lee, V., and Burkam, D. 2002. "Inequality at the Starting Gate: Social Background Differences in Achievement as Children Begin School." Economic Policy Institute. http://www.epsl.asu.edu/epru/articles/EPRU-0603-138-OWI.pdf

Lehrman, S. 2003. "The Reality of Race." *Scientific American* 288(2):32–34.

Leinbach, M. D., and Fagot, B. I. 1991. "Attractiveness in Young Children: Sex-Differentiated Reactions of Adults." *Sex Roles* 25(5–6):269–284.

Leite, R., and McKenry, P. 2002. "Aspects of Father Status and Postdivorce Father Involvement with Children." *Journal of Family Issues* 23(5):601–623.

Leland, J., and Wilgoren, J. 2005. "Living with Social Security: Small Dreams and Safety Nets." *New York Times* (June 19, 2005):1.

Lelyveld, J. (Ed.). 2001. *How Race Is Lived in America: Pulling Together, Pulling Apart.* New York: Times Books.

Lemert, E. 1951. *Social Pathology: A Systematic Approach to the Theory of Sociopathic Behavior.* New York: McGraw-Hill.

Lennon, M. C. 1989. "The Structural Contexts of Stress." *Journal of Health and Social Behavior* 30(3):261–268.

Leonard, S. 1996. "Feeling Appealing." *Psychology Today* 29(1):18.

Lerer, L. 2007. "Do You Lie on Your Resume?" http://www.forbes.com/careers/2007/02/07/leadership-resume-jobs-lead-careers-cx_ll_0207resume.html

Levin, S., VanLaar, C., and Sidanius, J. 2003. "The Effects of Ingroup and Outgroup Friendships on Ethnic Attitudes in College: A Longitudinal Study." *Group Processes & Intergroup Relations* 6(1):76–92.

LeVine, R. A., and White, M. 1992. "The Social Transformation of Childhood." In A. S. Skolnick and J. H. Skolnick (Eds.), *Family in Transition.* New York: HarperCollins.

Levine, R. V. 1993. "Is Love a Luxury?" *American Demographics* 15(2):27–28.

Levi-Strauss, C. 1964. *The Raw and the Cooked: Introduction to a Science of Mythology.* New York: Harper & Row.

Levy, B. R., Slade, M. D., Kunkel, S. R., and Kasl, S. V. 2002. "Longevity Increased by Positive Self-Perceptions of Aging." *Journal of Personality and Social Psychology* 832(2):261–270.

Levy, G., Sadovsky, A., and Troseth, G. 2000. "Aspects of Young Children's Perceptions of Gender-Typed Occupations." *Sex Roles* 42(11–12):993–1006.

Lewis, M. 1978. *The Culture of Inequality.* New York: New American Library.

Lichter, D., Graefe, D., and Brown, B. 2003. "Is Marriage a Panacea? Union Formation Among Economically Disadvantaged Unwed Mothers." *Social Problems* 50(1):60–86.

Liddell, C., and Lycett, J. 1998. "Simon or Sipho: South African Children's Names and Their Academic Achievement in Grade One." *Applied Psychology* 47(3):421–437.

Lieberson, S. 2000. *A Matter of Taste.* New Haven: Yale University Press.

Liebler, C. A., and Sandefur, G. D. 2002. "Gender Differences in the Exchange of Social Support with Friends, Neighbors, and Co-Workers at Midlife." *Social Science Research* 31(3):364–391.

Lillard, L., and Waite, J. 1995. "'Til Death Do Us Part: Marital Disruption and Mortality." *American Journal of Sociology* 100 (March):1131–1156.

Lin, N., Ye, X., and Ensel, W. W. 1999. "Social Support and Depressed Mood: A Structural Analysis." *Journal of Health and Social Behavior* 40:344–359.

Lindner, K. 2004. "Images of Women in General Interest and Fashion Magazine Advertisements from 1955 to 2002." *Sex Roles* 51(7/8):409–421.

Lindsey, E., and Mize, J. 2001. "Contextual Differences in Parent-Child Play: Implications for Children's Gender Role Development." *Sex Roles* 44(3–4):155–176.

Lindstrom, C., and Lindstrom, M. 2006. "Social Capital, GNP per Capita, Relative Income, and Health: An Ecological Study of 23 Countries." *International Journal of Health Services* 36:4:679–696.

Lino, M. 2007. "Expenditures on Children by Families, 2006." U.S. Department of Agriculture, Center for Nutrition Policy and Promotion. Miscellaneous Publication No. 1528–2006.

Lips, H. 1993. *Sex and Gender: An Introduction.* Mountain View, CA: Mayfield.

Liptak. 2002. "In the Name of Security, Privacy for Me, Not Thee." *New York Times* (November 24): Week in Review.

Litke, M. 2006. "Forget Child's Play, Japanese Toymakers Target Adults." http://abcnews.go.com/Technology/story?id=2623174&page=1

Livingston, R. W. 2001. "What You See Is What You Get: Systematic Variability in Perceptual-Based Social Judgment." *Personality and Social Psychology Bulletin* 27(9):1086–1096.

Lleras-Muney, A. 2004. "The Relationship Between Education and Adult Mortality in the United States." http://www.princeton.edu/~alleras/papers/mortalityrevision2.pdf

Lloyd, C. 2000. "Why Should a Baby Get the Father's Last Name?" *Salon.com* http//archive.salon.com/mwt/feature/2000/01/20/surnames/index.html

Lord, W. 1981. *A Night to Remember.* New York: Penguin.

Lovejoy, M. 2001. "Disturbances in the Social Body: Differences in Body Image and Eating Problems Among African American and White Women." *Gender & Society* 15(2): 239–261.

Lucas, R. 2007. "In Case You Haven't Heard." *Mental Health Weekly* 17(15):8.

Lucas, S. R. 1999. *Tracking Inequality: Stratification and Mobility in American High Schools.* New York: Teachers College Press.

Ludwig, J. 2005. "Perception or Reality? The Effect of Stature on Life Outcomes." http://www.galluppoll.com/

Lumsden, L. 1997. "Expectations for Students." *Emergency Librarian* 25(2).

Luo, Y., and Waite, L. J. 2005. "The Impact of Childhood and Adult SES on Physical, Mental, and Cognitive Well-Being in Later Life." *Journal of Gerontology:* Series B: Psychological and Social Sciences: 60B: 2: S93-S101.

Lupart, J., and Cannon, E. 2002. "Computers and Career Choices: Gender Differences in Grades 7 and 10 Students." *Gender, Technology & Development* 6(2):233–248.

Lynn, M., and Simons, T. 2000. "Predictors of Male and Female Servers' Average Tip Earnings." *Journal of Applied Social Psychology* 30(2):241–252.

Lytton, H., and Romny, D.1991. "Parents' Differential Socialization of Boys and Girls: A Meta-Analysis." *Psychological Bulletin* 109:267–296.

Macmillan, R. 2001. "Violence and the Life Course: The Consequences of Victimization for Personal and Social Development." *Annual Review of Sociology* 27:1–22.

Madrick, J. 2002. "A Rise in Child Poverty Rates Is at Risk in U.S." *New York Times* (June 13):C2.

Madrid, L. D., Canas, M., and Ortega-Medina, M. 2007. "Effects of Team Competition Versus Team Cooperation in Classwide Peer Tutoring." *Journal of Educational Research* 100:3:155–161.

Malley, J., Beck, M., and Adorno, D. 2001. "Building an Ecology for Non-Violence in Schools." *International Journal of Reality Therapy* 21(1):22–26.

Manning, P. 1974. "Police Lying." *Urban Life* 3:283–306.

———. 1984. "Lying, Secrecy, and Social Control." In J. Douglas Newton (Ed.), *The Sociology of Deviance* (pp. 268–279). Newton, MA: Allyn & Bacon.

Marcus, A. 2002. "When Janie Came Marching Home: Women Fought in the Civil War." *New York Times* (March 25).

Marks, G., Miller, N., and Maruyama, G. 1981. "Effects of Targets' Physical Attractiveness on Assumptions of Similarity." *Journal of Personality and Social Psychology* 41:198–206.

Marlar, M. R., and Joubert, C. E. 2002. "Liking of Personal Names, Self-Esteem, and the Big Five Inventory." *Psychological Reports* 91(2):407–410.

Marlowe, C. M., Schneider, S. L., and Nelson, C. E. 1996. "Gender and Attractiveness Biases in Hiring Decisions: Are More Experienced Managers Less Biased?" *Journal of Applied Psychology* 81(1):11–21.

Martin, J., Hamilton, B., Sutton, P., Ventura, S., Menacker, F., and Kirmeyer, S. 2006. "Births: Final Data for 2004." *National Vital Statistics Report* 55(1) CDC. http://www.cdc.gov/nchs/data/nvsr/nvsr55/nvsr55_01.pdf

Martin, P., and Midgley, E. 2006. "Immigration: Shaping and Reshaping America Revised and Updated 2nd Edition." *Population Bulletin* 61(4). http://www.prb.org/pdf06/61.4USMigration.pdf

Martin, R. A., and Svebak, S. 2001. "Stress." In M. J. Apter (Ed.), *Motivational Styles in Everyday Life*. Washington, DC: American Psychological Association.

Martin, S. P., and Robinson, J. P. 2007. "The Income Digital Divide: Trends and Predictions for Levels of Internet Use." *Social Problems* 54:1:1–22.

Martin, T. C., and Bumpass, L. L. 1989. "Recent Trends in Marital Disruption." *Demography* 26:41.

Marx, G. T. 1999. "What's in a Name? Some Reflections on the Sociology of Anonymity." *Information Society* 15(2):99–112.

Mastro, D., and Stern, S. 2003. "Representations of Race in Television Commercials: A Content Analysis of Prime-Time Advertising." *Journal of Broadcasting & Electronic Media* 47(4):638–647.

Mather, M. 2007. "The New Generation Gap." *Population Reference Bureau*. http://www.prb.org/Articles/2007/NewGenerationGap.aspx

Mathews, V. P., Kronenberger, W. G., Wang, Y., Lurito, J. T., Lowe, M. J., and Dunn, D. W. 2005. "Media Violence Exposure and Frontal Lobe Activation Measured by Functional Magnetic Resonance Imaging in Aggressive and Nonaggressive Adolescents." *Journal of Computer Assisted Tomography* 29:3:287–292.

Mathisen, J. A. 1989. "A Further Look at 'Common Sense' in Introductory Sociology." *Teaching Sociology* 17(3):307–315.

Matousek, M. 2007. "Long-Distance Living." *AARP: The Magazine* (July/August):36–37.

Mawson, A. R. 2005. "Understanding Mass Panic and Other Collective Responses to Threat and Disaster." *Psychiatry-Interpersonal and Biological Processes* 68:2:95–113.

May, E. 1988. *Homeward Bound: American Families in the Cold War Era*. New York: Basic Books.

Mazzeo, C., Rab, S., and Eachus, S. 2003. "Work-First or Work-Only: Welfare Reform, State Policy, and Access to Postsecondary Education." *Annals of the American Academy of Political and Social Science* 586 (March):144–171.

McCabe, M. P., and Ricciardelli, L. A. 2003. "Sociocultural Influences on Body Image and Body Changes Among Adolescent Boys and Girls." *Journal of Social Psychology* 143(1):5–26.

McConahay, J. B. 1981. "Reducing Racial Prejudice in Desegregated Schools." In W. D. Hawley (Ed.), *Effective School Desegregation*. Beverly Hills, CA: Sage.

McDonald, P. 2001. "Low Fertility Not Politically Sustainable." *Population Today* (August/September):3–8.

McDonald, W. F. 2003. "Immigrant Criminality: In the Eye of the Beholder?" http://www.stranieriinitalia.com/briguglio/immigrazione-e-asilo/2003/maggio/mcdonald-criminalita'.html

McLanahan, S. 2002. "Life Without Father: What Happens to the Children?" *Contexts* 1(1):35–44.

McLean, C. 1998. "Name Your Baby Carefully." *Alberta Report* 25(23):34–36.

McLeod, J. D., and Owens, T. J. 2004. "Psychological Well-Being in the Early Life Course: Variations by Socioeconomic Status, Gender, and Race/Ethnicity." *Social Psychology Quarterly* 67:3:257–278.

McPherson, M., Smith-Lovin, L., and Brashears, M. E. 2006. "Social Isolation in America: Changes in Core Discussion Networks over Two Decades." *American Sociological Review* 71:3:353–375.

McPherson, M., Smith-Lovin, L., and Cook, J. M. 2001. "Birds of a Feather: Homophily in Social Networks." *Annual Review of Sociology* 27:415–444.

McSwain, C., and Davis, R. 2007. *College Access for the Working Poor: Overcoming Burdens to Succeed in Higher Education*. Prepared by Institute for Higher Education Policy. http://www.ihep.org/assets/files/publications/a-f/College AccessWorkingPoor.pdf

MDRC. 2003. "Fast Fact: Welfare Policies and Adolescent School Performances." http://www.mdrc.org/area_fact_10.html

Mehan, H., Hubbard, L., Lintz, A., and Villanueva, I. 1994. *Tracking Untracking: The Consequences of Placing Low Track Students in High Track Classes* (Research Report 10). Santa Cruz, CA: National Center for Research on Cultural Diversity and Second Language Learning.

Mehrabian, A. 2000. "Beyond IQ: Broad-Based Measurement of Individual Success Potential or 'Emotional Intelligence.'" *Genetic, Social, and General Psychology Monographs* 126(2):133–239.

———. 2001. "Characteristics Attributed to Individuals on the Basis of Their First Names." *Genetic, Social and General Psychology Monographs* 127(1):59–89.

Mencimer, S. 2002. "You Call This a Vacation?" *New York Times Magazine* (June 12).

Mental Health America. 2007. "Alzheimer's Disease." Mentalhealthamerica.net. http://www.mentalhealthamerica.net/go/alzheimers

Merskin, D. 2007. "Three Faces of Eva: Perpetuation of the Hot-Latina Stereotype in *Desperate Housewives*." *Howard Journal of Communications* 18(2):133–151.

Merton, R. K. 1938."Social Structure and Anomie." *American Sociological Review* 3:672–682.

———. 1957. *Social Theory and Social Structure*. Glencoe, IL: Free Press.

Meyers, P. M., and Crull, S. R. 1994. "Question Order Effect: A Preliminary Analysis." Paper Presented at the Annual Meetings of the Association of Applied Sociology, Detroit, MI.

Miceli, T. J. 1992. "The Welfare Effects of Non-Price Competition Among Real Estate Brokers." *Journal of the American Real Estate and Urban Economics Association* 20(4):519–532.

Mignon, S., Larson, C., and Holmes, W. 2002. *Family Abuse: Consequences, Theories, and Responses*. Boston: Allyn & Bacon.

Mihailescu, M. 2005. "Dampening the Powder Keg: Understanding Interethnic Cooperation in Post-Communist Romania (1990–96)." *Nationalism & Ethnic Politics* 11:1:25–59.

Milburn, S. S., Carney, D. R., and Ramirez, A. M. 2001. "Even in Modern Media, the Picture Is Still the Same: A Content Analysis of Clipart Images." *Sex Roles* 44:277–294.

Milkie, M. A. 1999. "Social Comparisons, Reflected Appraisals, and Mass Media: The Impact of Pervasive Beauty Images on Black and White Girls' Self-Concepts." *Social Psychology Quarterly* 62(2):190–210.

Miller, E. 2006. "Other Economies are Possible! Special Collaboration with Grassroots Economic Organizing: Organizing toward an Economy of Cooperation and Solidarity." *Dollars and Sense* 266:11:5.

Miller, J. 2004. *Writing About Numbers: Effective Presentation of Quantitative Information*. Chicago: University of Chicago Press.

Miller, L. 2002. "Charities Hope 9/11 Inspires 'e-Philanthropy.'" *USA Today* (March 18).

Millman, M. 1980. *Such a Pretty Face: Being Fat in America*. New York: W. W. Norton.

———. 2002. *Seven Stories of Love*. New York: Harper Collins.

Mills, C. 1992. "The War on Drugs: Is It Time to Surrender?" In K. Finsterbusch and G. McKenna (Eds.), *Taking Sides: Clashing Views on Controversial Social Issues*. 7th ed. Guilford, CT: Dushkin Publishing.

Mills, C. W. 1959. *The Sociological Imagination*. London: Oxford University Press.

Mills, R. 2001. "Health Insurance Coverage: 2000." *Current Population Reports*. Washington, DC: U.S. Government Printing Office.

Minas, J. S., Scodel, A., Marlowe, D., and Rawson, H. 1960. "Some Descriptive Aspects of Two-Person, Zero-Sum Games." *Journal of Conflict Resolution* 4:193–197.

Mintz, S., and Kellogg, S. 1988. *Domestic Revolutions: A Social History of American Family Life.* New York: Free Press.

Miron, L. 1997. *Resisting Discrimination. Affirmative Strategies for Principals and Teachers.* Thousand Oaks, CA: Corwin.

Mirowsky, J., and Ross, C. E. 1989. *Social Causes of Psychological Stress.* New York: Aldine de Gruyter.

Mirowsky, J., Ross, C. E., and Reynolds, J. 2000. "Links Between Social Status and Health Status." In C. Bird, P. Conrad, and A. Fremont (Eds.), *Handbook of Medical Sociology* (pp. 47–67). 5th ed. Upper Saddle River, NJ: Prentice Hall.

Mirsky, S. 2000."What's in a Name?" *Scientific American* 283(3):112.

Mitra, A. 2002. "Mathematics Skill and Male-Female Wages." *Journal of Socio-Economics* 31(5):443–456.

Mok, T. A. 1998. "Asian Americans and Standards of Attractiveness: What's in the Eye of the Beholder?" *Cultural Diversity and Mental Health* 4(1):1–18.

Molnar, S. 1991. *Human Variation: Races, Types and Ethnic Groups.* 3d ed. Englewood Cliffs, NJ: Prentice Hall.

Mondschein, E., Adolph, K., and Tamis-LeMonda, C. 2000. "Gender Bias in Mothers' Expectations About Infant Crawling." *Journal of Experimental Child Psychology* 77(4):304–316.

Monge, P. T., and Kirste, K. K. 1980."Measuring Proximity in Human Organizations." *Social Psychology Quarterly* 43:110–115.

Montenegro, X. 2004. "Spirituality and Religion Among Americans Age 45 and Older." *AARP the Magazine.* http://assets.aarp.org/rgcenter/general/american_spirituality.pdf

Monthly Labor Review. 2003. "Working Poor and Education." http://www.bls.gov/opub/ted/2003/jun/wk5/art02.htm

Moore, J. F. 1997. *The Death of Competition: Leadership and Strategy in the Age of Business Ecosystems.* New York: Harper Business.

Morgan, S. P., and Taylor, M. 2006. "Low Fertility at the Turn of the Twenty-First Century." *Annual Review of Sociology* 32:375–399.

Morrongiello, B., and Hogg, K. 2004. "Mothers' Reactions to Children Misbehaving in Ways That Can Lead to Injury: Implications for Gender Differences in Children's Risk Taking and Injuries." *Sex Roles* 50(1–2).

Mortimer, J. T., and Simmons, R. G. 1978. "Adult Socialization." *Annual Review of Sociology* 4:421–454.

Moss, N. 2002. "Gender Equity and Socioeconomic Inequality: A Framework for the Patterning of Women's Health." *Social Science and Medicine* 54(5):649–661.

Moss, P., and Tilly, C. 2001. *Stories Employers Tell: Race, Skill, and Hiring in America.* New York: Russell Sage.

Mruk, C. 2006. *Self-Esteem: Research, Theory, and Practice.* 3d ed. New York: Springer.

Muftic, L. R. 2006. "Advanced Institutional Anomie Theory: A Microlevel Examination Connecting Culture, Institutions, and Deviance." *Institutional Journal of Offender Therapy and Comparative Criminology* 50:6:630–653.

Mughal, S., Walsh, J., and Wilding, J. 1996. "Stress and Work Performance: The Role of Trait Anxiety." *Personality and Individual Differences* 20(6):685–691.

Mui, A. C. 2001. "Coping and Depression Among Elderly Korean Immigrants." *Journal of Human Behavior in the Social Environment* 3(3–4):281–299.

Mulford, M., Orbell, J., Shatto, C., and Stockard, J. 1998. "Physical Attractiveness, Opportunity, and Success in Everyday Exchange." *American Journal of Sociology* 103(6):1565–1592.

Mullen, B., and Smyth, J. M. 2004. "Immigrant Suicide Rates as a Function of Ethnophaulisms: Hate Speech Predicts Death." *Psychosomatic Medicine* 66:343–348.

Murstein, B. I. 1999. "The Relationship of Exchange and Commitment." In J. M. Adams and W. H. Jones (Eds.), *Handbook of Interpersonal Commitment and Relationship Stability* (pp. 205–219). New York: Plenum.

Muthusamy, S. K., Wheeler, J. V., and Simmons, B. L. 2005. "Self-Managing Work Teams: Enhancing Organizational Innovativeness." *Organizational Development Journal* 23:3:53–66.

Myers, D. G. (2002). *Social Psychology*. 7th ed. New York: McGraw-Hill.

Myers, D., and Cranford, C. 1998. "Temporal Differentiation in the Occupational Mobility of Immigrant and Native-Born Latina Workers." *American Sociological Review* 63(1):68–93.

Myers, P. N. Jr., and Biocca, F. A. 1992. "The Elastic Body Image: The Effect of Television Advertising and Programming on Body Image Distortions in Young Women." *Journal of Communication* 42(3):108–134.

Myers, P. N. Jr., Biocca, F. A., Wilson, G., Nias, D., Kaiser, S. B., Frank, M. G., Gilovich, T., Furlow, F. B., and Aune, R. K. 1999. "Appearance and Adornment Cues." In L. K. Guerro, J. A. DeVito, and M. Hecht (Eds.), *The Nonverbal Communication Reader: Classic and Contemporary Readings*. 2d ed. Prospect Heights, IL: Waveland.

NAACP. 2005. *Looking to the Future. Voluntary K-12 School Integration*. The NAACP Legal Defense and Education Fund, The Civil Rights Project at Harvard, The Center for the Study of Race and Law at the University of Virginia Law School. http://www.naacpldf.org/content/pdf/voluntary/Voluntary_ K-12_School_Integration_Manual.pdf

———. 2006. "African Americans: The State of the Disparity." http://www.naacp .org/advocacy/research/State.of.the.Disparity.12.3.06version32.pdf

Nabi, R. L., and Sullivan, J. L. 2001. "Does Television Viewing Relate to Engagement in Protective Action Against Crime? A Cultivation Analysis from a Theory of Reasoned Action Perspective." *Communication Research* 28(6):802–825.

Nagata, M. L. 1999. "Why Did You Change Your Name? Name Changing Patterns and the Life Course in Early Modern Japan." *History of the Family* 4(3):315–338.

Nass, C. I., and Brave, S. 2007. *Wired for Speech: How Voice Activates and Advances the Human-Computer Relationship*. Cambridge: MIT Press.

Nass, C., and Moon, Y. (2000). "Machines and Mindlessness: Social Responses to Computers." *Journal of Social Issues* 56(1):81–103.

Nass, C., Moon, Y., and Carney, P. (1999). "Are Respondents Polite to Computers? Social Desirability and Direct Responses to Computers." *Journal of Applied Social Psychology* 29(5):1093–1110.

National Association for Legal Professionals. 2007a. "Market for New Law Graduates Up, Topping 90% for First Time Since 2000." Association for Legal Career Professionals. http://www.nalp.org/assets/768_classof06selectedfindings.pdf

———. 2007b. "Employment Patterns 1982–2004." Association for Legal Career Professionals. http://www.nalp.org/content/index.php?pid=385

National Center for Children in Poverty. 2007. "Demographics of Young, Poor Children." http://www.nccp.org/profiles/index_9.html

National Center for Health Statistics. 2006. *Health, United States, 2002, with Chartbook on Trends in the Health of America.* Hyattsville, MD.

National Center for Injury Prevention and Control. 2007. "Suicide: Fact Sheet." Injury Center. CDC http://www.cdc.gov/ncipc/factsheets/suifacts.htm

National Center for Public Policy and Higher Education. 2003. *College Affordability in Jeopardy.* http://www.highereducation.org/reports/affordability_supplement/affordability_supplement.pdf

———. 2006. "A National Overview: Improvements, Declines, and Disparities." *Measuring Up. The National Report Card on Education.* http://measuringup.highereducation.org/nationalpicture/default.cfm

National Center for State Courts. 2005. "An Empirical Overview of Civil Trial Litigation." *Caseload Highlights* 11:1.

National Child Care Information Center. 2004. "Promoting Responsible Fatherhood Through Child Care." Child Care Bureau. http://www.nccic.org/pubs/resp-fatherhood.pdf

National Climate Data Center. 2007. *Climate of 2007 Preliminary Annual Report.* http://www.ncdc.noaa.gov/oa/climate/research/2007/ann/global.html

National Coalition for the Homeless. 2006. "Who Is Homeless?" NCH Fact Sheet # 3. http://www.nationalhomeless.org/publications/facts/Whois.pdf

National Coalition on Health Care. 2007. "Health Insurance Coverage." http://www.nchc.org/facts/coverage.shtml

National Council of Churches. 2003. "Status of Child Care Legislation." http://www.ncccusa.org/ publicwitness/tanf-may2003report.html

National Fair Housing Alliance. 2007. *The Crisis of Housing Segregation.* http://www.nationalfairhousing.org/resources/newsArchive/2007%20Fair%20Housing%20Trends%20Report.pdf

National Governors Association. 2006. "Factsheet: Fast Facts: Civic Engagement and Older Americans—Volunteerism." NGA Center for Best Practices. http://www.nga.org/portal/site/nga/menuitem.9123e83a1f6786440ddcbeeb501010a0/?vgnextoid=296faf3550d7c010VgnVCM1000001a01010aRCRD

National Highway Traffic Safety Administration. 2007. "2006 Traffic Safety Annual Assessment: A Preview." http://www.nhtsa.gov

National Institute for Literacy. 2007a. "Fact Sheet Overview." http://www.nifl.gov/nifl/facts/facts_overview.html

———. 2007b. "Correctional Education Facts." National Institute for Literacy. http://www.nifl.gov/nifl/facts/correctional.html#correctional

National Institute of Mental Health. 2001. "The Numbers Count: Mental Disorders in America" (NIH Publication # 01–4584). http://www.nimh.nih.gov/publicat/numbers.cfm

———. 2003. "In Harm's Way: Suicide in America." http://www.nimh.nih.gov/publicat/harmsway.cfm

———. 2006. "The Numbers Count: Mental Disorders in America." http://www.nimh.nih.gov/health/publications/the-numbers-count-mental-disorders-in-america.shtml

National Institutes of Health. 2004. "High School Graduates from Immigrant Families Just as Likely to Succeed in College as American-Born Peers." http://www.nichd.nih.gov/news/releases/children_immigrants.cfm

National Marriage Project. 2004. *The State of Our Unions 2004.* http://marriage.rutgers.edu

———. 2006. *The State of Our Unions 2006.* http://marriage.rutgers.edu

National Mental Health Association. 2003. "Elderly—Alzheimer's Disease." *Factsheet.* http://www.nmha.org/infoctr/factsheets/101.cfm

National Oceanic and Atmospheric Administration. 2007. "Climate of 2006—in Historical Perspective." National Climatic Data Center. U.S. Department of Commerce. http://www.ncdc.noaa.gov/oa/climate/research/2006/ann/ann06.html#Majorhighlights

National Park Service. 1998. "Peak Immigration Years." Ellis Island Exhibit, New York.

National Television Violence Study. 1996–1998 (Vols. 1–3). Center for Communication and Social Policy, University of California at Santa Barbara (Ed.). Thousand Oaks, CA: Sage.

National Women's Law Center. 2006. "The Paycheck Fairness Act: Helping to Close the Wage Gap for Women." http://www.pay-equity.org/PDFs/PaycheckFairnessActApr06.pdf

Nationmaster. 2007. "Crime Statistics." http://www.nationmaster.com/cat/cri-crime

Nelson, D. L., and Simmons, B. L. 2005. "Eustress and Attitudes at Work: A Positive Approach." In A. G. Antoniou and C. L. Cooper (Eds.), *Research Companion to Organizational Health Psychology* (pp. 102–110). Northhampton, MA: Edward Elgar Publishing.

Nelson, T. 2001. "Tracking, Parental Education and Child Literacy Development: How Ability Grouping Perpetuates Poor Education Attainment Within Minority Communities." *Georgetown Journal on Poverty Law and Policy* VIII(2):363–375.

———. 2002. *Ageism: Stereotyping and Prejudice Against Older Persons.* Cambridge, MA: MIT Press.

Nemours Foundation. 2004. "Stress." http://www.kidshealth.org/teen/your_mind/emotions/stress.html

Nes, L. S., and Segerstrom, S. C. 2006. "Dispositional Optimism and Coping: A Meta-analytic Review." *Personality and Social Psychology Review* 10(3):235–251.

Netreach.com. 2003. "Physicians." http://www.netreach.net/~bhohlfeld/career_project/shal/8s_medical.htm

Networkforgood.org. 2007. "About Networkforgood." http://www.networkforgood.org/Npo/about/

Neumark-Sztainer, D., Faulkner, N., Story, M., Perry, C., Hannan, P. J., and Mulert, S. 2002. "Weight-Teasing Among Adolescents: Correlations with Weight Status and Disordered Eating Behaviors." *International Journal of Obesity and Related Metabolic Disorders* 26(1):123–131.

NewsHour. 2006. "Melding Denominations" Broadcast on WNET, New York City (June 19).

Newsweek Poll, 2007. MSNBC.com. July 6. http://www.msnbc.msn.com/id/19623564/site/newsweek/

New York Times. 2003a. "Suits Accuse Toyota of Bias in Lending" (April 10).

———. 2003b. "The Terrorism Link That Wasn't" (September 19). Editorial/Op-Ed.

———. 2006. "A New Name For Sale? No Way For A Marine" (December 13):27.

New Zealand Herald. 2004. "South Korean Teens Buy Dreams of Beauty in Plastic Alley" (August 28).

Nie, N., and Erbring, L. 2000. *Internet and Society*. http://www.stanford.edu/group/siqss/itandsociety/v01i01/v01i01a18.pdf

Nippert-Eng, C. 1996. *Home and Work*. Chicago: University of Chicago Press.

Nock, S. 1993. *The Costs of Privacy: Surveillance and Reputation in America*. New York: Aldine de Gruyter.

Northern Trust. 2006. "Wealth in America 2007." http://www-ac.northerntrust.com/content/media/attachment/data/white_paper/0702/document/wealth_america 2007.pdf

Office of Management and Budget. 2007. "Analytical Perspectives: Budget of the United States Government, Fiscal Year 2008." http://www.whitehouse.gov/omb/budget/fy2008/pdf/apers/estimates.pdf

Office of Research on Women's Health. 2007. "FY 2007 NIH Research Priorities for Women's Health." http://orwh.od.nih.gov/research/FY07ResearchPriorities.html

Olbrich, R. 1986. "Attribution Psychology: An Approach to Explaining Productive Psychotic Symptoms." *Fortschritte der Neorologie-Psychiatre* 54(12):402–407.

Oliker. S. 2000. "Examining Care at Welfare's End." In M. Meyer (Ed.), *Care Work: Gender, Class and the Welfare State* (pp. 167–185). New York: Routledge.

Olson, I. R., and Marshuetz, C. 2005. "Facial Attractiveness Is Appraised in a Glance." *Emotion* 5(4):498–502.

Omotani, B., and Omotani, L. 1996. "Expect the Best: How Your Teachers Can Help All Children Learn." *The Executive Educator* 18(8):27–31.

Online Newshour. 2007. "Pulitzer-Winning Book Examines Media and Civil Rights Movement." http://www.pbs.org/newshour/bb/social_issues/jan-june07/race beat_05-18.html

Ono, H. 2006. "Homogamy Among the Divorced and the Never Married on Marital History in Recent Decades: Evidence from Vital Statistics." *Social Science Research* 35(2):356–383.

Orbuch, T., Thornton, A., and Cancio, J. 2000. "The Impact of Marital Quality, Divorce, and Remarriage on the Relationships Between Parents and Their Children." *Marriage & Family Review* 29(4):221–246.

Orfield, G., and Eaton, S. 2003. "Back to Segregation." *Nation* 276(8):5–8.

Orfield, G., Eaton, S., and the Harvard Project on Desegregation. 1996. *Dismantling Desegregation: The Quiet Reversal of Brown v. Board of Education*. New York: New Press.

Orfield, G., and Yun, J. 1999. "Resegregation in American Schools." The Civil Rights Project. Harvard University, Cambridge, MA. http://www.civilrightsproject.ucla.edu/research/deseg/Resegregation_American_Schools99.pdf

Ottati, V. C., and Deiger, M. 2002. "Visual Cues and the Candidate Evaluation Process." In V. C. Ottati and R. S. Tindale (Eds.), *The Social Psychology of Politics: Social Psychological Applications to Social Issues* (pp. 75–87). New York: Kluwer Academic/Plenum.

Owsley, H. 1977. "The Marriage of Rachel Donelson." *Tennessee Historical Quarterly* 36 (Winter):479–492.

Pace, T. M., Mullins, L. L., Beesley, D., Hill, J. S., and Carson, K. 1999. "The Relationship Between Children's Emotional and Behavioral Problems and the Social Responses of Elementary School Teachers." *Contemporary Educational Psychology* 24(2):140–155.

Padavic, I., and Reskin, B. 2002. *Women and Men at Work.* 2d ed. Thousand Oaks, CA: Pine Forge.

Pahl, R. 2005. "Are All Communities in the Mind?" *Sociological Review* 53: 4:621–640.

Pahl, R., and Pevalin, D. J. 2005. "Between Family and Friends: A Longitudinal Study of Friendship Choice." *British Journal of Sociology* 56(3):433–450.

Pahl, R., and Spencer, L. 2004. "Capturing Personal Communities." In C. Phillipson et al. (Eds.), *Social Networks and Social Exclusion* (pp. 72–96). Aldershot, England: Ashgate.

Park, S. 2006. "The Influence of Presumed Media Influence on Women's Desire to Be Thin." *Communication Research* 32(5):594–614.

Parker-Pope, T. 1997. "Avon Is Calling, with New Way to Make a Sale." *Wall Street Journal* (October 27):B1.

Parloff, R. 2007. "Reyes Jury Out, but Overall Message In." http://legalpad.blogs .fortune.cnn.com/2007/07/31/reyes-jury-out-but-overall-message-in/

Parrott, S., and Mezey, J. 2003. "New Child Care Resources Are Needed to Prevent the Loss of Child Care Assistance for Hundreds of Thousands of Children in Working Families." Center for Law and Social Policy. Center on Budget and Policy Priorities. http://www.cbpp.org/7-15-03tanf.htm

Parrott, S., and Sherman, A. 2006. "TANF at 10: Program Results Are More Mixed Than Often Understood." Center on Budget and Policy Priorities. www.cbpp .org/8-17-06tanf.htm

Parsons, T. [1951] 1964. *The Social System.* Glencoe, IL: Free Press.

Patzer, G. L. 2006. *The Power and Paradox of Physical Attractiveness.* Boca Raton, FL: Brown/Walker Press.

Pearlin, L. I. 1989. "The Sociological Study of Stress." *Journal of Health and Social Behavior* 30(3):242–256.

Pearlin, L. I., Menaghan, E. G., Lieberman, M. A., and Mullan, J. T. 1981. "The Stress Process." *Journal of Health and Social Behavior* 22(4):337–356.

Pearlin, L. I., Schieman, S., Fazio, E. M., and Meersman, S. C. 2005. "Stress, Health, and the Life Course: Some Conceptual Perspectives." *Journal of Health and Social Behavior* 46(2):205–219.

Pearlin, L. I., and Skaff, M. M. 1996. "Stress and the Life Course: A Paradigmatic Alliance." *Gerontologist* 36(2):239–247.

Pearson, D. E. 1993. "Post Mass Culture." *Society* 30(5):17–22.

Perlini, A. H., Marcello, A., Hansen, S. D., and Pudney, W. 2001. "The Effects of Male Age and Physical Appearance on Evaluations of Attractiveness,

Social Desirability, and Resourcefulness." *Social Behavior and Personality* 29(3):277–287.

Persell, C., and Cookson, P. 1990. "Chartering and Bartering: Elite Education and Social Class." In P. Kingston and L. Lewis (Eds.), *The High Status Track*. Albany: SUNY Press.

Pescosolido, B., Grauerholz, E., and Milkie, M. 1997. "Culture and Conflict: The Portrayal of Blacks in U.S. Children's Picture Books Through the Mid and Late Twentieth Century." *American Sociological Review* 62(3):443–464.

Peterson, J. 2002a. "Feminist Perspectives on TANF Reauthorization: An Introduction to Key Issues for the Future of Welfare Reform." Institute for Women's Policy Research. http://www.iwpr.org/pdf/e511.html#impact2

———. 2002b. "Issues for the Future of Welfare Reform." Briefing Paper. Institute for Women's Policy Research. http://www.iwpr.org/pdf/e511.html#tanf7

Peterson, K. 1992. "The Maquilladora Revolution in Guatemala" (Occasional Paper Series 2). New Haven, CT: Yale Law School, Orville H. Schell Jr. Center for International Human Rights.

Peterson, R. 1996. "A Re-Evaluation of the Economic Consequences of Divorce." *American Sociological Review* 61:528–536.

Peterson, T. J. 2007. "Another Level: Friendships Transcending Geography and Race." *Journal of Men's Studies* 15(1):71–82.

Pew Foundation. 2007. "Internet and American Life Project: Demographics of Internet Users." http://www.pewinternet.org/trends/User_Demo_1.11.07.htm

Pew Research Center. 2005. "The Black and White of Public Opinion." (October 31), http://people-press.org/commentary/display.php3?AnalysisID=121

———. 2007. "As Marriage and Parenthood Drift Apart, Public Is Concerned About Social Impact." http://pewresearch.org/pubs/526/marriage-parenthood

Pfeiffer, S. 2007. "Many Female Lawyers Dropping Off Path to Partnership." *Boston Globe* (May 2).

Pfohl, S. 1977. "The Discovery of Child Abuse." *Social Problems* 24(3):310–323.

Pham, L. B., Taylor, S. E., and Seeman, T. E. 2001."Effects of Environmental Predictability and Personal Mastery on Self-Regulatory and Physiological Processes." *Personality and Social Psychology Bulletin* 27:611–620.

Philipson, I. 2002. *Married to the Job: Why We Live to Work and What We Can Do About It*. New York: Free Press.

Phillips, R. 2007. "Pentecostalism vs. Fundamentalism." http://www.beliefnet.com/features/pentecostal_chart.html

Phillips, R. G., and Hill, A. J. 1998. "Fat, Plain, but Not Friendless: Self-Esteem and Peer Acceptance of Obese Adolescent Girls." *International Journal of Obesity* 22(4):287–295.

Philogene, G. 1999. *From Black to African American: A New Social Representation*. Westport, CT: Praeger.

Pierce, J. W. and Wardle, J. 1997. Cause and effect beliefs and self-esteem of overweight children. *Journal of Child Psychology and Psychiatry* 38(6) Sep:645–650.

PIRG. 2002. "The Burden of Borrowing." http://www.pirg.org/ highered/burdenof borrowing.html

Poblete, P. 2000. "The Price to Pay for an 'American' Nose and Eyes Is More Than $2,500." *San Francisco Chronicle* (February 24):E1.

———. 2001. "Beauty Ideals Still in the Dark Ages." *San Francisco Chronicle* (June 24):B4.

Polakow, V. 1993. *Lives on the Edge.* Chicago: University of Chicago Press.

Policy Alert. 2005. "Income of U.S. Workforce Projected to Decline if Education Doesn't Improve." National Center for Public Policy and Education. http://www .highereducation.org/reports/pa_decline/index.shtml

Pollack, A. 2000. "Is Everything for Sale? Patenting a Human Gene as if It Were an Invention." *New York Times* (June 28):C2.

PollingReport.com. 2007. "Race and Ethnicity." ABC News/Washington Post Poll (April 12–15). http://www.PollingReport.com/race.htm

Population Reference Bureau. 2000. "The Aging of the United States, 1999–2025." http://www.prb.org

———. 2003a. "Traditional Families Account for Only 7% of U.S. Households." http://www.prb.org

———. 2003b. "World Population Data Sheet." http://www.prb.org

Portes, A. 2002."English-Only Triumphs, but the Costs Are High." *Contexts* 1(1):10–15.

Portes, A., and Rumbaut, R. 1996. *Immigrant America: A Portrait.* Berkeley, CA: University of California Press.

Poulin-Dubois, D., Serbin, L., Eichstedt, J., Sen, M., and Beissel, C. 2002. "Men Don't Put on Make-Up: Toddlers' Knowledge of the Gender Stereotyping of Household Activities." *Social Development* 11(2):166–181.

Powell, K., and Abels, L. 2002. "Sex-Role Stereotypes in TV Programs Aimed at the Preschool Audience: An Analysis of *Teletubbies* and *Barney and Friends.*" *Women and Language* 25(1):14–22.

Prabhakaran, V. 1999. "A Sociolinguistic Analysis of South African Teluga Surnames." *South African Journal of Linguistics* 17(2/3):149–161.

Preidt, R. 2007. "Marriage of Great Benefit to the Depressed." MedicineNet.com. http://www.medicinenet.com/script/main/art.asp?articlekey=81529

President's Commission on Law Enforcement and Administration of Justice. 1968. *The Challenge of Crime in a Free Society.* Washington, DC: U.S. Government Printing Office.

President's Council on Bioethics. 2005. *Taking Care: Ethical Caregiving in our Aging Society.* http://bioethics.gov/reports/taking_care/index.html

Press, K. 2007. "Divide and Conquer? The Role of Governance for the Adaptability of Industrial Districts." *Advances in Complex Systems* 10(1):3–92.

Preston, J. 2006. "Public Misled on Air Quality After 9/11 Attack, Judge Says." *New York Times* (February 3) B:4.

———. 2007. "Surge Seen in Applications for Citizenship." *New York Times* (July 5).

Progressive. 2000."The Housing Crunch." *Progressive* 64(5):8–10.

Psychology Matters. 2005. "Emotional Fitness in Aging: Older Is Happier." *Psychology Matters. APAOnline.* http://www.psychologymatters.org/fitness.html

Pullella, Philip. 2007. "A Boy by Any Other Name." *Reuters* (December 18) http://toothdigger.blogspot.com/2007/12/boy-by-any-other-name.html

Purdum, T. 2006. "Go Ahead, Try to Stop K Street." *New York Times* (January 8).

Putnam Investments. 2005. "Retirement Only a Breather: 7 Million Go Back to Work." Putnam Investment News. 2005. http://www.putnam.com/shared/pdf/ press_working_retired.pdf

Putnam, R. 1995. "Bowling Alone: America's Declining Social Capital." *Journal of Democracy* (January):65–78.

———. 1998. "The Strange Disappearance of Civic America." *New Prospect Inc.* http://epn.org/prospect/24/24putn.html

———. 2000. *Bowling Alone: The Collapse and Revival of American Community.* New York: Simon and Schuster.

Putnam, R. D., Feldstein, L., and Cohen, D. J. 2004. *Better Together: Restoring American Community.* New York: Simon and Schuster.

Quarantelli, E. L. 2001. "Sociology of Panic." In P. B. Baltes and N. Smelse (Eds.), *International Encyclopedia of the Social and Behavioral Sciences* 22:271–298.

Quick, J. C., Cooper, C. L., Nelson, D. L., Quick, J. D., and Gavin, J. H. 2003. "Stress, Health, and Well-Being at Work." In J. Greenberg (Ed.), *Organizational Behavior: The State of the Science* (pp. 53–89), 2d ed. Mahwah, NJ: Lawrence Erlbaum Associates.

Quiggin, J. 2006. "Blogs, Wikis and Creative Innovation." *International Journal of Cultural Studies* 9(4):481–496.

Quigley, S. J. 2003. "That's My Name, Don't Wear It Out." *American Journalism Review* 25(3):49–52.

Quint, J., Widom, R., and Moore, L. 2001. "Post-TANF Food Stamp and Medicaid Receipt." Project on Devolution and Urban Change. Manpower Demonstration Research Corporation.

Rabois, D., and Haaga, D. A. F. 2002. "Facilitating Police-Minority Youth Attitude Change: The Effects of Cooperation Within a Competitive Context and Exposure to Typical Exemplars." *Journal of Community Psychology* 30(2):189–195.

"Race: The Power of an Illusion." 2003. PBS. http://www.pbs.org/race/000_General/ 000_00-Home.htm

Rada, J., and Wulfemeyer, K. T. 2005. "Color Codes: Racial Descriptors in Television Coverage of Intercollegiate Sports." *Journal of Broadcasting & Electronic Media* 49(1):65–85.

Radin, P. 2006. "To Me, It's My Life: Medical Communication, Trust, and Activism in Psyberspace." *Social Science and Medicine* 62(3):591–601.

Raffini, J. 1993. *Winners Without Losers: Structures and Strategies for Increasing Student Motivation to Learn.* Needham Heights, MA: Allyn and Bacon.

Raley, S., Bianchi, S., Cook, K., and Massey, D. 2006. "Sons, Daughters, and Family Processes: Does Gender of Children Matter?" *Annual Review of Sociology* 32(1):401–421.

Ram, R. 2006. "Further Examination of the Cross-Country Association Between Income Inequality and Population Health." *Social Science & Medicine* 62(3):779–791.

Ramsey, J. L., and Langlois, J. H. 2002. "Effects of the 'Beauty Is Good' Stereotype on Children's Information Processing." *Journal of Experimental Child Psychology* 81(3):320–340.

Ramsey, J. L., Langlois, J. H., Hoss, R. A., Rubenstein, A. J., and Griffin, A. M. 2004. "Origins of a Stereotype: Categorization of Facial Attractiveness by 6 Month Old Infants." *Developmental Science* 7(2):201–211.

RAND. 2007. "Anatomy of an Insurance Class Action." Research Brief. RAND Institute for Civil Justice. http://www.rand.org/pubs/research_briefs/2007/RAND_RB9249.pdf

Rangarajan, A. 1998. "Keeping Welfare Recipients Employed: A Guide for States Designing Job Retention Services." Mathematica Policy Research Inc. (June).

Rapoport, A. 1960. *Fights, Games, and Debates*. Ann Arbor: University of Michigan Press.

Rawlins, W. 1992. *Friendship Matters: Communication, Dialectics, and the Life Course*. New York: Aldine de Gruyter.

Reeves, B., and Nass, C. 1996. *The Media Equation: How People Treat Computers, Television, and New Media Like Real People and Places*. New York: Cambridge University Press.

Regan, P. C. 2002. *The Mating Game: A Primer on Love, Sex, and Marriage*. Thousand Oaks, CA: Sage.

Reifman, A., Villa, L., Amans, J., Rethinam, V., and Relesca, T. 2001. "Children of Divorce in the 1990s: A Meta-Analysis." *Journal of Divorce and Remarriage* 36(1–2):27–36.

Reiman, J. 2006. *The Rich Get Richer and the Poor Get Prison*. 8th ed. Boston: Allyn & Bacon.

Reis, H. T., Nezlek, J., and Wheeler, L. 1980. "Physical Attractiveness in Social Interaction." *Journal of Personality and Social Psychology* 38:604–617.

Rensberger, B. 1981. "Racial Odyssey." *Science Digest* (January/February).

Rentner, D., Chadowsky, N., Fagan, T., Gayles, K., Hamilton, M., Jennings, J., and Kober, N. 2003. "From the Capital to the Classroom: State and Federal Efforts to Implement the No Child Left Behind Act." Center on Educational Policy and American Youth Policy Forum. http:// wwwaypf.org

Renzetti, C. M., and Curran, D. J. 1989. *Women, Men and Society: The Sociology of Gender*. Boston: Allyn & Bacon.

Renzulli, L., and Evans, L. 2005. "School Choice, Charter Schools, and White Flight." *Social Problems* 52(3):398–418.

Reskin, B. 2000. "Getting It Right: Sex and Race Inequality in Work Organizations." *Annual Review of Sociology* 26:707–709.

Reskin, B., McBrier, D., and Kmec, J. 1999. "The Determinants and Consequences of Workplace Sex and Race Composition." *Annual Review of Sociology* 25:335–361.

Reuters. 2007a. "Is It a Bird? Is It a Plane? No, It's a Baby" (August 8). http://www.reuters.com/article/oddlyEnoughNews/idUSWEL7556320070808?feedType=RSS

———. 2007b. "Chinese Couple to Name Baby "@"" (August 16). http://thehermes project.blogspot.com/2007/08/chinese-couple-to-name-baby.html

Rhodes, G., Geddes, K., Jeffrey, L., Dziurawiec, S., and Clark, A. 2002. "Are Average and Symmetric Faces Attractive to Infants' Discrimination and Looking Preferences?" *Perception* 31(3):315–321.

Richard, J. F., Fonzi, A., Tani, F., Tassi, F., Tomada, G., and Schneider, B. H. 2002. "Cooperation and Competition." In P. K. Smith and C. H. Hart (Eds.), *Blackwell Handbook of Child Social Development* (pp. 515–532). Malden, MA: Blackwell.

Richardson, L. W. 1988. *The Dynamics of Sex and Gender: A Sociological Perspective.* New York: Harper and Row.

Riley, D. 1988. *Am I That Name?* Minneapolis: University of Minnesota Press.

Riley, G. [1991] 1997. *Divorce: An American Tradition.* Lincoln, NE: University of Nebraska Press.

Riniolo, T. C., Johnson, K. C., Sherman, T. R., and Misso, J. A. 2006. "Hot or Not: Do Professors Perceived as Physically Attractive Receive Higher Student Evaluations?" *Journal of General Psychology* 133(1):19–35.

Ritzer, G. 1995. *Expressing America: A Critique of the Global Credit Card Society.* Thousand Oaks, CA: Pine Forge.

———. 2001. *Explorations in the Sociology of Consumption: Fast Food, Credit Cards, and Casinos.* Thousand Oaks, CA: Sage.

Rivera, C. 2003. "Study Says Welfare-to-Work Reforms Leave Recipients Below Poverty Line." *Los Angeles Times* (July 23):B3.

Robert Half International 2007. "Top Five Professions in Demand for 2007." http://hotjobs.yahoo.com/jobseeker/tools/ept/careerArticlesPost.html?post=33

Robert, S. A., and House, J. S. 2000. "Socioeconomic Inequalities in Health: An Enduring Sociological Problem." In C. Bird, P. Conrad, and A. Fremont (Eds.), *Handbook of Medical Sociology* (pp. 79–97). 5th ed. Upper Saddle River, NJ: Prentice Hall.

Roberts, D. F. 1975. "The Dynamics of Racial Intermixture in the American Negro: Some Anthropological Considerations." *American Journal of Human Genetics* 7:361–367.

Roberts, G., and Klibanoff, H. 2006. *The Race Beat: The Press, the Civil Rights Struggle and the Awakening of a Nation.* New York: Knopf.

Robinson, J. 2003. *Work to Live.* New York: Perogee.

Roediger, D. 2005. *Working Toward Whiteness: How America's Immigrants Became White.* New York: Basic Books.

Rofé, Y. 2006. "Affiliation Tendencies on the Eve of the Iraqi War: A Utility Theory Perspective." *Journal of Applied Social Psychology* 36(7):1781–1789.

Rosenhan, D. L. 1973. "On Being Sane in Insane Places." *Science* 179:250–258.

Rosenkrantz, L., and Satran, P. R. 2004. *Beyond Jennifer and Jason, Madison and Montana: What to Name Your Baby Now.* New York: St. Martin's Griffin.

Rosenthal, R., and Jacobson, L. 1968. *Pygmalion in the Classroom.* New York: Holt, Rinehart and Winston.

Ross, C. E., and Broh, B. A. 2000. "The Roles of Self-Esteem and the Sense of Personal Control in the Academic Achievement Process." *Sociology of Education* 73(4):270–284.

Ross, C. E., and Huber, J. 1985. "Hardship and Depression." *Journal of Health and Social Behavior* 26(4):312–327.

Ross, C., and Mirowsky, J. 2002. "Family Relationships, Social Support and Subjective Life Expectancy." *Journal of Health and Social Behavior* 43(4):469–489.

Ross, H., and Taylor, H. 1989. "Do Boys Prefer Daddy or His Physical Style of Play?" *Sex Roles* 20 (January):23–33.

Rossi, A. S., and Rossi, P. 1990. *Of Human Bonding: Parent-Child Relations Across the Life Course.* New York: Aldine de Gruyter.

Roussi, P. K., Vagia, H., and Koutri, I. 2007. "Patterns of Coping and Psychological Distress in Women Diagnosed with Breast Cancer." *Cognitive Therapy and Research* 31(1):97–109.

Roxburgh, S. 2005. "Parenting Strains, Distress, and Family Paid Labor: A Modification of the Cost-of-Caring Hypothesis." *Journal of Family Issues* 26(8):1062–1081.

Royo, S. 2006. "Beyond Confrontation." *Comparative Political Studies* 38:8:969–995.

Ruane, J. 1993."Tolerance Revisited: The Case of Spousal Force." *Sociological Focus* 26(4):333–343.

———. 2005. *Essentials of Research Methods.* Malden, MA: Blackwell.

Ruane, J., Cerulo, K., and Gerson, J. 1994. "Professional Deceit: Normal Lying in an Occupational Setting." *Sociological Focus* 27(2):91–109.

Rubenstein, A. J., Kalakanis, L., and Langlois, J. H. 1999. "Infant Preferences for Attractive Faces: A Cognitive Explanation." *Developmental Psychology* 35(3):848–855.

Rubin, B. 1996. *Shifts in the Social Contract: Understanding Change in American Society.* Thousand Oaks, CA: Pine Forge.

Rubin, J. Z., Provenzano, F. J., and Luria, Z. 1974. "The Eye of the Beholder: Parents' Views on Sex of Newborns." *American Journal of Orthopsychiatry* 44:512–519.

Rubin, L. B. 1993. *Just Friends: The Role of Friendship in Our Lives.* New York: Harper and Row.

Rubin, N., Shmilovitz, C., and Weiss, M. 1993. "From Fat to Thin: Informal Rites Affirming Identity Change." *Symbolic Interaction* 16(1):1–17.

———. 1994. "The Obese and the Slim: Personal Definition Rites of Identity Change in a Group of Obese People Who Became Slim After Gastric Reduction Surgery." *Megamot* 36(1):5–19.

Rubinstein, S., and Caballero, B. 2000. "Is Miss America an Undernourished Role Model?" *Journal of the American Medical Association* 283(2):1569.

Rudd, N. A., and Lennon, S. J. 1999. "Social Power and Appearance Management Among Women." In K. K. P. Johnson and S. J. Lennon (Eds.), *Appearance and Power: Dress, Body, Culture* (pp. 153–172). New York: Oxford University Press.

Rudman, L., Feinberg, J., and Fairchild, K. 2002. "Minority Members' Implicit Attitudes: Automatic Ingroup Bias as a Function of Group Status." *Social Cognition* 20(4):294–320.

Rust, J., Golombok, S., Himes, M., Johnston, K., and Golding, J. 2000. "The Role of Brothers and Sisters in the Gender Development of Preschool Children." *Journal of Experimental Child Psychology* 77(4):292–303.

Ryan, A. 1996. "Professional Liars." *Social Research* 63 (Fall):619–641.

Saad, L. 2007a. "A Downturn in Black Perceptions of Racial Harmony." *Gallup Poll* (July 6).

———. 2007b. "Black–White Education Opportunity Widely Seen as Equal." *Gallup Poll* (July 2).

Sacks, H. 1975. "Everyone Has to Lie." In M. Sanches and B. Blount (Eds.), *Sociocultural Dimensions of Language Use* (pp. 57–79). New York: Academic Press.

Sadker, M., and Sadker, D. 1985. "Sexism in the Schoolroom of the '80s." *Psychology Today* 19:54–57.

———. 1998. "Failing at Fairness: How America's Schools Cheat Girls." In P. Rothenberg (Ed.), *Race, Class, and Gender in the United States* (pp. 503–509). 4th ed. New York: St. Martin's.

Sahadi, J. 2006. "Top 10 Millionaire Counties." CNNMoney.com. http://money.cnn.com/2006/03/28/news/economy/millionaires/

Salmon, M. 1986. *Women and the Law of Property in Early America*. Chapel Hill: University of North Carolina Press.

Sanabria, H. 2001. "Exploring Kinship in Anthropology and History: Surnames and Social Transformation in the Bolivian Andes." *Latin American Research Review* 36(2):137–155.

Sanderson, C. A., Darley, J. M., and Messinger, C. S. 2002. "I'm Not as Thin as You Think I Am: The Development and Consequences of Feeling Discrepant from the Thinness Norm." *Personality and Social Psychology Bulletin* 28(2):172–183.

Sands, E. R., and Wardle, J. 2003. "Internalization of Ideal Body Shapes in 9–12 Year-Old Girls." *International Journal of Eating Disorders* 33(2):193–204.

Sangmpam, S. N. 1999. "American Civilization, Name Change, and African-American Politics." *National Political Science Review* 7:221–248.

Sapkidis, O. 1998. "To Whom Do You Belong?: Catholic and Orthodox Names at Syros (Greece)." In P. H. Stahl (Ed.), *Naming and Social Structure: Example From Southeast Europe*. New York: Columbia University Press.

Saporta, I., and Halpern, J. J. 2002. "Being Different Can Hurt: Effects of Deviation from Physical Norms on Lawyers' Salaries." *Industrial Relations* 41(3):442–466.

Saris, W. E., and Gallhofer, I. N. 2007. *Design, Evaluation, and Analysis of Questionnaires for Survey Research*. Boston: John Wiley and Sons.

Satran, O. R., and Rosenkrantz, L. 2003. *Cool Names for Babies*. New York: St. Martin's Griffin.

Scassa, T. 1996. "National Identity, Ethnic Surnames and the State." *Canadian Journal of Law and Society* 11(2):167–191.

Schachter, S. 1959. *The Psychology of Affiliation*. Stanford, CA: Stanford University Press.

Schaeffer, N. C., and Presser, S. 2003. "The Science of Asking Questions." *Annual Review of Sociology* 29:65–88.

Schaffner, B., and Gadson, M. 2004. "Reinforcing Stereotypes? Race and Local Television News Coverage of Congress." *Social Science Quarterly* 85(3):604–621.

Scharrer, E., Kim, D., Lin, K., and Liu, Z. 2006. "Working Hard or Hardly Working? Gender, Humor, and the Performance of Domestic Chores in Television Commercials." *Mass Communication & Society* 9(2):215–238.

Schatz, Amy. 2007. "Long Races Force Ad Ingenuity." *Wall Street Journal* (June 19). http://online.wsj.com/article/SB118221211658539826.html?mod=hpp_us_editors_picks

Schein, E. H. 2004. "Learning When and How to Lie: A Neglected Aspect of Organizational and Occupational Socialization." *Human Relations* 57(3):260–273.

Schlosser, E. 2005. *Fast Food Nation*. Harper Perennial.

Schmid, R. E. 2007. "Raising Prices Enhances Wine Sales." *Yahoo News*. http://news .yahoo.com/s/ap/20080114/ap_on_bi_ge/costs_more_tastes_better

Schmidley, D. 2003. "The Foreign-Born Population in the U.S.: March 2002." *Current Population Reports* (P20-539). Washington, DC: U.S. Census Bureau.

Schmitt, C. 2005. "Medical Malpractice Payout Trends 1991–2004: Evidence Shows Lawsuits Haven't Caused Doctors' Insurance Woes." http://www.citizen.org/ documents/Malpracticeanalysis_final.pdf

Schneiderman, R. 1967. *All for One*. New York: P.S. Eriksson.

Schopler, J., Insko, C. A., Drigotas, S., and Graetz, K. A. 1993. "Individual/Group Discontinuity: Further Evidence for Mediation by Fear and Greed." *Personality and Social Psychology Bulletin* 19(4):419–431.

Schott, L. 2000. "Ways That States Can Serve Families That Reach Welfare Time Limits." Center on Budget and Policy Priorities. http://www.cbpp.org

Schroeder, K., and Ledger, J. 1998. *Life and Death on the Internet*. Menasha, WI: Supple.

Schul, Y., and Vinokur, A. 2000. "Projection in Person Perception Among Spouses as a Function of the Similarity in Their Shared Experiences." *Personality and Social Psychology Bulletin* 26:987–1001.

Schulman, D. 2004. "Labeling Theory." In G. Ritzer (Ed.), *Handbook of Social Theory*. Thousand Oaks, CA: Sage.

Schulman, K. 2000. *The High Cost of Child Care Puts Quality Care Out of Reach for Many Families*. Washington, DC: Children's Defense Fund.

Schultz, J. W., and Pruitt, D. G. 1978. "The Effect of Mutual Concern on Joint Welfare." *Journal of Experimental Social Psychology* 14:480–492.

Schuman, D., and Olufs, R. 1995. *Diversity on Campus*. Boston: Allyn & Bacon.

Schur, E. 1984. *Labeling Women Deviant*. Philadelphia: Temple University Press.

Schwartz, M. A., and Scott, B. 2007. *Marriages and Families: Diversity and Change*, 5th ed. Upper Saddle River, NJ: Prentice Hall.

Scott, D., and Church, T. 2001. "Separation/Attachment Theory and Career Decidedness and Commitment: Effects of Parental Divorce." *Journal of Vocational Behavior* 58(3):328–347.

Segrin, C., and Nabi, R. 2002. "Does Television Viewing Cultivate Unrealistic Expectations About Marriage?" *Journal of Communication* 52(2):247–263.

Seiter, J., Bruschke, J., and Bai, C. 2002. "The Acceptability of Deception as a Function of Perceivers' Culture, Deceiver's Intention, and Deceiver-Deceived Relationship." *Western Journal of Communication* 66(2):158–180.

Sennett, R. 1977. *The Fall of Public Man*. New York: Knopf.

Sennett, R., and Cobb, J. 1972. *The Hidden Injuries of Class*. New York: Vintage.

Serbin, L., Poulin-Dubois, D., and Eichstedt, J. 2002. "Infants' Responses to Gender-Inconsistent Events." *Infancy* 3(4):531–542.

Shaffer, D. R., Crepaz, N., and Sun, C. 2000. "Physical Attractiveness Stereotyping in Cross-Cultural Perspective: Similarities and Differences Between Americans and Taiwanese." *Journal of Cross-Cultural Psychology* 31(5):557–582.

Shalala, D. 2003. "Older Americans: Living Longer, Living Better." *World Almanac and Book of Facts 2003*. New York: World Almanac Books.

Shapiro, A., and Leone, R. 1999. *The Control Revolution: How the Internet Is Putting Individuals in Charge and Changing the World We Know.* New York: Public Affairs/Century Foundation.

Share, D., and Silva, P. 2003. "Gender Bias in IQ-Discrepancy and Post-Discrepancy Definitions of Reading Disability. *Journal of Learning Disabilities* 36(1):4–15.

Sharma, U., and Black, P. 2001. "Look Good, Feel Better: Beauty Therapy as Emotional Labor." *Sociology* 35(4):913–931.

Shavit, Y., and Featherman, D. 1988. "Schooling, Tracking, and Teenage Intelligence." *Sociology of Education* 61:5.

Shaw, A. 2006. "The Arranged Transnational Cousin Marriages of British Pakistanis: Critique, Dissent and Cultural Continuity." *Contemporary South Asia* 15(2):209–220.

Sheldon, J. 2004. "Gender Stereotypes in Educational Software for Young Children." *Sex Roles* 51(7–8):433–444.

Sherif, M. 1966. *In Common Predicament: Social Psychology of Intergroup Conflict and Cooperation.* Boston: Houghton Mifflin.

Sherif, M., Harvey, O. J., White, B. J., Hood, W. R., and Sherif, C. W. 1961. *Intergroup Conflict and Cooperation: The Robbers' Cave Experiment.* Norman, OK: University Book Exchange.

Sherman, A., and Aron-Dine, A. 2007. "New CBO Data Show Income Inequality Continues to Widen After-Tax-Income for Top 1 Percent Rose by $146,000 in 2004." Center on Budget and Policy Priorities. http://www.cbpp.org/1–23–07inc.htm#_ftn4

Shipler, D. 2005. *The Working Poor: Invisible in America.* New York: Vintage.

Shipman, P. 1994. *The Evolution of Racism: Human Differences and the Use and Abuse of Science.* New York: Simon and Schuster.

Sigelman, L., Sigelman, C. K., and Fowler, C. 1987. "A Bird of a Different Feather? An Investigation of Physical Attractiveness and the Electability of Female Candidates." *Social Psychology Quarterly* 50(1):32–43.

Signorielli, N., and Bacue, A. 1999. "Recognition and Respect: A Content Analysis of Prime-Time Television Characters Across Three Decades." *Sex Roles* 40(7–8):527–544.

Signorielli, N., Gerbner, G., and Morgan, M. 1995. "Violence on Television: The Cultural Indicators Project." *Journal of Broadcasting and Electronic Media* 39 (Spring):278–283.

Signorielli, N., and Vasan, M. 2005. *Violence in the Media: A Reference Handbook.* Santa Barbara, CA: ABC-CLIO Publishers.

Silverman, R. M. 2005. "Redlining in a Majority Black City?: Mortgage Lending and the Racial Composition of Detroit Neighborhoods." *Western Journal of Black Studies* 29(1):531–541.

Silverstein, M. J., and Fiske, N. 2003. "Luxury for the Masses." *Harvard Business Review* (April):48–54.

Simanski, J. 2007. "Naturalizations in the United States: 2006." *Annual Flow Report.* Homeland Security. Office of Immigration Statistics.

Simendinger, A. 2003. "Week in Review" Transcript. PBS (September 19).

Simmel, G. 1950a. "The Lie." In K. Wolff (Ed.), *The Sociology of Georg Simmel* (pp. 312–316). New York: Free Press.

———. 1950b. "The Stranger." In K. Wolff (Ed.), *The Sociology of Georg Simmel* (pp. 402–408). New York: Free Press.

Simmons, J. L. 1966. "Public Stereotypes of Deviants." *Social Problems* 13:223–232.

Simmons, T., and O'Neill, G. 2001. "Households and Families" (C2KBR/01–8 Census 2000 Brief). Washington, DC: U.S. Census Bureau.

Simon, R. W. 1997. "The Meanings Individuals Attach to Role Identities and Their Implications for Mental Health." *Journal of Health and Social Behavior* 38(3):256–274.

Simon, R., and Marcussen, K. 1999. "Marital Transitions, Marital Beliefs, and Mental Health." *Journal of Health and Social Behavior* 40(2):111–125.

Simpson, J., Campbell, B., and Berscheid, E. 1986. "The Association Between Romantic Love and Marriage: Kephart (1967) Twice Revisited." *Personality and Social Psychology Bulletin* 12:363–372.

Simpson, R. 2004. "Masculinity at Work: The Experiences of Men in Female Dominated Occupations." *Work, Employment and Society* 18(2):349–368.

Skolnick, A. 1991. *Embattled Paradise: The American Family in an Age of Uncertainty*. New York: Basic Books.

Slater, A., Bremner, G., Johnson, S. P., Sherwood, P., Hayes, R., and Brown, E. 2000. "Newborn Infants' Preference for Attractive Faces: The Role of Internal and External Facial Features." *Infancy* 1(2):265–274.

Slater, P. 1970. *The Pursuit of Loneliness: American Culture at the Breaking Point*. Boston: Beacon.

Slavin, R. E., and Madden, N. A. 1979. "School Practices That Improve Race Relations." *American Educational Research Journal* 16:169–180.

Smedley, A., and Smedley, B. 2005. "Race as Biology Is Fiction; Racism as a Social Problem Is Real." *American Psychologist* 60(1):16–26.

Smith, A. 1991. *National Identity*. Reno: University of Nevada Press.

Smith, J. C. 2007. *Supreme Conflict: The Inside Story of the Struggle for Control of the United States Supreme Court*. New York: Penguin.

Smith, K. 2000. "Who's Minding the Kids? Child Care Arrangements: Fall 1995." *Current Population Reports* (P70–70). Washington, DC: U.S. Census Bureau.

Smith, S. 2006. "Counter Culture." *MediaWeek* 16(27):24–25.

Smith, S. 2007. "AFL-CIO: Nation's Workplaces Too Unsafe." http://www.occupational hazards.com/News/Article/54902/AFLCIO_Nations_Workplaces_Too_Unsafe .aspx

Smith, T. 2004. "America's Protestant Majority Is Fading NORC Research Shows." http://www.norc.uchicago.edu/about/press07202004.asp

Snyder, M. 2001. "Self-Fulfilling Stereotypes." In A. Branaman (Ed.), *Self and Society* (pp. 30–35). Malden, MA: Blackwell.

Sobal, J., and Maurer, D. (Eds.). 1999. *Interpreting Weight: The Social Management of Fatness and Thinness*. New York: Aldine de Gruyter.

Social Security Online. 2006. "Annual Statistical Supplement, 2005." Office of Policy http://www.ssa.gov/policy/docs/statcomps/supplement/2006/

Solman, P. 2006a. "Emissions Exchange Program Aims to Reduce Greenhouse Gases." Online NewsHour (June 7). http://www.pbs.org/newshour/bb/environment/jan-june06/globalwarming_06–07.html

———. 2006b. "Global Warming Presents New Business Opportunities." Online NewsHour (June 5). http://www.pbs.org/newshour/bb/environment/jan-june06/globalwarming_06–05.html

———. 2006c. "Biofuels as Oil Alternative." Online NewsHour (April 13). http://www.pbs.org/newshour/bb/economy/jan-june06/biofuels_4–13.html

———. 2006d. "Researchers Scramble to Create CO_2-Busting Technologies." Online NewsHour (June 8). http://www.pbs.org/newshour/bb/environment/jan-june06/globalwarming_06–08.html

Solomon, D., Battistich, V., and Hom, A. 1996. "Teacher Beliefs and Practices in Schools Serving Communities That Differ in Socioeconomic Level." *Journal of Experimental Education* 64(4):327–347.

Sorenson, A. 1990. "Estimating the Economic Consequences of Separation and Divorce: A Cautionary Tale from the U.S." In L. Weitzman and M. Maclean (Eds.), *Economic Consequences of Divorce: The International Perspective.* Oxford, England: Clarendon.

Sourcebook of Criminal Justice Statistics. 2005. Online Table 2.34. http://www.albany.edu/sourcebook/pdf/t2342005.pdf

South, S. 2001. "Time-Dependent Effects of Wives' Employment on Marital Dissolution." *American Sociological Review* 66(2):226–245.

South, S., and Lloyd, K. 1995. "Spousal Alternatives and Marital Dissolution." *American Sociological Review* 60(1):21–35.

South China Morning Post. 2006. "Slaves to the Notion of 'Beauty.'" New: Out of the Box: p. 15 (April 24).

Spain, D. 1999. "America's Diversity: On the Edge of Two Centuries." *PBR Reports on America* 1(2).

Spencer, L., and Pahl, R. 2006. *Rethinking Friendship: Hidden Solidarities Today.* Princeton, NJ: Princeton University Press.

Spreafico, A. 2005. "The Community Between Solidarity and Acknowledgement." *International Review of Sociology* 15(3):471–492.

Sprecher, S., and Regan, P. C. 2002. "Liking Some Things (in Some People) More Than Others: Partner Preferences in Romantic Relationships and Friendships." *Journal of Social and Personal Relationships* 19(4):463–481.

Squires, G., and Chadwick, J. 2006. "Linguistic Profiling." *Urban Affairs Review* 41(3):400–415.

Stack, S., and Eshleman, J. 1998. "Marital Status and Happiness: A 17-Nation Study." *Journal of Marriage & Family* 60(2):527–537.

Stafford, L., and Merolla, A. 2007. "Idealization, Reunions, and Stability in Long-Distance Dating Relationships." *Journal of Social & Personal Relationships* 24(1):37–54.

Stake, J., and Nickens, S. 2005. "Adolescent Girls' and Boys' Science Peer Relationships and Perceptions of the Possible Self as Scientist." *Sex Roles* 52(1–2):1–11.

Stapel, D. A., and Koomen, W. 2005. "Competition, Cooperation, and the Effects of Others on Me." *Journal of Personality and Social Psychology* 88(6):1029–1038.

Steinke, J., and Long, M. 1996. "A Lab of Her Own? Portrayals of Female Characters on Children's Educational Science Program." *Science Communication* 18(2):91–115.

Stenson, J. 2003. "Extra Stress Stresses Immune System Too." preventdisease.com/news/articles/extra_stress_stresses_immune_system.shtml

Stevens, J. 1999. *Reproducing the State.* Princeton, NJ: Princeton University Press.

St.-Hilaire, A. 2002. "The Social Adaptation of Children of Mexican Immigrants: Educational Aspirations Beyond Junior High School." *Social Science Quarterly* 83(4):1026–1043.

Stice, E., Spangler, D., and Agras, W. S. 2001. "Exposure to Media-Portrayed Thin-Ideal Images Adversely Affects Vulnerable Girls: A Longitudinal Experiment." *Journal of Social and Clinical Psychology* 20(3):270–288.

Stinchcombe, A. 1963. "Some Empirical Consequences of the Davis-Moore Theory of Stratification." *American Sociological Review* 28(5):805–808.

———. 1997. "On the Virtues of the Old Institutionalism." *Annual Review of Sociology* 23:1–18.

Stock, P. 1978. *Better Than Rubies: A History of Women's Education.* New York: G. P. Putnam.

Stockard, J., and Mayberry, M. 1992. *Effective Educational Environments.* Newbury Park, CA: Corwin Press.

Stodder, J. 1998. "Double Surnames and Gender Equality: A Proposition and the Spanish Case." *Journal of Comparative Family Studies* 29(3):585–593.

Stolberg, S. 2003a. "Senate Refused to Consider Cap on Medical Malpractice Awards." *New York Times* (July 10).

———. 2003b. "Senate Becomes OK Corral for a Surgeon and a Lawyer." *New York Times* (July 11).

Stoll, M. 2005. "Geographical Skills Mismatch, Job Search and Race." *Urban Studies* 42(4):695–717.

Stone, L. 1989. "The Road to Polygamy." *New York Review of Books* (March):13.

Strand, K., and Mayfield, E. 2000. "The Effects of 'Female Friendly' Teaching Strategies on College Women's Persistence in Mathematics." Presentation at Southern Sociological Society.

Straughan, R., and Lynn, M. 2002. "The Effects of Salesperson Compensation on Perceptions of Salesperson Honesty." *Journal of Applied Social Psychology* 32(4):719–731.

Straus, M. (with Donnelly, D.). 2001. *Beating the Devil out of Them: Corporal Punishment in American Families and Its Effects on Children.* New Brunswick, NJ: Transaction.

Straus, M., and Gelles, R. 1990. *Physical Violence in American Families: Risk Factors and Adaptations to Violence Families.* New Brunswick, NJ: Transaction.

Straus, M., Gelles, R., and Steinmetz, S. 1980. *Behind Closed Doors: Violence in American Families.* New York: Doubleday.

Strobino, D., Grason, H., and Mikovitz, C. 2002. "Charting a Course for the Future of Women's Health in the United States: Concepts, Findings and Recommendations." *Social Science and Medicine* 54(5):839–848.

Strum, C. 1993. "School Tracking: Efficiency or Elitism?" *New York Times* (April 1): B5.

Studentdoc.com. 2007. "Physician Salaries." http://www.studentdoc.com/july_surv.html

Suarez, E. 1997. "A Woman's Freedom to Choose Her Surname: Is It Really a Matter of Choice?" *Women's Right Law Reporter* 18(2):233–242.

Sue, C., and Telles, E. 2007. "Assimilation and Gender in Naming." *American Journal of Sociology* 12(5):1383–1415.

Suitor, J., Mecom, D., and Feld, I. 2001. "Gender, Household Labor, and Scholarly Productivity Among University Professors." *Gender Issues* 19(4):50–67.

Sullins, P. 2000. "The Stained Glass Ceiling: Career Attainment for Women Clergy." *Sociology of Religion* 61(3):243–266.

Sum, A., Kirsch, I., and Taggart, R. 2002. "The Twin Challenges of Mediocrity and Inequality: Literacy in the U.S. from an International Perspective 2002." Educational Testing Service. http://www.ets.org/Media/Research/pdf/PICTWIN.pdf

Sumner, W. G. 1963. "Sociology." In *Social Darwinism: Selected Essays of William Graham Sumner* (pp. 9–29). Englewood Cliffs, NJ: Prentice Hall.

Swarthout, L. 2007. "Testimony, Subcommittee on Higher Education, Lifelong Learning and Competitiveness." May 1st. http://www.uspirg.org/html

Swartz, D. 2003. "From Correspondence to Contradiction and Change: Schooling in Capitalist America Revisited." *Sociological Forum* 18(1):167–186.

Sweeney, J., and Bradbard, M. R. 1988. "Mothers' and Fathers' Changing Perceptions of Their Male and Female Infants over the Course of Pregnancy." *Journal of Genetic Psychology* 149:393–404.

Swidler, A. 2001. *Talk of Love: How Culture Matters.* Chicago: University of Chicago Press.

Sykes, G., and Matza, D. 1957. "Techniques of Neutralization: A Theory of Delinquency." *American Sociological Review* 22:664–670.

Tait, C. 2006. "Namesakes and Nicknames: Naming Practices in Early Modern Ireland." *Continuity and Change* 21(2):313–340.

Tajfel, H. 1982. "Social Psychology of Intergroup Relations." *Annual Review of Psychology* 33:1–39.

Takeuchi, S. A. 2006. "On the Matching Phenomenon in Courtship: A Probability Matching Theory of Mate Selection." *Marriage & Family Review* 40(1):25–51.

Taleporos, G., and McCabe, M. P. 2002. "The Impact of Sexual Esteem, Body Esteem and Sexual Satisfaction on Psychological Well-Being in People with Physical Disability." *Sexuality and Disability* 20(3):177–183.

Tannen, M. 2006. "For Mature Audiences." *New York Times Magazine* (January 22).

Tanur, J. 1992. *Questions About Questions.* New York: Russell Sage Foundation.

Teachout, T. 2002. "Is Tony Soprano Today's Ward Cleaver?" *New York Times* (September 15).

Teichner, G., Ames, E., and Kerig, P. 1997. "The Relation of Infant Crying and the Sex of the Infant to Parents' Perceptions of the Infant and Themselves." *Psychology—A Quarterly Journal of Human Behavior* 34(3–4):59–60.

Teigen, K. H. 1986. "Old Truths or Fresh Insights? A Study of Students' Evaluations of Proverbs." *Journal of British Social Psychology* 25(1):43–50.

TenBensel, R., Rheinberger, M., and Radbill, S. 1997. "Children in a World of Violence: The Roots of Child Maltreatment." In M. Helfer, R. Kempe, and R. Krugman (Eds.), *The Battered Child*. Chicago: University of Chicago Press.

Tennen, H., and Affleck, G. 1999. "Finding Benefits in Adversity." In C. R. Snyder (Ed.), *Coping: The Psychology of What Works*. New York: Oxford University Press.

Thernstrom, M. 2005. "The New Arranged Marriage." *New York Times Magazine* (December 13).

Thoits, P. 1983. "Dimensions of Life Events That Influence Psychological Distress: An Evaluation and Synthesis of the Literature." In H. Kaplan (Ed.), *Psychosocial Stress: Trends in Theory and Research* (pp. 33–103). New York: Academic Press.

———. 1994. "Stressors and Problem-Solving: The Individual as Psychological Activist." *Journal of Health and Social Behavior* 35(1):143–160.

———. 1995. "Stress, Coping, and Social Support Processes: Where Are We? What Next?" *Journal of Health and Social Behavior* 36 (extra issue):53–79.

———. 2006. "Personal Agency in the Stress Process." *Journal of Health and Social Behavior* 47(4):309–323.

Thomas, B., and Reskin, B. 1990. "A Woman's Place Is Selling Homes: Occupational Change and the Feminization of Real Estate Sales." In B. Reskin and P. Roos (Eds.), *Job Queues, Gender Queues. Explaining Women's Inroads into Male Occupations*. Philadelphia: Temple University Press.

Thompson, J. K., and Stice, E. 2001. "Thin-Ideal Internalization: Mounting Evidence for a New Risk Factor for Body-Image Disturbance and Eating Pathology." *Current Directions in Psychological Science* 10(5):181–183.

Thompson, R. 2006. "Bilingual, Bicultural, and Binominal Identities: Personal Name Investment and the Imagination in the Lives of Korean-Americans." *Journal of Language, Identity and Education* 5(3):179–208.

Thompson, S. H., Sargent, R. G., and Kemper, K. A. 1996. "Black and White Adolescent Males' Perceptions of Ideal Body Type." *Sex Roles* 34 (March):391–406.

Thomsen, S. R., Weber, M. M., and Beth-Brown, L. 2002. "The Relationship Between Reading Beauty and Fashion Magazines and the Use of Pathogenic Dieting Methods Among Adolescent Females." *Adolescence* 37(145):1–18.

Thorne, B. 1995. "Girls and Boys Together . . . But Mostly Apart: Gender Arrangements in Elementary School." In D. M. Newman (Ed.), *Sociology: Exploring the Architecture of Everyday Life* (pp. 93–102). Thousand Oaks, CA: Pine Forge.

Tierney, K., Bevc, C., and Kuligowsky, E. 2006. "Metaphors Matter: Disaster Myths, Media Frames, and Their Consequences in Hurricane Katrina." *Annals of the American Academy of Political and Social Science* 604:57–81.

Tierney, K. J., Lindell, M. K., and Perry, R. W. 2001. *Facing the Unexpected: Disaster Preparedness and Response in the United States*. Washington, DC: Joseph Henry Press.

Time-Life Books. 1988. *This Fabulous Century 1920–1930*. New York: Time-Life Books.

Tippet, S. 1993. "I've Got the Family I Always Wanted." *Ladies Home Journal* (April):150.

TodaysSeniorNetwork.com. 2007. "By the Numbers . . . Census Bureau Facts for Features: Older Americans Month Celebrated in May." http://www.todays seniorsnetwork.com/Aging_Facts_by_Numbers.htm

Tourangeau, R., Couper, M. P., and Conrad, F. 2004. "Spacing, Position, and Order: Interpretive Heuristics for Visual Features of Survey Questions." *Public Opinion Quarterly* 68(3):368–393.

Trebay, G. 2003. "From Woof to Warp." *New York Times* (April 6) Section 9:1.

Treharne, G. J., Lyons, A. C., and Tupling, R. E. 2001. "The Effects of Optimism, Pessimism, Social Support, and Mood on Lagged Relationship Between Daily Stress and Symptoms." *Current Research in Social Psychology* 7(5):60–81.

Trehub, S., Hill, D., and Kamenetsky, S. 1997. "Parents' Sung Performances for Infants." *Canadian Journal of Experimental Psychology* 51(4):385–396.

Tropp, L. 2003. "The Psychological Impact of Prejudice: Implications for Intergroup Contact." *Group Processes & Intergroup Relations* 6(2):131–149.

Tuggle, J., and Holmes, M. 1997. "Blowing Smoke Status Politics and the Smoking Ban." *Deviant Behavior* 18:1.

Tumin, M. 1967. *Social Stratification: The Forms and Functions of Inequality*. Englewood Cliffs, NJ: Prentice Hall.

Turetsky, V. 2005. "The Child Support Program: An Investment That Works." Center for Law and Social Policy. http://www.clasp.org/publications/cs_ funding2_072605.pdf

Turkel, G. 2002. "Sudden Solidarity and the Rush to Normalization: Toward an Alternative Approach." *Sociological Focus* 35(1):73–79.

Turkle, S. 1996. *Life on the Screen*. New York: Simon and Schuster.

———. 1997. "Multiple Subjectivity and Virtual Community in the End of the Freudian Century." *Sociological Inquiry* 67(1):72–84.

———. 2007. *Evocative Objects: Things We Think With*. Cambridge, MA: MIT Press.

Twenge, J. M., and Manis, M. 1998. "First-Name Desirability and Adjustment: Self-Satisfaction, Others' Ratings, and Family Background." *Journal of Applied Social Psychology* 28(1):41–51.

UCLA Internet Project. 2002. "Surveying the Digital Future." UCLA Center for Communication Policy. http://www.ccp.ucla.edu

Umberson, D. 1996. "Relations Between Adult Children and Their Parents: Psychological Well-Being." *Journal of Marriage and the Family* 51:999–1012.

UnderGodProCon.org. 2006. http://www.undergodprocon.org/pop/PledgeHistory.htm.

UNESCO. 2003. "Education in a Multilingual World." UNESCO Education Position Paper. http://unesdoc.unesco.org/images/0012/001297/129728e.pdf

UNICEF. 2006. "Immunization." http://www.childinfo.org/areas/immunization/ countrydata.php

———. 2007a. "Child Mortality. Infant Mortality Country Data." http://www.child info.org/areas/childmortality/infantdata.php

———. 2007b. "At a Glance." http://www.unicef.org/infobycountry/

Union of Concerned Scientists. 2005. "Crichton's Thriller *State of Fear:* Separating Fact from Fiction." http://www.ucsusa.org/global_warming/science/crichton-thriller-state-of-fear.html

———. 2006a. "Frequent Questions About Global Warming." http://www.ucsusa.org/global_warming/science/global-warming-faq.html#4

———. 2006b. "Recognizing Forests' Role in Climate Change." http://www.ucsusa.org/global_warming/solutions/recognizing-forests-role-in-climate-change.html#4

———. 2007a. "Findings of the IPCC Fourth Assessment Report: Climate Change Science." http://www.ucsusa.org/global_warming/science/ipcc-highlights1.html#end3

———. 2007b. "Authoritative Report Confirms Human Activity Driving Global Warming." http://www.ucsusa.org/news/press_release/authoritative-report-confirms-0008.html

United Nations. 2002. *2000 Demographic Yearbook.* New York: Author.

———. 2004. *Demographic Yearbook 2004.* New York: Author.

———. 2005. "Fostering Economic Policy Coordination in Latin America: The RED-IMA Approach to Escaping the Prisoner's Dilemma." New York: United Nations.

Urban Institute. 1999. "Do We Need a National Report Card on Discrimination?" http://www.urban.org/url.cfm?ID=900310

———. 2003. "A Foot in the Door? New Evidence on Housing Discrimination." http://www.urban.org/publications/900587.html

———. 2006. "Five Questions for Harry Holzer." http://www.urban.org/toolkit/fivequestions/HHolzer.cfm

U.S. Bureau of Labor Statistics. 2007a. "May 2006 National Occupational Employment and Wage Estimates United States." http://www.bls.gov/oes/current/oes_nat.htm

———. 2007b. "Lawyers." http://www.bls.gov

———. 2007c. "National Compensation Survey: Occupational Wages in the United States, June 2006." www.bls.gov/ncs/ocs/compub.htm

U.S. Census Bureau. 1993. "Money Income of Households, Families and Persons in the United States: 1992." *Current Population Reports* (Series P-60, no. 184). Washington, DC: U.S. Government Printing Office.

———. 2000. Table 1: "Nativity of the Population and Place of Birth of the Native Population: 1850–1990." http://www.census.gov/population/www/documentation/twps0029/tab01.html

———. 2002. *Statistical Abstract of the United States: 2002.* 122d ed. Washington, DC: U.S. Census Bureau.

———. 2004a. Table MS-2: "Estimated Median Age at First Marriage." http://www.census.gov/population/socdemo/hh-fam/tabMS-2.pdf

———. 2004b. "America's Families and Living Arrangements, 2003." http://www.census.gov/prod/2004pubs/p20-553.pdf

———. 2005a. "American Fact Finder. Poverty Rates in U.S. 2005." http://factfinder.census.gov/home/saff/main.html?_lang=en

———. 2005b. "The Living Arrangements of Children in 2005." Population Profile of the United States: Dynamic Version. http://www.census.gov/population/pop-profile/dynamic/LivArrChildren.pdf

———. 2006a. Current Population Survey, 2006 Annual Social and Economic Supplement. Annual Demographic Survey. March Supplement. "2005 Poverty Table of Contents." http://pubdb3.census.gov/macro/032006/pov/toc.htm

———. 2006b. "Fact Sheet." American Fact Finder. U.S. 2006 American Community Survey, Data Profile Highlights. http://fastfacts.census.gov/servlet/ACSSAFFFacts?_submenuId=factsheet_0&_sse=on

———. 2006c. Current Population Survey, 2006 Annual Social and Economic Supplement. "Person Income Table of Contents." http://pubdb3.census.gov/macro/032006/perinc/toc.htm

———. 2006d. "Poverty: 2005 Highlights." http://www.census.gov/hhes/www/poverty/poverty05/pov05hi.html

———. 2007a. "State and County Quick Facts." http://quickfacts.census.gov/qfd/states/23000.html

———. 2007b. "Fast Facts for Congress: People, Relationships." http://fastfacts.census.gov/home/cws/main.html

———. 2007c. International Data Base. "Population Pyramids." http://www.census.gov/ipc/www/idb

———. 2007d. *The 2007 Statistical Abstract: The National Data Book.* http://www.census.gov/compendia/statab/

———. 2007e. "America's Families and Living Arrangements 2006." Current Population Survey 2006. http://www.census.gov/population/www/socdemo/hh-fam/cps2006.html

———. 2007f. "Current Population Survey." Annual Social and Economic (ASEC) Supplement. http://pubdb3.census.gov/macro/032007/perinc/new02_000.htm

———. 2007g. "Poverty: Poverty Thresholds 2006." http://www.census.gov/hhes/www/poverty/threshld/thresh06.html

———. 2007h. "The American Community—Asians: 2004." The American Community Survey Reports. The U.S. Department of Commerce. http://www.census.gov/prod/2007pubs/acs-05.pdf

———. 2007i. "Facts for Features. Hispanic Heritage Month 2007: Sept 15–Oct 15." http://www.census.gov/Press-Release/www/releases/archives/facts_for_features_special_editions/010327.html

———. 2007j. "The American Community—Hispanics: 2004." The American Community Survey Reports. U.S. Department of Commerce. http://www.census.gov/prod/2007pubs/acs-03.pdf

———. 2008. *The 2008 Statistical Abstract: The National Data Book.* http://www.census.gov/compendia/statab/

U.S. Conference of Catholic Bishops 2006. "Poverty in America." http://www.usccb.org/cchd/povertyusa/povfacts_age.shtml

U.S. Department of the Army. 2003. "Stress and Combat Performance." *Leader's Manual for Combat Stress Control* (Chapter 2). Washington, DC: Headquarters, Department of the Army.

U.S. Department of Education. 1997. *The Condition of Education 1997* (NCES 97–388). T. Smith, B. Aronstamm, B. Young, Y. Bae, S. Choy, and N. Alsalam. Washington, DC: U.S. Government Printing Office.

———. 2001. *The Condition of Education 2002* (NCES 2001–072). Washington, DC: U.S. Government Printing Office.

———. 2002. *The Condition of Education 2002* (NCES 2002–025). Washington, DC: U.S. Government Printing Office.

———. 2003. *The Condition of Education 2003* (NCES 2003–067). Washington, DC: U.S. Government Printing Office.

———. 2004. *Digest of Education Statistics: 2004.* http://nces.ed.gov/programs/digest/d04/tables/dt04_257.asp

———. 2005a. *Digest of Education Statistics: 2005.* http://nces.ed.gov/programs/digest/2005menu_tables.asp

———. 2005b. Youth Indicators: 2005. Indicator 41: Voting Behaviors. http://nces.ed.gov/programs/youthindicators/Indicators.asp?PubPageNumber=41&ShowTablePage=TablesHTML/41.asp

———. 2006. *The Condition of Education 2006.* National Center for Educational Statistics (NCES 2006–071). Washington, DC: U.S. Government Printing Office.

———. 2007a. *The Condition of Education 2007.* National Center for Educational Statistics. Washington, DC: U.S. Government Printing Office. http://nces.ed.gov/programs/coe/list/index.asp

U.S. Department of Health and Human Services. 2005. "2005 National Household Survey on Drug Use and Health." http://www.oas.samhsa.gov/nsduh/2k5nsduh/2k5Results.htm#2.10

———. 2006. "Indicators of Welfare Dependence: Annual Report to Congress 2006." http://aspe.hhs.gov/hsp/indicators06/index.htm

———. 2007a. "Health, United States, 2006, Special Excerpt: Trend Tables on 65 and Older Population." DHHS Publication # 2007–0152 http://www.cdc.gov/nchs/data/hus/hus06_SpecialExcerpt.pdf

———. 2007b. Administration on Children, Youth and Families. *Child Maltreatment 2005.* Washington, DC: U.S. Government Printing Office.

U.S. Department of Housing and Urban Development. 2005. "Homeownership Gaps Among Low-Income and Minority Borrowers and Neighborhoods." U.S. Department of Housing and Urban Development. Office of Policy Development and Research. http://www.huduser.org/publications/pdf/HomeownershipGapsAmongLow-IncomeAndMinority.pdf#xml=http://65.214.34.132/highlight/pdf-painter.html?url=http%3A//www.huduser.org/publications/pdf/HomeownershipGapsAmongLow-IncomeAndMinority.pdf&fterm=racial&fterm=discrimination&fterm=loans&fterm=racial+discrimination+in+loans&la=en&charset=iso8859-1

U.S. Department of Justice. 2000. "Crimes Against Persons Age 65 or Older, 1992–97." Bureau of Justice Statistics (NCJ 176352). Washington, DC: Author.

———. 2001. *Uniform Crime Reports: Crime in the United States—2000.* http://www.fbi.gov/ucr/ 01cius.htm

———. 2005. "Violent Crime Rate Unchanged During 2005: Theft Rate Declined." http://www.ojp.gov/bjs/pub/press/cv05pr.htm

———. 2006a. "Violent Victimization Rates by Age, 1973–2005." http://www.ojp.usdoj .gov/bjs/glance/tables/vagetab.htm

————. 2006b. "Violent Crime." http://www.fbi.gov/ucr/05cius/offenses/violent_crime/index.html

————. 2006c. "Criminal Victimization." http://www.ojp.usdoj.gov/bjs/cvictgen.htm

————. 2006d. "Crime in the United States." http://www.fbi.gov/ucr/05cius/data/table_01.html

————. 2006e. "Crime Clock 2005." http://www.fbi.gov/ucr/05cius/about/crime_clock.html

————. 2007a. "Victim Characteristics." http://www.ojp.usdoj.gov/bjs/cvict_v.htm#income

————. 2007b. "Criminal Victimization in the United States, 2005." http://www.ojp.usdoj.gov/bjs/, accessed 7/18/07.

U.S. Department of Labor. 2005a. "Fastest Growing Occupations 2004–2014." http://www.bls.gov/emp/emptab21.htm

————. 2005b. "Tomorrow's Jobs." Occupational Outlook Handbook. http://www.bls.gov/oco/oc02003.htm

————. 2005c. "A Profile of the Working Poor, 2003." Report 983. http://www.bls.gov/cps/cpswp2003.pdf

————. 2006a. "American Time Use Survey, 2005." http://www.bls.gov/tus/

————. 2006b. "Current Population Survey. Characteristics of the Employed." Table 11 ftp://ftp.bls.gov/pub/special.requests/lf/aat11.txt

————. 2006c. *Women in the Labor Force: A Databook.* http://www.bls.gov/cps/wlf-databook2006.htm

————. 2006d. "Rate of Working Poor Up in 2004." http://www.bls.gov/opub/ted/2006/jun/wk3/art01.htm

————. 2007a. "American Time Use Survey, 2006." http://www.bls.gov/tus/

————. 2007b. "Quick Stats." http://www.dol.gov/wb/stats/main.htm

————. 2007c. "Employment Status of Women and Men in 2006." Women's Bureau. http://www.dol.gov/wb/factsheets/Qf-ESWM06.htm

U.S. PIRG. 2007. "Student Debt." http://www.uspirg.org/higher-education/student-debt

U.S. Social Security Administration. 2007. "Fast Facts & Figures About Social Security, 2007." http://www.socialsecurity.gov/policy/docs/chartbooks/fast_facts/2007/fast_facts07.html#generalinfo

USA Today. 2003. "News." http://www.usatoday.com/snapshot/news/2001-07-06-familysize.htm?loc=interstitialskip

Useem, M., and Karabel, J. 1986. "Pathways to Top Corporate Management." *American Sociological Review* 51.

Vago, S. 1997. *Law and Society.* 5th ed. Englewood Cliffs, NJ: Prentice Hall.

————. 2003. *Law and Society.* 7th ed. Englewood Cliffs, NJ: Prentice Hall.

Van Avermaet, E., Buelens, H., Vanbeselaere, N., and Van Vaerenbergh, G. 1999. "Intragroup Social Influence Processes in Intergroup Behavior." *European Journal of Social Psychology* 29(5–6):815–823.

Van den Buick, J. 2000. "Is Television Bad for Your Health? Behavior and Body Image of the Adolescent 'Couch Potato.'" *Journal of Youth and Adolescence* 29(3):273–288.

van der Lippe, T., and van Dijk, L. 2002. "Comparative Research on Women's Employment." *Annual Review of Sociology* 28:221–241.

van Dijk, J. A. G. M. 2005. *The Deepening Divide: Inequality in the Information Society.* Thousand Oaks, CA: Sage.

Vanfossen, B., Jones, J., and Spade, J. 1987. "Curriculum Tracking and Status Maintenance." *Sociology of Education* 60:104–122.

Vanman, E. J., Paul, B. Y., and Ito, T. A. 1997. "The Modern Face of Prejudice and the Structural Features That Moderate the Effect of Cooperation on Affect." *Journal of Personality and Social Psychology* 73 (November):941–959.

Van Overwalle, F. 1997. "Dispositional Attributions Require the Joint Applications of the Methods of Difference and Agreement." *Personality and Social Psychology Bulletin* 23:974–980.

Vartanian, L. R., Giant, C. L., and Passino, R. M. 2001. "Ally McBeal vs. Arnold Schwarzeneggar: Comparing Mass Media, Interpersonal Feedback and Gender as Predictors of Personal Satisfaction with Body Thinness and Muscularity." *Social Behavior and Personality* 29(7):2001.

Verhaeghe, R., Vlerick, P., Gemmel, P., Van Maele, G., and De Backer, G. 2006. "Impact of Recurrent Changes in the Work Environment on Nurses' Psychological Well-Being and Sickness Absence." *Journal of Advanced Nursing* 56(6):646–656.

Vernez, G., and Abrahamse, A. 1996. *How Immigrants Fare in U.S. Education.* Santa Monica, CA: RAND.

Veroff, J., Douvan, E., and Kulka, R. 1981. *The Inner American: A Self-Portrait from 1957 to 1976.* New York: Basic Books.

Vinorskis, M. 1992. "Schooling and Poor Children in 19th Century America." *American Behavioral Scientist* 35(3):313–331.

Visher, E., Visher, J., and Pasley, K. 2003. "Remarriage Families and Stepparenting." In F. Walsh (Ed.), *Normal Family Processes: Growing Diversity and Complexity* (pp. 153–175). 3d ed. New York: Guilford.

Vogel, C. 2006. "A Pollock Is Sold, Possibly for a Record Price." *New York Times* (November 2) http://www.nytimes.com/2006/11/02/arts/design/02drip.html?ei=5090 &en=53ef078e6646b854&ex=1320123600&adxnnl=1&partner=rssuserland& emc=rss&adxnnlx=1162883074-hD7+iTcDZc6SWlkvwJtuPQ

VolunteerMatch.org. 2007. *2006 Annual Report.* http://www.volunteermatch.org/about/annual_report_06.pdf

Von Ah, D., Kang, D., and Carpenter, J. S. 2007. "Stress, Optimism, and Social Support: Impact on Immune Responses in Breast Cancer." *Research in Nursing and Health* 30(1):72–83.

Voss, K., Markiewicz, D., and Doyle, A. B. 1999. "Friendship, Marriage, and Self-Esteem." *Journal of Social and Personal Relationships* 16(1):103–122.

Vrij, A., and Firmin, H. R. 2002. "Beautiful Thus Innocent? The Impact of Defendants' and Victims' Physical Attractiveness and Participants' Rape Beliefs on Impression Formation in Alleged Rape Cases." *International Review of Victimology* 8(3):245–255.

Walker, K. 1995. "Always There for Me: Friendship Patterns and Expectations Among Middle and Working Class Men and Women." *Sociological Forum* 10(2):273–296.

Wallerstein, J., and Blakeslee, S. 1990. *Second Chances: Men, Women, and Children a Decade After Divorce.* New York: Ticknor and Fields.

Wang, M. K. 2002. "The Ancient Foundations of Modern Nation-Building in China: The Case of the Offspring of Yan and Yellow Emperors." *Bulletin of the Institute of History and Philology Academia Sinica* 73(3):583–624.

Wapnick, J., Mazza, J. K., and Darrow, A. A. 2000. "Effects of Performer Attractiveness, Stage Behavior, and Dress on Evaluation of Children's Piano Performances." *Journal of Research in Music Education* 48(4):323–336.

Ward, L. M., Hansbrough, E., and Walker, E. 2005. "Contributions of Music Video Exposure to Black Adolescents' Gender and Sexual Schemas." *Journal of Adolescent Research* 20(2):143–166.

Warschauer, M. 2004. *Technology and Social Inclusion: Rethinking the Digital Divide.* Cambridge, MA: MIT Press.

Wartik, N. 2002."Hurting More, Helped Less?" *New York Times* (June 23).

Washington Post. 2007. "At Least Half of Students Admit to Cheating"(June 4), B:2.

Waskul, D. D., and van der Riet, P. 2002. "The Abject Embodiment of Cancer Patients: Dignity, Selfhood, and the Grotesque Body." *Symbolic Interaction* 25(4):487–513.

Waters, M., and Jimenez, T. 2005. "Assessing Immigrant Assimilation: New Empirical and Theoretical Challenges." *Annual Review of Sociology* 31:105–125.

Watkins, L. M., and Johnston, L. 2000. "Screening Job Applicants: The Impact of Physical Attractiveness and Application Quality." *International Journal of Selection and Assessment* 8(2):76–84.

Watson, D., Hubbard, B., and Wiese, D. 2000. "Self-Other Agreement in Personality and Affectivity: The Role of Acquaintanceship, Trait Visibility, and Assumed Similarity." *Journal of Personality and Social Psychology* 78:546–558.

Watson, S., and Jones, A. 2006. "Scientific Poll: 84% Reject Official 9/11 Story." InforWars.com. http://www.infowars.com

Watson, W. H., and Maxwell, R. J. (Eds.). 1977. *Human Aging and Dying: A Study in Sociocultural Gerontology.* New York: St. Martin's.

Wattenberg, L. 2005. *The Baby Name Wizard: A Magical Method for Finding the Perfect Name for Your Baby.* New York: Broadway.

Weber, M. [1922] 1968. *Economy and Society.* New York: Bedminster.

WebMD. 2007. "Frequently Asked Questions About Body Image and Beauty." http://www.webmd.com/skin-beauty/frequently-asked-questions-about-body-image

Webster, B., and Bishaw, A. 2006. "Income, Earnings and Poverty Data from the 2005 American Community Survey Data." *American Community Survey Reports.* http://www.census.gov/prod/2006pubs/acs-02.pdf

Weisberg, K. 1975. "'Under Great Temptations Here': Women and Divorce in Puritan Massachusetts." *Feminist Studies* 2(2/3):183–193.

Weiss, M. 1998. "Parents' Rejection of Their Appearance-Impaired Newborns: Some Critical Observations Regarding the Social Myth of Bonding." *Marriage and Family Review* 27(3–4):191–209.

Weiss, R. 2005. *The Experience of Retirement*. Ithaca, NY: Cornell University Press.

Wellman, B. 2001. "Physical Place and Cyberplace: The Rise of Personalized Networking. *International Journal of Urban and Regional Research* 25(2):227–252.

———. 2004. "Connecting Communities: On and Offline." *Contexts* 3(4):22–28.

Wellman, B., Boase, J., and Chen, W. 2002. "The Networked Nature of Community Online and Offline." *Information Technology and Society* 1(1):51–165.

Wells, J., and Lewis, L. 2006. "Internet Access in U.S. Public Schools and Classrooms: 1994–2005." U.S. Department of Education. Washington, DC: National Center for Education Statistics (NCES 2007–020).

Wells, R. 1982. *Revolutions in Americans' Lives: A Demographic Perspective on the History of Americans, Their Families and Their Society*. Westport, CT: Greenwood.

Wertheimer, B. 1977. *We Were There: The Story of Working Women in America*. New York: Pantheon.

West, C. 1994. *Race Matters*. Boston: Beacon.

Wetzel, D. 2007. "Products of the System." *Yahoo! Sports* (September 11). http://sports.yahoo.com/nfl/news?slug=dw-productsofthesystem091107& prov=yhoo&type=lgns

Wheaton, B. 1982. "A Comparison of the Moderating Effects of Personal Coping Resources on the Impact of the Exposure to Stress in Two Groups." *Journal of Community Psychology* 10:293–311.

———. 1983. "Stress, Personal Coping, Resources, and Psychiatric Symptoms: An Investigation of Interactive Models." *Journal of Health and Social Behavior* 24(3):208–229.

———. 1990. "Life Transitions, Role Histories, and Mental Health." *American Sociological Review* 55(2):209–223.

White, M. A., Kohlmaier, J. R., Varnado-Sullivan, P., and Williamson, Donald A. 2003. "Racial/Ethnic Differences in Weight Concerns: Protective and Risk Factors for the Development of Eating Disorders and Obesity Among Adolescent Females." *Eating and Weight Disorders* 8(1):20–25.

Whitehead, B. 1993."Dan Quayle Was Right." *Atlantic Monthly* (April):47–84.

Wichman, H. 1970. "Effects of Isolation and Communication on Cooperation in a Two-Person Game." *Journal of Personality and Social Psychology* 16:114–120.

Wilcox, W. B., Waite, L., and Roberts, A. 2007. "Marriage and Mental Health in Adults and Children." Research Brief #4. Center for Marriage and Families. http://center.americanvalues.org/?p=55

Wilder, D. A., and Shapiro, P. N. 1984. "Role of Outgroup Cues in Determining Social Identity." *Journal of Personality and Social Psychology* 47:342–348.

Wilkinson, I., and Young, L. 2002. "On Cooperating: Firms, Relations, and Networks." *Journal of Business Research* 55(2):123–132.

Will, J. A., Self, P. A., and Dalton, N. 1976. "Maternal Behavior and Perceived Sex of Infant." *American Journal of Orthopsychiatry* 49:135–139.

Williams, D. 2005. "Controversial Issues Coming to the Fore at Bishops' Gathering: Vatican Moves to Limit Information Provided to Public." *Washington Post* (October 6) A:18.

Williams, K., and Dunne-Bryant, A. 2006. "Divorce and Adult Psychological Well-Being: Clarifying the Role of Gender and Child Age." *Journal of Marriage & Family* 68(5):1178–1196.

Williams, P. 2002. "Test, Tracking and Derailment." *Nation* 274(15):9.

Williams, R. M., Jr. 1970. *American Society: A Sociological Interpretation.* 3d ed. New York: Alfred A. Knopf.

Williams, S. 2001. "Sexual Lying Among College Students in Close and Casual Relationships." *Journal of Applied Social Psychology* 31(November): 2322–2338.

Williamson, D. A., Zucker, N. L., Martin, C. K., and Smeets, M. A. M. 2001. "Etiology and Management of Eating Disorders." In P. B. Sutker and H. E. Adams (Eds.), *Comprehensive Handbook of Psychopathology.* New York: Kluwer Academic/Plenum.

Willis, F. N., Willis, L. A., and Grier, J. A. 1982. "Given Names, Social Class, and Professional Achievement." *Psychological Reports* 54:543–549.

Wilson, J. 2000. "Volunteering." *Annual Review of Sociology* 26:215–240.

Wilson, W. J. 1980. *The Declining Significance of Race: Blacks and Changing American Institutions.* 2d ed. Chicago: University of Chicago Press.

———. 1990. *The Truly Disadvantaged: The Inner City, the Underclass, and Public Policy.* Chicago: University of Chicago Press.

Winneg, K., Kenski, K., and Jamieson, K. H. 2005. "Detecting the Effects of Deceptive Presidential Advertisements in the Spring of 2004." *American Behavioral Scientist* 49(1):114–129.

Winter, G. 2003. "Tens of Thousands Will Lose College Aid, Report Says." *New York Times* (July 18):A13.

Wirthlin Report. 2001. "Americans' Attitudes Toward Crime and Prevention." McLean, VA: Wirthlin Worldwide.

Wiseman, C. V., Gray, J. J., Mosimann, J. E., and Ahrens, A. H. 1992. "Cultural Expectations of Thinness in Women: An Update." *International Journal of Eating Disorders* 11(1):85–89.

Wisman, J. D. 2000. "Competition, Cooperation, and the Future of Work." *Peace Review* 12(2):197–203.

Witkin-Lanoil, G. 1984. *The Female Stress Syndrome: How to Recognize and Live With It.* New York: Newmarket.

Wolf, N. 1991. *The Beauty Myth: How Images of Beauty Are Used Against Women.* New York: W. Morrow.

Wolfe, T. 1976. "The Me Decade and the Third Great Awakening." In *Mauve Gloves and Madmen Clutter and Vine* (pp. 126–167). New York: Farrar, Straus and Giroux.

Wong, F. Y., McCreary, D. R., Bowden, C. C., and Jenner, S. M. 1991. "The Matching Hypothesis: Factors Influencing Dating Preferences." *Psychology* 28(3–4):27–31.

Wong, J. 2002. "What's in a Name?: An Examination of Social Identities." *Journal for the Theory of Social Behavior* 32(4):451–464.

Wood, N. T., Solomon, M. R., and Englis, B. G. 2003. "No One Looks That Good in Real Life! Projections of the Real Versus Ideal Self in the Online Visual Space." In L. M. Scott and R. Batra (Eds.), *Persuasive Imagery: A Consumer Response Perspective* (pp. 383–395). Mahwah, NJ: Lawrence Erlbaum.

World Almanac and Book of Facts 1998. 1998. Mahwah, NJ: Funk and Wagnall.

World Almanac and Book of Facts 2007. 2007. New York: World Almanac Books.

World Bank. 2005. "Education and Development." http://web.worldbank.org/WBSITE/EXTERNAL/TOPICS/EXTEDUCATION/0,,contentMDK:20591648~menuPK:1463858~pagePK:148956~piPK:216618~theSitePK:282386,00.html

World Christian Database. 2004. "Denominations Represented." http://worldchristiandatabase.org/wcd/about/denominations.asp

World Health Organization. 2007a. "Poverty and Health." http://www.who.int/hdp/poverty/en/

———. 2007b. "Core Health Indicators." http://www.who.int/whosis/database/core/core_select.cfm

Wu, Z., and MacNeill, L. 2002. "Education, Work, and Childbearing After Age 30." *Journal of Comparative Family Studies* 33(2):191–213.

Wuthnow, R. 1998. *Loose Connections: Civic Involvement in America's Fragmented Communities*. Cambridge, MA: Harvard University Press.

Yahoo News. 2003. "Majority in US Believes Bush 'Stretched Truth' About Iraq: Poll." http://www.informationclearinghouse.info/article3989.htm

Zagorin, P. 1996. "The Historical Significance of Lying and Dissimulation." *Social Research* 63 (Fall):863–912.

Zaidel, D. W., Bava, S., and Reis, V. A. 2003. "Relationship Between Facial Asymmetry and Judging Trustworthiness in Faces." *Laterality* 8(3):225–232.

Zebrowitz, L. A., Collins, M. A., and Dutta, R. 1998. "The Relationship Between Appearance and Personality Across the Life Span." *Personality and Social Psychology Bulletin* 24(7):736–749.

Zebrowitz, L. A., Hall, J., Murphy, N. A., and Rhodes, G. 2002. "Looking Smart and Looking Good: Facial Cues to Intelligence and Their Origins." *Personality and Social Psychology Bulletin* 28(2):238–249.

Zeitlin, M., Lutterman, K. G., and Russell, J. W. 1977. "Death in Vietnam: Class, Poverty, and the Risks of War." In M. Zeitlin (Ed.), *American Society Incorporated* (pp. 143–155). 2d ed. Chicago: Rand McNally.

Zelizer, V. 1985. *Pricing the Priceless Child*. New York: Basic Books.

Zernike, K. 2006. "The Remarrying Kind." *New York Times* (January 29).

Zimmer-Gembeck, M. J., and Locke, E. M. 2007. "The Socialization of Adolescent Coping: Relationships at Home and School." *Journal of Adolescence* 30(1):1–16.

Zimmerman, T., Haddock, S., Ziemba, S., and Rust, A. 2001. "Family Organizational Labor: Who's Calling the Plays?" *Journal of Feminist Family Therapy* 13(2–3):65–90.

Zitner, A. 2003. "Nation's Birthrate Drops to Its Lowest Level Since 1909." *Los Angeles Times* (June 26):1.

Zogby International. 2006. "Government/Corporate Scandals Damage Public Trust in Institutions at the Bedrock of Society." http:/www.zogby.com/news/Read News.dbm?ID=1116

Zuckerman, M., Miyake, K., and Elkin, C. S. 1995. "Effects of Attractiveness and Maturity of Face and Voice on Interpersonal Impressions." *Journal of Research in Personality* 29(2):253–272.

Glossary/Index

Aliens Citizens of a foreign country. The
United States distinguishes four legal
statuses for aliens: legal immigrants,
temporary legal migrants, refugees,
and unauthorized migrants, 247

Allan, G., 44

Alper, S., 16

Alt, M., 163

Alternative dispute resolution, 191

Altheide, D., 178

Altheimer, E., 114–115

Amablile, T. M., xvii

Amans, J., 220

Amato, P. R., 44, 220–221, 225

Amber Alert system, 24

American Association of Retired Persons,
55–57, 64, 67, 225, 294

American Bar Association, 189

American Cancer Society, 152

American Civil Liberties Union, 186, 193

American Heart Association, 48, 152

American Institute of Stress, 48

American Library Association, 193

American Medical Association, 150, 190

American Obesity Association, 113

American Patriots, 193

American Psychological Association,
48, 60

American Religious Identity Survey,
294, 297–298

American Society of Plastic Surgery, 112

American Tax Reform Association, 190

Ames, E., 141

Amodeo, N. P., 20

Andre, T., 145

Andreoletti, C., 111

Andrews, E., 160

Andrews, K., 162

Aneshensel, C., 48–49

Angier, N., 166

Aniston, Jennifer, 97

Anistopoulou, Jennifer, 97

Anit-smoking campaigns, 187–188

Anticipatory socialization Socialization
that prepares a person to assume a
future role, 61

AOL, 264

Appearance norms Society's generally
accepted standards of appropriate
body height, body weight,
distribution or shape, bone structure,
skin color, etc., 114

Apter, A., 49

Arichi, M., 103

Aries, P., 105

Arikian, N. J., 49

Aristotle, 113

Aron-Dine, A., 239

Aronson, E., 16, 17

Ascribed status Status assigned or given
without regard to persons' efforts or
desires, 168

Ashcroft, John, 193

Ashenfelter, D., 186

Asian Americans
contribution of, 250–251
household income, 253
prejudice against, 256
success of, 256

Assimilation The process by which
immigrant groups come to adopt the
dominant culture of their new
homeland as their own, 252

Associated Press, 198, 199, 201

Association for Children for Enforcement
of Support, 28

Asylees *See* Refugees

Atkin, C., 144

Atlas, 196

Auerbach, J. A., 103

Aune, R. K., 115–116

Aupy, A., 252

Austin, A. M. B., 17

Azaryahu, M., 101

Babbie, Earl, 4, 6

Babri, K. B., xviii

Baby Boomers
population, 63–64, 66
religion and, 294
retirement, 67–68

Back, K., 43

Bacue, M., 143

Badr, L. K., 110–111

Bagilhole, B., 149

Bai, C., 199

Baker, Cody C., 99

Baker, M., 84

Baker, S., 250

Balcom, D., 221

Baldas, T., 162

Baldasty, G., 165

Baloff, P., 112

Bamburg, J., 284

About the Authors

Janet M. Ruane (PhD, Rutgers University) is Professor of Sociology at Montclair State University. She has served as her department's Coordinator of Undergraduate Advising and as the Advisor of the Graduate Program in Applied Sociology. Professor Ruane's research interests include formal and informal social control mechanisms, domestic violence, media and technology, research methods, and applied sociology. She is the author of *Essentials of Research Methods* (Blackwell) and has contributed articles to several journals, including *Sociological Inquiry, Law and Policy, Communication Research, Sociological Focus, Journal of Applied Sociology, Science as Culture, Simulation and Games,* and *Virginia Review of Sociology.* Over the years, Professor Ruane has gained considerable classroom experience, teaching both introductory and advanced-level sociology courses as well as graduate courses in applied sociology.

Karen A. Cerulo (PhD, Princeton University) is Professor of Sociology at Rutgers University. Her research interests include culture and cognition, symbolic communication, media and technology, and comparative historical studies. Professor Cerulo's articles appear in a wide variety of journals, including the *American Sociological Review, Contemporary Sociology, Poetics, Social Forces, Sociological Forum, Sociological Inquiry,* and *Communication Research,* and annuals such as the *Annual Review of Sociology* and *Research in Political Sociology.* She is the author of three books: *Identity Designs: The Sights and Sounds of a Nation,* a work that won the ASA Culture Section's award for the best book of 1996 (Rose Book Series of the ASA, Rutgers University Press); *Deciphering Violence: The Cognitive Order of Right and Wrong* (Routledge); and *Never Saw It Coming: Cultural Challenges to Envisioning the Worst* (University of Chicago Press). She also has edited a collection entitled *Culture in Mind: Toward a Sociology of Culture and Cognition* (Routledge). Professor Cerulo's teaching earned her the Rutgers University Award for Distinguished Contributions to Undergraduate Education.